P9-EEA-756

MATHEMATICS IN THE SOCIAL AND LIFE SCIENCES:

Theories, Models and Methods

M. A. BALL, B.A., Ph.D., M.Inst.P.
Department of Applied Mathematics and Theoretical Physics
University of Liverpool

ELLIS HORWOOD LIMITED
Publishers · Chichester

Halsted Press: a division of
JOHN WILEY & SONS
New York · Chichester · Brisbane · Toronto

Mathematics and its applications

Series Editor: G. M. BELL, Professor of Mathematics, King' College (KQC), University of London

Mathematics and its applications are now awe-inspiring in their scope, variety and depth. Not only is there rapid growth in pure mathematics and its applications to the traditional fields of the physical sciences, engineering and statistics, but new fields of application are emerging in biology, ecology and social organisation. The user of mathematics must assimilate subtle new techniques and also learn to handle the great power of the computer efficiently and economically.

The need of clear, concise and authoritative texts is thus greater than ever and our series will endeavour to supply this need. It aims to be comprehensive and yet flexible. Works surveying recent research will introduce new areas and up-to-date mathematical methods. Undergraduate texts on established topics will simulate student interest by including applications relevant at the present day. The series will also include selected volumes of lecture notes which will enable certain important topics to be presented earlier than would otherwise be possible.

In all these ways it is hoped to render a valuable service to those who learn, teach, develop and use mathematics.

Baldock, G. R. & Bridgeman, T. — **Mathematical Theory of Wave Motion**
Ball, M. A. — **Mathematics in the Social and Life Sciences: Theories, Models and Methods**
de Barra, G. — **Measure Theory and Integration**
Berry, J. S., Burghes, D. N., Huntley, I. D., James, D. J. G. & Moscardini, A. O. — **Teaching and Applying Mathematical Modelling**
Burghes, D. N. & Borrie, M. — **Modelling with Differential Equations**
Burghes, D. N. & Downs, A. M. — **Modern Introduction to Classical Mechanics and Control**
Burghes, D. N. & Graham, A. — **Introduction to Control Theory, including Optimal Control**
Burghes, D. N., Huntley, I. & McDonald, J. — **Applying Mathematics**
Burghes, D. N. & Wood, A. D. — **Mathematical Models in the Social, Management and Life Sciences**
Butkovskiy, A. G. — **Green's Functions and Transfer Functions Handbook**
Butkovskiy, A. G. — **Structure of Distributed Systems**
Cao, Z-Q., Kim, K. H. & Roush, F. W. — **Incline Algebra and Applications**
Chorlton, F. — **Textbook of Dynamics, 2nd Edition**
Chorlton, F. — **Vector and Tensor Methods**
Crapper, G. D. — **Introduction to Water Waves**
Cross, M. & Moscardini, A. O. — **Learning the Art of Mathematical Modelling**
Cullen, M. R. — **Linear Models in Biology**
Dunning-Davies, J. — **Mathematical Methods for Mathematicians, Physical Scientists and Engineers**
Eason, G., Coles, C. W. & Gettinby, G. — **Mathematics and Statistics for the Bio-sciences**
Exton, H. — **Handbook of Hypergeometric Integrals**
Exton, H. — **Multiple Hypergeometric Functions and Applications**
Exton, H. — **q-Hypergeometric Functions and Applications**
Faux, I. D. & Pratt, M. J. — **Computational Geometry for Design and Manufacture**
Firby, P. A. & Gardiner, C. F. — **Surface Topology**
Gardiner, C. F. — **Modern Algebra**
Gasson, P. C. — **Geometry of Spatial Forms**
Goodbody, A. M. — **Cartesian Tensors**
Goult, R. J. — **Applied Linear Algebra**
Graham, A. — **Kronecker Products and Matrix Calculus: with Applications**
Graham, A. — **Matrix Theory and Applications for Engineers and Mathematicians**
Griffel, D. H. — **Applied Functional Analysis**

Harris, D. J. — Mathematics for Business, Management and Economics
Hanyga, A. — Mathematical Theory of Non-linear Elasticity
Harris, D. J. — Mathematics for Business, Management and Economics
Hoskins, R. F. — Generalised Functions
Hunter, S. C. — Mechanics of Continuous Media, 2nd (Revised) Edition
Huntley, I. & Johnson, R. M. — Linear and Nonlinear Differential Equations
Jaswon, M. A. & Rose, M. A. — Crystal Symmetry: The Theory of Colour Crystallography
Johnson, R. M. — Linear Differential Equations and Difference Equations: A Systems Approach
Kim, K. H. & Roush, F. W. — Applied Abstract Algebra
Kosinski, W. — Field Singularities and Wave Analysis in Continuum Mechanics
Lord, E. A. & Wilson, C. B. — The Mathematical Description of Shape and Form
Marichev, O. I. — Integral Transforms of Higher Transcendental Functions
Meek, B. L. & Fairthorne, S. — Using Computers
Moore, R. — Computational Functional Analysis
Muller-Pfeiffer, E. — Spectral Theory of Ordinary Differential Operators
Nonweiler, T. R. F. — Computational Mathematics: An Introduction to Numerical Analysis
Oldknow, A. & Smith, D. — Learning Mathematics with Micros
Ogden, R. W. — Non-linear Elastic Deformations
Rankin, R. — Modular Forms
Ratschek, H. & Rokne, Jon — Computer Methods for the Range of Functions
Scorer, R. S. — Environmental Aerodynamics
Smith, D. K. — Network Optimisation Practice: A Computational Guide
Srivastava, H. M. & Karlsson, P. W. — Multiple Gaussian Hypergeometric Series
Srivastava, H. M. & Manocha, H. L. — A Treatise on Generating Functions
Sweet, M. V. — Algebra, Geometry and Trigonometry in Science, Engineering and Mathematics
Temperley, H. N. V. & Trevena, D. H. — Liquids and Their Properties
Temperley, H. N. V. — Graph Theory and Applications
Thom, R. — Mathematical Models of Morphogenesis
Townend, M. Stewart — Mathematics in Sport
Toth, G. — Harmonic and Minimal Maps
Twizell, E. H. — Computational Methods for Partial Differential Equations
Wheeler, R. F. — Rethinking Mathematical Concepts
Willmore, T. J. — Total Curvature in Riemannian Geometry
Willmore, T. J. & Hitchin, N. — Global Riemannian Geometry

Statistics and Operational Research

Editor: B. W. CONOLLY, Professor of Operational Research, Queen Mary College, University of London

Beaumont, G. P. — Introductory Applied Probability
Beaumont, G. P. — Basic Probability and Random Variables*
Conolly, B. W. — Techniques in Operational Research: Vol. 1, Queueing Systems
Conolly, B. W. — Techniques in Operational Research: Vol. 2, Models, Search, Randomization
French, S. — Sequencing and Scheduling: Mathematics of the Job Shop
French, S. — Decision Theory
Griffiths, P. & Hill, I. D. — Applied Statistics Algorithms
Hartley R. — Linear Methods of Mathematical Programming
Jones, A. J. — Game Theory
Kemp, K. W. — Dice, Data and Decisions: Introductory Statistics
Oliveira-Pinto, F. — Simulation Concepts in Mathematical Modelling
Oliveira-Pinto, F. & Conolly, B. W. — Applicable Mathematics of Non-physical Phenomena
Schendel, U. — Introduction to Numerical Methods for Parallel Computers
Stoodley, K. D. C. — Applied and Computational Statistics A First Course
Stoodley, K. D. C., Lewis, T. & Stainton, C. L. S. — Applied Statistical Techniques
Thomas, L. C. — Games, Theory and Applications
Whitehead, J. R. — The Design and Analysis of Sequential Clinical Trials

**In preparation*

First published in 1985 by

ELLIS HORWOOD LIMITED
Market Cross House, Cooper Street, Chichester, West Sussex, PO19 1EB, England

The publisher's colophon is reproduced from James Gillison's drawing of the ancient Market Cross, Chichester.

Distributors:

Australia, New Zealand, South-east Asia:
Jacaranda-Wiley Ltd., Jacaranda Press,
JOHN WILEY & SONS INC.,
G.P.O. Box 859, Brisbane, Queensland 4001, Australia

Canada:
JOHN WILEY & SONS CANADA LIMITED
22 Worcester Road, Rexdale, Ontario, Canada.

Europe, Africa:
JOHN WILEY & SONS LIMITED
Baffins Lane, Chichester, West Sussex, England.

North and South America and the rest of the world:
Halsted Press: a division of
JOHN WILEY & SONS
605 Third Avenue, New York, N.Y. 10158, USA .

British Library Cataloguing in Publication Data
Ball, M.A.
Mathematics in the social and life sciences: theories, models and methods –
(Ellis Horwood series in mathematics and its applications)
1. Social sciences – Mathematics
I. Title
300'.1'51 H61.25

Library of Congress Card No. 85–4546

ISBN 0–85312–486–8 (Ellis Horwood Limited – Library Edn.)
ISBN 0–85312–887–1 (Ellis Horwood Limited – Student Edn.)
ISBN 0–470–20191–6 (Halsted Press)

Typeset by Heather FitzGibbon, Fleet, nr. Aldershot, Hants.
Printed in Great Britain by R.J. Acford, Chichester

Table of Contents

Preface

Applied mathematics is a wonderful and exciting subject. It is the essence of the theoretical approach to science and engineering. In scientific subjects, applied mathematics uses the language of mathematics and the concepts of the subject to develop a richer, more precise, more quantitative theory than is possible with words. These theories can give predictions which may be tested by experiment. In this way applied mathematics contributes to the working of the scientific method. In engineering there is design work as well as the acquisition of knowledge; there, mathematics can also make an indispensable contribution.

In the physical sciences and in the engineering subjects based on them, the role of mathematics is straightforward. In the life and social sciences, however, the use of mathematics is more questionable; there are advantages and disadvantages in its use. It is important to be aware of these and not to form opinions about the applicability of mathematics from prejudices, fears and ignorance. In this book our aim is to show not only where mathematics is of use, but also where its use causes difficulties.

Despite the problems, considerable success in these uses of mathematics has been achieved in the last 60 years. University teaching of applied mathematics, however, has remained rather restricted, and there is a need to broaden the curriculum. This book tries to fill this gap. Although a few new models and methods are introduced, most of the book's contents are available elsewhere, but in a lot of disparate, inaccessible places and often not in an appropriate form. For example, some economics books are dogmatic, some books treat Game

Theory almost as a branch of pure mathematics, and some books treat population dynamics as an exercise in differential equations. An applied mathematics textbook, when not dealing with mathematical methods, should always be relevant to the topic under consideration, should always be questioning the assumptions made and testing the models and their results. I hope this book achieves this and treats the topics in a scientific and 'systematic' way.

This book is designed as a textbook; I would not claim to be an expert in any of the subjects in the book. I have tried, through copious reading and through conversations with others, to avoid any serious errors and omissions; I apologize if there are any. Being an 'amateur' does, however, have its advantages: it has made me more aware of the difficulties of understanding that a beginner in a subject encounters. It may also have given me a wider view of the totality of the subject matter and may have allowed me to approach it in a scientific way.

The author is an applied mathematician/theoretical physicist whose research interests are mainly in condensed matter physics. Why, you may ask, is a solid-state physicist writing a book on subjects such as microeconomics and population theory? – partly out of personal interest, partly because there seems to be a need and partly by accident. The book grew out of a lecture course given to second-year mathematical students at the University of Liverpool. The Department of Applied Mathematics and Theoretical Physics there felt that the uses of mathematics which were being taught to mathematics students were too much limited to physical topics so that at the instigation of two colleagues, Roger Bowers and Roland Graham, and myself, the course was born. I would like to thank them for their help and inspiration, for many discussions about points of interest and for reading parts of the book. Many other colleagues at Liverpool have contributed to the book in various ways and I would like to thank them – in particular Archie McKerrell, who read large sections of the book and made detailed comments. Nevertheless all omissions, errors, etc. are the fault of the author. I would also like to thank my family for encouragement and for forbearance.

On Using This Book

The types of model or theory of interest in this book are those in which the use of mathematical language is appropriate and in which the development conforms as far as possible with the methods of a scientific investigation or of an engineering design. The **aim** of this book is to show how such models and theories are developed in the social and life sciences.

This is done firstly by seeing how mathematical languages are used to develop models in general and secondly (the main part of the book) by developing the basic theory of three particular subject areas, i.e. microeconomics, 'games', and population dynamics. This approach will enable the reader to develop his own models or theories when he needs to. As encouragement in this process, a few questions (marked$^{(m)}$) suggest further topics which might be modelled using mathematical language.

The first chapter (SM1) on Systems and Models introduces the way in which mathematics is used in the pursuit of knowledge and in design. The ideas of mathematical modelling and systems are introduced. Some of this may seem abstract and vague at first and need not be studied closely on a first reading. The ideas of SM1 occur frequently in later chapters so that the reader is advised to refer back, both to understand the ideas better and to see how the general approach is working.

The three main parts are: part E on Microeconomics, part G on Conflict and Cooperation and part P on Population Dynamics. Each part is designed to show how mathematics can be used to provide a clear foundation of the subject. There is also sufficient development in each subject for the reader to feel he has got somewhere. Topics which would only be of interest to the specialist but are not helpful towards the main aim (e.g. Giffen goods) have been omitted. All topics are approached along the lines set out in SM1, i.e. a tentative model is produced, based on experimental results, the concepts of the subject and some mathematical concepts; then the model is developed to produce some results and the credibility of the model is tested for its reasonableness and by these results. The reader is advised to take note of this procedure as it is an important part of his education.

The three main parts are self-contained, so that each part can be read separately. Nevertheless some of the concepts and many of the mathematical techniques are common to more than one subject. There are also advantages in taking a broad, general view rather than a specialist's: many of the most exciting advances are taking place at present in interdisciplinary subjects and many advances in knowledge occur when an approach to one topic is applied to some different topic, e.g. the use of Game Theory in evolution (see P4.8). It is thus hoped that the reader, even if studying only one subject, will read the book as a whole.

At the end of most chapters there is a set of exercises. Most are of a standard type, designed to test the reader's understanding. In the open-ended questions (marked $^{(m)}$) the reader is asked to develop models for himself. These can be long or short exercises and should prove worth while – it would be even better if the reader could think of his own topics to model.

This book grew out of a course for second-year mathematics students at an English university. It is mainly directed at such students, but other students, particularly economists, life scientists, computer scientists and social scientists, should also find it useful. Some of the material is suitable for first- and for third-year students, as this is an introductory text leading on to more advanced material.

The mathematics is fairly elementary; anyone with 'A' level mathematics and some first year algebra, calculus and elementary probability should be capable of understanding all the mathematics in the book. Any additional mathematical topics needed are explained, with the exception of equivalence relations, abstract vectors, and eigenvalues and eigenvectors; the reader may need to learn about these topics before all the book can be understood. The unstarred sections are reasonably easy and the sections with stars (*) and (**) contain the more difficult parts. These can be omitted on a first reading: the remainder should contain enough material for 36 lectures.

The reader needs no more than an acquaintance with the subjects of micro-economics, conflict studies, population studies or genetics. Some prior reading (see the book list) is useful but not essential.

Reading List

There are many books on the subjects covered in this book. Some are worth reading. Others are not suitable for mathematics undergraduates; they may have misleading titles, or be too simple or too hard. The following can be recommended, with the reservations made in the comments. Those marked * are more advanced than this book. The abbreviations are for reference purposes.

PRELIMINARY READING

Burghes, D., and Wood, A.D., *Mathematical Models in the Social, Management and Life Sciences* (Ellis Horwood).
Introduces elementary mathematical methods and shows how they can be applied in 'real' situations.

Burghes, D. and Borrie, M.S., *Modelling with Differential Equations* (Ellis Horwood). (MBB)
Mathematical methods with plenty of applications.

Kemeny, J.G., Snell, J.L. and Thompson, G.L., *Introduction to Finite Mathematics* (Prentice-Hall). (MKST)
It introduces aspects of Game Theory, Markov chains and the Simplex Method.

Burghes, D., Huntley, I. and McDonald, J., *Applying Mathematics* (Ellis Horwood).
A set of situations with appropriate, easy mathematical models; it also contains some suggestions of situations to model.

Donaldson, P., *Economics of the Real World* (Pelican).
Descriptive economics, suitable for background reading.

Samuelson, P., *Economics* (McGraw-Hill). Please note that the earlier editions were called 'Economics: an introductory analysis' but present editions are just called 'Economics'.

GENERAL

Andrews, J.G. and McClone, R.R., *Mathematical Modelling* (Butterworths).
A set of situations with appropriate models.

Haberman, R., *Mathematical Models* (Prentice-Hall).
It uses a modelling approach to the topics of mechanical vibrations, population dynamics, and traffic flow. About the same standard as this book.

MICROECONOMICS

Henderson, J.M. and Quandt, R.E., *Microeconomic Theory* (McGraw-Hill). (EHQ)
A standard textbook. Readable but never queries the correctness of the theory.

Varian, H.R., *Microeconomic Analysis* (Norton).

*Intrilligator, M.D., *Mathematical Optimization and Economic Theory* (Prentice-Hall). (EI)

*Malinvaud, E., *Lectures in Microeconomic Theory* (North-Holland).

Dewey, D., *Microeconomics* (O.U.P.).
One of the better, 'less mathematical', textbooks.

*Gale, D., *The Theory of Linear Economic Models* (McGraw-Hill). (EG)

GAMES THEORY

*Thomas, L.C., *Games Theory and Applications* (Ellis Horwood).
Readable and gives a broad survey of Game Theory.

*Jones, A.J., *Game Theory* (Ellis Horwood). (GJ)

*Owen, G., *Game Theory* (Academic Press). (GO)
Both (GO) *and* (GJ) *require a strong background in pure mathematics.*

Bacharach, M., *Economics and the Theory of Games* (Macmillan). (GB)
Written for economists, not mathematicians; full of interesting ideas and comments.

POPULATION DYNAMICS

Maynard Smith, J., *Models in Ecology* (C.U.P.). (PS1)

*Maynard Smith, J., *Evolution and the Theory of Games* (C.U.P.). (PS2)
The original theory. Sometimes lacks clarity but contains much of interest.

May, R.M., *Stability and Complexity in Model Ecosystems* (Princeton University Press).
An advanced, but interesting book.

MATHEMATICS

Feller, W., *Probability Theory and Its Applications* (John Wiley). (MF)

Boyce, W.E. and diPrima, R.C., *Elementary Differential Equations and Boundary Problems* (John Wiley). (MBdP)

Burden, R.L., Faires, J.D. and Reynolds, A.C., *Numerical Analysis* (Prindle, Weber, and Schmidt). (MBFR)

Part SM:

SYSTEMS AND MODELS

CHAPTER SM1

Systems and Models

SM1.1 AIMS

We can view a branch of mathematics as a **language**. Such a language provides a description of the relationships between the objects involved. For example, classical mechanics describes the relationship between the forces acting on particles and their movement, and group theory describes the possible relations between the elements of a group.

A mathematical language is **precise** and this is its main distinction from everyday language. Precision is an advantage in certain situations, e.g. the use of vectors for the description of space. In other situations it may be inappropriate or even a disadvantage, e.g. in poetry or in diplomacy.

It was usually as a description of some real system that a branch of mathematics was devised; for example, arithmetic was invented in order to count the number of apples a man had, or the number of his wives. Many other branches of mathematics occurred because of the need to explain the phenomena of physics and engineering; for example, Euclidean geometry was developed in order to describe and discover the properties of the space in which we live. It has been mainly in the last 60 years that mathematical languages have been devised to deal with **non-physical systems**, e.g. traffic flow, population growth, telephone or nerve networks. In this book we shall be looking at some of these areas of study and the mathematical languages and techniques which have been devised to help in the understanding of such subjects: the first third of the book is devoted to microeconomics, the middle third to the theory of conflict and cooperation, and the last third to the theory of populations.

The book aims then:

(a) to show how mathematical languages can be developed to help in the understanding of non-physical subjects;
(b) to show the advantages, and dangers, of mathematical theories in such situations;
(c) in particular to see how far the development of such theories is in accord with the methods used in a scientific investigation or in an engineering design study;
(d) to illustrate some of the main mathematical techniques involved.

The subject is usually more important than the mathematical language devised to help in its description. Thus the book is designed around the subjects and contains some meaty (and digestible) chunks of economics and ecology for the reader to get his teeth into. This is, however, an introductory book and can do little more than whet the reader's appetite and encourage him to go further into these subjects and/or to look at other non-physical subjects.

Although this book concentrates on only three subjects the reader should not get the idea that all non-physical subjects can be described by a few mathematical languages. Just as there are lots of branches of mathematics that deal with physics, e.g. Euclidean geometry, electromagnetic theory, quantum mechanics, there are many that deal with non-physical subjects.

With so many different mathematical languages needed to describe so many different subjects, let us look at the way mathematical theories are developed and at the structural aspects they have in common. This is described in the **general theory of systems**, which is a way of approach to a subject. Our aim here is not a complete exposition of 'systems theory', but to pick out the common structural ideas which occur in many subjects, and in particular in the three subjects in this book, so that when *the reader is confronted by some new topic, he knows whether a mathematical approach is appropriate and how to devise a mathematical language to help towards its understanding*. The ability to do this is very useful: its acquisition is no easy matter but some of the skills involved should become clearer as we progress through this chapter and through the book.

These ideas occur at the beginning of the book to help the reader recognize the structural ideas common to microeconomics, conflict theory, and population dynamics, and to their development. As progress is made through the book, the reader should try to see how this development is related to the general scheme presented here.

SM1.2 SYSTEMS THEORY

When we think, we do so mainly, if not wholly, in terms of 'concepts'. These can be categorized as **objects, attributes, relationships**, and **systems**.

Definition: A system is a set of objects together with relationships between their attributes.

Objects are simply the parts of a system; for example, in a gas of molecules, they would be the molecules, or in a market they would be the sellers and the buyers. The attributes are properties of the objects, e.g. the mass, the size, the velocity, the position of each molecule, or the goods and the money possessed by a buyer or seller. Note that an object is only perceived and recognized because of its attributes. The relationships only exist between the attributes of the objects; these relationships tie the system together (they make the system a system), e.g. the forces between the molecules, or the number of goods a seller is willing to sell at a given price.

At this stage these ideas are so general as to be almost useless – any description in words describes a 'system'. It is when we characterize the systems that we start to gain something. For example, a system is said to be **static** if the attributes do not change with time, and it is **dynamic** if they do. Examples of static and dynamic systems are commonplace in physics, e.g. a bridge or an oscillating spring, but this classification is also very useful in other subjects.

Another useful concept is that of **subsystem**: a subsystem can itself be considered as a system but is part of the original system under consideration. The subsystems can sometimes be considered as 'objects' in the larger system.

Environment

The **environment** of a system is the set of all objects which are outside the system and which are related to the objects of the system. An **open** system is one in which the interactions of the system with its environment are considered. A **closed** system is one in which these interactions are neglected. The distinction between the system and its environment is at the choice of the observer and should be chosen to gain accuracy and convenience.

It is obviously nonsensical to talk about a particular system unless it can be distinguished from its environment. This is easy if the system can be considered as closed in some context and/or in some approximation.

Real systems

A **real system** is a description of a real situation, as in the examples above. The description can be in any language, ordinary or mathematical, that is convenient. It is important to realize that *real systems are descriptions*: they are not the situation itself. For this reason such systems are sometimes called **descriptive**.

Real systems which do not incorporate the conscious behaviour of human beings are called **natural** systems. These occur for example in the natural sciences, i.e. physics, chemistry, biology, etc. The aim in devising a natural system is to understand the underlying real situation and to predict its behaviour.

Systems which incorporate the conscious behaviour of human beings can be called **social systems**. The understanding of the behaviour of the real situation in this case is not easy because of the involvement of Man; so the devising of realistic social systems is particularly difficult and full of dangers.

Many aspects of a real situation are irrelevant and cloud our understanding: indeed Man has a finite brain and cannot expect to know everything. Thus to achieve a better understanding, extraneous details have to be omitted when devising descriptive systems: for example, if we want to find out how fast a car will go, we do not study the colour of the car; we study its engine, its carburretor, etc. Which details are important and which are irrelevant comes with experience.

Design

Besides the desire to understand and predict there is also the wish to design. In engineering, for example, a natural system may be modified in order to try to achieve certain requirements or **norms**. These usually give rise to problems which in turn require **solutions**. The creation of norms and the designing of a system which satisfies them is called a **normative** study.

For example, suppose we want to design a car which goes as fast as possible. This then is the norm and creates problems in designing the engine, the bearings, etc..

Thus the study of engineering is both descriptive and normative.† There is also in engineering the requirement that the design can be carried out, e.g. that the design for the fastest car can be used to build a prototype which will perform as required. We shall call this function the **practical** role of engineering.

In the social sciences, the study may be descriptive, normative and practical. For example, the way we organize our economic life is open to choice (to some extent at least!) so that the study of economics has normative as well as descriptive aspects. Unfortunately it is often difficult to distinguish between the descriptive and normative aspects in many studies of the social sciences, and it is sometimes claimed that they cannot be distinguished as every description implies a norm in the form of a value judgement. Such deliberations need not concern us here, but the reader may like to try to distinguish between the descriptive and normative aspects of microeconomics and Game Theory as he reads the book; when he has discovered the norms he might ask himself whether the resulting problems have solutions and whether the solutions are practical.

Abstract systems

These are systems which have no direct relation to anything other than thought-processes, i.e. they bear no direct relation to the outside world (or 'reality' if the

† Thus in some ways engineering is a more difficult, interesting and imaginative subject than the natural sciences.

reader prefers the term). The obvious example of such a system is a branch of pure mathematics, e.g. group theory, but some people may also consider metaphysics or theology as abstract systems. Here we are only interested in abstract mathematical systems, and this is what we mean when we use the term **abstract system**.

A simple example is a *set* with various *elements*, which have certain properties and bear a relation to each other. The elements are then the objects of the system and their properties are the attributes.

Consider the set $\{x_1, x_2\}$ of two real variables. The 'objects' then are x_1 and x_2 and the attribute of x_i is its magnitude. Suppose the variables satisfy the equations

$$\begin{aligned} a_{11}x_1 + a_{12}x_2 &= b_1 \\ a_{21}x_1 + a_{22}x_2 &= b_2. \end{aligned} \qquad \text{(SM1.2.1)}$$

Then these equations are the relations between x_1 and x_2, and the system is a static one. Suppose, however, the variables are functions of time and satisfy the equations

$$\begin{aligned} \frac{dx_1}{dt} &= a_{11}x_1 + a_{12}x_2 \\ \frac{dx_2}{dt} &= a_{21}x_1 + a_{22}x_2. \end{aligned} \qquad \text{(SM1.2.2)}$$

Then the equations are the relations between x_1 and x_2, but the system is a dynamic one.

SM1.3 MATHEMATICAL MODELS

The language used in a real system may be an ordinary one such as English, a mathematical one, or a mixture. Real systems using ordinary languages are sometimes called **word models**. The precision of mathematical languages, however, means that it is useful to incorporate them into the system. Not only is the precision an advantage in itself but it also makes prediction of the system behaviour easier and more reliable. How, then, can mathematical languages be used? One way, given a word model, is to associate with it an abstract system so that its objects, attributes and relationships are in one-to-one correspondence and have the same behaviour as the word model. This abstract system is termed the **abstract model** and the original system is called the **realization** of the abstract model.† A simple example from classical mechanics is of two particles connected by a string passing over a pulley, the string hanging vertically: this is

† For more details of this approach, see *Mathematical Foundations of Thermodynamics* by R. Giles (Pergamon Press).

the system and the abstract model will be the set of equations which describe the positions of the particles.

The prediction of system behaviour in this procedure is carried out as follows: the word model is mapped onto the abstract model. The logic of the abstract model is then applied so that its behaviour is predicted. This behaviour is then interpreted in terms of the word model so that we know the behaviour of the word model.

In practice, however, there are considerable difficulties with this approach in which the word model and abstract model are kept separate. For a system to be completely amenable to the creation of a perfect abstract model, it must possess some special properties, e.g. the relationships must be known explicitly, and the attributes must be quantifiable, not too numerous, and their behaviour under the relationships must be known. It is a rare system that has all these properties.

How, then, can we use mathematics in describing a general situation? We suggest that the best way is to use a **mathematical model** † in which the system itself uses both mathematical and non-mathematical language. In this way the situation under consideration can often be described more adequately and the models of the situation refined more readily. Some of the subsystems of the mathematical model will be abstract systems, but by mixing the mathematics and the technical non-mathematical language together instead of keeping them separate, it is possible to use mathematics in many more situations. This is because the arrangement is more flexible, allowing a more speculative approach, but using the deductive power of mathematics whenever possible.

The harnessing of the mathematical and more intuitive, non-mathematical approaches in a mathematical model is advantageous to both approaches: it ensures that the abstract systems considered are realistic, and it forces the intuitive models to be more logical, rigorous and precise. It is also helpful when approximations have to be made as the real implications of the approximations are immediately apparent. Mathematical models have often been used in physics and have contributed to the rapid development of the subject. They have also produced new concepts both in physics and in mathematics. The use of mathematical models has in some cases been essential as some physical phenomena are describable only in mathematical terms, e.g. the wave and corpuscular natures of the electron. It might have been advantageous in other subjects, e.g. economics, if the disciplines of mathematical modelling had been used.

The research approach

Mathematical modelling requires imagination, craftmanship, and a knowledge of both mathematics and the subject involved. In this book the subjects and the mathematical language are intertwined in order to show the reader how

† The reader is warned that other books may use this term to mean an *abstract* model. The terminology varies from author to author.

mathematical models are developed. Nevertheless the only way for the reader to develop the skills involved in mathematical modelling is for him to try to model some situations for himself, i.e. do some research. The modelling exercises (marked $^{(m)}$) should be helpful in this.

When reading the book the reader should ask himself: 'what should be done next so that we can achieve a better understanding?' before he moves on to another section. The reader should thus try, whenever possible, to put himself in the shoes of the originators of the subjects, and try to think of the questions that they asked themselves.

The place of logic

Understanding, prediction and possibly design are the three reasons for building a mathematical model. To get these, however, the model usually needs simplifying, with some approximations being made, in order to obtain a tractable abstract model. To find the predictions of the abstract model, the rules of logic are used. These predictions can then be interpreted in terms of the original mathematical model.

Logic plays an essential part in the use of a mathematical model. To get results, predictions, etc., however, it is sometimes necessary to make jumps in the deductive process, i.e. it is not essential to deduce *rigorously* each step from previous steps. The steps in the deductive process have to be highly plausible and must not be illogical, but they need not be rigorously deductible. Any results obtained in this way have to be justified by the process of **verification**, as does the original mathematical model.

Verification

It is the aim of every academic subject (although it is not always obviously so in some subjects!) to see that their descriptions are in accord with reality. Scientific method requires the prediction of a theory to be tested against reality and the test tells us whether the mathematical model is a suitable model of the real situation. Such tests cannot tell us that the system is a perfect model, but if it passes all possible tests, then it models the real situation within the limits of attainable information.

In most branches of physics (except, for example, cosmology), theories are testable, because it is possible to set up experiments. In non-physical subjects, verification is usually difficult and often impossible: thus models in these subjects often do not have this check (of verification) and so we must be doubly careful in the way we set about making models, and in the way we use the predictions of the models.[†]

Flow-chart

The whole procedure by which a mathematical model is produced and is verified is shown in Fig. SM1.1.

† It is terrifying to see the certainty some economists have in their own predictions.

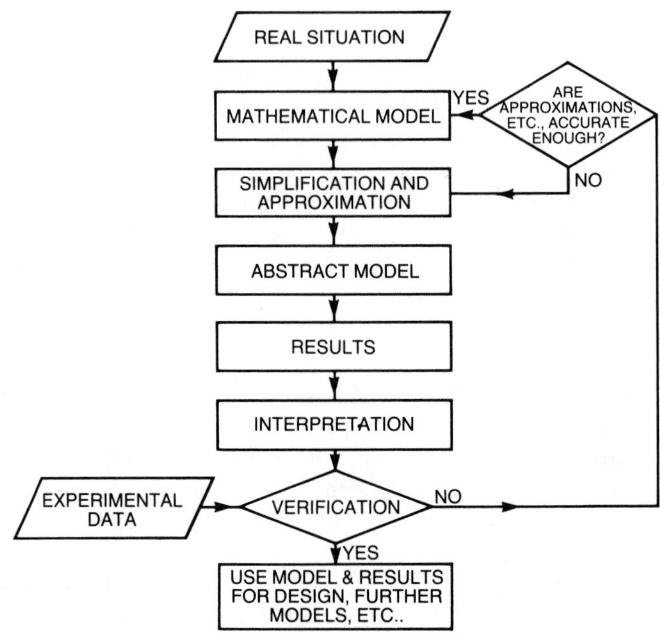

Fig. SM1.1. Flow chart of procedure used in mathematical modelling of a descriptive system.

An Analogy

The roles of mathematics, the subject, and skills in the building of a mathematical model can be illustrated by analogy to the mortar, the bricks, and the skills in the building of a wall (see Fig. SM1.2). The verification process is illustrated in Fig. SM1.3!

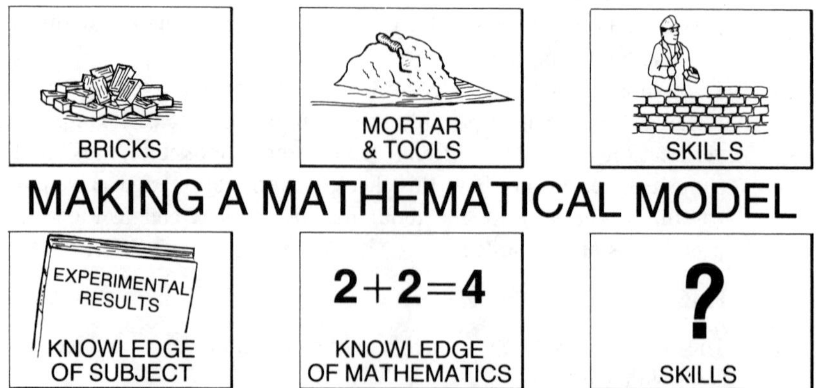

Fig. SM1.2. Analogy between building a wall and building a mathematical model

Fig. SM1.3. The verification process

In practice the lumps of knowledge of a real situation are not nicely-shaped objects such as bricks; they are more like lumps of stone which are jagged and have awkward corners. Of course it is possible to build walls with such stones without the use of mortar; there are plenty of them in the North of England. However, they take an immense amount of skill and time to build, if they are to last, and of course they are not so useful as walls which use mortar. The walls without mortar are analogous to word models.†

Some mathematicians are under the impression that mathematical models require a lot of mathematics and only a small knowledge of the subject involved. Such people need to be reminded that anyone who builds a wall which is 90% mortar is rather foolish.

Practicality

This plays the same role in design work that verification does in the pursuit of knowledge: the solutions of the mathematical model have to be tested to see if they are practical. If they are not, not only the mathematical model but also the descriptive system and the norms on which the solutions are based have to be

† Note the quotation by Henri Poincaré: 'Le savant doit ordonner; on fait la science avec des faits comme une maison avec des pierres; mais une accumulation de faits n'est pas plus une science qu'un tas de pierres n'est une maison'.

examined to see if they are accurate and sensible respectively. Even if the solutions are practical, it is wise to consider the norms in the light of the solutions and the knowledge gained. For example, it may be possible to improve the specification of a car's engine because the solution to a problem in road-holding has been obtained.

A flow-chart for design work is given in Fig. SM1.4.

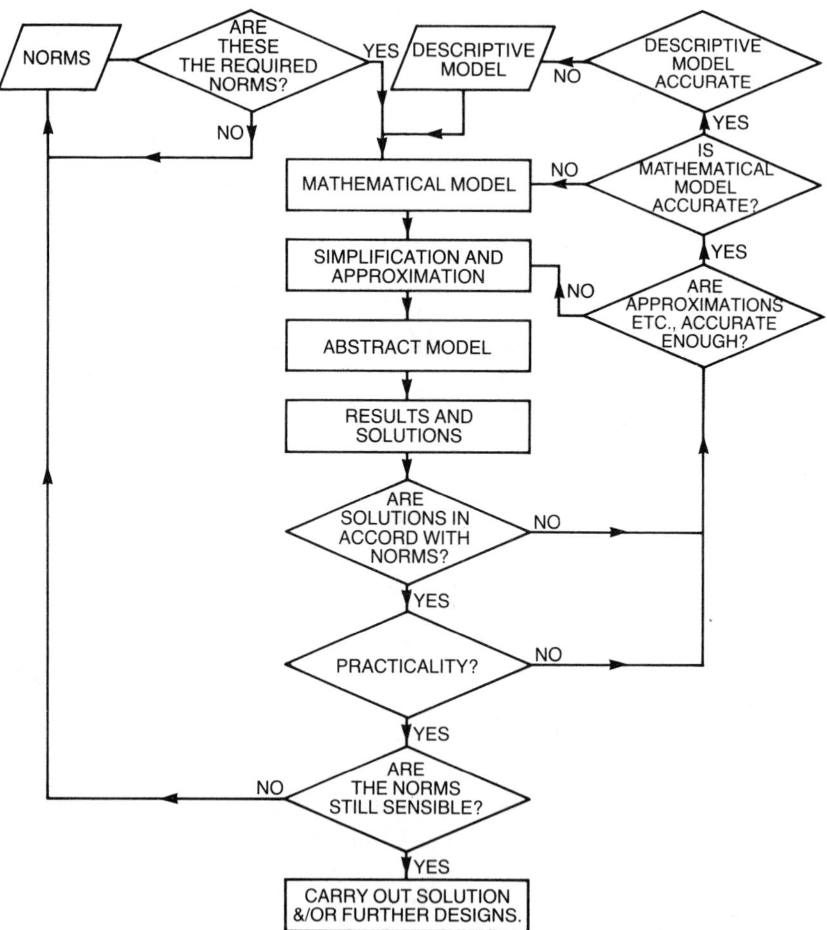

Fig. SM1.4. Flow chart of procedure when mathematical modelling is used in design.

SM1.4 FURTHER CLASSIFICATION

One of the advantages of using abstract models is that they can be classified more precisely and more systematically than systems in general. This classification can be extended to most, if not all, mathematical models and usually to systems in general.

Sometimes the variables of the abstract model correspond to actual attributes of its realization. We might call such models **classical** although the word **deterministic** is often used.

In other cases we might only be interested in the probabilities that the attributes of the realization have certain values. In this case the variables in the abstract model would be probability distributions and the model is called **stochastic.**

The **state** (at a given time t, if time is involved) of an abstract model is given by the values taken by the variables of the model at time t, i.e. the 'state' is the set of all the properties of the model at a particular time. Both classical and stochastic models have 'states'.

A **causal** model would be one in which the state at time t_2 is determined by the states at times $t \leqslant t_1$, where t_1 is the time immediately prior to t_2; for example, in a model where time is continuous, $t_1 = t_2 - \delta T$, but if we are considering time in discrete units T, where $t_2 = NT$, then $t_1 = (N-1)T$.

A causal model is called **state-determined** when the state at time t_2 is determined completely by the state at time t_1. A typical classical, state-determined model for a closed system with time taken as continuous has variables $x_1, \ldots, x_n$, satisfying a system of equations of the form

$$\frac{\mathrm{d}x_i}{\mathrm{d}t} = f_i(x_1, \ldots, x_n) \quad i = 1, \ldots, n. \tag{SM1.4.1}$$

We could take axes, with x_1 taking values along the first axis, and so on, and then the state of the model is fixed by a point in this space, which we call **phase-space** or **state-space**. When t is continuous, the state traces a path in phase-space; for a state-determined system, such paths do not cross. The reader might like to prove this.

Equilibrium and stability

Equilibrium in a state-determined system means no change with time; for example, for the equation (SM1.4.1)

$$\frac{\mathrm{d}x_i}{\mathrm{d}t} = 0 \quad \text{for all } i. \tag{SM1.4.2}$$

This requires

$$f_i(x_1, \ldots, x_n) = 0. \tag{SM1.4.3}$$

There is a possibility that there are no solutions to this set of equations. There may be, of course, only one solution or there may be several. When we are considering complex systems such as economics, it is important to know whether equilibrium solutions exist. (This is obviously an important question for the Treasury!) Sometimes our mathematical knowledge is such that we do not know whether they exist or not and it is necessary to introduce some mathematical assumptions to ensure their existence; we would then investigate what these assumptions correspond to in the realization of the model.

Of interest is the behaviour of the system near an equilibrium point. A system may veer away from an equilibrium point, or travel in towards it, or just oscillate around it. In the latter two cases the system is said to be **stable** and in the former it is **unstable.**

Large systems

Consider a large system consisting of a large number of identical objects, e.g. a gas of molecules or the population of a species. We are more likely to be interested in overall (i.e. macroscopic) properties of the system rather than in the properties of the individual objects. Indeed it is usually impossible to calculate the attributes of a particular object because of the complexity of the system.

There are two ways to attempt to calculate these macroscopic properties. One way, called the macroscopic approach, is to try to develop equations which relate these macroscopic properties to each other without ever referring to the behaviour of individual objects. For example, it is sometimes possible to relate the rate of change of a species' population at time t to the population itself at time t.

The other approach, the microscopic one, looks at the behaviour of the individual objects and then tries to calculate the average behaviour of the attributes. It is then usually possible to get the macroscopic properties from these averages.

Input and output systems

Many systems can be viewed as machines which turn **inputs** into **outputs.** An example is a car factory where steel, rubber, labour, etc. are the inputs and cars are the outputs. Another example is a cow, where grass, water, etc. are the inputs and milk is the output.

In these systems we are often not interested in the interior workings of the system but only on the relationship of the outputs to the inputs.

SM1.5 CONCLUSION

This book is designed to show how mathematical language is used in the development of economics, games theory and population dynamics.

The author hopes that the reader will also learn about the skills and the process of mathematical modelling. The subjects are in general less precise and more complex than the usual physical subjects studied by mathematicians, but this means that the procedures of mathematical modelling are more easily seen.

One reservation, however, needs to be made. The acquisition of data and its interpretation (i.e. the methods of statistics) plays an enormous part in the development of a mathematical model and in the validation procedure. This book, as can be seen from its aim (see SM1.1), does not attempt any statistical analysis. Thus although the book describes the construction and validation of mathematical models in the various subjects covered, these descriptions omit the statistical methods involved.

In the social and life sciences, quantitative results are often not possible and only qualitative results can be achieved. These results should not be denigrated, however, as they are useful. The book shows how much easier it is to obtain such results, and to find the limits of their validity, by using mathematical models rather than by using word models.

Finally, a word about the choice of topics, about which the reader may be curious. The subjects were partly chosen because of their own importance and partly because of their appropriateness to the aims of the book. They show up the advantages and disadvantages of using mathematical models, and they exhibit most of the categories of systems already mentioned.

Part E:
MICROECONOMICS

CHAPTER E1

Introduction

Economics affects our daily lives. For example, taxes may be increased, we might be offered a job with more pay, or the prices of some foods such as peas or margarine may rise rapidly. Not surprisingly, the majority of humans are very concerned about such effects.

What is economics? In his book, *Economics* (see note on p. 15), Samuelson suggests several definitions. One is that economics is the study of how mankind tries to organize its consumption and production activities. This definition is sufficient for now; a fuller picture should emerge after further study.

The subject of economics can be divided into three related areas: microeconomics, macroeconomics, and econometrics. **Microeconomics** studies the pricing and production of individual commodities, e.g. the price of a kg of peas or the number of nails produced by a firm in Liverpool in a year. **Macroeconomics** is interested in the national aggregate production of such goods and in topics such as inflation and the gross national product. **Econometrics** is concerned with the *measurement* of economic quantities. The distinction between microeconomics and macroeconomics is analogous to the distinction between micro-physics and macro-physics: micro-physics studies the behaviour of individual particles, e.g. individual electrons or individual molecules, whereas macro-physics is interested in the behaviour of aggregates of such particles, e.g. fluids and solids. Microeconomics and macroeconomics are connected: microeconomic changes give rise to macroeconomic changes: macroeconomic effects, such as inflation and rates of exchange, affect microeconomic behaviour just as macroscopic effects in physics, such as temperature and pressure, affect microscopic behaviour.

In this section we study microeconomics, our aim being to see how the language of mathematics can be used to construct a theory of microeconomics, so that, for example, the price changes of commodities such as margarine and peas can be understood.

Unlike physics, many simplifications and assumptions, some of them rather drastic, have to be made in order to obtain a usable theory. The results of the theory may turn out to be unrealistic, and the reader will have to constantly use his judgement whether to accept the whole, a part, or none of these results.

The best way to test a theory is to conduct laboratory experiments. In such an experiment, the conditions are controlled and the behaviour of the system is measured; the measurements are then compared with the predictions of the theory. To set up a controlled experiment, however, is not always possible. For example, in cosmology we cannot control the conditions governing the behaviour of distant galaxies – the conditions just occur and all we can do is to observe the resulting behaviour. Similarly in economics we usually cannot control the conditions governing the behaviour of prices, jobs, etc. Consequently in economics the testing of theories and models is not as strict as in other disciplines such as chemistry; theories can only be tested against observations of economic behaviour which occur in the natural course of events.

The discipline of getting economic information from data is the task of econometrics. It is a complex subject and we are not concerned with it in this book. We are aiming to build some models of microeconomic behaviour and to see how realistic these models are: it is in testing the realism of our models that the results of econometrics are relevant.

This section of the book assumes no previous knowledge of economics. Most of the economic concepts are straightforward and easy to grasp. The reader should have no difficulty with the economic ideas. Indeed the mathematically-inclined reader should find the economic ideas clarified by the use of mathematical language. The section is nevertheless not meant to be a comprehensive textbook on microeconomics: in the short space available, we cover only the fundamentals of the traditional theory, and do not consider the interesting off-shoots of the theory. Anyone interested in these topics should consult one of the standard textbooks.

Microeconomics is concerned with the interplay of consumers' demand and the producers' supply of commodities and it is this interplay, known as the market, which determines the price of a given commodity. Thus in E2 we develop the theory of demand and in E3 we look at the theory of supply. In E4 we discuss the market and how prices are determined in some particular types of market. In E5 we look at linear systems in microeconomics: practical problems can be solved if they can be approximated as linear: in particular we look at linear programming techniques and at input–output systems.

CHAPTER E2

Utility and the Theory of Demand

E2.1 INTRODUCTION

The demand for a particular commodity (or good) depends simultaneously on many factors, e.g. its price, the prices of other commodities, the tastes of the consumers, the incomes of the consumers and the distribution of income within the population. The purpose of the theory of demand is to ascertain quantitatively the way in which the various factors affect the demand for certain goods. Such a theory might be used by individual manufacturers wishing to know how much of a commodity to manufacture and hence how much manufacturing plant to install; or by the government or academic economists wanting to know how changes in various economic levers, such as taxes, will affect the overall economy.

The nature of demand in the real world is complicated: it depends on many more factors than those already mentioned, e.g. the amount of advertising for the good, the cost and availability of credit, etc. In addition the types of good under consideration are extremely varied: some goods, e.g. bread, are bought almost every day whereas a consumer may buy a house only two or three times in a lifetime: some goods are bought almost exclusively by manufacturers, e.g. machine tools, and other goods are bought first by retailers and then mainly by domestic consumers, e.g. shoes: there may be a finite stock of some goods, e.g. uranium, whereas other goods, e.g. air, are so plentiful that they are free; and some goods, e.g. leisure, are not easy to define or to price.

In order to construct a theory, we must at first ignore most of these complexities. This means imposing some restrictions on the factors involved and on the type of goods we consider. When we have 'understood' our constructed theory, we may then be able to relax these restrictions. Thus we only consider the factors mentioned in the first paragraph. We confine our considerations to goods which are always of the same quality and meet the same specifications, e.g. 'good quality' peas, or iron nails of a certain length and shape. In general we ignore the effect of 'brand' names (for example, when talking about washing-powders, we neglect the effect of the names 'Persil' or 'Ariel' on the consumer). For convenience we assume that the quantities of the good can be specified in infinitely small divisions of standard units, e.g. specification by weight or by volume. This restriction is not essential but it makes the mathematics easier by letting us use the tools of analysis and in particular of calculus. For simplicity we assume that there is an infinite stock of each good.

Please note then that the theory developed here does not fit exactly the economic behaviour of many types of good in the real world; nevertheless, we proceeed with it in the hope that the analysis and the results of the model can be used to understand the behaviour of demand in many real situations.

E2.2 CONSUMER PREFERENCE

Why is the demand for one commodity, e.g. peas, greater than that for another, e.g. spinach? Is there a way of measuring quantitatively this difference?

To try to answer these questions we consider the preferences of a particular consumer. To measure them we can imagine the consumer in a room with two tables, on each of which there are a collection of goods; he then chooses between the two collections. By varying these collections a complete picture of his preferences can be obtained.

The collections do not have the prices of goods displayed, so that the preferences are made independently of price. It is in the market that the preferences and prices together are supposed to determine the consumer's demands. This assumption of the separation of preferences and prices may be unrealistic. Indeed, there are circumstances when price does influence preference, for example when the consumer wishes to impress by his wealth and buys in a lavish, ostentatious manner. It is also assumed that the quality of the goods is fixed and known: for example the consumer knows whether the lettuces have slugs in them or whether the car batteries are good. Of course a higher price is sometimes a guarantee of quality; such an effect is ignored in our theory.

A consumer's preferences vary considerably with time; for example, in the evening he may prefer a pint of beer to a bowl of cornflakes, whereas in the morning he prefers the cornflakes to the beer. From the producer's viewpoint, he may consume both the pint of beer and the bowl of cornflakes in the period in which the producers make their decisions to increase or decrease the manufacture of beer and cornflakes. Thus in economics we average the preferences of a consumer over such a period. We assume that such a period is long enough to average the rapid fluctuations in the consumer's preferences but short enough not to mask any slow variation in the tastes of the consumer.

We thus, in principle, know the order of the consumer's preferences. We now develop this mathematically to see how it affects the demand for a commodity.

Vector notation

In a unit period of time the amounts of two different commodities, labelled can be specified by putting the quantities q_1, q_2 in a particular order, i.e. (q_1, q_2). We thus adopt a vector notation, i.e. write $\mathbf{q} = (q_1, q_2)$. With n different types of commodity, a vector $\mathbf{q}$ becomes $(q_1, q_2, q_3, \ldots, q_n)$.

The set of these vectors is the cone formed by the positive quadrant. It is called the **commodity space**. (This space is convex and connected; there are no regions not available to the consumer.) This space is not a vector space as the quantities $q_1, q_2, \ldots, q_n$ are always non-negative. Thus it is only permissible to subtract two vectors if the resultant lies in commodity space.

The usual scalar product is defined:

$$\mathbf{q}.\mathbf{r} = \sum_i q_i r_i. \tag{E2.2.1}$$

Preference. To signify that consumer A prefers the quantities $\mathbf{q}$ $(= (q_1, q_2, \ldots, q_n))$ to $\mathbf{r}$ $(= (r_1, r_2, \ldots, r_n))$ we write

$$\mathbf{q} \underset{A}{\succ} \mathbf{r} \quad \text{or} \quad \mathbf{r} \underset{A}{\prec} \mathbf{q}. \tag{E2.2.2}$$

To show that he does not prefer $\mathbf{q}$ to $\mathbf{r}$ we write

$$\mathbf{q} \underset{A}{\not\succ} \mathbf{r}.$$

Indifference. If $\mathbf{q} \underset{A}{\not\succ} \mathbf{r}$ and $\mathbf{r} \underset{A}{\not\succ} \mathbf{q}$, consumer A is said to be indifferent between $\mathbf{q}$ and $\mathbf{r}$, and this is written $\mathbf{q} \underset{A}{\sim} \mathbf{r}$.

If A either is indifferent or prefers $\mathbf{q}$ to $\mathbf{r}$ we write $\mathbf{q} \underset{A}{\succsim} \mathbf{r}$.

A's preferences can be expressed in terms of his utility (see E2.3). One way of deriving utility theory is to study the properties of the preference relations. Alternatively it can be assumed directly and the following paragraphs omitted.

***Properties of the preference relations**

Completeness: the set of preference relations ($\underset{A}{\succ}$, $\underset{A}{\prec}$, $\underset{A}{\sim}$) is complete, i.e. for any bundles $\mathbf{q}, \mathbf{r}$ of commodities

$$\text{either} \quad \mathbf{q} \underset{A}{\succ} \mathbf{r}, \quad \mathbf{r} \underset{A}{\succ} \mathbf{q}, \quad \text{or } \mathbf{q} \underset{A}{\sim} \mathbf{r}. \tag{E2.2.3}$$

Transitivity:

$$\text{if } \mathbf{q} \underset{A}{\succ} \mathbf{r} \text{ and } \mathbf{r} \underset{A}{\succsim} \mathbf{s} \text{ then } \mathbf{q} \underset{A}{\succ} \mathbf{s};$$

$$\text{if } \mathbf{q} \underset{A}{\succ} \mathbf{r} \text{ and } \mathbf{r} \underset{A}{\succsim} \mathbf{s} \quad \text{then} \quad \mathbf{q} \underset{A}{\succ} \mathbf{s}. \tag{E2.2.4}$$

Monotony: for all $\mathbf{q} \neq \mathbf{0}, \mathbf{s} \neq \mathbf{0} \quad \mathbf{q} + \mathbf{s} \succ_A \mathbf{q}$. (E2.2.5)

The first property, completeness, follows from the definitions, Both transitivity and monotony are reasonable if the consumer behaves rationally and if discommodities such as rubbish, for which monotony does not hold, are not considered. It can be argued that a consumer 'can have too much of commodity', but he can always give any surplus away, so that (E2.2.5) holds even when $\mathbf{q}$ has a large component. Of course a consumer may become satiated, i.e. his desire for a commodity decreases with increasing amounts of it. This is discussed in E2.5.

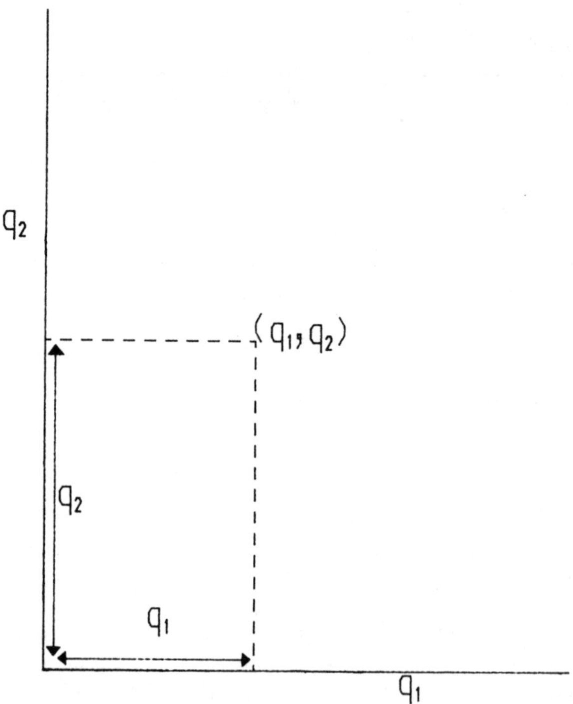

Fig. E2.1. Commodity space for two commodities Q_1, Q_2 showing the vector (q_1, q_2).

***Preference zones**

From the monotony property (E2.2.5) we can, for a given $\mathbf{r}_1$, partition commodity space into various zones. (See Fig. E2.2.) Zone (1) is such that for vectors $\mathbf{q}$ in this zone, $(\mathbf{q} - \mathbf{r}_1)$ is a commodity vector, so that $\mathbf{q} \succ_A \mathbf{r}_1$. Thus vectors in Zone (1) (hatched with a \\\\\ pattern in Fig. (E2.2) are preferred to $\mathbf{r}_1$. In Zone (2), $(\mathbf{r}_1 - \mathbf{q})$ is a commodity vector, so that $\mathbf{r}_1 \succ_A \mathbf{q}$, i.e. $\mathbf{r}_1$ is preferred to any vector in Zone (2) (hatched with a ///// pattern in Fig. E2.2). In Zones (3) and (4) we are ignorant as to whether a vector in these zones is, or is not, preferred to $\mathbf{r}_1$.

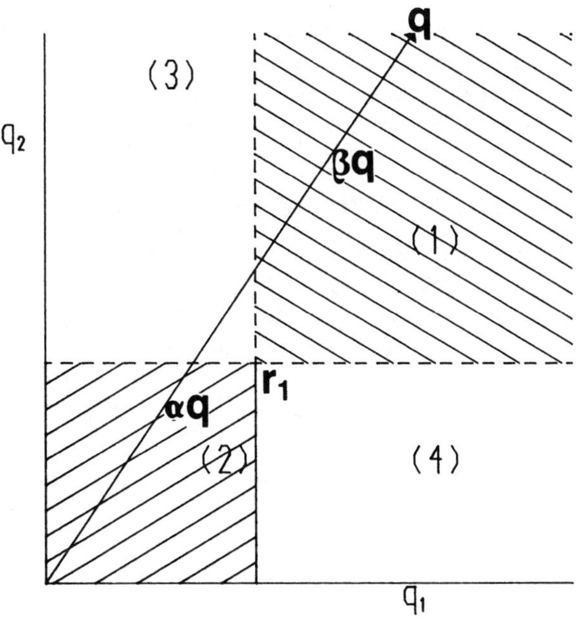

Fig. E2.2. Preference zones for a given point $\mathbf{r}_1$. For definition of the points $\alpha\mathbf{q}$ and $\beta\mathbf{q}$, see E2.5.

** Equivalence classes under the relation ~

The properties ensure that if $\mathbf{q} \underset{A}{\sim} \mathbf{r}$, then $\mathbf{r} \underset{A}{\sim} \mathbf{q}$; they also ensure

Theorem E2.2.1 If $\mathbf{q} \underset{A}{\sim} \mathbf{r}$ *and* $\mathbf{r} \underset{A}{\sim} \mathbf{s}$, *then* $\mathbf{q} \underset{A}{\sim} \mathbf{s}$. (E2.2.6)

We leave the proof of this to the reader, suggesting the *reductio ad absurdum* method.

The relation $\underset{A}{\sim}$ thus satisfies the requirements for an equivalence relation, which are:

(i) $\mathbf{q} \underset{A}{\sim} \mathbf{q}$;

(ii) if $\mathbf{q} \underset{A}{\sim} \mathbf{r}$ then $\mathbf{r} \underset{A}{\sim} \mathbf{q}$;

(iii) if $\mathbf{q} \underset{A}{\sim} \mathbf{r}$ and $\mathbf{r} \underset{A}{\sim} \mathbf{s}$ then $\mathbf{q} \underset{A}{\sim} \mathbf{s}$. (E2.2.7)

As $\underset{A}{\sim}$ is an equivalence relation, it partitions the set of commodity vectors into equivalence classes. These equivalence classes are in fact surfaces, as can be seen from the following:

Theorem E2.2.2. On any straight line with a positive gradient, there is at most one point belonging to a particular equivalence class. (E2.2.8).

If there were two points belonging to a given equivalence class, the monotony property (E2.2.5) would be violated.

These equivalence classes are known as indifference surfaces or when only two goods are involved, indifference curves.

E2.3 INDIFFERENCE SURFACES AND UTILITY

An **indifference surface** for consumer A is a set of points in commodity space such that for any two points r_1, r_2 on that surface, $r_1 \underset{A}{\sim} r_2$. When only two goods are involved, the surfaces are called **indifference curves**. Indifference surfaces do not cross, and they can only touch at infinity. Each indifference surface partitions the commodity space into two regions (Fig. E2.3), the one further from the origin being preferred to the one closer to the origin.

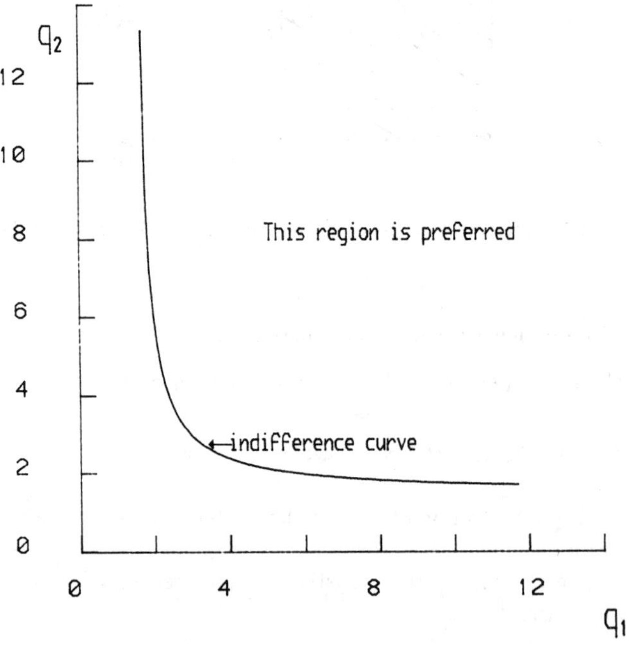

Fig. E2.3. An indifference curve partitions commodity space into two regions.

These indifference surfaces are usually considered, as we do here, to be **smooth**, i.e. expressible by equations involving continuous, differentiable functions. Continuity is proven in E2.5 using a new assumption but little is learned from that proof, and that section may be omitted if desired.

Typical examples of some indifference curves are given by the equations $(q_1 - U)(q_2 - U) = U^2$ for various values of U. In this example, U increases with distance from the origin, i.e. with increasing preference, so that U looks like a measure of preference. Note that these curves have negative slope, i.e. $\mathrm{d}q_2/\mathrm{d}q_1 < 0$.

This is a requirement for all indifference curves, as can be seen from Fig. E2.4. In addition these curves are convex, i.e. $d^2 q_2/dq_1^2 > 0$. The convexity of indifference surfaces is often assumed in microeconomic theory, because it facilitates certain uniqueness proofs. It is justified by the concept of satiation: a consumer is likely to prefer roughly equal amounts (in appropriate units!) of two goods to having a large amount of one and none of the other. We investigate this further in E2.5.

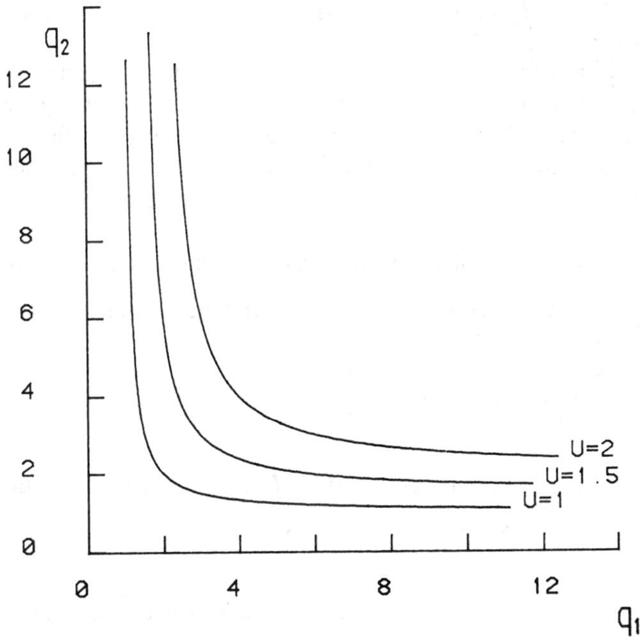

Fig. E2.4. Indifference curves $(q_1 - U)(q_2 - U) = U^2$ for various values of U.

Utility

We assign to each indifference curve a number U_A known as utility such that U is monotonically strictly increasing with the preference of the indifference surfaces. Thus, if $\mathbf{q}$ is a point and $U_A(\mathbf{q})$ is the number assigned to the unique indifference surface on which $\mathbf{q}$ lies, then $U_A(\mathbf{q})$ is known as A's **utility function** for the bundle $\mathbf{q}$. A particular indifference surface on which the utility is U_0 has the equation

$$U_A(\mathbf{q}) = U_0. \tag{E2.3.1}$$

As this surface is smooth we assume that it is possible to choose $U_A(\mathbf{q})$ as continuous and differentiable. Then, from the monotony property,

$$\partial U_A/\partial q_i \geqslant 0. \tag{E2.3.2}$$

The properties required of $U_A(\mathbf{q})$ are that for all $\mathbf{x}$ and $\mathbf{y}$

$$U_A(\mathbf{x}) > U_A(\mathbf{y}) \Leftrightarrow \mathbf{x} \underset{A}{\succ} \mathbf{y};$$

$$U_A(\mathbf{x}) = U_A(\mathbf{y}) \Leftrightarrow \mathbf{x} \underset{A}{\sim} \mathbf{y}. \tag{E2.3.3}$$

These properties do not uniquely define $U_A(\mathbf{q})$. For a given function $U_A(\mathbf{q})$, any monotically increasing function of $U_A(\mathbf{q})$ also satisfies the conditions (E2.3.1) and so is suitable. Thus utility in our theory is not a measurable quantity – only the indifference surfaces and their order are 'measurable'. A utility function need not be introduced – it just makes the mathematics and the verbal reasoning easier.

To each consumer a utility function can be assigned but none of them is uniquely defined. Thus in most circumstances it is not possible to compare one person's utility function with another's. Hence to sum individual utilities to obtain an overall utility for a group of people does not give a useful quantity, and to talk of the greatest good of the greatest number is meaningless!

Rate of Commodity Substitution (or Marginal Rate of Substitution)

On an indifference surface, U_A is constant, so that its differential $\mathrm{d}U_A$ is zero. Now

$$\mathrm{d}U_A = \sum_i (\partial U_A/\partial q_i)\, \mathrm{d}q_i \tag{E2.3.4}$$

so that on an indifference surface, $U(q_1, \ldots, q_n)$ is a constant and

$$\sum_i (\partial U_A/\partial q_i)\, \mathrm{d}q_i = 0. \tag{E2.3.5}$$

Suppose that q_3, q_4, etc. are kept constant and the amount of good Q_1 that consumer A has is reduced by a small amount δq_1. Then A can maintain his utility by increasing the amount of Q_2 he has by an amount δq_2 in such a way that he stays on the same indifference surface. $(-\delta q_2/\delta q_1)$ is known as the rate of commodity substitution (RCS) of Q_2 for Q_1, and is non-negative: from (E2.3.3) it is given by

$$(\partial U_A/\partial q_1)_{2,3,4,\ldots,} / (\partial U_A/\partial q_2)_{1,3,4,\ldots}. \tag{E2.3.6}$$

In the example of Fig. E2.4, RCS $= (q_2^2/q_1^2)$.

E2.4 DEMAND

The maximization of utility

Our aim is to find consumer A's demand for the goods Q_1, Q_2, etc., given that he has a certain amount of money, y_A, to spend on these goods. This demand function is obtained by maximizing the utility function, subject to the constraint of only spending y_A units of money. The maximization procedure ensures that A gets what he most wants over the unit period of time. (Is impulse buying taken into account in our theory?)

Suppose the price of good i is p_i units of money. Then the total cost of buying $\mathbf{q}$ goods is

$$\sum_i p_i q_i \equiv \mathbf{p}.\mathbf{q}. \qquad \text{(E2.4.1)}$$

If consumer A has y_A units of money, then the budget constraint on A is

$$\mathbf{p}.\mathbf{q} \leqslant y_A. \qquad \text{(E2.4.2)}$$

For various reasons (see below), microeconomic theory usually ignores the 'less than' (<) condition in (E2.4.2), so that the budget constraint becomes

$$\mathbf{p}.\mathbf{q} = y_A. \qquad \text{(E2.4.2a)}$$

We aim to maximize $U_A(\mathbf{q})$ subject to this constraint. The maximization of a function subject to several constraints is an important and common mathematical problem; the usual procedure for this is the method of Lagrange multipliers, described in the next chapter (E3). Our problem here is so simple that we can solve it directly.

The constraint (E2.4.2) constitutes a hyperplane (a line in two-dimensions: see Fig. E2.5) in commodity space. If an indifference surface cuts this plane,

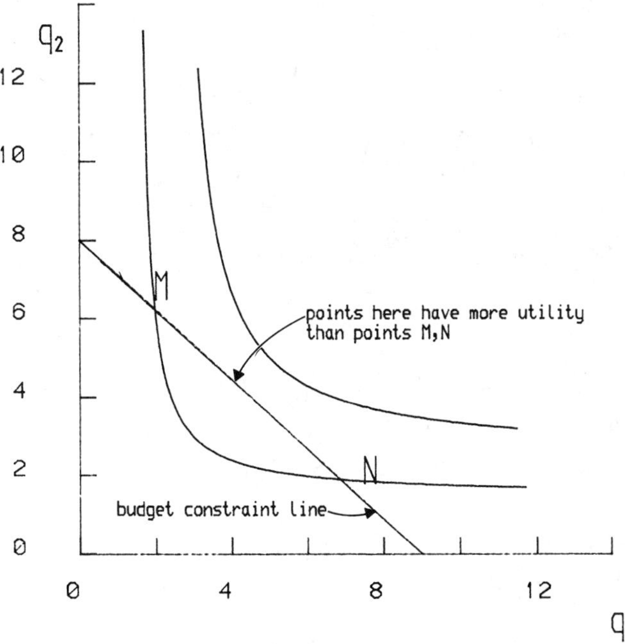

Fig. E2.5. An indifference curve crossing the budget constraint line MN.

there are points on the plane with higher values of utility than the points common to both the plane and the indifference surface. Thus the points with the highest values of utility occur either at places where an indifference surface is tangential to the plane or at the edges of the plane.

Let us consider the former case first. Then at a maximum point, the surface must have the same gradients as the plane of budget constraint, i.e.

$$(\partial U_A/\partial q_j)\,(\partial U_A/\partial q_i) = p_j/p_i \tag{E2.4.3}$$

which can be interpreted as saying that the rate of commodity substitution must be equal to the ratio of the prices. From (E2.4.3) we see that there exists a non-zero number λ such that, for all i,

$$\partial U_A/\partial q_i = \lambda p_i \tag{E2.4.4}$$

or in vector form

$$\nabla U_A = \lambda \mathbf{p}. \tag{E2.4.5}$$

The above equation is the one we would get if we used the technique of Lagrange multipliers. Together with the constraint equation (E2.4.2) these equations yield values of $\mathbf{q}$ which correspond to the turning points of U_A. There may be several of these, some of which are maxima and some of which may be minima. Assuming that there is at least one, we choose the absolute maximum value of U_A, so that for a given value of $\mathbf{p}$ and y_A, this value of U_A is unique. Let us here assume that this procedure gives rise to a unique value of $\mathbf{q}$, so that we can write

$$\mathbf{q} = \mathbf{D}_A(\mathbf{p}, y_A) \tag{E2.4.6}$$

where $\mathbf{D}_A$ is a one-valued function of $\mathbf{p}$ and y_A. The ith component is known as A's demand function for Q_i.

When the highest values of utility occur on the edges of the plane, one or more of the components q_i of $\mathbf{q}$ are zero; we then have to solve (E2.4.3) and (E2.4.2) in a restricted commodity space with these components. We can still assume that $\mathbf{q}$ is a unique function of $\mathbf{p}$ and y_A so that equation (E2.4.6) still applies.

Example. Suppose a consumer's utility function U for two goods, butter and margarine, is given implicitly by

$$(M + 6 - U)\,(B + 6 - 2U) = 2U^2$$

where B, M are the amounts in 1/100 kg of butter and margarine respectively. Suppose their prices in £ per 1/100 kg are b and m respectively. What are the demand funtions?

In Fig. E2.6 are drawn some typical indifference curves. Note that for $U > 3$ the curves do not reach the M-axis and for $U > 6$ they do not reach the B-axis either.

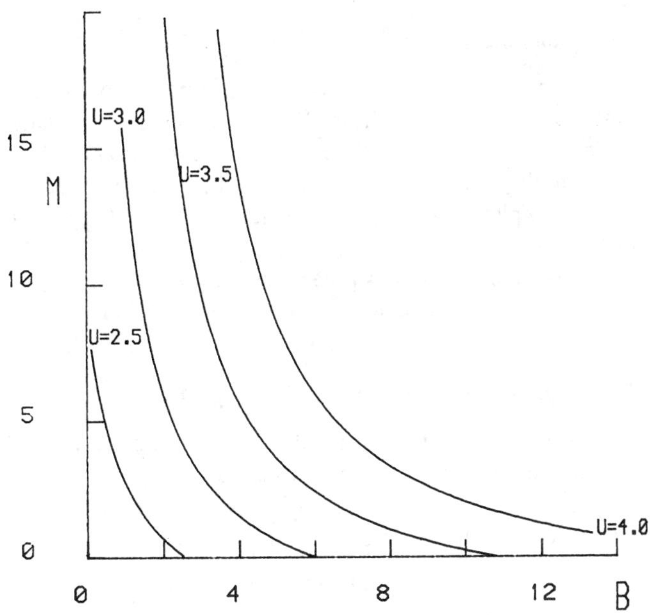

Fig. E2.6. Some indifference curves for the 'butter' and 'margarine' example.

To find the demand functions we write

$$U = (M + 6)(B + 6)/(B + 2M + 18)$$

and assume that the maximization of U occurs at a point where both M and B are non-zero. Differentiating with respect to B and then M, we get from (E2.4.3)

$$(B + 6)/(M + 6) = (2m/b)^{1/2}.$$

The budget constraint is

$$Bb + Mm = y$$

where y is the amount of money per unit time available for spending on both butter and margarine. The demand functions are

$$B = (2/b)^{1/2}(6m + 6b + y)/(m^{1/2} + (2b)^{1/2}) - 6$$

$$M = (1/m)^{1/2}(6m + 6b + y)/(m^{1/2} + (2b)^{1/2}) - 6.$$

If one of these is negative, the corresponding good is not bought. Thus if

$$y \leqslant 6m^{1/2}(-m^{1/2} + (b/2)^{1/2}), \quad \textit{then } B = 0, M = y/m,$$

and if

$$y \leqslant 6(2b)^{1/2}(m^{1/2} - (b/2)^{1/2}), \quad \textit{then } M = 0, B = y/b.$$

These two results occur when the maximum of U is on one of the axes.

Budget and income

Let Y_A be A's income. The budget y_A for the goods under consideration is a function of Y_A. If A partitions Y_A into amounts for his various wants, then y_A is a function of Y_A only. It then follows that A gains no utility by not spending all of y_A on these goods, so that equation (E2.4.2a) is correct.

It is simplest, but a bit unrealistic, to assume that y_A is linearly proportional to Y_A.

The assumption that y_A depends only on Y_A and not on prices etc. is also unrealistic but it is difficult to improve on it without complicating the theory.

The Aggregate Demand Function

This is the sum of the individual demand functions. It is a function of **p** and of the amounts $y_A, y_B, \ldots,$ spent by the various customers on the commodity Q_i. As these amounts are functions of the consumers' incomes $Y_A, Y_B, \ldots,$ etc., we write the aggregate demand function for Q_i as

$$D_i(\mathbf{p}, Y_A, Y_B, \ldots). \tag{E2.4.7}$$

The demand for particular commodities varies in different ways with different incomes; for example, the demand for slippers is fairly constant over the population whereas the demand for luxury yachts is restricted to the rich. It is thus convenient to write D_i as a function of Y, the average income, and of $\mathscr{D}$, the distribution of income within the population:

$$q_i = D_i(\mathbf{p}, Y, \mathscr{D}). \tag{E2.4.8}$$

Having shown the existence of D_i, our aim now is to find some of its properties.

Money Illusion

Demand functions are homogeneous of degree zero in prices and incomes. This follows from the linearity of the budget constraint (E2.4.2); if all prices and budgets are multiplied by the same factor, the quantities demanded do not change. (If **p** and y_A are multiplied by z, equations (E2.4.2) and (E2.4.3) are unchanged, i.e. z cancels out. The result (E2.4.6) occurs whether $(\mathbf{p}, y_A)$ or $(z\mathbf{p}, zy_A)$ are the prices and budgets respectively.) As budgets and incomes are linearly related, our conclusion follows.

This condition on the demand functions can be empirically tested. A consumer's utility increases if his income alone increases, but if prices also increase in the same proportion, the increase in utility is illusory.

Demand Curves

If Y, $\mathscr{D}$, and all the prices of goods except Q_i are assumed constant, q_i, the aggregate demand for Q_i, is a function of p_i:

$$q_i = D_i(p_i). \tag{E2.4.9}$$

This is the demand function with which we are mostly concerned. The actual curve depends on the utility functions, on the other prices, etc., but it is generally assumed to be negatively sloped, i.e. the lower the price, the greater the demand.

*Quality

Important though D_i is, quantities such as utility and indifference surfaces also have their uses. Consider an average consumer: we can picture him as having a utility function from which the aggregate demand function is derived. Suppose his utility function for butter and margarine is as given in our example. Then to achieve a utility of $U = 3.5$ requires only 11/100 kg of butter on its own but requires enormous quantities of margarine on its own, i.e. the average consumer prefers butter to margarine. The consumer considers that butter has more **quality** than its substitute commodity (see E2.6), margarine. The concept of quality can be very useful to a manufacturer when trying to sell more of a product.

**E2.5 SMOOTHNESS AND CONVEXITY

Topology

A surface without breaks is called **topological**; the indifference surfaces can be shown to have this property. This implies that there are the same number of surfaces as there are points on the real line, so that to each surface a utility value can be assigned. There are examples of similar types of 'surfaces' which are not topological and to which utility values cannot be assigned. This property is thus important in ensuring that utility is a sensible concept.

We now establish the existence of this property. Firstly, we prove the following:

Theorem E2.5.1. For a given $\mathbf{r}_1$ *and any* $\mathbf{q}$*, there exist real numbers* α, β *such that* $\alpha\,\mathbf{q} \prec_A \mathbf{r}_1$ *and* $\beta\,\mathbf{q} \succ_A \mathbf{r}_1$. (E2.5.1)

This can be seen to be true from Fig. E2.3, i.e. $\alpha\mathbf{q}$ lies in the zone in which $\mathbf{r}_1$ is preferred, and $\beta\mathbf{q}$ lies in the zone of vectors preferred to $\mathbf{r}_1$. Algebraically it can be seen that there always exist numbers α, β such that $(\mathbf{r}_1 - \alpha\mathbf{q})$ and $(\beta\mathbf{q} - \mathbf{r}_1)$ are commodity vectors and hence from the monotony assumption (E2.2.5), we have the result (E2.5.1).

Using the monotony assumption we also have the following:

Theoren E2.5.2. For any real positive numbers λ, μ *such that* $\lambda > \mu$*, and for any* $\mathbf{q} \neq 0$

$$\lambda\mathbf{q} \succ_A \mu\mathbf{q}. \tag{E2.5.2}$$

This can be proved in the same way as (E2.5.1) was proved.

Suppose we travel along the ray in the direction of $\mathbf{q}$ starting at the origin O. At first we are at points $\alpha\mathbf{q}$ such that $\alpha\mathbf{q} \not\succsim_A \mathbf{r}_1$; then suddenly we are at points $\beta\mathbf{q}$ such that $\beta\mathbf{q} \succ_A \mathbf{r}_1$. Let γ be the least upper bound of the set $\{\alpha\}$ – then γ is the greatest lower bound of the set $\{\beta\}$ and

$$\beta \geqslant \gamma \geqslant \alpha. \tag{E2.5.3}$$

The problem for us is that we want γ to belong to neither set $\{\alpha\}$ nor set $\{\beta\}$. In that case

$$\gamma\mathbf{q} \underset{A}{\sim} \mathbf{r}_1 \tag{E2.5.4}$$

by the completeness property (E2.2.3).

The appropriate way to ensure that γ belongs to neither $\{\alpha\}$ nor $\{\beta\}$ is to require these sets to be open, *i.e. the sets of real numbers* $\{\alpha\colon \alpha\mathbf{q} \not\succsim_A \mathbf{r}_1\}$ *and* $\{\beta\colon \beta\mathbf{q} \succ_A \mathbf{r}_1\}$ *are open at the upper and lower boundaries respectively* (E2.5.4).

This, then, is an additional assumed property of the preference relations. From this property we see that for any $\mathbf{q}$, there always exists one and only one real number γ such that $\gamma\mathbf{q} \underset{A}{\sim} \mathbf{r}_1$.

From this property it is easy to demonstrate that the indifference surfaces are topological. From Fig. E2.2 we see that in any neighbourhood of $\mathbf{r}_1$, no matter how small, we can find a point $\gamma\mathbf{q}$ such that $\gamma\mathbf{q} \underset{A}{\sim} \mathbf{r}_1$. The point $\gamma\mathbf{q}$ has to be close to $\mathbf{r}_1$ because of the monotony property (E2.2.5). We leave a formal proof, if so desired, to the reader.

Theorem E2.2.2 shows that through every point $x\mathbf{q}$ along a ray there passes one indifference surface, so that there are the same number of indifference surfaces as there are points on the positive real line. Consequently, $U(x\mathbf{q})$ can be chosen as a differentiable function of x, with the property that

$$\partial U(x\mathbf{q})/\partial x > 0. \tag{E2.5.5}$$

The general differentiability of $U(\mathbf{q})$ cannot be proved†: however, for smooth surfaces and sensibly chosen functions U, utility is differentiable.

Convexity

It is often assumed that indifference surfaces are convex. To see why, consider the case with only two commodities, Q_1, Q_2. If all indifference curves are convex and do not touch the axes for finite q_1, q_2, then the constraint equation (E2.4.2) is tangential at only one point of contact to only one indifference curve. This makes the equations (E2.4.3) simpler to solve: more importantly it means that there is only one value of $\mathbf{q}$ for given values of $\mathbf{p}$ and y so that the demand function can be defined unambiguously everywhere and is continuous.

Convexity can be defined when there are more than two commodities:

† When defined over the surfaces of E5.2, a function like $U(\mathbf{q})$ is not differentiable.

'a function $U(\mathbf{q})$ is said to be **convex (concave)** in the region R if

$$U(\lambda\mathbf{q}^1 + (1-\lambda)\mathbf{q}^2) \leqslant (\geqslant)\ \lambda U(\mathbf{q}^1) + (1-\lambda)\,U(\mathbf{q}^2) \text{ for all } \mathbf{q}^1, \mathbf{q}^2 \text{ in } R.\text{'} \tag{E2.5.6}$$

With no equality sign in (E2.5.6), $U(\mathbf{q})$ is said to be strictly convex (concave). If the utility function is strictly concave, the indifference surfaces are convex. (See EE2.11.)

The convexity of the indifference surfaces is usually justified by the idea of **satiation**: it is thought that a consumer prefers approximately equal amounts (in appropriate units) of two goods to having a large amount of one and a small amount of the other. This seems reasonable in general but there may well be exceptions and is hardly sufficient to justify assuming that all utility functions are concave globally (i.e. at all points of commodity space).

* E2.6 ELASTICITIES

Empirical information about the demand functions is difficult to obtain. Estimates of their derivatives at certain points are easier to get, and the information obtained is usually formulated in terms of quantities known as 'elasticities'.

The own-elasticity of demand for Q_i is written ϵ_{ii} and is defined as

$$\epsilon_{ii} = \frac{p_i}{q_i}\,(\partial q_i/\partial p_i)_{p_{j\neq i}}. \tag{E2.6.1}$$

At given values of $\mathbf{p}$, $\mathbf{q}$, this elasticity is a number, independent of the units in which $\mathbf{p}$ and $\mathbf{q}$ are measured. It is negative, as demand curves are downward sloping.

The expenditure on Q_i is $p_i q_i$, so that the change in this expenditure when the price p_i increases to $(p_i + \delta p_i)$ is

$$\delta p_i \partial(p_i q_i)/\partial p_i = q_i\left(1 + \frac{p_i}{q_i}\,\partial q_i/\partial p_i\right)\delta p_i = q_i(1+\epsilon_{ii})\,\delta p_i. \tag{E2.6.2}$$

Thus the expenditure increases if $\epsilon_{ii} > -1$ but decreases if $\epsilon_{ii} < -1$. It is thus critical for a manufacturer to have a reasonable estimate of ϵ_{ii} before he increases his prices.

An increase in p_i affects the demand for Q_j $(j \neq i)$. A cross-price elasticity describes this effect:

$$\epsilon_{ji} = \frac{p_i}{q_j}\,(\partial q_j/\partial p_i)_{p_{k\neq i}}. \tag{E2.6.3}$$

The increase in p_i may increase the demand for Q_j because consumers substitute Q_j for Q_i; or it may decrease the demand, because consumers have less money to spend on Q_j as the amount they have spent on Q_i has increased.

From the individual budget constraint equation (E2.4.2), we have

$$\mathbf{p}.\mathbf{q} = \sum_A y_A \equiv y \tag{E2.6.4}$$

where $\mathbf{q}$ now represents the aggregate quantity of goods, and y represents the aggregate amount of money spent. Then, when all prices except p_i remain constant,

$$q_i + p_i\,(\partial q_i/\partial p_i)_{p_{j\neq i}} + \sum_{j\neq i} p_j(\partial q_j/\partial p_i)_{p_{k\neq i}} = 0,$$

i.e.

$$1 + \epsilon_{ii} + \sum_{j\neq i} \frac{p_j q_j}{p_i q_i}\,\epsilon_{ji} = 0. \tag{E2.6.5}$$

This equation (E2.6.5) shows that if the expenditure on Q_i increases (i.e. if $1 + \epsilon_{ii} > 0$) then at least one of the cross-elasticities must be negative, but if the expenditure decreases, then the cross-elasticities can all be positive.

Of interest also is the way that the demand for goods varies with income, and in particular how it varies with average income Y. We define an **income elasticity** of demand for good i

$$\eta_i = \frac{Y}{q_i}\left(\frac{\partial q_i}{\partial Y}\right)_p. \tag{E2.6.6}$$

Income elasticities are usually considered as positive, although they can sometimes be negative as when an increase in income allows more luxurious items to be bought; for example, the demand for public transport decreases when consumers can afford to buy private cars.

The budget constraint equation (E2.6.4) gives some relations between the income elasticities. Assuming that y is linearly proportional to Y,

$$\mathbf{p}\,.\,(\partial\mathbf{q}/\partial Y) = y/Y, \tag{E2.6.7}$$

which gives on rearrangement

$$\sum_i p_i q_i \eta_i = y. \tag{E2.6.8}$$

** The Slutsky Equation

An increase in the price p_i changes both the slope and the position of the hyperplane (E2.4.2) caused by the budget-constraint. We can get to the new hyperplane from the old one in two steps:

(i) we first find the hyperplane which is parallel to the new hyperplane and which is tangential to the old indifference surface, i.e. the utility U is kept fixed;

(ii) then we move to the new hyperplane.

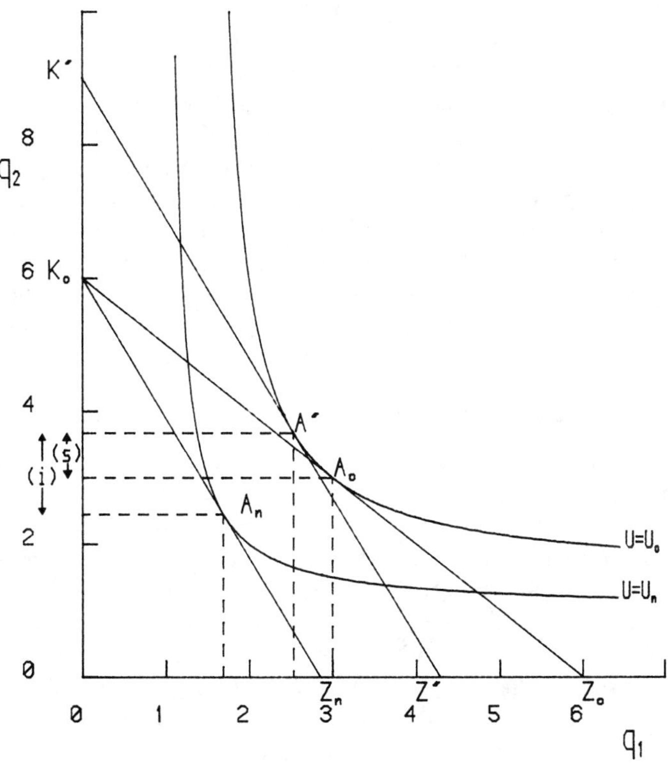

Fig. E2.7. Indifference curves and constraint lines illustrating the Slutsky equation.

In Fig. E2.7, the old hyperplane is the line K_0Z_0: this touched the utility surface $U = U_0$ at the point A_0. The new hyperplane caused by a change in price of good Q_1 is K_0Z_n. To get from K_0Z_0 to K_0Z_n, the first step is to draw $K'Z'$ parallel to K_0Z_n and touching $U = U_0$ at A'. Step (ii) moves from $K'Z'$ to K_0Z_n touching the new utility curve $U = U_n$ at the point A_n.

The first step (i) is not possible unless the income is allowed to increase, i.e. U is kept constant by increasing the income and the price p_i at the same time. The second step decreases the income to its original value, keeping the prices constant. The distance between the two parallel hyperplanes is δy, the change in y required to keep U constant when p_i is changed by the amount δp_i.

In terms of differentials

$$dq_j = (\partial q_j/\partial p_i)_Y dp_i + (\partial q_j/\partial Y)_p dY$$

so that

$$(\partial q_j/\partial p_i)_y = (\partial q_j/\partial p_i)_U - (\partial q_j/\partial Y)_p \left(\frac{\partial Y}{\partial p_i}\right)_U . \qquad \text{(E2.6.9)}$$

Equation (E2.6.9) is known as the Slutsky equation, and shows the two steps discussed above.

The importance of the Slutsky equation is the distinction it makes between the first and second terms in (E2.6.9). The first term keeps the utility constant, and so measures the amount that Q_j substitutes for Q_i (c.f. 'Rate of Commodity Substitution' in E2.3). The second term measures the effect of the decrease in the purchasing power of the income due to an increase in prices. The first is called a **substitution** effect and the second an **income** effect. These are illustrated in Fig. E2.7 on goods Q_1 and Q_2 when the price of Q_1 is increased. The projections of A_0A' and $A'A_n$ on the axes represent the substitution and income effects respectively. On Q_1, both effects are negative, whereas on Q_2 the substitution effect is positive and in this particular case is smaller than the negative income effect, thereby making ϵ_{21} negative.

Substitutes and Complements

Goods may be related to each other in different ways; for example, orange juice and apple juice can be substituted for each other, whereas petrol and cars are complementary, i.e. for travel purposes one cannot be used without the other. Two commodities are called **substitutes** if one commodity can be substituted for the other and satisfy a similar need, whereas they are **complements** if they are both needed in order to satisfy a particular need. These definitions can be made more precise and quantitative by using the substitution effect from the Slutsky equation, i.e. goods i, j are substitutes if $(\partial q_i/\partial p_j)_U > 0$ and complements if $(\partial q_i/\partial p_j)_U < 0$. It is thus useful to introduce a new type of elasticity ξ, which we call a compensated elasticity, i.e.

$$\xi_{ji} = \frac{p_i}{q_j}(\partial q_j/\partial p_i)_U. \qquad \text{(E2.6.10)}$$

The Slutsky equation can thus be written, assuming Y and y are linearly related,

$$\epsilon_{ji} = \xi_{ji} - (\partial q_j/\partial Y)q_i\, Y/y \qquad \text{(E2.6.11)}$$

$$= \xi_{ji} - p_i q_i \eta_j/y. \qquad \text{(E2.6.12)}$$

The compensated own-elasticity ξ_{ii} measures the amount of substitution that occurs when p_i is increased. It is non-positive. If Q_j is a close substitute for Q_i, then ξ_{ji} is large and positive and ξ_{ii} is large and negative. This relationship can be made quantitative as follows:

$$\sum_i \left(\frac{\partial U}{\partial q_i}\right)\left(\frac{\partial q_i}{\partial p_j}\right) = \frac{\partial U}{\partial p_j} \qquad \text{(E2.6.13)}$$

so that when p_j varies, but U is kept constant,

$$\sum_i p_i(\partial q_i/\partial p_j)_U = 0 \qquad \text{(E2.6.14)}$$

using (E2.4.4). This can be written

$$\sum_i p_i q_i \xi_{ij} = 0. \qquad \text{(E2.6.15)}$$

* The concept of an industry

Many commodities are very similar but are distinguishable in small ways, e.g. trade mark, packaging, design, quality. It would be very difficult to gather information about the economy of a nation if each commodity had to be distinguished from closely similar products. It would also be difficult to carry out any overall microeconomic analysis. It is thus worth while to group various similar products into an 'industry'.

The set of products which forms an industry can be chosen by using the compensated cross-elasticities ξ_{ij}. If ξ_{ij} is large, products i and j would be grouped in the same industry. The criterion for the minimum value of ξ_{ij} for products i and j to be in the same industry depends on the kind of classification required. To illustrate this, let us consider cars. Let i be a family saloon car. Then ξ_{ij} is large when j is also a family saloon car with a comparable engine size, but ξ_{ij} is smaller but not zero when j is a sports car. Thus if we want to consider only the industry for family saloon cars, the minimum ξ_{ij} considered would be large; if, however, we wanted to consider the whole car industry, including luxury and sports cars, the minimum for ξ_{ij} would be smaller.

**Duality

In E2.4 we maximized $U(\mathbf{q})$ subject to the constraint of keeping $\mathbf{p}$ and y fixed. Why, however, did we not minimize y with $\mathbf{p}$ and U fixed? This behaviour assumption, i.e. minimizing the cost while keeping the prices and the utility fixed, is as reasonable as our previous one. However, we again get the equations (E2.4.3), so that if there is only one value of $\mathbf{q}$ obtained, the results of this assumption are the same as before. This result can also be got using Lagrange multipliers, as we shall see in E3.

This approach is known as the **dual** to the original problem. Dual problems often occur in microeconomics (see E3 and E5). To approach a problem by its dual is sometimes helpful as it gives fresh insights and new concepts.

In this case we define first the **indirect utility function** $u(\mathbf{p}, y)$ which is the maximum value of utility attainable for given $\mathbf{p}$ and y. It is a unique function of $\mathbf{p}$ and y. Because of (E2.5.5) and the slope of the budget constraint,

$$\partial u(\mathbf{p}, y)/\partial y > 0. \tag{E2.6.16}$$

Thus this function can be inverted to give y as a function of $\mathbf{p}$ and u, i.e.

$$y = C(\mathbf{p}, u). \tag{E2.6.17}$$

This is known as the **consumer cost function**, and is to the dual problem what u is to the original one.

Assuming that $C(\mathbf{p}, u)$ is differentiable with respect to $\mathbf{p}$, then from the budget constraint,

$$(\partial C/\partial p_i)_u = q_i, \tag{E2.6.18}$$

where q_i is the **compensated demand function**, as it was derived with utility kept constant. Differentiating again we get

$$p_j \xi_{ij}/q_i = (\partial q_i/\partial p_j)_u = (\partial^2 C/\partial p_i \partial p_j)_u = (\partial q_j/\partial p_i)_u \tag{E2.6.19}$$

so that

$$\xi_{ij} p_j q_j = \xi_{ji} p_i q_i. \tag{E2.6.20}$$

E2.7 APPLICATIONS

The theory of demand is a general theory so that direct application of it is often not possible without knowledge of the actual utility functions, or demand functions†. We give below two applications: further applications can be found in other books.

Two-person, two-commodity exchange

Suppose two people A and B have initially some quantities (q_{1A}^0, q_{2A}^0) and (q_{1B}^0, q_{2B}^0) of two goods. Why should they wish to exchange with each other any of these quantities? What quantities would they exchange?

These questions can be answered using indifference curves and the device of the Edgeworth Box. Consider A's commodity space with origin O_A and let O_B be the point $(\mathbf{q}_A^0 + \mathbf{q}_B^0)$. Then we draw the rectangular box $O_A M O_B N$. If we view the box from O_B, it can appear as part of B's commodity space with axes $O_B M$, $O_B N$ for the commodities 1 and 2 (see Fig. E2.8). Indifference curves for A and B can be drawn as shown; we assume that the curves are convex. Let G be the point $\mathbf{q}_A^0$, through which can be drawn the curves $U_A(\mathbf{q}_A) = U_A^0$ (i.e. GRH). In the region GTHR contained within these two curves, every point represents an allocation of commodities to A and B which increases the utilities of both A and B above their utility level at G. At any given point X within $GTHR$ there may be different points at which the utilities of both A and B are increased above the utilities at X. As both A and B want to achieve a maximum for their respective utilities, they choose points within $GTHR$ from which it is impossible to increase simultaneously both the utility of A and the utility of B. What is the locus of such points?

The indifference curves touch each other; each one of A's indifference curves touches one and only one of B's indifference curves. The locus of tangent points is known as Edgeworth's **contract curve**, and is shown dashed in Fig. E2.8. Within the region $GTHR$, the curve is RST. From any point on RST, any movement will decrease the utility of either A or B or both. Thus the curve RST represents the locus of points required.

† The theory is in many respects very similar to thermodynamics; for example, utility plays a similar mathematical role to entropy. Direct application of thermodynamics is also difficult without knowledge of the fundamental equation, or the equations of state of a thermodynamic system.

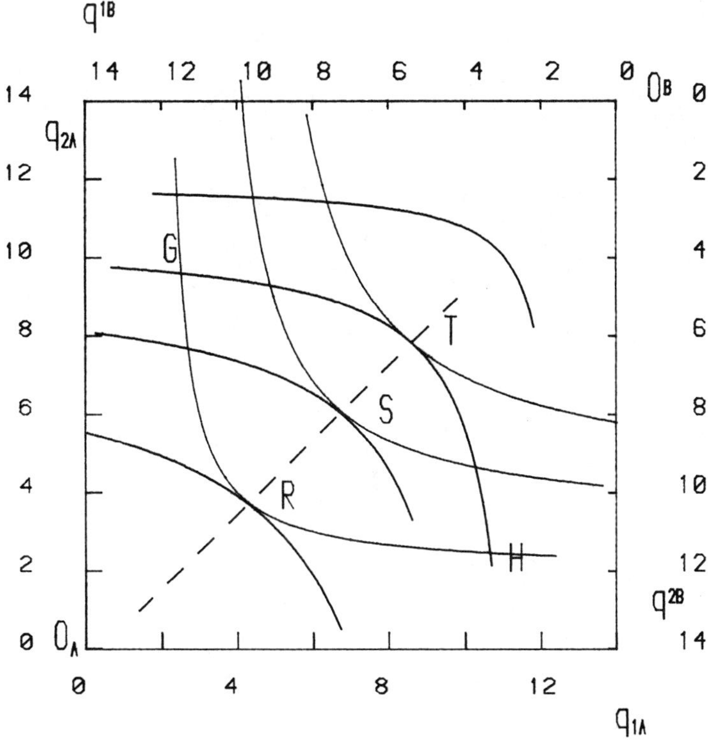

Fig. E2.8. The Edgeworth Box.

This means that A and B exchange quantities of goods until they have amounts corresponding to some point on RST. These criteria do not give a unique point, i.e. they on their own do not tell us exactly what quantities of each good are exchanged, only a range of possible quantities. Incorporation of a budget constraint will, in general, give a unique point (see E4.7).

***Leisure, income and overtime**

Income and leisure are goods in an economic sense, but are qualitatively different from nails or peas: how do we price them or find the demand for them?

Consider an employee A who works for a wage rate r units of money per working hour. What range of income is available to him? Suppose he is asked to work a standard number of hours, 35 say, in a week. He may be allowed to work more than this, thereby increasing his income and decreasing his leisure. He may be able to work less, for example by being late for work, or by absenteeism, or by taking unpaid holidays. This increases his leisure, but decreases his income.

There is thus a range of possible incomes Y_A and leisures l (measured in hours) for a given wage rate, and these form a commodity space. The consumer A can choose between different points in this commodity space and so indifference curves can be drawn (see Fig. E2.9) and a utility function $U(l, Y_A)$ derived. The variables l and Y_A have a finite range: let us take the minimum of l as zero and the maximum of Y_A as $Y_{\max}$. Now l and Y_A are linearly related

$$Y_A + rl = Y_{\max} \tag{E2.7.1}$$

and this acts as a budget constraint. The 'price' of leisure is thus r.

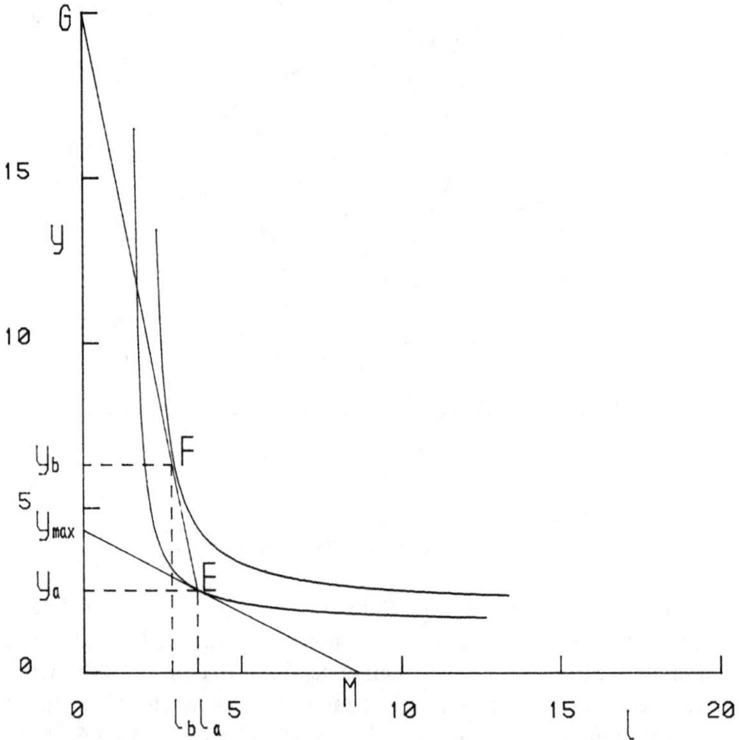

Fig. E2.9. Indifference curves and constraints for income y and leisure l.

The actual values Y_a, l_a are determined by the point E where an indifference curve touches the line (E2.7.1). At E, then, the indifference has slope $(-r)$, i.e.

$$-(\partial U/\partial l_A)/(\partial U/\partial Y_A) = -r. \tag{E2.7.2}$$

Thus the rate of substitution of income for leisure equals the wage rate.

How would an employer induce an employee to work longer? Increasing the wage rate would increase the downward slope of the constraint line, but this line still goes through M, the maximum of l. Where the new constraint line touches an indifference curve depends on the curves, and the new value of l_a may be larger than the original one.

To get the employee freely to work longer, his utility must be increased. The employer can do this by offering a higher wage rate for extra hours worked. This puts a kink in the constraint equation. Let W be the hours worked, so that $(W + l)$ is a constant, Z say. Then the wage rate is r for $W < (Z - l_a)$ and r' for $W > (Z - l_a)$. The budget constraint goes along ME and then along EG, touching a different indifference curve at F. On this curve the utility is greater. The new income and leisure are given by the coordinates of F.

EE2 EXERCISES

2.1 The utility function for the quantities x_1, x_2 of two goods is $U(x_1, x_2) = [x_1^\gamma + 3x_2^\gamma]$. Draw indifference curves for the cases $\gamma = 2$: $\gamma = \frac{2}{3}$: $\gamma = -1$.

2.2 Quantities of whisky and orange juice are denoted by x and y. A consumer's utility function for these goods is $U(x, y) = -(x + 3y) + \sqrt{(x^2 + 10xy + 9y^2)}$:

(i) Derive the rate of commodity substitution by partial differentiation.
(ii) Find the shape of the indifference curves by getting an implicit relation between x, y and U not involving a square root. Derive the rate of commodity substitution from the slopes of the indifference curves and show that the result is the sames as in (i).

2.3 Derive the demand function for the goods in Exercise 2.1 when $\gamma = \frac{2}{3}$.

2.4 A consumer's utility function for two goods is $U(x_1, x_2) = x_1^\alpha x_2^\beta$. Show that the share of this consumer's budget spent on either goods is independent of the price of the goods.

2.5 In a unit of time, a consumer's desires for the quantities x and y of sugar and marmalade respectively are given by the utility function $U(x, y) = (2x^{-1} + y^{-1})^{-1}$. Sketch three indifference curves.

Unit quantities of sugar and marmalade cost p_1 and p_2 units of money respectively. In a unit of time, the consumer has 30 units of money to spend on these items. Show that his demand function for sugar is $30\sqrt{(2/p_1)} / (\sqrt{p_2} + \sqrt{2p_1})$.

If $p_1 = 18$ and $p_2 = 16$, how many units of sugar and marmalade does he buy and how much does he spend on each?

2.6 Suppose that, in Exercise 2.5, the consumer has b units of money. Calculate now the demand functions for sugar and marmalade. Then calculate the six elasticities.

2.7 In a unit of time, a consumer's desires for the quantities x and y of tea and coffee respectively are given by the utility function $U(x, y) = (2x^{1/2} + y^{1/2})^2$. Unit quantities of tea and coffee cost p_x and p_y units of money respectively. In a unit of time, this consumer has B units of money to spend on these items. Find his demand function for tea and the cross-price elasticity for tea.

Show that the own-elasticity for tea is $-2(p_x + 2p_y) / (p_x + 4p_y)$. Show that, if the price of tea increases, the amount that the consumer spends on tea decreases.

2.8 Mr. Smith's preferences between x kg of potatoes and y kg of rice per week are described by the indifference curves

$$U = x^2 y^2 / (2y^2 + x^2)$$

for various values of u. Explain why $f(u(x, y))$, where f is any monotonically increasing function, is a suitable utility function for Mr. Smith.

Given that the prices for a kg of potatoes and a kg of rice are p_1 and p_2 pence respectively, derive Mr. Smith's demand function for potatoes given that he has z pence per week to spend on these goods. Show that this demand function is independent of the particular choice of f.

The values of p_1, p_2 and z are 16, 27 and 153 respectively; how many kilos of potatoes does Mr. Smith buy? The value of p_1 is increasing at ½ pence per week, but both p_2 and z remain constant at the above values. How fast is the amount of money spent by Mr. Smith per week on potatoes increasing, when p_1 is 16?

2.9 If the consumer's utility function with respect to butter, B, and margarine, M, is described by

$$U = (0.7B^{1/2} + 0.3M^{1/2})^2,$$

(a) what is the rate of commodity substitution of butter for margarine?

(b) if the price of butter is twice that of margarine, what is the share of butter in total expenditure y on the two commodities (provided both are bought)?

(c) what parameters in the utility function reflect the quality of butter and margarine? If butter prices rise by 5% a year and margarine prices by 10% a year, by how much would producers of margarine have to raise its relative quality, i.e. change these parameters, to prevent its share in expenditure from falling?

2.10 Show that the utility functions defined in Exercise 2.1 are convex when $0 < \gamma < 1$.

2.11 For a utility U of two quantities x_1 and x_2, find the rate of change of the slope of an indifference curve in terms of the partial derivatives of U. If U is strictly concave, show that the indifference curves are convex.

2.12 Which of the following utility functions are equivalent:

$$U_1 = xy + 1$$
$$U_2 = x^2y^2 + 2xy + 5$$
$$U_3 = xy^2.$$

Give reasons for your answer.

2.13 A consumer's utility function is

$$U = x^2 + 5xy + 4y^2$$

where x and y are the quantities of two commodities X and Y respectively. Sketch three indifference curves. For such curves show that $dy/dx < 0$ and $d^2y/dx^2 > 0$. (Hint: express them in terms of x and y.) Hence show that $-\frac{5}{8} < dy/dx < -\frac{2}{5}$.

In your sketch, draw a line

$$x \cos \alpha + y \sin \alpha = c$$

where α is an acute angle, and indicate α. Taking this equation to be a budget constraint, show that for $\cot \alpha < \frac{2}{5}$, the consumer only buys X, and for $\cot \alpha > \frac{5}{8}$, only Y. What proportion of the budget does the consumer spend on X if $\cot \alpha = \frac{1}{2}$?

2.14 Differentiate (E2.4.4) and (E2.4.2a) to obtain the relations

$$p_i q_i \, \xi_{ij} = p_j q_j \, \xi_{ji} \quad \text{and} \quad \sum_j \xi_{ij} = 0.$$

2.15 Obtain the demand function from the indirect utility function,

$$D_i(p, y) = -(\partial u(\mathbf{p}, y)/\partial p_i)/(\partial u(\mathbf{p}, y)/\partial y).$$

(Roy's identity. Hint: differentiate u and the budget constraint w.r.t. p_i.)

2.16$^{(m)}$ Construct a model to discover how demand is related to quality for a commodity with different levels of quality but with no close substitutes.

Some steps in the procedure might be as follows:

(i) suppose at first there are just two quality levels. Sketch some indifference curves. See whether there are any limits on the **RCS**, and how the indifference curves behave near the axes;

(ii) see how the budget constraint effects the maximization of the utility, and search for any unusual features in the demand functions;

(iii) what are the implications for the pricing of the better quality product?

2.17$^{(m)}$ What factors affect the relation between the budget y_A for a certain set of goods and the income Y_A? Consider a wide variety of goods from food to luxury goods. Investigate how the elasticities and the Slutsky equation are affected.

CHAPTER E3

The Supply Side

E3.1 THE FIRM

The **firm** is the technical name for the unit which, from inputs, produces particular commodities. The firm is thus a typical **input–output** system, turning inputs into commodities. An input (sometimes known as a **factor**) is any good or service which contributes to the production of an output; for example, raw materials such as oil are inputs for making plastics. An example of a service is the labour of the employees. Some goods are outputs for one firm but inputs for another. For example, steel is an input for a car manufacturer but an output for a steel producer.

Input and output levels are rates of flow per unit time. This unit of time is chosen to be long enough to allow the completion of a commodity from a given set of inputs (e.g. in agriculture the unit of time might well be a year). Nevertheless we would want this unit of time to be short enough to consider the technology of making the commodity to be constant.

Technology, in economics, means the way the commodity is made, i.e. the machines and the business and personnel management. Economics does not deal with improving the way commodities are made, which is the task of engineering etc., nor does it deal with improving the output given certain numbers of men and machines. That is the job of business management. Economics assumes that these jobs are done and that the technology decisions have been taken.

The outputs of a firm are thus single-valued functions of the inputs and we can write the output q_i of the ith commodity as

$$q_i = q_i(x_1, x_2, x_3, \ldots, x_n) \qquad \text{(E3.1.1)}$$

where $x_1, x_2, x_3, \ldots, x_n$ are the quantities per unit time of the inputs, X_1, X_2, X_3, etc. q_i is known as the **production function** of the ith commodity. To keep matters simple, we only discuss firms which produce one commodity.

In a firm, various economic decisions are taken, e.g. what inputs are to be used, how many commodities are to be produced? The decision-maker is called the **entrepreneur**; this may be one person, e.g. the owner or the managing-director, or it may be a group, e.g. the management committee or a mass-meeting of all the workers. How decisions are taken is not a concern here, nor are any connotations of the word 'entrepreneur'. It is just a technical term for the decision-maker.

There are many different values of $x_1, x_2, \ldots, x_n$ which lead to a given output. One task of theoretical economics is to find out what choice of the above values the entrepreneur makes and to find the consequences of this choice. This is the main aim of this chapter.

Central to the discussion is the distinction between **fixed** and **variable inputs**. It may not be possible to alter certain inputs (e.g. factories) except over several units of time; such inputs are called 'fixed'. The production function is thus independent of the fixed variables during this length of time. The inputs which can be varied rapidly are called the variable inputs, and the entrepreneur alters these in the **short run** to achieve the required production.

E3.2 THE PRODUCTION FUNCTION

Consider the first m inputs as variable, and the rest as fixed. Then we can write the production function as $q(\mathbf{x}, \xi)$, where $\mathbf{x} \equiv (x_1, x_2, \ldots, x_m)$ represents the amounts of the variable inputs and ξ represents the amounts of the fixed ones. In the short run, i.e. in the time in which ξ is fixed, we can ignore the variation of q with ξ and write the production function simply as

$$q = q(\mathbf{x}). \qquad \text{(E3.2.1)}$$

The vector $\mathbf{x}$ is just like the vector in E2.2, i.e. the vectors cannot have negative components. Here, however, we are dealing with a different space called the **input space**.

The production function is a single-valued function of $\mathbf{x}$, but does not have to be well behaved; in E5 we consider linear production functions which cannot be differentiated at certain points. In this chapter we assume that the production function has continuous first- and second-order partial derivatives.

We could now proceed directly to learn how the entrepreneur makes the decision about the values of x_1, x_2, etc. to be used; the reader can omit the rest of this section. Nevertheless to get an understanding of the subject it is important to see the kind of function that the production function is. It should also be remembered that in practice the production function is not completely known, and that only certain aspects of it are measurable. This is a problem for anyone who wants to get quantitative results from the theory.

Thus in the remainder of the section we introduce various concepts and terms which provide some understanding of the nature of the production function and its measurement.

Isoquants

The entrepreneur can use many different combinations of the inputs to gain a particular level of output, i.e. there are many different **x** which give the same value of $q(\mathbf{x})$. In input space, the equation

$$q^0 = q(\mathbf{x}) \tag{E3.2.2}$$

defines a surface, known as an **isoquant**. This has very similar properties to the indifference surfaces discussed in E2.3. Each isoquant partitions the input space into two regions, the one further from the origin giving a larger output than the one closer to the origin. Note, however, that the amount q^0 of commodity produced is a well-defined and measurable quantity, in contrast to the concept of utility.

*Productivity

If the input variables x_j for $j \neq i$ are kept constant, q becomes a function of x_i alone. This function is known as the productivity of the ith input. A series of productivity curves of q against x_i can be drawn for the different values of the other inputs: in general an increase in these inputs will decrease the quantity x_1 required to reach a given output level.

The average productivity of the input X_i is defined as q/x_i. The marginal productivity, written MP (X_i), is $\partial q/\partial x_i$. Typical curves for these quantities are shown in Fig. E3.1. To make the marginal productivity independent of the units, i.e. 'dimensionless', a quantity ω_i known as the output elasticity of X_i is sometimes defined:

$$\omega_i = (x_i/q)\,(\partial q/\partial x_i). \tag{E3.2.3}$$

It is usually assumed that MP (X_i) will eventually decline as x_i is increased. This is known as the *law of diminishing marginal productivity*. An obvious example is the provision of labour in agricultural production, e.g. wheat: as labour is increased, there is an increased production of wheat for a fixed area of land. However, increasing applications of labour will result in smaller and smaller increases in the output of wheat.

Rate of Technical Substitution

A quantity of particular interest to the entrepreneur and which can sometimes be measured approximately is the rate at which one input can be substituted for another. We define the rate of technical substitution (RTS) of X_1 for X_2 as that

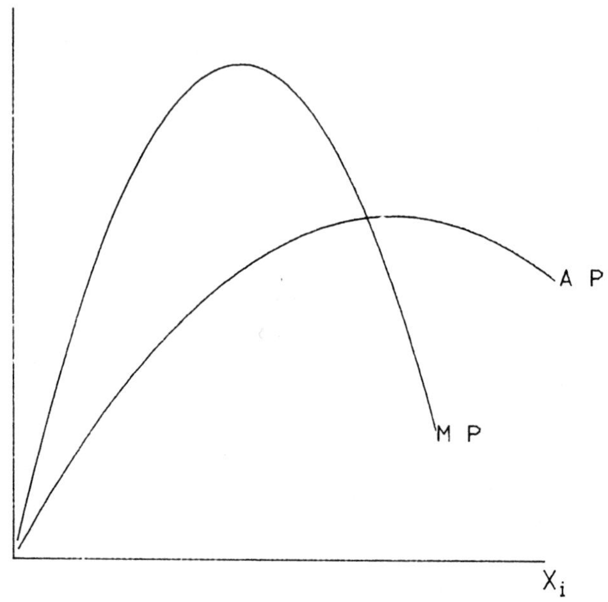

Fig. E3.1. Typical curves of average and marginal productivity.

rate at which X_2 must be replaced by X_1 to maintain a given output level while all other inputs are fixed.

Consider the (x_1, x_2)-plane in input space: this cuts the isoquant in a curve. The negative of the slope of this curve is the RTS, i.e. along this isoquant curve

$$\text{RTS} = -\,\mathrm{d}x_2/\mathrm{d}x_1. \quad \text{(E3.2.4)}$$

This can be shown to be equal to the ratio of the marginal productivities: using differentials

$$\mathrm{d}q = \sum_i (\partial q/\partial x_i)\mathrm{d}x_i. \quad \text{(E3.2.5)}$$

Along an isoquant, $\mathrm{d}q = 0$. When the variables x_i are kept constant the differentials are zero, so that

$$0 = (\partial q/\partial x_1)\mathrm{d}x_2 + (\partial q/\partial x_2)\,\mathrm{d}x_2 \quad \text{(E3.2.6)}$$

and

$$\text{RTS} = (\partial q/\partial x_1)/(\partial q/\partial x_2) = \text{MP}(X_1)/\text{MP}(X_2). \quad \text{(E3.2.7)}$$

It may occur that the marginal productivity of X_1 becomes negative. The example of wheat-growing is a case in point: if the amount of labour is increased too much, the workmen get in each others way and may even destroy part of the crop. If MP (X_2) is positive, then the RTS of X_2 for X_1 is negative. In Fig. E3.2 is drawn an isoquant for two inputs X_1 and X_2 with a x_2 negative RTS at the point R. In going from R to S along the isoquant the variables x_1 and x_2 both decrease; the **rational** entrepreneur is going to choose the inputs specified by the point S rather than those specified by R. We say that S **dominates** R. Dominated inputs are never used.

It is often assumed, as it is with indifference surfaces, that isoquants are convex.

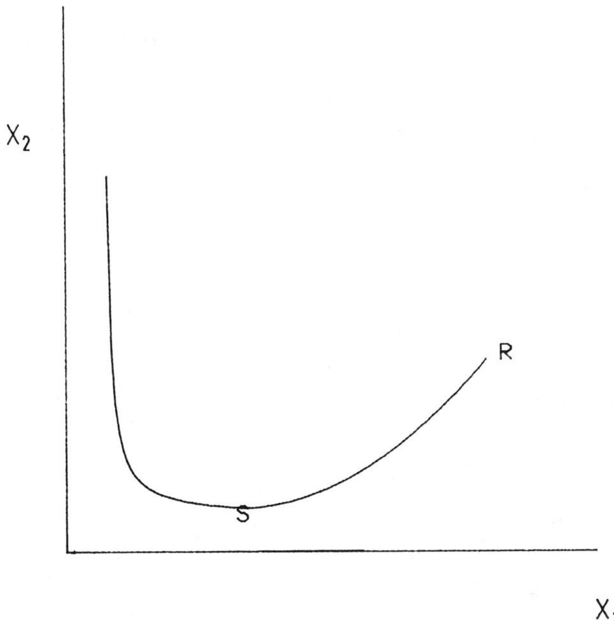

Fig. E3.2. A convex isoquant exhibiting a negative RTS in the right of S.

Returns to scale

The entrepreneur often wants to know what the output response will be if all inputs are increased by the same proportion, i.e. what is $q(t\mathbf{x})/q(\mathbf{x})$? This is known as **returns to scale**, and a suitable precise index for it which is independent of t is

$$k = \left(\frac{\mathrm{d}}{\mathrm{d}t}\,(q(t\mathbf{x}))\right)_{t=1} \Big/ q(\mathbf{x}). \tag{E3.2.8}$$

Returns to scale are increasing if $k > 1$, constant if $k = 1$ and decreasing if $k < 1$. From (E3.2.3) and (E3.2.8)

$$k = \sum_i \omega_i. \tag{E3.2.9}$$

It is sometimes assumed that production functions are homogeneous, i.e.

$$q(t\mathbf{x}) = t^k q(\mathbf{x}). \tag{E3.2.10}$$

The degree of homogeneity is the same as the returns-to-scale index. Two commonly used homogeneous production functions for two inputs are the Cobb–Douglas function

$$q = Ax_1^{\alpha} x_2^{1-\alpha}, \tag{E3.2.11}$$

and the CES function

$$q = A(\alpha x_1^{-\rho} + (1-\alpha)x_2^{-\rho})^{-1/\rho} \quad 0<\alpha<1. \tag{E3.2.12}$$

E3.3 OPTIMIZATION AND THE THEORY OF LAGRANGE MULTIPLIERS

The total cost of producing q goods in a unit time is C where

$$\begin{aligned} C &= \sum_i r_i x_i + b \\ &= \mathbf{r}.\mathbf{x} + b. \end{aligned} \tag{E3.3.1}$$

In the above equation, x_i is the amount of input X_i used, r_i is the price per unit quantity of X_i and b is the fixed cost, i.e. the cost of the fixed inputs. The prices r_i are likely to be slowly increasing functions of x_i, because in the short run, prices tend to rise as the amounts purchased increase.

With knowledge of the cost of using the inputs $\mathbf{x}$, how does the entrepreneur decide on the value of $\mathbf{x}$? There are two behaviour assumptions: the first is that the entrepreneur chooses the value of $\mathbf{x}$ which maximizes the production for a given cost, and the second is that he chooses a value of $\mathbf{x}$ which minimizes the cost for a given value of production. These assumptions lead (see below) to the same result.

The theory which we shall develop depends on psychological assumptions such as the above. If the assumptions are not true, the theory may be unrealistic.

The mathematical problem to which the first assumption leads is the maximization of $q(\mathbf{x})$ subject to the requirement

$$C(\mathbf{x}) = C_0 \tag{E3.3.2}$$

where C_0 is the given cost. This problem of the maximization of a function of several variables subject to constraints is a common one so that it is worth tackling in a general way. We do this next.

Lagrange multipliers

We consider first the problem where there is only one constraint, and generalize later. The aim is to maximize a function $f(x_1, \ldots, x_m)$ subject to the constraint

$$g(x_1, \ldots, x_m) = G. \tag{E3.3.3}$$

One method might be to use (E3.3.3) to express one of the variables, x_1 say, in terms of the others and then eliminate it from f. This treats, however, the variables in an asymmetrical way; it is also not always possible because the variable x_1 cannot always be expressed as a unique function of the other variables.

A better way to proceed is via the method of Lagrange multipliers. An extra variable λ known as a Lagrange multiplier is introduced and a function V is defined:

$$V(x_1, \ldots, x_m, \lambda) = f(x_1, \ldots, x_m) + \lambda\,(g(x_1, \ldots, x_m) - G). \qquad \text{(E3.3.4)}$$

The stationary points (SPs) of this function V are then found, treating all $(m+1)$ variables as independent. These points are given by the equations

$$\partial f/\partial x_i + \lambda\ \partial g/\partial x_i = 0, \qquad \text{(E3.3.5)}$$

$$g(x_1, \ldots, x_m) = G. \qquad \text{(E3.3.6)}$$

This ensures that the constraint is satisfied, which means that the function V is then identical with f. Thus finding the SPs of V is equivalent to finding the SPs of f subject to the constraint.

The equations (E3.3.5) and (E3.3.6) are $(m+1)$ equations in the $(m+1)$ unknowns $\mathbf{x}$ and λ. There may be several solutions of these equations and we have to go to the second-order conditions (see below) to find out the nature of the SPs. Having to solve these equations means solving for one extra variable: this is a drawback to the method, but the advantage of treating the variables symmetrically and of the significance of the Lagrange multiplier (see below) outweigh this disadvantage.

** Geometrical Interpretation

The equations (E3.3.5) can be written

$$\nabla f + \lambda \nabla g = \mathbf{0}, \qquad \text{(E3.3.7)}$$

where ∇f is the vector $(\partial f/\partial x_1, \partial f/\partial x_2, \ldots)$ and ∇g is similarly defined. The above equations show that at a TP $\mathbf{x} = \mathbf{a}$, the tangent planes of the surfaces

$$f(\mathbf{x}) = f(\mathbf{a}) \qquad \text{(E3.3.8)}$$

and (E3.3.3) are the same.

Let us see this in the case of two input variables. Draw some curves $f(x_1, x_2) = c$ for different values of x_2 (see Fig. E3.3) of c. Suppose the curve $f(x_1, x_2) = c$ meets $g(x_1, x_2) = G$ at the point $\mathbf{a} \equiv (a_1, a_2)$. Then if the two curves do not touch at this point $\mathbf{a}$, then there is a point near $\mathbf{a}$ on the curve $f(\mathbf{x}) = c + \delta c$. Then the point $\mathbf{a}$ cannot be a stationary point. We can thus deduce that the point $\mathbf{x} = \mathbf{a}$ is an SP of $f(x)$ subject to the constraint $g(x) = G$ if and only if the tangents to the two surfaces at $\mathbf{x} = \mathbf{a}$ are the same.

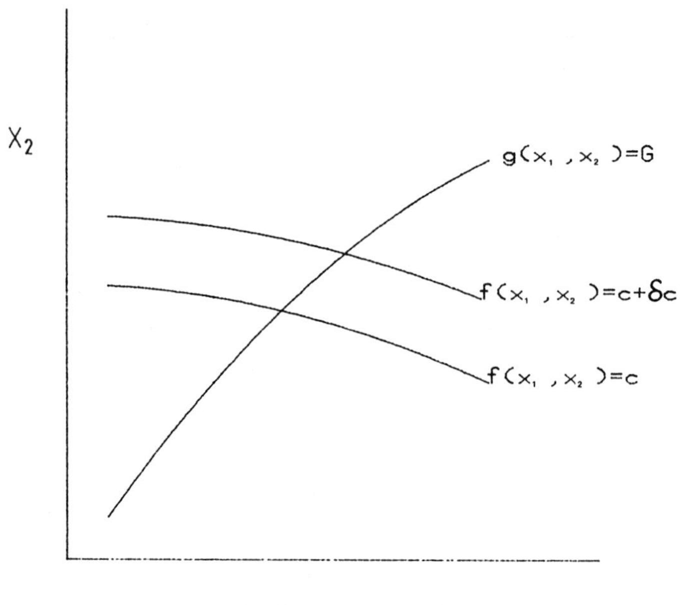

Fig. E3.3. Curves $f(x_1, x_2) = c$ and $f(x_1, x_2) = c + \delta c$ crossed by the constraint curve $g(x_1, x_2) = G$.

* Second-order conditions

The equations (E3.3.5) and (E3.3.6) only determine the SPs; they do not tell us whether the SPs are maxima, minima or saddle-points. In a specific case it is usually best to examine the behaviour of f near the SP along the constraint surface. It may sometimes be useful to look at the behaviour of V to second order in displacements from the SP. The Lagrange multiplier λ is fixed by the first-order equations (E3.3.5) and (E3.3.6). Thus the second-order variation in V is

$$\frac{1}{2}\sum_{ij}\left(\frac{\partial^2 f}{\partial x_i\,\partial x_j} + \lambda\,\frac{\partial^2 g}{\partial x_i\,\partial x_j}\right)\delta x_i\,\delta x_j. \tag{E3.3.9}$$

The variations δx_i are, however, subject to the requirement of lying on the constraint surface. To first order this is

$$\sum_i \partial g/\partial x_i\,\delta x_i = 0. \tag{E3.3.10}$$

This requirement is, however, only needed to first order, because substitution of second-order terms for δx_i in (E3.3.9) would only give third-order contributions.

The expression (E3.3.9) is a quadratic form in δx_i. We want to test whether this expression is positive-definite, negative-definite, indefinite or zero, when the displacements are subject to the constraint (E3.3.10). The appropriate way to do this is to eliminate one of the δx_i using (E3.3.10) and testing the resulting quadratic form. If it is zero, other methods must be used. If it is none of these, the SP is a saddle-point.

It may, of course, occur that the quadratic form (E3.3.9) itself is positive- or negative-definite, in which case it is unnecessary to use the constraint equation (E3.3.10).

Dual problem

We have been considering the problem of maximizing $f(\mathbf{x})$ subject to the constraint $g(\mathbf{x}) = G$. Suppose $\mathbf{x} = \mathbf{a}$ is such a maximum point. Let us write

$$F \equiv f(\mathbf{a}). \tag{E3.3.11}$$

Let us now consider the problem of minimizing $g(\mathbf{x})$ subject to the constraint

$$f(\mathbf{x}) = F. \tag{E3.3.12}$$

We can again use a Lagrange multiplier μ to get the equations

$$\nabla g + \mu \nabla f = \mathbf{0} \tag{E3.3.13}$$

$$f(\mathbf{x}) = F. \tag{E3.3.14}$$

Equations (E3.3.13) are the same as equations (E3.3.7) with

$$\mu = 1/\lambda. \tag{E3.3.15}$$

Thus $\mathbf{x} = \mathbf{a}$ is also an SP of this problem. Is it a minimum?

The second-order variation is now

$$\frac{1}{2}\frac{1}{\lambda}\sum_{ij}\left(\frac{\partial^2 f}{\partial x_i\, \partial x_j} + \lambda\frac{\partial^2 g}{\partial x_i\, \partial x_j}\right)\delta x_i\, \delta x_j \tag{E3.3.16}$$

using (E3.3.9). The constraint equation (E3.3.10) is also the same, from (E3.3.13) and (E3.3.14). Thus if $\mathbf{x} = \mathbf{a}$ is a maximum of f subject to the constraint $g = G$, then $\mathbf{x} = \mathbf{a}$ is a $\left\{\begin{matrix}\text{maximum}\\ \text{minimum}\end{matrix}\right\}$ of g subject to the constraint $f = F$ if λ is $\left\{\begin{matrix}\text{positive}\\ \text{negative}\end{matrix}\right\}$.

*** Several Constraints**

This problem is easily overcome: for each constraint of the form (E3.3.6), an extra Lagrange multiplier is used. Thus if there are l constraints of the form

$$g_j(x_1, \ldots, x_m) = G_j \quad j = 1, 2, \ldots, l \tag{E3.3.17}$$

then we define l Lagrange multipliers λ_j such that (E3.3.5) becomes

$$\partial f/\partial x_i + \sum_{j=1}^{l} \lambda_j \, \partial g_j/\partial x_i = 0. \qquad \text{(E3.3.18)}$$

There are then $(m + l)$ unknowns, i.e. m variables and l Lagrange multipliers, and there are $(m + l)$ equations, i.e. m equations (E3.3.18) and l constraints (E3.3.17).

** Significance of Lagrange Multipliers

Suppose the constraint equation is altered slightly, i.e. it becomes

$$g(\mathbf{x}) = G + \delta G. \qquad \text{(E3.3.19)}$$

What is the change δF in the maximum value of f? Suppose the position of the maximum value changes by a small amount, i.e.

$$\mathbf{a} \to \mathbf{a} + \delta \mathbf{a}. \qquad \text{(E3.3.20)}$$

Then

$$\begin{aligned} \delta F = f(\mathbf{a} + \delta \mathbf{a}) - f(\mathbf{a}) &= \delta \mathbf{a}.\nabla f(\mathbf{a}) + O(|\delta a|^2) \\ &= -\lambda \delta \mathbf{a}.\nabla g(\mathbf{a}) \\ &= -\lambda(g(\mathbf{a} + \delta \mathbf{a}) - g(\mathbf{a})) + O(|\delta a|^2) \\ &= -\lambda \delta G. \qquad \text{(E3.3.21)} \end{aligned}$$

Thus

$$\lambda = -\delta F/\delta G, \qquad \text{(E3.3.22)}$$

i.e. the Lagrange multiplier is the negative of the rate of change of the maximum value of f with respect to the change in the constraint.

E3.4 THE EXPANSION PATH

Let us now see what results come from the behaviour assumptions introduced at the beginning of E3.3.

Output Maximization

Suppose the entrepreneur wishes to maximize the production $q(\mathbf{x})$ subject to the requirement (E3.3.2), i.e. that the cost remain constant. The resulting equations are

$$\nabla q(\mathbf{x}) + \lambda \nabla C(\mathbf{x}) = \mathbf{0}. \qquad \text{(E3.4.1)}$$

The entrepreneur always chooses a region where the marginal productivities are positive (see E3.2). We also have

$$\frac{\partial C}{\partial x_i} = r_i + \sum_j \frac{\partial r_j}{\partial x_i} . x_j \qquad \text{(E3.4.2)}$$

which we assume to be positive†. Thus the Lagrange multiplier λ is negative.

The entrepreneur then wants to solve the equations (E3.4.1) to find the input **x**. Does he get a unique result?

Surfaces with constant cost are called isocost surfaces. Typical examples of isoquants and isocost lines are shown in Fig. E3.4. In that diagram the isocosts and isoquants give only one point **x** where the equations (E3.4.1) are satisfied. This is the usual case and the mathematical condition of convexity of the isoquants and concavity of the isocost surfaces ensures this. If, however, such conditions are not true globally (i.e. everywhere) there may be several solutions of (E3.4.1) and (E3.3.2), but only one of these is chosen, the one that gives the largest value of $f(\mathbf{x})$. Let us write this point as **a**. Thus as the cost C_0 varies, the point **a** traces a path in input space. This path is known as the **expansion path.**

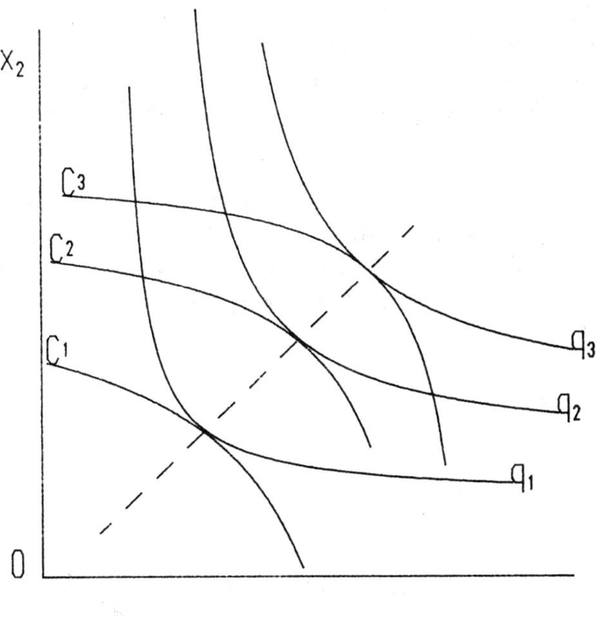

Fig. E3.4. Typical isocost lines $C^{(1)}$, $C^{(2)}$, $C^{(3)}$ and isoquants $q^{(1)}$, $q^{(2)}$, $q^{(3)}$. The expansion path is shown dashed.

Cost Minimization

Suppose the entrepreneur wishes to minimize the cost $C(\mathbf{x})$ of a given amount of production $q(\mathbf{x})$, i.e. minimize $C(\mathbf{x})$ subject to

$$q(\mathbf{x}) = q_0. \tag{E3.4.3}$$

† $r_i > 0$, $\partial r_i/\partial x_i \geqslant 0$ and it is most likely that $\partial r_j/\partial x_i \geqslant 0$.

The resulting Lagrange multiplier equations are

$$\nabla C + \mu \nabla q(\mathbf{x}) = \mathbf{0}. \tag{E3.4.4}$$

As we saw in E3.3 this equation is the same as (E3.4.4). When q_0 is the value $q(\mathbf{a})$, equations (E3.4.3) and (E3.4.4) give the point $\mathbf{x} = \mathbf{a}$ among their solutions. As λ is negative this solution minimizes $C(\mathbf{x})$.

Thus the two behaviour assumptions lead to the same expansion path.

E3.5 COST FUNCTIONS

The constrained production maximization procedure showed that for each value C of the cost, there was a unique point $\mathbf{a}$ on the expansion path, giving rise to a unique value $q(\mathbf{a})$ of the production. The constrained cost minimization procedure showed that for each value q of production, there was a unique value C for the cost. This shows that there is a one-to-one relation between the cost C and the production q, i.e. we can write the cost as a unique function of q. This function, written $C(q)$, is the **short-run cost function**, and satisfies

$$C(q) = \phi(q) + b, \tag{E3.5.1}$$

where b are the fixed costs, and $\phi(q)$ is the variable cost, i.e. the cost due to the variable input. Note that $\phi(0)$ is zero.

A typical curve for the cost function is shown in Fig. E3.5. When $q = 0$, $C = b$. As q increases the costs rise because variable inputs have to be bought.

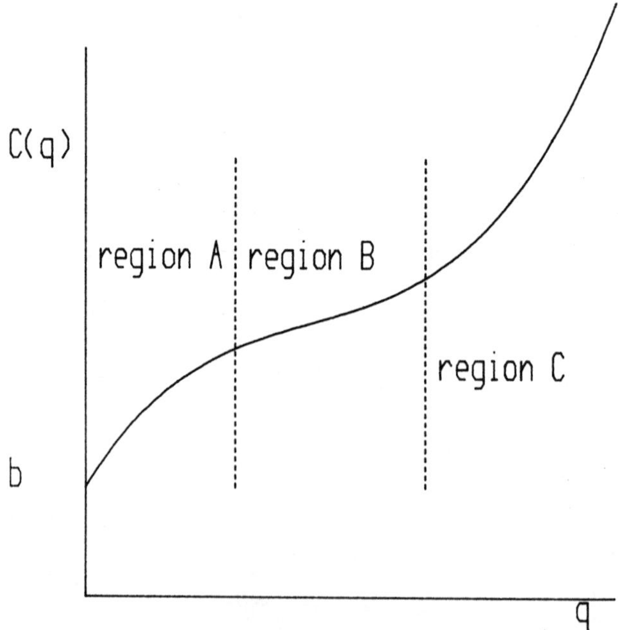

Fig. E3.5. A typical cost function $C(q)$.

These should vary linearly with the amounts bought if these amounts are small, so that $C(q)$ increases linearly with q for q small (Region A). As q increases the costs might level out, as machinery and labour are being used more productively (Region B). When q becomes large, costs increase quite considerably (Region C); this is mainly because the price of the variable inputs increases. For example, the price of the raw materials may increase because of demand, and the price of labour may increase because of overtime working. A cubic function is commonly used to represent the cost function.

Several other functions can be derived from the cost function. These are the **Average Total Cost** (ATC) which is $(\phi(q) + b)/q$; the **Average Variable Cost** (AVC) which is $\phi(q)/q$ and the **Marginal Cost** (MC) which is $dC(q)/dq$. The MC curve passes through the minimum points of both the AVC and the ATC curves. If $C(q)$ is cubic, the ATC, AVC and MC first decline and then increase as q increases (see Fig. E3.6).

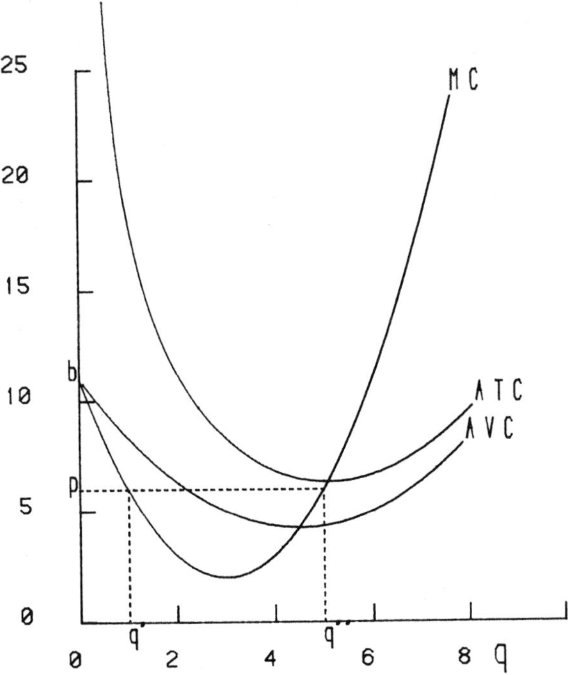

Fig. E3.6. Typical examples of MC, AVC and ATC curves.

* The Long Run

The short-run cost function is a function of the fixed variables ξ, and so we can write

$$C(q, \xi) = \phi(q, \xi) + b(\xi). \quad \text{(E3.5.2)}$$

Thus for a given production q, there is a set of cost functions depending on ξ.

The rational entrepreneur is going to choose the value of ξ which minimizes the cost. We can thus define a long-run cost function $C_L(q)$:

$$C_L(q) = \min_{\xi} \; C(q; \xi). \tag{E3.5.3}$$

This function touches the minimum cost function and so is the lower envelope of all the cost functions.

E3.6 PROFIT MAXIMIZATION IN AN IDEAL MARKET

The price p at which a commodity is sold is often determined by the market, and the entrepreneur has no influence over it. This happens for instance, in an ideal market (see E4). The entrepreneur in these circumstances adjusts his production to this price. We make the behaviour assumption that he chooses a value q of his production that maximizes his profit at this price.

We consider only the short-run situation. The **profit** π is given by the difference between the revenue and the cost. The **revenue** is the money from the sale of the commodities, i.e. pq. Thus

$$\pi = pq - C(q). \tag{E3.6.1}$$

To maximise this, we must look at all possible maxima, which can occur not only at stationary points of the function but at the end-points of the function's domain. Let us return to this latter point after we have investigated the SPs. These are given by

$$\frac{d\pi}{dq} = p - dC/dq = 0, \tag{E3.6.2}$$

i.e.

$$p = C'(q). \tag{E3.6.3}$$

Thus to maximize his profit he chooses the value of q such that the MC is equal to the price.

There may of course be several values of q satisfying (E3.6.3). The one chosen is the one that gives an absolute maximum for π. A requirement for a maximum is that

$$\frac{d^2\pi}{dq^2} < 0 \tag{E3.6.4}$$

and this implies

$$d^2C/dq^2 > 0, \tag{E3.6.5}$$

i.e. MC is increasing. In Fig. E3.6 there are two values, q' and q'', corresponding to the price p. For q', the MC is decreasing and gives a minimum for π: for q'', MC is increasing, and π has a maximum.

Let us return, however, to the consideration of the end-point of π's domain; in this case there is only one, at $q = 0$. This gives the same value of π, irrespective of p:

$$\pi = -C(0) = -b. \qquad \text{(E3.6.6)}$$

In this case the profit is negative and is equal to the fixed costs. To decide whether this profit is an absolute maximum, it must be compared with the profit obtained when (E3.6.3) holds. This is

$$qC'(q) - \phi(q) - b = q(\text{MC} - \text{AVC}) - b. \qquad \text{(E3.6.7)}$$

Thus if MC is less than the AVC at the value of q determined by (E3.6.3), the value of π given by (E3.6.6) is chosen and the entrepreneur ceases production, i.e. puts $q = 0$.

Now the minimum of the AVC occurs when

$$\phi'(q)/q - \phi(q)/q^2 = 0, \qquad \text{(E3.6.8)}$$

i.e. where MC is equal to the AVC. Assuming that the AVC has only one minimum, which is usually true, we see that MC < AVC for $q < q_A$ and MC > AVC for $q > q_A$, where q_A is the value of q where the AVC has a minimum.

The final result, then, is that if $p >$ min (AVC), the solution of (E3.6.3) which gives the maximum profit is chosen but if $p \leqslant$ min (AVC), zero production is the optimal choice.

Even though (E3.6.3) may have several solutions, a particular solution is always chosen, so that there is always a one-to-one relationship between p and q for $p >$ min (AVC). Thus we can write q as a function of p, i.e.

$$q = S_f(p) \qquad \text{(E3.6.9)}$$

where

$$\begin{aligned} S_f(p) &= 0 \qquad\qquad\qquad\qquad\qquad\quad, \quad p < \min(\text{AVC}) \\ &= \max\{q : q \text{ satisfies } p = C'(q)\}, \quad p \geqslant \min(\text{AVC}). \end{aligned} \qquad \text{(E3.6.10)}$$

If $C(q)$ is independent of p, and if $C'(q)$ is a one-to-one function, then finding q from (E3.6.3) is the same as finding the inverse function of $C'(q)$.

The function $S_f(p)$ is known as the **supply function** for the firm. This supply function is the amount the firm produces and sends to the market when the price of the commodity in the market is p.

It should be noted that the process of maximization imposes conditions on possible production functions (see EE3.7). For example, the Cobb-Douglas function is not suitable. This is why it is often assumed that production functions are strictly concave.

E3.7 THE AGGREGATE SUPPLY FUNCTION

For a given market, this function $S(p)$ is just the sum of the supply functions of all the firms supplying the commodity to the market:

$$S(p) = \sum_f S_f(p). \tag{E3.7.1}$$

The slope of this function is of great interest. For an individual firm, if its cost function $C_f(q)$ is independent of the price p, then its supply function $S_f(p)$ is an increasing function of p; this is because $C_f'(q)$ is an increasing function of q, as required by the profit maximization procedure. In this case, $S(p)$ has positive slope.

If, however, $C_f(q)$ depends on p, then it is mathematically possible for $S_f(p)$, and hence $S(p)$, to have a negative slope.

What economic mechanisms could cause this? One mechanism could be that an increase in the price of a commodity leads directly to the increase in the price of the raw materials needed to make the commodity. For example, an increase in the price of tyres increases the price of transport and hence the price of rubber, steel, etc. needed to make the tyres. Other mechanisms may arise from the different production functions and costs of the firms involved. These effects do not always act to increase prices; they may act in an advantageous manner. In all cases, however, they are due to effects external to each firm involved. We say the effects are due to **externalities.**

Thus, in general, the aggregate supply function has a positive slope but in some markets where externalities are present it may have a negative slope.

EE3 EXERCISES

3.1 Draw some isoquants for the following production functions:

(i) $q = x_1^a x_2^{(1-a)}$ $\qquad a = \frac{1}{4};\ a = \frac{1}{2};$

(ii) $q = (x_1^{-\alpha} + x_2^{-\alpha})^{-1/\alpha}$ $\qquad \alpha = 1;\ \alpha = 2;$

(iii) $q = x_1^2 x_2^2 - x_1^3 x_2^3/6$ $\qquad (x_1 x_2 < 4);$

(iv) $q = (x_1 + x_1^2)(x_2 + x_2^2)/(x_1 + x_1^2 + x_2 + x_2^2).$

Are the isoquants convex?

3.2 Calculate the RTS for the production functions of Exercise 3.1.

3.3 Draw the marginal productivity curves for the production functions of Exercise 3.1 and check whether they satisfy the law of diminishing returns.

3.4 Verify that the Cobb–Douglas and the CES production functions are homogeneous and that their *returns-to-scale* parameter is one.

3.5 Find the *returns-to-scale* index of the production functions of Exercise 3.1 (iii) and (iv) when $x_1 = x_2$, and see how they vary with q.

3.6 A firm produces a good Q using two inputs X_1 and X_2. The short-run production function is

$$q = Ax_1^{\alpha} x_2^{(1-\alpha)},$$

where x_1 and x_2 are the amounts of the inputs used in producing an amount q of the product and A, α and $(1-\alpha)$ are positive constraints. The prices paid by the firm for unit quantities of X_1 and X_2 are respectively r_1 and r_2 units of money. In the short run the firm has a fixed cost of b units of money.

Determine the expansion path of the firm and find the maximum short-run output for a total cost of C units of money.

In the case $\alpha = \frac{1}{3}$, $r_1 = \frac{1}{3}$, $r_2 = \frac{2}{3}$, $A = 1$ and $b = 15$, determine directly, i.e. without using any general theoretical results, the minimum cost for a short-run output of 15 units of Q. What is the significance of your results?

3.7 The Cobb–Douglas production function is $q(x_1, x_2) = Ax_1^{\alpha} x_2^{1-\alpha}$, where $0 < a < 1$. Show that the corresponding expansion path is a straight line, given that the cost is $C = r_1x_1 + r_2x_2 + b$. Find the cost function in terms of q, α, r_1, r_2 and b. Show that an absurd result is obtained if we use these results to maximize profits at fixed prices.

3.8 The following are short-run cost functions for different entrepreneurs. In each case, sketch the graphs of the marginal cost (M.C.) and the average variable cost (A.V.C.) curves on the same axes in each case:

(i) $q^3 - 10q^2 + 33q + 66$;
(ii) $q^3 - 12q^2 + 48q + 36$;
(iii) $3q^3 - 18q^2 + 127q + 300$;
(iv) $q^3 - 7q^2 + 16q + 90$.

Are any of these unrealistic? If so, why?

3.9 For the cost functions of Exercise 3.8 determine the price at which the entrepreneur ceases production in an ideal market. Derive also the supply function in each case.

3.10 In Exercise 3.8 (i) determine the output level in an ideal market and the rate of profit for the entrepreneur when the price is 16 units of money.

3.11 Consider the cost function $C(q)$ shown in Fig. E3.5. Let P_1 be the point $(0, b)$ and P_2 be the foot of the tangent from P_1 to the curve. Suppose that the coordinates of P_2 are $(q_2, C(q_2))$. Show that, if storage costs are negligible, the entrepreneur can cut his costs and obtain a new cost function which is the straight line P_1P_2, i.e. for $q \leqslant q_2$

$$C = (C(q_2) - b)\, q/q_2 + b,$$

and is the original cost function $C(q)$ for $q > q_2$. Show that in an ideal market, this reduction has no effect.

3.12 A manufacturing plant has a cost function

$$C(q) = 25 + 55q - 6q^2 + 2q^3.$$

Find the minimum price per unit for production to be sustained. Find also the supply function. Show that, if the price is 75 units, q is approximately 3.08. Show that the minimum price that would induce an entrepreneur to start a new plant with this cost function is 62.5 units.

Given that the aggregate demand is

$$D(p) = 1000 - 10p$$

and that there are 90 identical plants, find the rate of production when the aggregate demand equals the supply.

In the long run, how many plants are used to supply the market?

3.13$^{(m)}$ Suppose the production function for a commodity is $q(x_1, x_2)$. Given that the price in an ideal market for the commodity is p units of money, construct a theory which determines the entrepreneur's demand function for X_1 and X_2. See what results you get when q is the Cobb-Douglas function?

(i) Is there any connection between the RTS and the demand elasticities? What 'measurable' parameters would be of use to the entrepreneur?
(ii) What does the 'law of diminishing marginal productivity' say about $\partial^2 q/\partial x_1^2$? Hence determine the sign of $\partial x_1/\partial r_1$ and interpret your result in terms of wages and employment.

3.14$^{(m)}$ Suppose an entrepreneur can produce two different commodities Q_1, Q_2 from two inputs X_1, X_2, so that he has two production functions

$$q_1 = q_1(x_1, x_2)$$
$$q_2 = q_2(x_1, x_2)$$

How does he determine the cost of producing quantities q_1 and q_2? If the prices of Q_1 and Q_2 in an ideal market are p_1 and p_2, how does he decide the size of q_1 and q_2? At what prices should production of one or other of the commodities cease?

Construct a theory which answers these questions.

Do you think that in practice it makes any difference if the commodities Q_1 and Q_2 are:

(i) substitutes, e.g. similar commodities of different quality;
(ii) complements;
(iii) unrelated, e.g. wool and mutton which both require the input of sheep.

CHAPTER E4

Market Behaviour

E4.1 INTRODUCTION

Market is the technical name for the conditions under which producers sell and consumers buy a certain commodity. The term market is used when only one commodity is being bought and sold, whereas the word **multi-market** is used when more than one commodity is involved. The price, demand and supply of any one good affects the prices etc. of many other goods and vice versa. Multi-market behaviour is thus very complicated.

The aim of our analysis is to discover how the price of a commodity is determined by the behaviour of the consumers and of the sellers. To achieve any understanding of this, drastic simplification of the multi-market system is needed. Thus we are often forced to examine a single market in which the prices etc. of all other goods and commodities are considered fixed and independent of the price of the good under consideration. In this chapter, except in sections E4.8 and E4.12, we make this assumption unless otherwise stated.

Such an idealization has its disadvantages. Not only does it make it difficult to validate any results we may get but it also means that it is difficult to use any empirical knowledge to set up a model for market behaviour. Knowledge of actual market behaviour is limited, and so the types of market considered are based on models. It is difficult to know how closely a real market approximates to any particular model, and hence whether the results of that model are applicable to the real market situation. For example, the **ideal competitive** market†, considered in E4.2, seems to have some advantages over other types of

† Sometimes known as a 'perfectly competitive' market.

markets (see E4.6). It is a matter of judgement (some would say political bias!) to decide whether these advantages exist in any real situation.

An ideal competitive market is one in which the actions of any single buyer or seller have no perceptible influence on the behaviour of the market. The conditions for such a market are considered in more detail in E4.2. In contrast, a market is said to be **imperfectly competitive** if the actions of one or more buyers or sellers have a perceptible influence on the market. A market with a single seller is a **monopoly**, a market with two sellers is a **duopoly** and a market with a small finite number of sellers is an **oligopoly**. A market with a single buyer is a **monopsony**, a market with two buyers is a **duopsony**, and a market with a small finite number of buyers is an **oligopsony**. Examples of such markets occur in retail and factor markets; in the retail clothing trade, big high-street stores such as 'Marks and Spencer' are buyers whose actions affect the whole market, and in motor-car production, large manufacturers such as 'Ford' are buyers whose actions affect the whole market for components.

The restriction to a single market is more realistic if we consider a homogeneous commodity, i.e. one where the buyers do not distinguish between the outputs of different firms. Many commodities, although very similar, are often distinguished by their brand labels, e.g. cigarettes, detergents and tea, and consumers may have particular feelings towards a brand. Such commodities are said to be **product differentiated** and one brand is in economic terms a substitute for another brand (see E2). In this chapter, product differentiation is ignored and it is assumed that the commodity under consideration has no close substitutes.

E4.2 THE IDEAL COMPETITIVE MARKET

Traditionally there are four conditions that a market must obey if it is to be called ideally competitive. These are as follows.

(1) Firms produce a homogeneous commodity and there are no advantages or disadvantages to any seller for selling to any consumer.
(2) There are a large number of both firms and consumers, there is no collusion between them, and the sales and purchases of each one are negligible in comparison to the total amounts transacted.
(3) Both firms and consumers know all the prices at which the commodity is offered or bought, and they take every opportunity to increase their profits or their utility.
(4) In the long run, entry into and exit from the market is free for firms and consumers.

Before considering the reality of these conditions, let us look at some of their consequences. A consequence of condition (1) is that consumers have no reason to prefer the product of one firm to that of another and that sellers have no reason to prefer selling to one consumer rather than to another, i.e. rules of selling such as 'looking after regular customers' or 'first come, first served' are not used. A more important consequence is that there is a universal price per unit of the commodity within the market and that this price does not vary with the amount bought or sold. The easiest way to verify this is to assume that it is untrue, i.e. assume that there is more than one price in the market. A consequence of condition (2) is that the individual firm can change his supply and the individual customer can change his demand without perceptibly altering the market price. Thus the individual buyer or seller acts as if he cannot influence the market price and consequently modifies his demand or supply respectively to the given market situation. Such buyers or sellers are often called **price-takers**.

Are conditions (1)–(3) realistic? As we have already seen, in many cases consumers often differentiate between different brands of the same product. Similarly, producers sometimes differentiate between customers, preferring ones they know and trust to an unknown customer. Condition (2) is also unlikely to be often fulfilled, but occasionally it may be, e.g. in a town-market where fruit is on sale. Condition (3) seems even more unlikely, as information about prices is difficult to obtain. For example, it is costly both in time and in money for a housewife to visit several stores to note down the prices, before she decides where to buy her groceries.

We leave the judgement of the importance of these criticisms to the reader. One point that needs to be stressed is that the response to the ideal competitive market to any change is supposedly instantaneous. Because of perfect information, buyers go immediately to the seller who is offering a product at the lowest price: sellers never lower their prices in order to build up goodwill: producers try immediately to alter their supply when the market price changes, and so on. Considerations such as these suggest that a more realistic model would incorporate some time-lag between a change in market conditions and the response of the market.

Condition (4) only affects the long-run behaviour of the market and in this book is not of much concern. For economic theory, however, it is very important and rather controversial. It ensures that in the long run, resources flow freely between alternative uses, seeking those uses from which the greatest advantages are gained. For example, firms move out of those markets where they incur losses and move into those markets where they make profits. Labour is supposed to make similar moves, whereas inefficient firms are in the long run eliminated from the market and are replaced by efficient ones. All these consequences sound delightful but in practice do not always occur. For example, labour does not readily move jobs, because of economic, social and legal reasons; changing jobs often involves moving from one's town or even one's country, and this may cost money, may involve leaving family and friends and may be illegal because of immigration laws. For new firms to be created in a market often requires capital and people with entrepreneurial desires. It is not clear that such requirements are always available†.

† This aspect is reminiscent of 'evolution': in a biological system there may well be niches for new species (e.g. rabbits could have prospered in Australia long before their introduction) but there are not necessarily the right type of animals or plants available to evolve to take advantage of the opportunities.

E4.3 SHORT-RUN EQUILIBRIUM IN THE IDEAL MARKET

In an ideal competitive market a single price prevails. Both buyers and sellers are price-takers, so that their desires are determined by the aggregate demand function and aggregate supply function respectively. If at a price p_e, demand equals supply, i.e. for $p = p_e$

$$D(p) = S(p) \tag{E4.3.1}$$

then the desires of buyers and sellers are satisfied and there is thus no reason for the price to change from p_e. An equilibrium state of a system is defined to be a state in which there is no tendency for the system to change, so that (E4.3.1) is the condition which determines when a market is in equilibrium.

For the idea of market equilibrium to be useful, the market must be dynamic, i.e. change with time, when not in equilibrium. Is this so? Consider a price p not satisfying (E4.3.1): then demand $D(p)$ is either greater than or less than supply $S(p)$. When the former occurs, buyers will be willing to pay more than p for the commodity; if the latter occurs the suppliers incur unnecessary costs in manufacturing and storing goods that are not sold, and will change their supply. In either case there is a tendency for the market to change. The strength, however, of this tendency is not known without research into real markets, so that whether states satisfying (E4.3.1) are truly distinctive from non-equilibrium markets is an open question. Of particular importance is how rapidly the market reaches equilibrium and whether markets are usually in their equilibrium states. These questions cannot be answered: we look briefly at them in E4.8 and E4.9.

Existence and Uniqueness of Equilibrium

The condition (E4.3.1) may have no, one, or many solutions for the price. The aggregate demand function $D(p)$ is a monotonically decreasing function of p. The aggregate supply function is usually monotonically increasing, so that the usual plot of $D(p)$ and $S(p)$ looks like Fig. E4.1. There is just one value of p where the two curves cross, and this is the equilibrium value p_e of the price.

It is possible to have unusual features even when $S(p)$ is monotonically increasing. For example, in Fig. E4.2, $S(p) > D(p)$ for all positive p. In this case the equilibrium value for p is zero. In this case the commodity is free and consumers can get as much as they want for nothing. Air is an obvious example. Another case is shown in Fig. E4.3: here the supoly is only non-zero at prices at which the demand is zero, i.e. the price at which a supplier is willing to sell the commodity is greater than any consumer is willing to pay. The equilibrium is thus $D = S = 0$.

It is usual, then, for there to be one and only one equilibrium when $S(p)$ is monotonically increasing. If there is no equilibrium it is probable that the model is incorrect. When $S(p)$ is decreasing, however, it is possible for there to be several equilibrium values. An example is shown in Fig. E4.4.

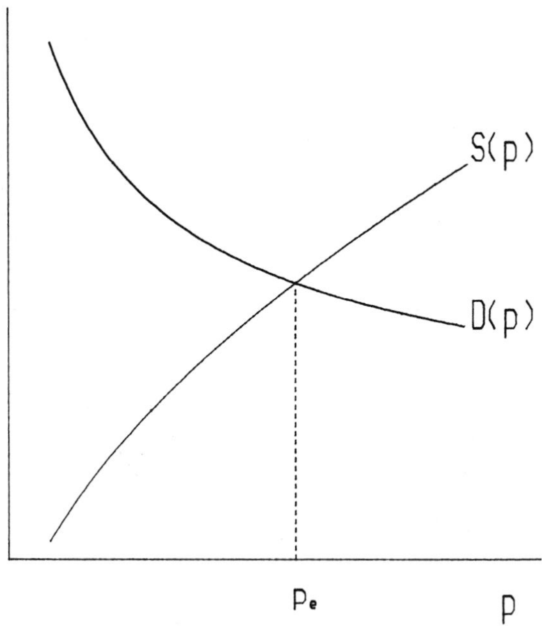

Fig. E4.1. The usual plot of demand $D(p)$ and supply $S(p)$ giving the equilibrium price p_e where they meet.

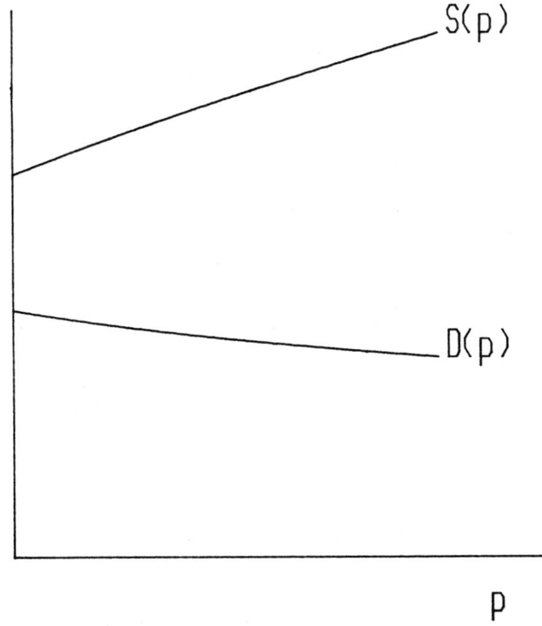

Fig. E4.2. A plot of supply and demand where the equilibrium value of p is zero.

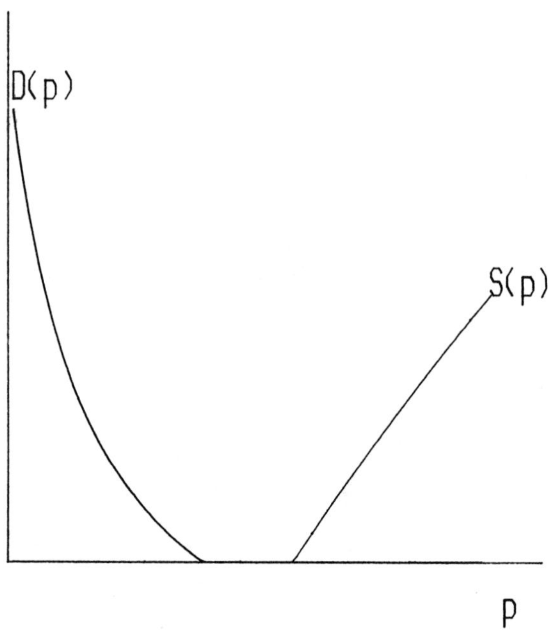

Fig. E4.3. Supply and demand must both be zero for equilibrium here.

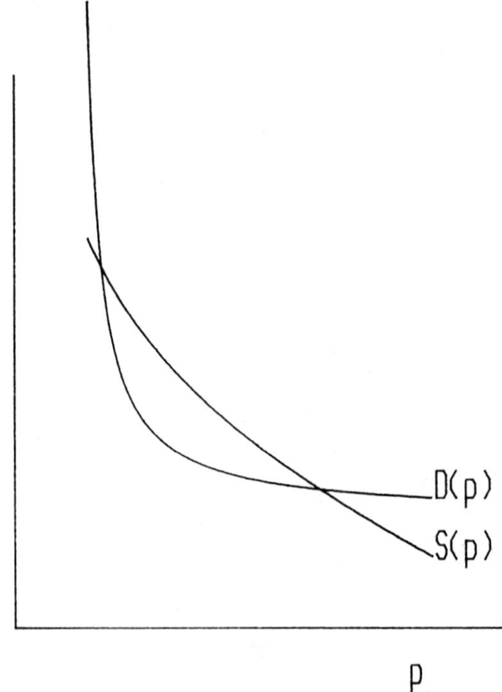

Fig. E4.4. In this case, the aggregate supply $S(p)$ is decreasing, and there are two equilibrium values of p.

E4.4 MONOPOLY

A market where there is only one seller but numerous buyers is known as a monopoly. The demand for the commodity is given by the aggregate demand function. The supply is determined by the wishes of the seller, who is free to do as he pleases. He is not a price-taker; he can influence the price of the commodity by his action.

Let us assume that he wishes to maximize his profit. Then he will arrange the supply to the market in such a way that the price is at a value which maximizes his profit. Let us see how this is done.

We assume that the buyers have perfect information and buy at the cheapest price, so that there is a single price per unit quantity in the market. His profit is then $\pi(q)$:

$$\pi(q) = R(q) - C(q), \tag{E4.4.1}$$

where $C(q)$ is his cost function, and $R(q)$ is the revenue,

$$R(q) = pq. \tag{E4.4.2}$$

The behaviour assumption is that the monopolist wants to maximize his profit. The latter is a continuous and differentiable function of q, so that maxima etc. occur when $d\pi/dq$ is zero, i.e. when

$$d\pi/dq = R'(q) - C'(q) = 0, \tag{E4.4.3}$$

and at the end-point, i.e.

$$q = 0.$$

$R'(q)$ is called the marginal revenue, so that to maximize profits, marginal revenue is put equal to marginal cost. The other possibility, i.e. an absolute maximum occurring at $q = 0$, is unlikely and is discussed below.

The revenue is a function of the amount bought. We know that customers want to buy $D(p)$ goods, where $D(p)$ is the aggregate demand function; thus

$$q = D(p). \tag{E4.4.4}$$

This equation is a one-to-one relation between price and quantity and can be inverted directly. We write

$$p = \widetilde{D}(q) \tag{E4.4.5}$$

where $\widetilde{D}$ is the inverse function of D. The revenue can thus be written

$$R(q) = q\,\widetilde{D}(q). \tag{E4.4.6}$$

The monopolist then chooses a value of q, q_m say, such that

$$q_m(d\widetilde{D}(q_m)/dq) + \widetilde{D}(q_m) = q_m\, d\widetilde{D}(q_m)/dq + p_m = C'(q_m). \tag{E4.4.7}$$

The corresponding price p_m is obtained from (E4.4.5).

A monopoly market is supposedly always in equilibrium, because the monopolist adjusts his production to the customers' demands. This assumes that he has an adequate knowledge of the aggregate demand function.

It is necessary to find out whether the condition for maximization (E4.4.3) really gives a maximum, when R is given by (E4.4.6). The function D is a decreasing function of p so that $\tilde{D}$ is a decreasing function of q. Thus

$$R'(q) < D(q). \tag{E4.4.8}$$

It is thus usually assumed that the marginal revenue R' is also a decreasing function of q, but is always positive. The second derivative R'' of R is then negative. The condition for (E4.4.3) to give a maximum is that

$$\frac{d^2\pi}{dq^2} = R'' - C'' < 0, \tag{E4.4.9}$$

which occurs when

$$R'' < C''. \tag{E4.4.10}$$

If the marginal cost C' is increasing, this is satisfied. Such an occurence is shown in Fig. E4.5.

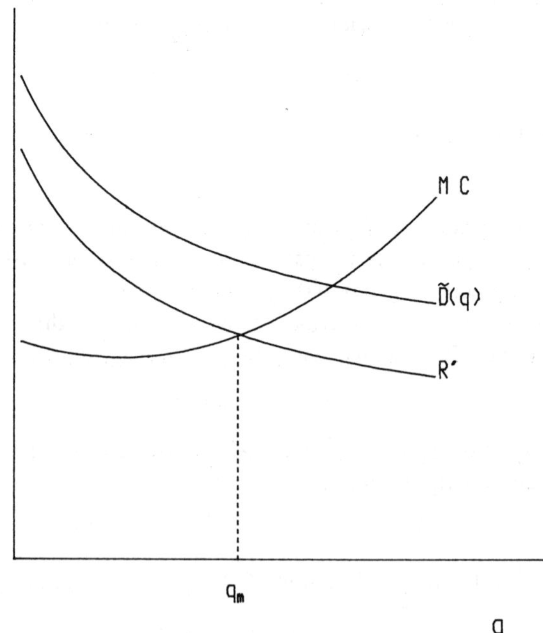

Fig. E4.5. The inverse demand function $\tilde{D}(q)$, the marginal revenue function $R'(q)$ and the marginal cost function $C'(q)$. The quantity q_m where $R' = C'$ is the amount the monopolist produces.

Whether the point $q = 0$ gives an absolute maximum depends on the particular demand and cost functions involved. The profit when $q = 0$ is $(-b)$, i.e. the fixed cost, as we saw in E3. The profit, when (E4.4.7) is used, is

$$-q_m \, dD(q_m)/dq + P(q_m) \tag{E4.4.11}$$

where $P(q)$ is a function with the same form as the profits in an ideal competitive market

$$P(q) = q\,C'(q) - C(q). \tag{E4.4.12}$$

The first term in (E4.4.11) is always positive. Thus when q_m is greater than the value giving the minimum of AVC (see E3), (E4.4.7) always gives the absolute maximum. When q_m is less, a numerical check has to be undertaken.

E4.5 COMPARISON

In this section we compare the behaviour of the ideal and monopoly markets. In E4.4 we saw how the monopolist maximizes his profit by choosing the amount q_m he produces to satisfy (E4.4.3). Suppose, however, he had acted as if he were in an ideal competitive market at equilibrium. Then the price p_e of his goods and the quantity q_e he produces would be derived from (E4.3.1). It is of interest to compare p_e with p_m, and q_e with q_m.

We show that when there are no externalities, i.e. when marginal cost is independent of price, and when $q_e > 0$ then $p_e < p_m$ and $q_e > q_m$. To do this we assume the opposite, i.e. assume $p_e \geqslant p_m$. Then as the demand function D is monotonically decreasing, $q_e \leqslant q_m$. Now

$$C'(q_m) = R'(q_m) = \widetilde{D}(q_m) + q_m \, d(\widetilde{D}(q_m)/dq), \tag{E4.5.1}$$

$$< \widetilde{D}(q_m), (= p_m), \tag{E4.5.2}$$

and

$$C'(q_e) = p_e. \tag{E4.5.3}$$

The marginal cost $C'(q)$ is a monotonically increasing function of q. Thus if $q_e \leqslant q_m$

$$C'(q_e) \leqslant C'(q_m)$$

which implies

$$p_e < p_m$$

which contradicts our hypothesis.

In a monopoly market then, under the above conditions, the price to the consumer is higher than in an ideal competitive market and the number of goods produced is less. Obviously the consumer prefers the latter type of market. The entrepreneur, however, prefers to produce his goods in the above type of monopolistic market because his profits are then as large as possible given his costs and the consumers' demand function.

In practice, however, the monopolist may not be able to make the profits our model predicts. If his profits are large, other entrepreneurs will be tempted to copy the original product and enter the market in competition. There are initial costs (e.g. building a factory) which an entrepreneur encounters when entering a market, so a monopolist may try to keep the price of his goods at a price p such that $p_e < p < p_m$ and the profits at this price of any entrepreneur entering the market would not merit the initial costs. Other monopolists may have a legal restraint on other entrepreneurs entering the market. Examples of these are people with a patent on their inventions, or government enterprises. Even in these cases, however, the entrepreneurs cannot always make the profits our model predicts: there may be substitutes for the goods being produced which the consumers may prefer if the price of the original commodity is too high.

Note that the benefits of the competitive market have only been shown for the case when that market is in equilibrium. Little is known about non-equilibrium markets. Similarly, when externalities are present, the above analysis does not apply and the situation is unclear. There may also be more than one equilibrium in this case.

There is, however, one clear situation where a monopoly market benefits the consumer. This is when q_e is zero, but q_m is non-zero. This can occur because the monopolist's profits are larger than the profits of a comparable firm in a competitive market, so that it may benefit a monopolist to keep manufacturing when the firms in the ideal market cease production.

E4.6 DUOPOLY AND OLIGOPOLY

The ideal competitive market is the one with the most competition between the producers: in the monopoly market there is no competition. These are markets with some competition but not as much as in the ideal case. For example, in the duopoly market there are just two producers, and there may be competition between them and/or there may be **cooperation**†. Similarly in an oligopoly there can be competition and/or cooperation between the several producers. The noteworthy aspects of both these types of market are that the actions of any producer have a perceptible influence on market behaviour.

The distinguishing feature of these types of market is the interdependence of the actions of the sellers. This is seen most simply in the duopoly market: consider such a market with two sellers labelled 1 and 2 with corresponding cost functions $C_1(q_1)$ and $C_2(q_2)$ where q_j is the quantity supplied by the jth seller. Then the profits $\pi_j(q)$ are given by

$$\pi_j = q_j \tilde{D}(q_1 + q_2) - C_j(q_j) \tag{E4.6.1}$$

where $\tilde{D}$ is the inverse of the demand function and is a function of $(q_1 + q_2)$. Suppose that seller 1 wants to maximize his profits. He can only alter q_1, but the value he chooses for q_1 depends on the value of q_2. Similarly the value of q_2 which seller 2 chooses depends on the value of q_1. Thus the values chosen for q_1 and q_2 are interdependent and so are the profits that are made.

† The concepts of 'competition' and 'cooperation' will be given a more quantitative analysis in the section on the Theory of Games.

This interdependence is reminiscent of the situation in a game; there the outcome for a player depends not only on his own actions but on the actions of others. This relationship is briefly discussed in the section on the Theory of Games.

There are many ideas about how duopolists behave. One idea, due to Cournot, is that they ignore each other, i.e. each one maximizes his profit as if the other's actions did not affect his own. Two equations can be got from maximizing π_1 w.r.t. q_1 and π_2 w.r.t. q_2, and together they can be solved to give values for q_1 and q_2. For a duopolist to behave in this way is unwise as there are ways in which he can make a bigger profit. It is also inconsistent, for a duopolist can hardly base his own reactions to the market on the theory that the other duopolist will not react.

**** Pareto Optimality**

To analyse the duopoly situation more fully we plot some constant-profit contours, i.e. the values of q_1 and q_2 that make π_1 (say) be constant. If $D(q)$ and $C_1(q_1)$ are known, these are easily derived, and in Fig. E4.6 some of these are sketched; we have taken $D(q)$ as linear and $C_1(q_1)$ and $C_2(q_2)$ as cubic. As the profit gets larger, the amount of curve available gets less.

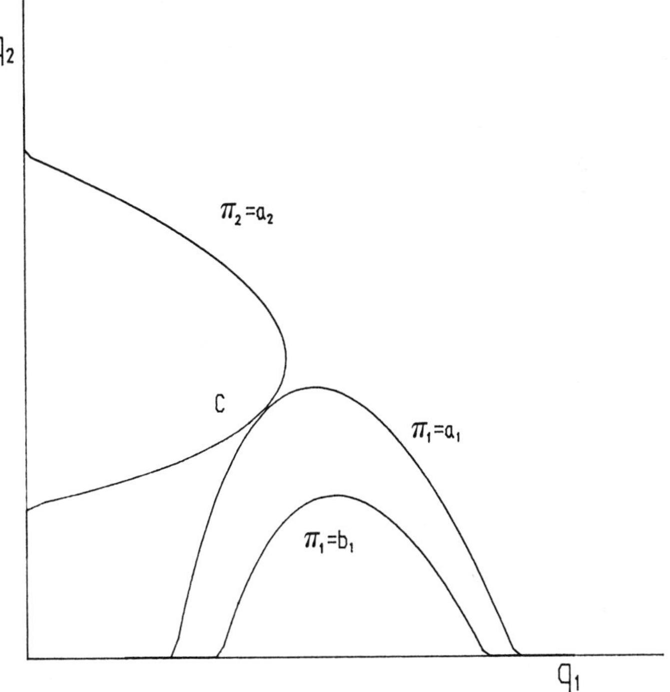

Fig. E4.6. Curves of constant profit: $\pi_1 = a_1$, $\pi_1 = b_1$ and $\pi_2 = a_2$, where a_1, a_2, b_1 are in units of money per unit time. Note that $a_1 < b_1$. C is a point of the contract curve.

Each seller wants to maximize his profits. To find a set of values of q_1, q_2 from which the sellers might choose we introduce the idea of Pareto optimality. A point (q_1^*, q_2^*) is said to be **Pareto optimal** if for every other point (q_1, q_2) either

$$\pi_1(q_1^*, q_2^*) > \pi_1(q_1, q_2) \quad \text{and/or} \quad \pi_2(q_1^*, q_2^*) > \pi_2(q_1, q_2). \tag{E4.6.2}$$

The set of such points is the Pareto Optimal Set (POS). Once the producers are selling quantities (q_1^*, q_2^*) which belong to the POS, one or other of the producers would dislike a change to some other quantities (q_1, q_2). So it can be argued that a point belonging to the POS is an equilibrium solution for a duopoly market.

The POS may be empty or may have one or more points in it. This situation is very similar to the situation with the Edgeworth Box where there were several solutions. The similarity is even greater than this because the POS in the duopoly market is formed from the points at which the curves of constant profit touch. The proof of this is left to the reader. These points form a **contract curve** as in the Edgeworth Box.

The maximum total profit is obtained by maximizing the single function

$$\pi_1(q_1, q_2) + \pi_2(q_1, q_2). \tag{E4.6.3}$$

The point (q_1^c, q_2^c) which gives the absolute maximum of this function belongs to the POS. Nevertheless this point is not necessarily the natural equilibrium of the duopoly market because one of the producers (the ith say) may be getting less profit by making the quantity q_i^c than he would if he were making a different quantity. If, however, the duopolists can cooperate, the other duopolist would find it worth while to give a side-payment to overcome this drawback. This solution to the duopoly market is known as the **collusion** solution, and in it the duopolists act together to form a monopoly. This is discussed further in G5.2.

The Cournot solution is not, in general, Pareto optimal. In Fig. E4.6 the Cournot solution is at the meet of the constant profit curves such that π_1 has a horizontal tangent and π_2 a vertical tangent. Thus π_1 and π_2 do not have a common tangent and hence the solution is not on the contract curve. Note, however, that the solution is an equilibrium solution, as each duopolist would lose if they separately moved away from it.

E4.7 MULTI-MARKET EQUILIBRIUM

To find the equilibrium price of one commodity we have so far assumed that the price of every other commodity was fixed. This assumption is obviously untenable. The price of one commodity affects the demand and the supply of other commodities and hence affects the price of these other commodities: in turn their prices affect the demand, supply and price of the original commodity.

The correct way to find the price of any good is to find simultaneously the prices of every good. As yet we only know how to find prices when there is equilibrium, so that in this section we investigate multi-market equilibrium, i.e. the equilibrium when many goods are involved. However, we do not know *a priori* that such an equilibrium exists.

To exhibit the criteria and the equations which govern the equilibrium prices of a set of goods, we consider an ideal competitive multi-market with a large number of sellers and buyers of each commodity and with the other conditions (see E4.2) of ideal competition also satisfied. We assume that the utility and production functions of all consumers and producers respectively are known and we make the usual behaviour assumptions that utility and profit are maximized.

The maximization of utility leads to an aggregate demand function for each good, and these are functions of the prices of all goods. As each market is competitive, the supply of a good to the market can be described in terms of an aggregate supply function. This is a function of the price of the good but may also be a function of the prices of the other goods if production involves other goods. An equilibrium condition is that supply equals demand in each market: if there are m goods, this gives rise to m equations. If these can be solved simultaneously it would seem that we had our set of prices.

This is, however, too simple. Every consumer's demand function depends on his income: this is determined by the price and quantity of goods that he sells. In equilibrium each consumer spends exactly the amount of money he receives. In a **closed** economy the money a consumer receives depends on the amount of goods he sells and the price at which he sells them.

This makes the system even more complex: demand depends on the income of the consumers and the prices of the goods: the supply of each good depends on the prices of all the goods: the income of the consumer depends on the amount of goods he sells and the prices of these goods: the amount of goods sold and the prices are determined by the requirement that supply equals demand.

To avoid complications and to get some idea of such a multi-market system, let us briefly look at an exchange multi-market in which there is no production.

Pure Exchange

Let us consider an economy in which N individuals buy and sell m types of commodity, and the total amount of each type is fixed. We denote individuals by capital subscripts and types of commodity by lower case subscripts. The total number N individuals is large and each has an initial endowment of each commodity, i.e. A has an endowment q_{Aj}^0 of commodity j. To ensure that the market is competitive we assume that each q_{Aj}^0 is of the same order, i.e. for each j there is no A such that q_{Aj}^0 is very much larger than q_{Bj}^0 for all $B \neq A$.

At given market prices, an individual may be able to increase his utility by selling a portion of his initial endowment of some commodities and adding to his stocks of other commodities. Trading takes place if two individuals can increase their utilities; we assume here that all N individuals are able so to do.

The **excess demand** E_{Aj} of A for the jth commodity is

$$E_{Aj} \equiv q_{Aj} - q^0_{Aj} \tag{E4.7.1}$$

where q_{Aj} is the final amount that A has. This has to be determined from the theory. A will buy or sell depending on the prices, so that even the sign of E_{Aj} is unknown *a priori.*

A's total wealth y_A is given by

$$y_A = \sum_{j=1}^{m} p_j q^0_{Aj} \tag{E4.7.2.}$$

where p_j is the price of the jth commodity. We assume that there is no desire to hold money, i.e. each individual wants to be in monetary equilibrium, so that his total wealth after trading

$$\sum_{j=1}^{m} p_j q_{Aj} \tag{E4.7.3}$$

must be equal to his initial wealth. Thus

$$\sum_{j=1}^{m} p_j E_{Aj} = 0. \tag{E4.7.4}$$

This, then, is A's budget constraint.

To determine E_{Aj}, we maximize A's utility function U_A, subject to the budget constraint. U_A is a function of q_{Aj} but it is more useful to express it as a function of E_{Aj}:

$$U_A(q_{A1}, q_{A2}, q_{A3}, \ldots, q_{Am}) \equiv U_A(E_{A1} + q^0_{A1}, \ldots). \tag{E4.7.5}$$

The maximization procedure is the same as the one described in E2. It leads to a unique function E_{Aj} in terms of the prices $p_1, \ldots, p_m$. Note that the incomes have not had to be included as an extra parameter, because the budget constraint (E4.7.4) has automatically taken care of the incomes. This budget constraint is satisfied by the E_{Aj} because to find E_{Aj}, the budget constraint had to be used.

The aggregate excess demand function E_j for commodity j is got by summing over all consumers A:

$$E_j = \sum_A E_{Aj}(p_1, \ldots, p_m). \tag{E4.7.6}$$

We can also aggregate the budget constraint

$$\sum_{j=1}^{m} p_j E_j = 0. \tag{E4.7.7}$$

This result is known as **Walras' law** and is an identity satisfied by any set of prices in our system, not necessarily equilibrium prices. Note that if E_j has been found correctly, Walras' law is automatically satisfied.

Supply and demand are all taken account of in the aggregate excess demand functions E_j. Thus a necessary and sufficient condition for equilibrium is that E_j is zero in every market, i.e.

$$E_j(p_1, \ldots, p_m) = 0, \quad j = 1, \ldots, m. \qquad \text{(E4.7.8)}$$

These equations look as if they determine the prices $p_1, \ldots, p_m$; note, however, that the m equations are not independent: if $(m - 1)$ of the equations are satisfied, the last one is also satisfied because of Walras' law so that if $(m - 1)$ of the markets are in equilibrium, the last market is in equilibrium. Thus there are $(m - 1)$ independent equations. Notice also that if all prices are multiplied by a positive constant μ, then the wealth of all individuals is multiplied by μ, so that E_{Aj} is the same function of μp_i as it was originally of p_i. Thus the aggregate excess demand functions E_j do not change under this transformation, so that the absolute prices of the commodities are not determined by the equilibrium conditions, only their ratios. The equations (E4.7.8) are really $(m - 1)$ independent equations in $(m - 1)$ unknowns.

The equilibrium equations (E4.7.8) have to be solved simultaneously, to find the price ratios of all the commodities. Solving the equations may be a difficult task: specific multi-market systems have been constructed, some of which have equilibrium solutions and others which do not. There may even be systems where there is more than one equilibrium solution. There has been much research into the mathematical conditions under which equilibrium does or does not exist. Much of this work involves abstruse mathematics, and seems a rather arid exercise as it has little contact with real economic systems. One justification is that to a large extent the benefits of the ideal competitive system only occur if equilibrium occurs, so that there is less need to try to ensure that the actual microeconomic system is ideally competitive if equilibrium does not generally occur in multi-market systems. If, however, research shows that equilibrium can exist under fairly general mathematical conditions, it may be a worthwhile economic policy to try to make the microeconomic system more competitive.

Introducing production into the multi-market system does not introduce any new principles into the analysis.

** Edgeworth Box Revisited

The previous analysis can be applied to the exchange of two types of commodity between two people as was discussed in E2.7. In this analysis we are assuming the conditions of the ideal competitive system, which are different from the conditions considered in E2.7.

The equilibrium solution(s) is obtained from the equation (E4.7.8), but to what point(s) in Fig. E2.8, the Edgeworth Box, does this solution(s) refer? To find this, we go through the steps of analysis again. The budget constraint (E4.7.4) for given values of p_1 and p_2 is a straight line through the point G, whose slope depends on the ratio p_1/p_2. Thus the point given by maximizing U_A (for given p_1, p_2) is the point where that straight line touches A's indifference curves. B's budget constraint is the same straight line, so the maximization of U_B gives a point where that straight line touches B's indifference curve. The equilibrium condition (E4.7.8) means that these two points coincide, i.e. that A's and B's indifference curves touch and that their common tangent goes through the point G.

The solution set then is a point (or at most a finite set of points) which lies on the contract curve. The reason why we did not get the whole of the contract curve is that the conditions for competition are an additional constraint.

E4.8 STABILITY

We now return to the discussion of the behaviour of the market for a single commodity and in this and the following two sections we shall look at behaviour away from equilibrium. This behaviour is known as **dynamics** and little is known about it. Nevertheless it is an important topic, because markets are rarely in equilibrium; as macroeconomics is the behaviour of aggregate microeconomic behaviour, it is difficult to see how dynamical macroeconomic behaviour can properly be understood without some knowledge of dynamics in microeconomics.

In this section we investigate the stability of the equilibrium of an ideal competitive market: that is, when the system is disturbed from equilibrium, will it or will it not return to equilibrium? Note that the probability of a system ever reaching an unstable equilibrium is zero.

The **excess demand function** $E(p)$ is defined by

$$E(p) \equiv D(p) - S(p), \tag{E4.8.1}$$

where $D(p)$ is the aggregate demand function and $S(p)$ is the aggregate supply function. All these are functions of the price, which is the same throughout the market (see E4.2). Now we assume, following Walras, that if supply exceeds demand, i.e. $E(p)$ is negative, the price will decrease.

Let the equilibrium price be p_e. For prices p not very different from p_e, $E(p)$ can be expanded in a Taylor series

$$\begin{aligned} E(p) &= E(p_e) + (p - p_e)E'(p_e) + O(|p - p_e|^2) \\ &= (p - p_e)E'(p_e) + O(|p - p_e|^2). \end{aligned} \tag{E4.8.2}$$

Now suppose that initially the market is disturbed in such a way that $E(p)$ is positive. Then p will increase and so $E(p)$ will $\left.\begin{matrix}\text{increase}\\ \text{decrease}\end{matrix}\right\}$ according as $E'(p_e)$ is $\left.\begin{matrix}\text{positive}\\ \text{negative}\end{matrix}\right\}$. The market will then $\left.\begin{matrix}\text{deviate from}\\ \text{return to}\end{matrix}\right\}$ equilibrium. The reader should verify that the same condition on $E'(p_e)$ leads to the same behaviour if $E(p)$ is negative initially.

The **Walrasian stability condition** thus leads to $\left.\begin{matrix}\text{instability}\\ \text{stability}\end{matrix}\right\}$ according as $E'(p_e)$ is $\left.\begin{matrix}\text{positive}\\ \text{negative}\end{matrix}\right\}$.

This Walrasian stability assumption looks reasonable provided that the buyers and sellers in the market have some means of learning about the sign of $E(p)$. They could learn this by noticing the rate of sale or by observing the quantity sold at the end of a period of trading: for example, if demand exceeds supply the sellers will sell out before the end of the trading period.

If this is a reasonable argument, it seems more sensible to consider market behaviour in terms of the quantity sold. To do this, Marshall defined the **excess demand price** $F(q)$:

$$F(q) \equiv \widetilde{D}(q) - \widetilde{S}(q) \qquad \text{(E4.8.3)}$$

where $\widetilde{D}$ and $\widetilde{S}$ are the inverse of the aggregate demand and supply functions respectively. The **Marshallian stability condition** is that the quantity q sold will $\left.\begin{matrix}\text{increase}\\ \text{decrease}\end{matrix}\right\}$ if $F(q)$ is $\left.\begin{matrix}\text{positive}\\ \text{negative}\end{matrix}\right\}$.

Let the quantity sold when the market is in equilibrium be q_e. Then for $|q - q_e|$ small, F can be expanded in a Taylor series

$$\begin{aligned} F(q) &= F(q_e) + (q - q_e)F'(q_e) + O(|q - q_e|^2) \\ &= (q - q_e)F'(q_e) + O(|q - q_e|^2). \qquad \text{(E4.8.4)} \end{aligned}$$

The Marshallian stability condition implies that the market is $\left.\begin{matrix}\text{unstable}\\ \text{stable}\end{matrix}\right\}$ according as $F'(q_e)$ is $\left.\begin{matrix}\text{positive}\\ \text{negative}\end{matrix}\right\}$. The details of the argument are left to the reader.

To compare the results of both conditions we note that

$$\mathrm{d}\widetilde{D}/\mathrm{d}q = 1/(\mathrm{d}D/\mathrm{d}p). \qquad \text{(E4.8.5)}$$

Then

$$\begin{aligned} F'(q_e) &= 1/(\mathrm{d}D/\mathrm{d}p)_e - 1/(\mathrm{d}S/\mathrm{d}p)_e \\ &= -(\mathrm{d}E/\mathrm{d}p)_e/((\mathrm{d}D/\mathrm{d}p)_e(\mathrm{d}S/\mathrm{d}p)_e). \qquad \text{(E4.8.6)} \end{aligned}$$

The demand function $D(p)$ always has a negative slope. In general, $S(p)$ has a positive slope. In these circumstances both conditions predict that the unique equilibrium is stable. If, however, $S(p)$ is negatively sloped at equilibrium, the two conditions lead to contradictory predictions about the stability of equilibrium, i.e. if the Walrasian stability condition predicts that the equilibrium is stable, the Marshallian condition predicts it to be unstable, and vice versa.

Markets with negatively-sloping supply curves all have their own characteristics, so that the correct assumption about the stability of the market is dependent on the market concerned: it may be Walrasian, Marshallian, or entirely different.

E4.9 A SIMPLE MODEL OF DYNAMICS

The Walrasian stability condition suggests that the rate at which the price changes in an ideal competitive market is a function of $E(p)$. If the period of time in which the price changes is small in comparison with the short-run period, time can be treated as a continuous variable. We can then write

$$dp/dt = f(E(p)/q_e) \tag{E4.9.1}$$

where f is some monotonically increasing function of its argument. To ensure that the argument is dimensionless we write it as $E(p)/q_e$. A necessary and sufficient condition for equilibrium is that $E(p)$ is zero, so that

$$f(0) = 0. \tag{E4.9.2}$$

If $E(p)/q_e$ is small, the function f can be expanded in a Taylor series to give

$$dp/dt = k\, E(p)/q_e \tag{E4.9.3}$$

to first order in $(E(p)/q_e)$. The constant k is positive and has the dimensions of price divided by time. The equation (E4.9.3) can be used to get some idea of market behaviour.

When $|p - p_e|$ is small, $E(p)$ can also be expanded in a Taylor series as in (E4.8.2). Then

$$dp/dt = k\, E'(p_e)\,(p - p_e)/q_e. \tag{E4.9.4}$$

This can be integrated to give

$$p - p_e = A \exp(-t/\tau) \tag{E4.9.5}$$

where A is a constant depending on the initial conditions and

$$\tau = -q_e/(k\, E'(p_e)). \tag{E4.9.6}$$

As can be seen, p tends to p_e, i.e. the equilibrium is stable, if $E'(p_e)$ is negative, in agreement with our former analysis.

The constant τ has dimensions of time and is known as the **relaxation time.** It measures the time which the market takes to reach equilibrium. If τ is small, the market reaches equilibrium quickly and if τ is large, the market takes a long time to reach equilibrium. Note that if τ is larger than the short-run period, equilibrium is not likely to be reached in the short run, and this model is not valid.

E4.10 A MARKET WITH A TIME-DELAY

There are a large number of markets in which time cannot be taken as a continuous variable. This happens for instance when entrepreneurs carry out production in batches or when buyers buy at fixed, long intervals. A typical example of the former is an agricultural crop, e.g. potatoes, and an example of the latter is fireworks which, in the U.K., are mainly bought just before 5th November each year.

In these cases we may consider time as a discrete variable and label each production run by an integer, n say. The market in which these goods are sold will also be labelled by the same integer. The entrepreneur will probably decide the amount of production for the $(n+1)$th production run on what has happened previously. Suppose he makes a decision based on the behaviour of the nth market (this assumption makes the system state-determined (see SM1.4)). Writing S_{n+1} as the aggregate supply to the $(n+1)$th market,

$$S_{n+1} = f(p(n)), \qquad \text{(E4.10.1)}$$

where $p(n)$ is the price in the nth market. Let us assume that equilibrium occurs rapidly in the market whenever buyers and sellers get together, i.e. that in the nth market, supply equals demand

$$D(p(n)) = S_n. \qquad \text{(E4.10.2)}$$

Suppose the market is an ideal competitive market. Then the supply S_n is determined by an aggregate supply function $S(p)$ and (E4.10.1) becomes

$$S_{n+1} = S(p(n)). \qquad \text{(E4.10.3)}$$

These two equations, (E4.10.2) and (E4.10.3), determine the price $p(n)$ in such a market. It is easy to calculate $p(n)$ by graphical means (see Fig. E4.7): draw the aggregate demand and supply functions with the same axes. Suppose $p(0)$ is the initial price: then the supply S_1 to the first market is $S(p(0))$ which is found by drawing the vertical (dotted) line through $p(0)$ till it reaches $S(p)$. The demand D_1 is equal to S_1. The price p_1 in this market is found by drawing the horizontal (dashed) line through S_1 till it reaches the demand curve, and then dropping a vertical (dotted) line to the axis. The process is then repeated. The result is known as a **cobweb** diagram.

Such diagrams can have many different types of behaviour, depending on the functions $D(p)$ and $S(p)$. In Fig. E4.7 we have drawn the conventional diagram in which $S(p)$ has a positive slope; the cobweb progresses inwards towards the point $p = p_e$ where $D(p)$ and $S(p)$ are equal. At this point the price does not change, i.e. the system is in equilibrium. This equilibrium is stable in Fig. E4.7, but it is not always so. We investigate the important question of the stability of equilibrium points below.

There is an interesting point to note about the behaviour in Fig. E4.7: the price $p(n)$ oscillates about p_e, for even n, $p(n)$ being higher than p_e with the supply less than $S(p_e)$, and for odd n, $p(n)$ lower than p_e and the supply greater than $S(p_e)$. An entrepreneur who knew or thought he knew that this was going to happen would modify his behaviour: he would use the predicted values of $p(n)$ to produce a quantity of goods for the nth market which would maximize his profit, and even if he could not guess $p(n)$ accurately he would at least increase his production when n is even. If many entrepreneurs did this, it would of course alter the conditions in the market and equations (E4.10.1) and (E4.10.3) would

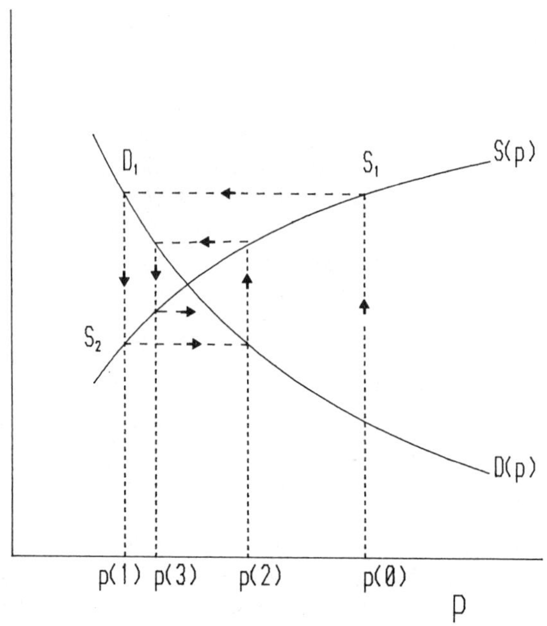

Fig. E4.7. Cobweb diagram for the dynamical behaviour of a market with a time-delay.

no longer be valid. Indeed the assumption of state-determined behaviour is invalid, and we need to ask: 'how does the entrepreneur make his decisions?' They are made on his **expectation** of how the market will behave. The assumption of state-determined behaviour means that the entrepreneur expects market $(n + 1)$ to be like market n. What the entrepreneur actually expects is almost impossible to know; indeed the system may not even be causal.

Let us return to the more mundane topic of the stability of equilibrium points for the equations (E4.10.2) and (E4.10.3). We investigate small deviations of p from p_e. To do this we expand $D(p)$ and $S(p)$ in a Taylor series about p_e:

$$D(p) = D(p_e) + (p - p_e)D'(p_e) + O(|p - p_e|^2); \tag{E4.10.4}$$

$$S(p) = S(p_e) + (p - p_e)S'(p_e) + O(|p - p_e|^2). \tag{E4.10.5}$$

Then to first order in $|p - p_e|$,

$$D(p_e) + (p(n) - p_e)E'(p_e) = S(p_e) + (p(n-1) - p_e)S'(p_e), \tag{E4.10.6}$$

so that

$$p(n)D'(p_e) - p(n-1)S'(p_e) = p_e(D'(p_e) - S'(p_e)). \tag{E4.10.7}$$

This equation can be solved in the same way as a differential equation with constant coefficients. Hence

$$p(n) = (S'(p_e)/D'(p_e))^n\, A + p_e, \tag{E4.10.8}$$

where A is a constant depending on the initial conditons. It is easy to see that

$$A = p(0) - p_e. \tag{E4.10.9}$$

The system is stable if

$$(S'(p_e)/D'(p_e))^n \to 0 \quad \text{as } n \to \infty. \tag{E4.10.10}$$

It is thus stable if $|D'(p_e)| > |S'(p_e)|$, i.e. if the demand curve is more strongly sloped than the supply curve no matter what its sign.

When $S'(p_e)$ is positive, the system is unstable if $S'(p_e) > |D'(p_e)|$, whereas for such a system with no time-delay the market is always stable. For all systems, economic or otherwise, a time-delay usually tends to make a system less stable†.

It is also interesting to note that in the general case with $S'(p_e) > |D'(p_e)|$ there is no stable equilibrium point, i.e. the system is never in equilibrium. As the benefits of the ideal market mainly come when the system is in equilibrium, this result has some significance for discussions about the virtues of different economic systems, which in reality involve time-delays.

* E4.11 MONEY

Money has two purposes, termed **accounting** and **circulating** respectively. Accounting money serves as a standard of value which measures the relative prices of different commodities. Circulating money serves as a store of value.

Accounting money serves as a standard, so that no one holds accounting money or desires to hold accounting money for its own sake. Indeed it is possible to dispense with a separate unit of money and use the quantity of a particular commodity instead. In E4.7, when considering a pure-exchange multi-market, we saw that the equilibrium equations only determine the relative prices of the commodities. Thus one good, known as the **numéraire**, can be chosen as the unit of value, and then the prices of all the other commodities are expressed in terms of the numéraire.

There are two disadvantages to this procedure. Firstly there are fluctuations in the price of the numéraire itself due to changes in its demand and supply, and these fluctuations are then reflected in the prices of the other commodities. Secondly it is inconvenient if the unit of account is being used for other purposes. For these reasons gold was often used.

Monetary units can overcome the second of these, and the first can be overcome by taking the unit as a suitable average of the prices of a large number of the commodities. This is what the Retail Price Index does.

The discussion of circulating money is difficult because we do not have realistic assumptions about an individual's demand for money. Let us see how our pure-exchange multi-market model is affected: we take money as the $(m + 1)$th good and assume the consumers have an intial stock of money, i.e. A

† In the section on population dynamics this also occurs (see P2.9).

has initial stock $q^0_{A,m+1}$ of money. If A wants to have $q_{A,m+1}$ units of money, his excess demand $E_{A,m+1}$ for money is

$$E_{A,m+1} = q_{A,m+1} - q^0_{A,m+1}, \tag{E4.11.1}$$

making the budget constraint

$$\sum_{j=1}^{m} p_j E_{A,j} + E_{A,m+1} = 0 \tag{E4.11.2}$$

as the price of money is unity. Walras' law now becomes

$$\sum_{j=1}^{m} p_j E_j + E_{m+1} = 0. \tag{E4.11.3}$$

The equilibrium equations are

$$E_j(p_1, \ldots, p_m) = 0 \quad j = 1, \ldots, m \tag{E4.11.4}$$

as in (E4.7.8) and the money equation is

$$E_{m+1}(p_1, \ldots, p_m) = 0. \tag{E4.11.5}$$

If the commodities are in equilibrium, then the money market is in equilibrium from Walras' law. Then consumers as a whole do not desire to exchange money for commodities or commodities for money.

Circulating money thus does not affect the equilibrium conditions for the m commodities, so that in equilibrium the ratio of the prices of the commodities is independent of the circulating money. Prices are determined by the quantity of money, but otherwise circulating money has no effect on the equilibrium situation. *It may, however, have an effect on the commodity sector in the non-equilibrium situation* because of Walras' law (E4.11.3), which is true even when there is not equilibrium.

* E4.12 TAXATION

As an application of our market analysis we look at the effect of taxation on an ideal competitive market. Taxation is a complicated topic; let us assume that the tax on an article is a percentage of its price, i.e. the producer gives tp to the government per article and keeps $(1 - t)p$ for himself. What is the effect of taxation on the price?

The cost to the ith manufacturer has now increased owing to the taxation: the new cost of producing q_i articles is

$$C_i(q_i) + tpq_i \tag{E4.12.1}$$

where $C_i(q)$ is the cost function when tax is not present (see E3.5). By maximizing the profit we get the equation

$$C_i'(q_i) + tp = p. \tag{E4.12.2}$$

This leads to the supply equation

$$q_i = S_i^0(p(1-t)), \tag{E4.12.3}$$

where S_i^0 is the ith manufacturer's supply function without taxation. The aggregate supply function is thus

$$q = S^0(p(1-t)), \tag{E4.12.4}$$

where S^0 is the aggregate supply function without taxation.

To find the price, draw the demand and supply curves (see Fig. E4.8) and suppose that the market is in equilibrium. Note that the supply curve $S^0(p(1-t))$ can be obtained from the curve $S^0(p)$ simply by changing the scale on the p-axis, so that the horizontal distance between the two curves is $xt/(1-t)$ when the curve S^0 is at x. Let p_0 be the equilibrium price without taxation. Then taking the general case as in Fig. E4.8, the price p_e with taxation satisfies

$$p_0 < p_e < p_0/(1-t). \tag{E4.12.5}$$

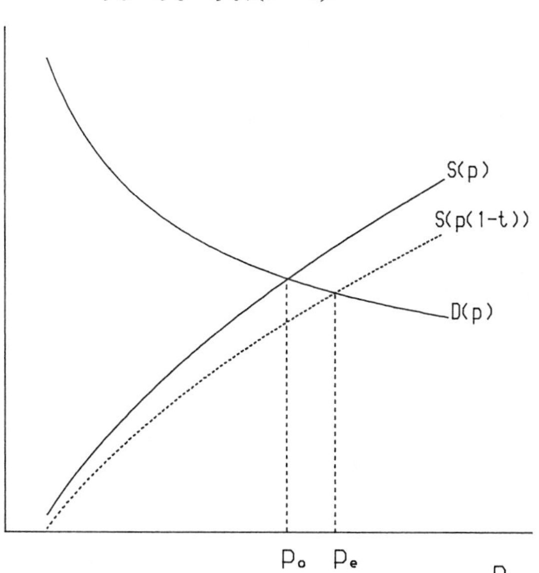

Fig. E4.8. Demand and supply curves when taxation is present.

Unless the demand curve is very flat (i.e. the elasticity is almost zero)

$$p_e < p_0(1+t), \tag{E4.12.6}$$

i.e. the price to the consumer does not include all the tax and the producer has had to pay some.

Note that this tax acts as an externality: the actual cost in (E4.12.2) involves the price p. The effect of this externality is to decrease the slope of the aggregate supply function.

EE4 EXERCISES

4.1 An ideal market is supplied by 100 firms, each with the supply function

$$S(p) = \begin{cases} 6p - 6 & p \geqslant 1 \\ 0 & p < 1 \end{cases}$$

where p is the price. The aggregate demand function is $(-300p + 3{,}000)$. Find the equilibrium price. Find also the equilibrium price in the presence of a tax of 1 unit of money per unit quantity of the commodity. Comment on your result.

4.2 Find the price obtained by a monopolist with cost function $C(q) = (25 + 10q)$ when faced by a demand function $D(p) = (25 - \frac{1}{2}p)$.

4.3 An ideal market is supplied by 50 firms, each with the supply function

$$S(p) = \begin{cases} 4p - 5 & p \geqslant \frac{5}{4} \\ 0 & p < \frac{5}{4} \end{cases}$$

and 50 firms each with the supply function

$$S(p) = \begin{cases} 3p - 4 & p \geqslant \frac{4}{3} \\ 0 & p < \frac{4}{3} \end{cases}$$

where p is the price. The aggregate demand function is $D(p) = 2{,}000 - 200p$. Find the equilibrium price.

4.4 The demand in a market is $D(p) = b - p$. The supply function is

$$S(p) = \begin{cases} (10 + (3p + 1)^{1/2})/3 & p \geqslant 8 \\ 0 & p < 8. \end{cases}$$

Find the equilibrium prices and corresponding quantities sold in an ideal market when (i) $b = 20$, (ii) $b = 13$, (iii) $b = 12$.

Suppose all the firms merged and formed a monopoly with cost function $C(q) = q^3 - 10q^2 + 33q + 66$. Find now the equilibrium prices and quantities sold.

4.5 There are N identical firms producing a particular commodity. The cost function for each firm when producing q units is $(q^3 + 2q^2 + 4q + 6)$ units of money. Show that the supply function for each firm is

$$S(p) = \begin{cases} (2 + (3p - 8)^{1/2})/3 & p \geqslant 3 \\ 0 & p < 3. \end{cases}$$

N is large. The demand function is $D(p) = N(\frac{22}{3} - p)$. Find the equilibrium price and the profit or loss each firm is making.

Suppose all the firms combine and form a monopoly such that the cost of producing Nq goods is $NC(q)$. Find the equilibrium price and the corresponding profit or loss of the monopoly.

4.6 In an ideal competitive market for a commodity, the cost in £ for a unit quantity is p. There are N identical producers and the cost for each of producing q units is £$(q^3 - 7q^2 + 16q + 90)$. Show that these producers stop production if $p < \frac{15}{4}$. Find the aggregate supply function.

The aggregate demand function is $N(b - p)$. Find the equilibrium price and the quantity sold when (i) $b = 16$, (ii) $b = 6$.

4.7 A profit-maximizing monopolist produces a quantity q of a commodity. His (short-run) cost function is $C(q) = 100 + 25q$. The demand is $D(p) = 30 - p/5$, where p is the price. Find the values of p, q, and the profit.

The same monopolist contrives to separate his consumers into two distinct markets with respective demand functions $D_1(p_1) = (225 - p_1)/20$ and $D_2(p_2) = (375 - 3p_2)/20$. Show that this is possible. Find the values of p_1, p_2, q_1, q_2 and the total profit which results from the new marketing procedure. What do you deduce from your results?

4.8 Find the equilibrium prices in a prefectly competitive market with supply function $S(p) = (-p^2 + 7)/3$ and the demand function $D(p) = -p + 3$. Determine whether these prices are stable using the static criteria of both Walras and Marshall.

The dynamic behaviour of the price p satisfies, in certain circumstances, the equation

$$\mathrm{d}p/\mathrm{d}t = k(D(p) - S(p)),$$

where k is a constant. Justify this equation on Walrasian grounds. Obtain the general solution of the equation and show that near an equilibrium price this solution leads to behaviour which accords with the Walraisan static stability hypothesis.

4.9 In a market for a commodity, the supply function $S(p)$ is $6p^2/(1 + 2p^2)$ units and the demand function $D(p)$ is $(3 - p)$ units, where p is the price in £ of a unit.

(i) Find the equilibrium price in an ideal competitive market and show that the equilibrium is stable according to the Walraisan stability criterion.

(ii) Invert the supply and demand functions and show that the above equilibrium is stable according to the Marshallian stability criterion.

(iii) Suppose the commodity is in a market with lagged adjustment, i.e. where the supply for year n is determined by the price $p(n - 1)$. Show that the equilibrium is unstable. Sketch a 'cobweb' diagram of the demand and supply against price for the years 1, 2, 3 when the price p_0 in year 0 is £2.00 per unit.

4.10 The supply function $S(p)$ for a commodity is $(4 + (4 + 3p)^{1/2})/3$. The demand function is $(4 - p)$. Find the equilibrium price p_e for this commodity in an ideal competitive market.

The dynamic behaviour of p satisfies, in certain circumstances, the equation $\mathrm{d}p/\mathrm{d}t = kE(p)$, where $E(p)$ is the excess demand function and k is a constant. What is the sign of k?

The initial price is $\frac{13}{27}$ units. Show that the supply S satisfies the equation $(3S)^4(7 - 3S)^3 = (\frac{19}{3})^4(\frac{2}{3})^3 \exp(-7kt/2)$. (Hint: put $(4 + 3p) = u^2$.)

4.11 Find the equilibrium price in an ideal market of a commodity with supply function $S(p) = -0.1p + 50$ and demand function $D(p) = -0.5p + 100$. Determine whether or not this price is stable using the criteria of both Walras and Marshall.

The dynamic behaviour of p satisfies in certain circumstances the differential equation $\mathrm{d}p/\mathrm{d}t = k_1(D(p) - S(p))$ and in other circumstances the difference equation $p_{(t+1)} - p_t = k_2(D(p_t) - S(p_t))$; k_1 and k_2 are constants; what are their signs?

Obtain the general solutions of each of the above equations for the above demand and supply functions. Compare these results with each other and with the results of the static stability analysis.

4.12 Adam and Eve had no money, and so went foraging for food in the Garden of Eden. Adam found six figs and Eve found 18 apples. They then met to bargain over the figs and apples. Explain the excess demand functions for figs and apples for Adam and Eve, and write down the budgetary constraints in terms of these functions and the prices p_f and p_a of figs and applies.

Adam's preferences are expressed by the utility function $x_f x_a/(9x_f + x_a)$ and Eve's by $y_f y_a/(y_f + y_a)$, where x_f, y_f and x_a, y_a are numbers of figs and apples. Obtain equations for the excess demand functions for figs for Adam and Eve in terms of the ratio p_f/p_a, and hence show that this ratio is 3. Hence find the number of figs Adam and Eve have after their bargaining session.

4.13$^{(m)}$ A retailer of perishable goods, e.g. strawberries, must have an adequate supply each season but must sell them all by the end of the season. Suppose he offers a price to the grower at the end of the season so that the grower supplies him with a supply for next season based on that price. He cannot know the demand accurately, so that as the season nears its end, he may lower the selling price, having kept it constant during the earlier part of the season. Model this situation in general terms, and consider the way the retailer fixes the selling price. Find some results by using some typical supply and demand functions.

The price offered to the grower may depend on last year's prices. Investigate the dynamics of this situation.

CHAPTER E5

Linear Models in Microeconomics

E5.1 LINEARITY IN MICROECONOMICS

There are many aspects of microeconomics which behave linearly or approximately so. For example, the output of shirts is linearly related to the input of cotton and buttons. Other inputs, e.g. labour, are not always linearly related to output, but in certain systems such non-linear aspects are not important and a linear model is reasonable. In this chapter we investigate some linear models in which the processes, and in particular the production processes or **activities**, are linear. Such models should be compared with the theory of E3 where the production functions had continuous first- and second-order partial derivatives: in a linear activity, one or more outputs are produced in fixed proportions from one or more inputs in fixed proportions. Such an activity is homogeneous of degree one and hence gives constant returns to scale (see E3.2).

Three reasons for studying linear models are firstly that they are reasonably realistic models in some situations, secondly that empirical values for the parameters are often available and thirdly that it is possible to solve these models. Thus industrial and commercial planners often use the techniques of linear programming (see E5.3–E5.4); these find the maximum or minimum values of a linear function, e.g. revenue or production cost, when the variables are subject to some linear constraints. The Leontief model (see E5.5) provides a linear multi-market system which can be solved and into which empirical results can be incorporated. This should be compared to the system discussed in E4.7. To introduce these ideas the chapter begins with a section, E5.2, on linear production functions.

Basic mathematical ideas

The mathematics required is quite different from that of previous chapters, as it involves the properties of point sets and inequalities. The reader will find these ideas and results useful in the section on the Theory of Games. Nevertheless he is warned (or relieved?) that we do not delve deeply into the mathematics and that the Fundamental Duality Theorem is only stated and not proved.

In multi-market systems, goods, e.g. steel, may be outputs of one process and inputs of another. With such complicated systems it is generally useful to describe quantities by a vector in commodity space (see E2.2) thereby not distinguishing between inputs and outputs. A general production process may produce several outputs; but in the linear models discussed here we simplify matters by assuming that each activity has only one output. An activity can then be represented by a position vector in commodity space. We write $\mathbf{a}_j$ as the **activity vector** (or **activity point**) of the jth activity; its component a_{ij} is the minimum amount of the ith commodity required to produce a unit amount of the output of activity j.

Suppose there are n commodities and l activities. It is useful to define a $(n * l)$ matrix A known as the **consumption matrix** with elements a_{ij}, all of which are non-negative. Suppose the output of the jth activity is z_j: the vector $\mathbf{z}$ with l components z_j is called the **intensity vector**. The minimum inputs required to operate all the activities giving these outputs is $A.\mathbf{z}$.

It oftens happens that each output commodity is produced by just one activity. Unless otherwise stated (as in E5.2) we make this assumption in this chapter. Activities and outputs can then be identified with each other, and there are l output commodities. For convenience, let the first l components of a vector in commodity space denote **secondary** commodities, i.e. the outputs of some activity, and the last m components, where

$$m = n - l, \tag{E5.1.1}$$

denote **primary** commodities, i.e. these are only inputs. Then $A.\mathbf{z}$ can be written

$$\begin{bmatrix} A' & O' \\ A'' & O'' \end{bmatrix} \begin{bmatrix} \mathbf{z} \\ \mathbf{0} \end{bmatrix}, \tag{E5.1.2}$$

where A' is an $(l * l)$ matrix and A'' an $(m * l)$ matrix. O', O'' are $(l * m)$ and $(m * m)$ matrices with every component zero. The matrix A' transforms secondary commodities into secondary commodities and A'' transforms primary commodities into secondary commodities.

In the more general input–output analysis (see E5.5), we need the above formalism. In many instances, however, no secondary commodities act as inputs and it is simpler to consider output space, of dimension l, and input space, of dimension m, separately and ignore commodity space entirely. The matrix A' is zero and we write A'' as A, i.e. A is considered as an $(m * l)$ matrix connecting input and output spaces. The activity vectors can be viewed as vectors in input space and $\mathbf{z}$ as a vector in output space. This is the easiest picture in which to discuss linear programming and we use it for that purpose in E5.3 and E5.4.

E5.2 LINEAR PRODUCTION FUNCTIONS

In this section we aim to find out what the production function looks like when there are several activities, each producing the same output commodity. The entrepreneur has to decide which combination of activities gives him the maximum output, from fixed quantities of each input. This is really a problem of 'technology' (see E5.1) rather than of economics; nevertheless it is of interest in practice and its solution will give further insight into the shape of production functions.

Firstly we note that the production function gives constant returns to scale, and the returns-to-scale index k is one. Thus the isoquants all have the same shape, and we only need to find the shape of one isoquant. This is usually the unit isoquant, the one that gives a unit amount of production.

Isoquants are surfaces in input space, and it is more convenient in this section to consider this space rather than the more general commodity space (see E5.1). Thus all commodity vectors in this section are vectors in input space. As in E3.1 we label the inputs as $X_1, X_2, \ldots, X_m$ and quantities of these inputs by $x_1, x_2, \ldots, x_m$. Suppose the entrepreneur has the amounts x'_i of X_i. Suppose also that he produces z_j amount of output using the jth activity. Then the entrepreneur wants to maximize q where

$$q = \sum_j z_j \tag{E5.2.1}$$

subject to the conditions

$$\sum_j a_{ij} z_j \leqslant x'_i \quad (i = 1, \ldots, m). \tag{E5.2.2}$$

These conditions (E5.2.2) ensure that no more than the variable input is used. The solution of this problem requires the techniques of linear programming, discussed in the next two sections.

Our aim here is to derive the isoquants, which is a different problem. Consider in input space a line with direction cosines l_i passing through the origin. Points on this line are given by

$$\mathbf{r} = r\mathbf{l}, \tag{E5.2.3}$$

where r is the distance from the origin and

$$\mathbf{l} = (l_1, l_2, \ldots, l_m). \tag{E5.2.4}$$

On this line there is, for a given output q', a set of values of r such that we can find z_j satisfying the two conditions:

$$\sum_j z_j = q', \tag{E5.2.5.}$$

$$\sum_j a_{ij} z_j \leqslant rl_i. \tag{E5.2.6}$$

(Condition (E5.2.6) can be expressed in vector form:

$$A\mathbf{z} = r\mathbf{l}. \tag{E5.2.7})$$

The minimum value r_m of this set gives the point $r_m\mathbf{l}$ lying on the isoquant for q'.

This can be seen as follows: let r' be some other value. Then by using the combination of activities that lead to the value r_m, then the inputs $r'\mathbf{l}$ are capable of producing the output qr'/r_m which is greater than q. Thus q is not the maximum production of the inputs $r'\mathbf{l}$, and so $r'\mathbf{l}$ does not lie on the isoquant corresponding to q. Thus if the line meets the isoquant it does so at $r_m\mathbf{l}$.

The calculation of the isoquant is now straightforward but rather complicated. To clarify the situation we look at some simple ideas and examples.

Domination

An activity k is said to be dominated if there exists a linear combination of other activities j such that $\sum_j z_j a_{ij} \leqslant a_{ik}$, where $\sum_j z_j = 1$, and there exists at least one value of i such that

$$\sum_j z_j a_{ij} < a_{ik}. \tag{E5.2.8}$$

Dominated activities are never used (cf. E3.2).

Isoquants for two inputs

Consider first the case with only one activity. Conditions (E5.2.6) become

$$a_{11} q' \leqslant rl_1, \; a_{21} q' \leqslant rl_2. \tag{E5.2.9}$$

The activity point $\mathbf{a}_1$ lies on the unit isoquant, and the lines parallel to the axes starting at $\mathbf{a}_1$ (see Fig. E5.1) constitute the rest of the isoquant. This means that the addition of only one of the inputs above the amounts $\mathbf{a}_1$ does not increase the production, and the additional amount of input is not used.

When two activities are involved, we need to look at the two activity points $\mathbf{a}_1$ and $\mathbf{a}_2$. If one of the activities is dominated, the isoquants are as in Fig. E5.1, with the corner at the point of the undominated activity, and the other activity point lying within the quadrant formed by the unit isoquant.

When neither of the activities is dominated, the two activity points lie on the unit isoquant, and so do all the points lying on the line joining the two activity points. Suppose, without loss of generality, that $a_{11} > a_{12}$. Then $a_{21} < a_{22}$. The rest of the unit isoquant is the lines (see Fig. E5.2)

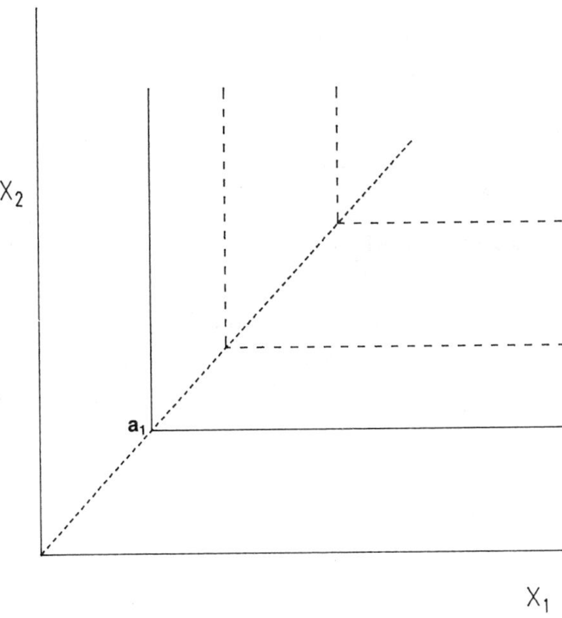

Fig. E5.1. The unit isoquant for two inputs, X_1 and X_2, and one activity, passing through the activity point $\mathbf{a}_1$ Other isoquants are shown dashed and have corners on the line (shown dotted) through the origin O and $\mathbf{a}_1$.

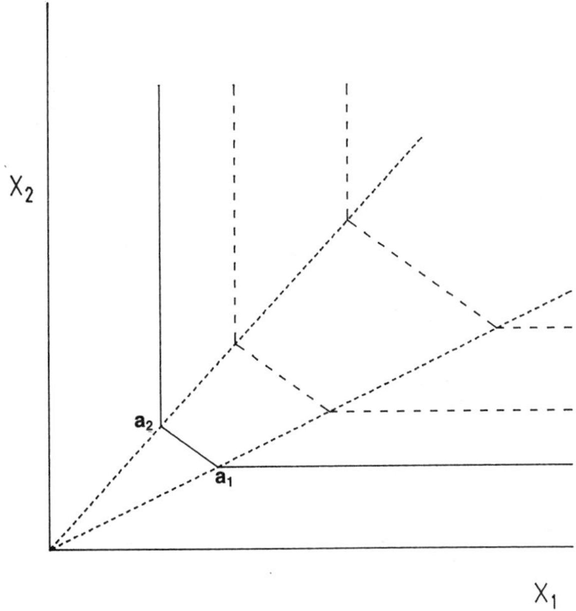

Fig. E5.2. The unit isoquant for two inputs X_1 and X_2 and two undominated activities with activity points $\mathbf{a}_1$ and $\mathbf{a}_2$. Another isoquant is shown dashed.

$$x_1 = a_{12}, \quad x_2 \geqslant a_{22}, \tag{E5.2.10}$$

$$x_2 = a_{21}, \quad x_1 \geqslant a_{11}. \tag{E5.2.11}$$

When three or more (n say) activities are involved we label the activities by the size of their x_1 coordinate, so that

$$a_{11} > a_{12} > a_{13} > \ldots > a_{1n}. \tag{E5.2.12}$$

Consider the polygon whose vertices are the activity points. Then the points

$$z_j \, \mathbf{a}_j \tag{E5.2.13}$$

are its interior and boundary points. If this set of points is convex†, none of the activities is dominated‡. The unit isoquant of an undominated set of activities is got (Fig. E5.3) by joining adjacent activity points by straight lines, plus the lines

$$x_2 = a_{21} \quad x_1 \geqslant a_{11},$$
$$x_1 = a_{1n}, \quad x_2 \geqslant a_{2n}. \tag{E5.2.14}$$

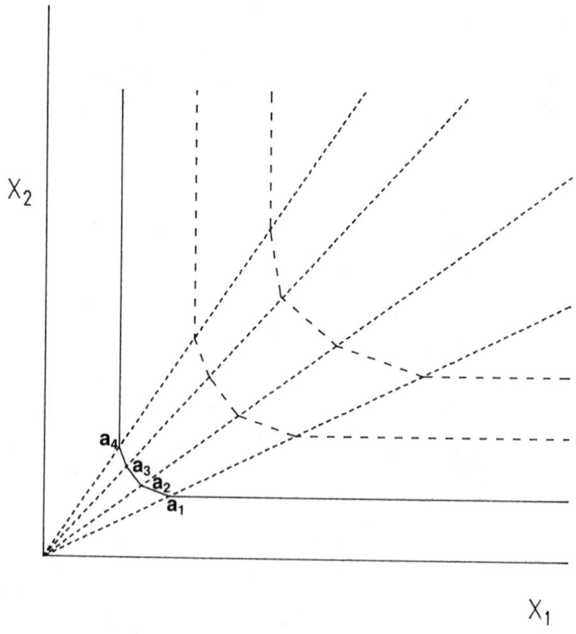

Fig. E5.3. Unit isoquant (continuous line) for system with two inputs X_1 and X_2 and four undominated activities. Another isoquant is shown dashed.

† A point set is said to be **convex** if every point on a straight line segment joining any two points of the set is also in the set.

‡ Otherwise one or more activity is dominated – we leave the proof to the reader.

Isoquants for many inputs

This situation is more complex and more difficult to visualize but the approach to it is similar to the approach used with two inputs and many activities. We consider the polyhedron formed by the activity points. If an activity point is not a vertex of this polyhedron, the activity is dominated and can be ignored. The polyhedron is thus taken to be convex. Part of the unit isoquant is got from the surfaces of the polyhedron which are nearest the origin. The remainder consists of the planar surfaces formed by the edges of the polyhedron and lines parallel to the axes drawn in the following way: suppose

$$a_{ij} = \min (a_{i1}, a_{i2}, a_{i3}, \ldots). \tag{E5.2.15}$$

Then the required line is

$$x_i = a_{ij}, \quad x_k > a_{kj} \quad (k \neq i). \tag{E5.2.16}$$

Once isoquants and production functions have been obtained, the actual inputs given the costs of the inputs are obtained (see E3) by maximizing the output for a given cost or by minimizing the cost for a given output.

E5.3 LINEAR PROGRAMMING 1

In this section we discuss some simple linear programming (l.p.) problems and show how, when there are only two variables, a solution can be found by a graphical method. A typical l.p. problem occurs as follows: consider a linear system where several outputs are produced from the same inputs. The problem is to choose the production of each output in order to maximize the profit or alternatively to minimize the cost. Let us consider the simplest situation in which the inputs and outputs are separate and A is an $(m * l)$ matrix connecting input and output spaces (see end of E5.1). An amount z_j of output j requires at least $a_{ij}z_j$ of the input X_i. Suppose the entrepreneur has the amount x_i of the input X_i and the price at which he can sell a unit quantity of the output j is p_j. Then he wants to maximize his revenue, i.e. find the values z_j which maximize

$$\sum_j p_j z_j, \tag{E5.3.1}$$

subject to the conditions

$$\sum_j a_{ij} z_j \leqslant x_i, \tag{E5.3.2}$$

$$z_j \geqslant 0. \tag{E5.3.3}$$

A typical minimizing l.p. problem is to find the inputs x'_i which minimize the variable cost

$$\sum_i r'_i x'_i \tag{E5.3.4}$$

where the price of a unit quantity of X_i is r_i'. The constraints are

$$\sum_i a_{ij} x_i' \geqslant q_j', \tag{E5.3.5}$$

$$x_i' \geqslant 0, \tag{E5.3.6}$$

where condition (E5.3.5) comes from the requirement that there must be enough of each input to produce the required amount q_j' of each output.

The above can be written in vector form: $\mathbf{x}$, $\mathbf{z}$, $\mathbf{p}$ are the vectors in the maximizing problem and $\mathbf{x}'$, $\mathbf{r}'$, $\mathbf{q}'$ in the minimizing one. Then the first problem is to find the vector $\mathbf{z}$ which maximizes

$$\mathbf{p} \,.\, \mathbf{z} \tag{E5.3.7}$$

subject to

$$A \,.\, \mathbf{z} \leqslant \mathbf{x}, \tag{E5.3.8}$$

$$\mathbf{z} \geqslant \mathbf{0}. \tag{E5.3.9}$$

The second is to find the input vector $\mathbf{x}'$ which minimizes

$$\mathbf{r}' \,.\, \mathbf{x}' \tag{E5.3.10}$$

subject to

$$\mathbf{x}' \,.\, A \geqslant \mathbf{q}' \tag{E5.3.11}$$

$$\mathbf{x}' \geqslant \mathbf{0}. \tag{E5.3.12}$$

The variables in (E5.3.7) are $\mathbf{z}$ with $\mathbf{x}$ fixed, and in (E5.3.10) are $\mathbf{x}'$ with $\mathbf{q}'$ fixed.

The mathematics in these problems is known as **linear programming**. The terms (E5.3.7) (and (E5.3.10)) are known as the **objective function** and the inequalities are known as the **constraints** with the simple inequalities (E5.3.9) (and (E5.3.12)) known as the **trivial** constraints. The **constraint equations** are got by replacing the constraints by equalities. If the variables satisfy the constraints, they are said to be a **feasible solution**, and the whole set of such solutions is said to form the **feasible region**. If there is at least one feasible solution, the l.p. problem is said to be **feasible**. The solution which is the maximum (or minimum) is known as the **optimal solution** and then the objective function is said to have the **value** of the l.p. problem.

To clarify these ideas let us look at a problem. Consider a simplified model of a furniture factory in which two items, tables and bookcases, are made from two materials, wood and composite. It takes 3 lots of wood and 1 lot of composite to make a table whereas it takes 1.5 lots of wood and 2 lots of composite to make a bookcase. Each day, 12 lots of wood and 7 lots of composite are delivered to the factory. The profit on a table is £10 and the profit on a bookcase is £6. We want to determine the number of tables and bookcases made each day.

In this problem the outputs are tables and bookcases, the inputs are the lots of wood and the lots of composite and the activities are making tables and making bookcases. In input space the activity vectors are (3, 1) and (1.5, 2) respectively, and the objective function is

$$10z_1 + 6z_2, \tag{E5.3.13}$$

where z_1 and z_2 are the number of tables and bookcases produced each day. The contraints are

$$3z_1 + 1.5z_2 \leqslant 12, \tag{E5.3.14}$$

$$z_1 + 2z_2 \leqslant 7. \tag{E5.3.15}$$

The effect of the constraints is best seen pictorally (see Fig. E5.4). The trivial constraints restrict z_1 and z_2 to the first quadrant. (E5.3.14) and (E5.3.15) show that the feasible region is the quadrilateral $OABC$ between the axes and the lines $3x_1 + 1.5x_2 = 12$ and $x_1 + 2x_2 = 7$. (These are the constraint equations.)

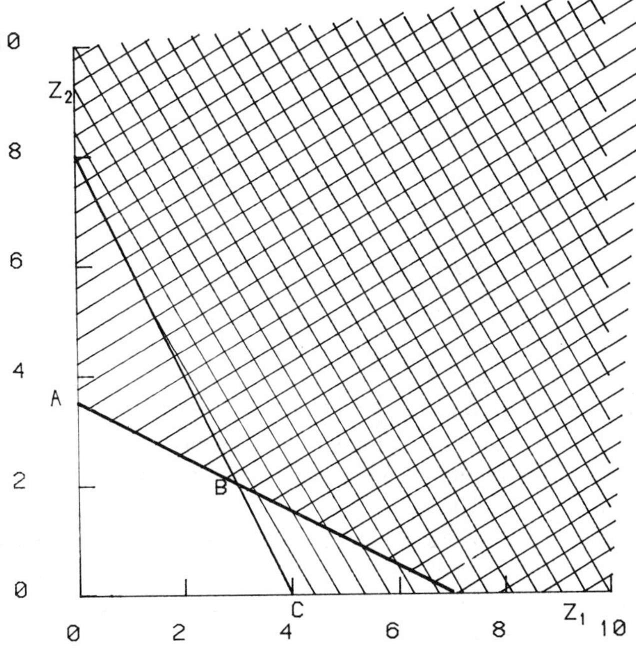

Fig. E5.4. The feasible region $OABC$ in the furniture factory problem. The region hatched ///// satisfies $z_1 + 2z_2 > 7$ and the region hatched \\\\\ satisfies $3z_1 + 1.5z_2 > 12$.

To find the values of z_1 and z_2 which give the objective function its maximum value within the feasible region, look at values which give a fixed size for the objective function (see Fig. E5.5). When it has size 10, z_1 and z_2 lie on a straight line close to the origin; for size 25, they lie on a parallel line further from the origin, and for size 40 the values lie on another parallel line even

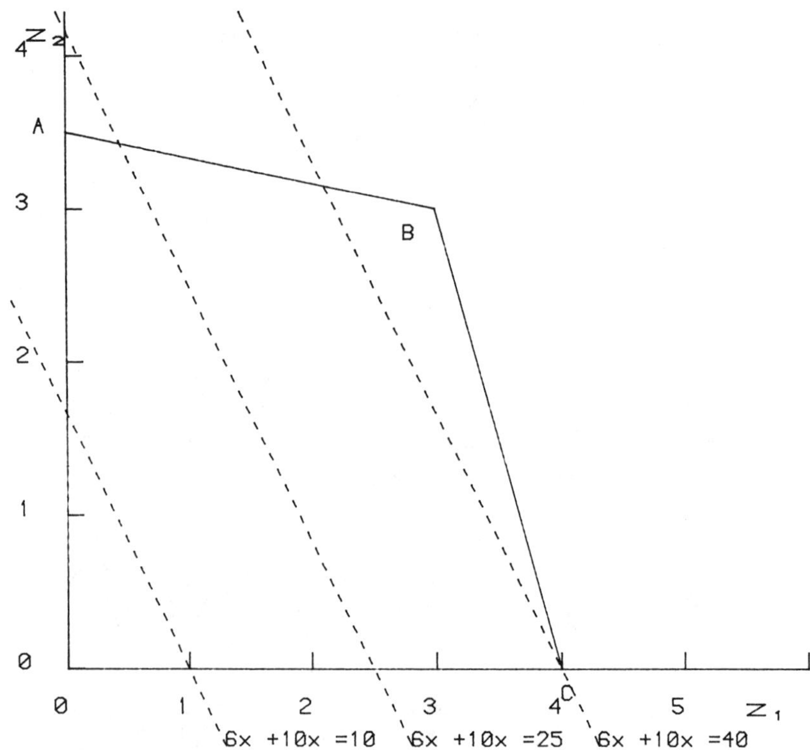

Fig. E5.5. The contours of the objective function $(10z_1 + 6z_2)$ of the furniture factory problem within the feasible region *OABC*.

further away. The contours of the objective function are parallel lines, the size increasing with distance from the origin. The maximum occurs at the vertex *B*, i.e. the point (3, 2). The l.p. problem thus has value 42.

This, then, is the solution of the mathematical problem. Its interpretation is that to make the maximum profit, of £42, the factory should make 3 tables and 2 bookcases per day.

With two variables, the contours of the objective function are straight laines. With many variables, these contours form hyperplanes, so that, if it exists, the optimal solution of the mathematical problem always lies at the boundary of the feasible region and usually at a vertex†.

If the linear programming problem involves more than three variables, a graphical method of solution is not possible. It is then necessary to work out the sizes of the objective function at the vertices of the feasible region. To calculate every vertex and the corresponding size of the objective function would take a

† Some real problems require a solution in integers: for example, if the vertex in our factory problem occurred at (3.1, 1.9) this solution would have been satisfactory mathematically but not in actuality as it is not possible to make 3.1 tables and 1.9 bookcases. The mathematics of finding such integer solutions is called integer programming and is difficult; it is not discussed here (see Reading List, EG).

considerable time and is not necessary. The best way is to start at one vertex, usually the origin if it belongs to the feasible region, and then find, if possible, an adjacent vertex which increases the size of the objective function. This strategy is continued until a vertex is obtained such that no adjacent vertex improves the objective function. This vertex is then the optimal solution.

The reader may like to prove that any vertex which is not the optimal solution always has an adjacent vertex which improves the objective function.

The above method is the strategy behind the **Simplex Method**, which is the standard way of finding the optimal solution. The calculations are heavy and tedious, but the method is well-suited for use on computers, and computer library routines are often available. The full theory of the method is complicated and is not given here. It is contained in many books (e.g. see EI Reading List).

L.p. problems are not always straightforward. For example, it is possible that the optimal solution is not unique. This happens when the contours of the objective function are parallel to one of the sides of the feasible region. In this case there are infinitely many optimal solutions.

Other difficulties occur when the feasible region is not finite. There are two possibilities. The first is that the feasible region is empty. This happens when the constraints are mutually contradictory. For example,

$$z < 1, \quad z > 2$$

are two such constraints. The problem is then said to be **infeasible.** The second possibility is that the feasible region is unbounded. An example is given in Fig. E5.6. In this case there may be a unique optimum, there may be infinitely many or the problem itself may be **unbounded**, i.e. the size of the objective function can be made arbitrarily large with the constraints still satisfied.

Linear programming problems are usually microeconomic in character but can occur in many different guises. Two of the most famous problems are known as the diet problem and the transportation problem: details of these can be found in most textbooks on the subject (see, also, EE5.5 and EE5.4). In most cases the conversion of the real problem into a linear programming problem requires both care and the other skills required in mathematical modelling.

E5.4 LINEAR PROGRAMMING 2: DUALITY

In this section we present some general theorems about linear programming and interpret the results in terms of general production processes (see E5.1).

We saw in E5.3 that l.p. problems could be either maximizing or minimizing problems; in linear programming there is to every maximizing problem of the form (E5.3.7–E5.3.9) a corresponding minimizing problem, known as the **dual**:

$$\textit{find the vector } \mathbf{r} \textit{ which minimizes } \mathbf{r} \,.\, \mathbf{x}, \tag{E5.4.1}$$

subject to

$$\mathbf{r} \,.\, A \geqslant \mathbf{p}, \tag{E5.4.2}$$

$$\mathbf{r} \geqslant \mathbf{0}. \tag{E5.4.3}$$

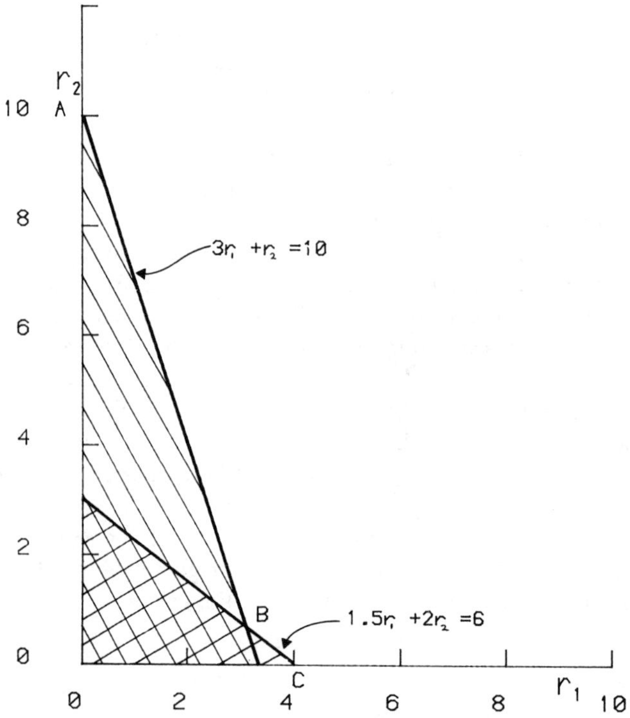

Fig. E5.6. An unbounded feasible region, given by the constraints $3r_1 + r_2 \geqslant 10$, $1.5r_1 + 2r_2 \geqslant 6$, $r_1 \geqslant 0$, $r_2 \geqslant 0$. The region hatched \\\\\\\\\\satisfies $3r_1 + r_2 < 10$ and is unavailable: the region hatched ///// satisfies $1.5r_1 + 2r_2 < 6$ and is unavailable. It is the unhatched part of the first quadrant which is the feasible region. (The constraints come from the dual of the furniture factory problem (see E5.3.13).)

Similarly, to every minimizing problem of the form (E5.4.1–E5.4.3) there is a dual maximizing problem given by (E5.3.7–E5.3.9). The original l.p. problem is known as the **primal**.

Note that in the problem (E5.4.1–E5.4.3) the variable is **r**. The units of this variable can be deduced from (E5.4.2): as **p** is a price vector in (E5.3.7), **r** is also a price vector, often known as the **shadow** price vector. The reader may like to speculate as to what prices **r** actually refers, before it is revealed at the end of the section. Now, however, it is more useful to derive some mathematical results.

By taking the scalar product of **x** with (E5.3.8) and of **z** with (E5.4.2) we get:

Theorem E5.4.1. If **z** *is a feasible solution of the maximum problem (E5.3.7) and* **r** *is a feasible solution of the dual minimizing problem (E5.4.1–EE5.4.3) then*

$$\mathbf{p.z} \leqslant \mathbf{r}.A.\mathbf{z} \leqslant \mathbf{r.x}. \qquad \text{(E5.4.4)}$$

Using this result the following theorem is easily proved:

Theorem E5.4.2. If there exists feasible solutions $\mathbf{z}_0$ *and* $\mathbf{r}_0$ *of the l.p. problems, such that*

$$\mathbf{p}.\mathbf{z}_0 = \mathbf{r}_0.\mathbf{x}, \tag{E5.4.5}$$

then $\mathbf{z}_0$ *and* $\mathbf{r}_0$ *are optimal solutions of their respective problems.*

The next result is difficult to prove, as it requires a lot of results from linear algebra. We state it without proof:

Theorem E5.4.3 (Fundamental Duality Theorem). If a standard linear programming problem and its dual are both feasible then they both have optimal solutions and both have the same value. If either problem is not feasible, then neither has an optimal solution.

From this and the previous theorems we can prove an equilibrium theorem:

Theorem E5.4.4. The feasible solutions $\mathbf{z}$ *and* $\mathbf{r}$ *of the maximum problem (E5.3.7–E5.3.9) and its dual (E5.4.1–E5.4.3) are optimal solutions if and only if*

$$r_i = 0 \quad \textit{whenever} \quad \sum_j a_{ij} z_j < x_i \tag{E5.4.6}$$

and

$$z_i = 0 \quad \textit{whenever} \quad \sum_i r_i a_{ij} > p_j. \tag{E5.4.7}$$

To prove this, let us first suppose that conditions (E5.4.6) and (E5.4.7) hold. Then

$$\mathbf{p}.\mathbf{z} = \sum_{i,j} r_i a_{ij} z_j = \mathbf{r}.\mathbf{x}$$

so that from Theorem E5.4.2, **r** and **z** are optimal solutions.

Suppose now that **r** and **z** are optimal solutions. Then

$$\mathbf{p}.\mathbf{z} = \mathbf{r}.\mathbf{x} = \mathbf{r}.A.\mathbf{z}$$

from Theorem E5.4.3. Thus

$$\sum_j \left(p_j - \sum_i a_{ij} r_i\right) z_j = 0$$

and as

$$p_j - \sum_i a_{ij} r_i < 0$$

the result (E5.4.7) follows. The result (E5.4.6) can be similarly obtained.

The dual problem, its interpretation and the theorems can be understood more easily if we look at our previous l.p. problem (see E5.3). The dual of that problem is to minimize

$$12r_1 + 9r_2$$

and the constraints are

$$3r_1 + r_2 \geqslant 10$$

$$1.5r_1 + 2r_2 \geqslant 6.$$

The reader should solve this problem graphically (noting that the feasible region is unbounded) and obtain the value 42 at

$$r_1 = \tfrac{28}{9}, \qquad r_2 = \tfrac{2}{3}. \tag{E5.4.8}$$

This is in agreement with Theorem E5.4.3. The reader should check that the other theorems are satisfied.

The meaning of the shadow prices can now be elucidated. Suppose there is available to the entrepreneur small extra amounts ϵ of wood and η of composite. He can then increase his profit by

$$(\tfrac{28}{9}\,\epsilon + \tfrac{2}{3}\,\eta),$$

i.e. the prices at which he values these extra inputs are the shadow prices. Thus the shadow prices $\mathbf{r}$ are the prices the entrepreneur would be willing to pay to increase his production. Theorems E5.4.1 and E5.4.2 show that if the entrepreneur values his stocks at the shadow prices, the gain π where

$$\pi = \mathbf{p}.\mathbf{z} - \mathbf{r}.\mathbf{x},$$

is less than or equal to the value of his stocks. Theorem E5.4.2 states that to find the maximum revenue, the entrepreneur should choose the production $\mathbf{z}$ and the shadow prices $\mathbf{r}$ to make π zero. The interpretation of Theorem E5.4.4 is obvious: (E5.4.6) says that if the required input of commodity i is less than the stock available, then the entrepreneur is unwilling to pay anything to increase his stock of commodity i to add to his production, i.e. the shadow price is zero. Similarly (E5.4.7) says that if the stock value of commodity j is greater than the price at which it can be sold, then the entrepreneur is unwilling to produce any of that commodity.

E5.5 INPUT–OUTPUT ANALYSIS

A multi-market analysis is necessary for planning the economy or predicting its behaviour because the quantity of any good produced depends not only on its own price but also on the prices and production of other goods. In E4.7 a simplified multi-market analysis was presented; it was very complicated and the introduction of production into that analysis would have complicated it even more. Indeed because of its complexity, it is not of much use in practical application nor can it incorporate empirical data.

Input–output analysis tries to be as simple as possible. It ignores consumer demand, and only considers production. It divides the economy (or the multi-market) into sectors and tries to find their production and their requirements. The sectors can be industries (see E2.6) but the production of individual goods is not considered. The model assumes that in the short term, production is a linear function of inputs. A consumption matrix can be defined and its elements estimated from empirical data. Thus data from one year, say, can be used to plan the productive part of the economy of the following year. This model is also known as the Leontief model, after its originator.

As commodities can be either inputs or outputs we usually work in commodity space. We use (E5.1.2) to define an $(n * n)$ matrix A and $\mathbf{z}$ as a vector in commodity space, i.e. $\mathbf{z}$ has its last m components zero. The matrix P, where

$$P = (I - A), \tag{E5.5.1}$$

with I the $(n * n)$ identity matrix, describes the final output and input because the vector $P.\mathbf{z}$ describes the amounts of each commodity production or consumed by the activities. If the component $(P.\,\mathbf{z})_i$ is positive (negative) the total production produces (consumes) that amount of the ith commodity.

The basic equation of input–output analysis is got from (E5.5.1):

$$(I - A)\,.\,\mathbf{z} = \mathbf{y} \tag{E5.5.2}$$

where $\mathbf{y}$ is written

$$\mathbf{y} = \mathbf{y}_1 - \mathbf{y}_2; \tag{E5.5.3}$$

$\mathbf{y}_1$ and $\mathbf{y}_2$ are respectively the total amounts produced and consumed. The components of $\mathbf{y}_2$ are assumed known and both $\mathbf{y}_1$ and $\mathbf{y}_2 \geqslant \mathbf{0}$. The analysis aims to find the value, if it exists, of $\mathbf{z}$ which gives rise to a required value of $\mathbf{y}_1$.

Closed systems

If there are no primary inputs into the system, $\mathbf{y}_2$ is zero and the system is called closed: all the inputs required are produced by the system itself. We show below that for these types of system, $(I - A)$ has an inverse. Thus the solution is

$$\mathbf{z} = (I - A)^{-1}\,.\,\mathbf{y}_1\,. \tag{E5.5.4}$$

This has a simple interpretation: it can be written (see Theorem E5.5.4),

$$\mathbf{z} = \mathbf{y}_1 + A\,.\,\mathbf{y}_1 + A^2\,.\,\mathbf{y}_1 + A^3\,.\,\mathbf{y}_1 + \ldots\,. \tag{E5.5.5}$$

In this expression, each term (except the first) on the right-hand side is the input required to produce the goods specified by the previous term. The first term $\mathbf{y}_1$ is the output sought, the second term is the input needed for the production of $\mathbf{y}_1$, the third term is the input needed for the production of $A\,.\mathbf{y}_1$, and so on. All these inputs have to be produced by the activities and so (E5.5.5) is the solution. Note that all the terms in (E5.5.5) are non-negative.

The closed system is economically uninteresting because it is unrealistic. It has no inputs and hence the outputs $\mathbf{y}_1$ can be as large as we like, just by making the intensity vector large enough. Mathematically, however, the matrices which occur in a closed system are of interest as similar matrices occur in open systems and in the theory of Markov chains (see P4.5); we now look at these matrices.

Productive matrices

If there exists a vector $\mathbf{z}' \geqslant \mathbf{0}$ such that the non-negative matrix A satisfies

$$\mathbf{z}' - A \,.\, \mathbf{z}' > \mathbf{0}, \tag{E5.5.6}$$

then that matrix is said to be **productive**. Any vector $\mathbf{z}'$ satisfying (E5.5.6) is in fact positive, i.e. $\mathbf{z}' > \mathbf{0}$, as $z_i' > \sum_j a_{ij} z_j' \geqslant 0$.

These matrices have some interesting properties which we now derive:

Theorem E5.5.1. If A *is productive and* $\mathbf{z} \geqslant \mathrm{A} \,.\, \mathbf{z}$, *then* $\mathbf{z} \geqslant \mathbf{0}$.

Suppose that $\mathbf{z} = (z_1, z_2, z_3, \ldots)$ satisfies $\mathbf{z} \geqslant A \,.\, \mathbf{z}$ but at least one coordinate is negative. Let $\mathbf{z}'$ be a vector such that $\mathbf{z}' > \mathbf{0}$ and $\mathbf{z}' > A \,.\, \mathbf{z}'$. Suppose $(-z_1/z_1')$ is the maximum value of $(-z_i/z_i')$. Then $(-z_1/z_1') > 0$. Consider the vector $\mathbf{x} = \mathbf{z} - (z_1/z_1')\mathbf{z}'$. Then $x_1 = 0$ and $\mathbf{x} \geqslant \mathbf{0}$. Now $\mathbf{x} > A \,.\, \mathbf{z} - (z_1/z_1') A \,.\mathbf{z}' > \mathbf{0}$. This implies that $\mathbf{x} > A \,.\mathbf{x} > \mathbf{0}$, which contradicts our supposition. Hence our theorem is proved.

Theorem E5.5.2. If A *is productive then* (I − A) *is non-singular.*

Suppose $(I - A)$ is singular: then there exists $\mathbf{x}$ such that $(I - A) \,.\mathbf{x} = \mathbf{0}$. Then $(I - A) \,.(-\mathbf{x}) = \mathbf{0}$. By Theorem E5.5.1, $\mathbf{x} \geqslant \mathbf{0}$ and $(-\mathbf{x}) \geqslant \mathbf{0}$. Thus $\mathbf{x} = \mathbf{0}$. Hence $(I - A)$ is non-singular.

Let $\mathbf{y} > \mathbf{0}$. Then the vector $\mathbf{x}$ such that $(I - A) \,.\, \mathbf{x} = \mathbf{y}$ satisfies $\mathbf{x} - A \,.\, \mathbf{x} > \mathbf{0}$. Then by Theorem E5.5.1, $\mathbf{x} > \mathbf{0}$. Thus the matrix $(I - A)$ maps non-negative vectors into non-negative vectors and so is itself non-negative.

Theorem E5.5.3. The matrix A *is productive if and only if* (I − A) *is non-negative.*

The details of the proof are left to the reader. It can be seen from Theorem E5.5.3 that for a productive matrix A there are numerous vectors $\mathbf{z}'$ satisfying (E5.5.6).

Theorem E5.5.4. If A *is a productive matrix,* $\lim_{n \to \infty} \mathrm{A}^n = 0$.

As A is productive there exists $\mathbf{z}$ such that $\mathbf{z} - A.\mathbf{z} \geqslant \mathbf{0}$ where $\mathbf{z} > \mathbf{0}$. Let $\lambda = \min_i \left(\left(z_i - \sum_j a_{ij} z_j\right)/z_i\right)$. Then $\lambda < 1$ and $A.\mathbf{z} < \mu\,\mathbf{z}$, where $\mu = 1 - \lambda/2 < 1$. Therefore $A^2.\mathbf{z} < \mu^2\,\mathbf{z}$ and so $\lim\,(A^n.\mathbf{z}) < \lim\,(\mu^n\,\mathbf{z}) = \mathbf{0}$. But $\mathbf{z} > \mathbf{0}$. Therefore the theorem is proved.

From this theorem the result (E5.5.5) can be easily obtained.

Open systems

In a production system the inputs may be raw materials (e.g. iron), machines, or services (e.g. labour). A sector of an open system can have inputs which are either primary or secondary, or both. For example, some goods such as steel and rubber are sometimes manufactured inside as well as imported into an economy.

The inclusion of the last type of commodity makes the analysis rather complex, so that we ignore them here and assume the sectors are only involved with commodities which are either primary or secondary, but not both.

Using the notation of E5.1, equation (E5.5.1) can be written

$$\mathbf{z} - A'.\mathbf{z} = \mathbf{y}_1, \tag{E5.5.7}$$

$$-A''.\mathbf{z} = -\mathbf{y}_2 \tag{E5.5.8}$$

but, strictly speaking, (E5.5.8) should be written:

$$A''.\mathbf{z} \leqslant \mathbf{y}_2. \tag{E5.5.9}$$

If A' and A'' are computed from empirical data, there is at least one solution of (E5.5.7) such that $\mathbf{y}_1 > \mathbf{0}$, so that A' is a productive matrix. Thus $(I - A')$ has an inverse, so that for given $\mathbf{y}_1$,

$$\mathbf{z} = (I - A')^{-1}.\mathbf{y}_1. \tag{E5.5.10}$$

To satisfy the input conditions (E5.5.9), a possible output $\mathbf{y}_1$ must satisfy

$$A''.(I - A')^{-1}.\mathbf{y}_1 \leqslant \mathbf{y}_2. \tag{E5.5.11}$$

This can be used to determine the inputs required for the production or, if the inputs are fixed, it will restrict the amount of production available.

Empirical systems

For the Leontief model to be useful, the elements of the consumption matrix must be deducible from empirical data. This can be done if the output and consumption of all the sectors for a particular period of time are known. The method should be clear from the following example: suppose that two industries, labelled 1 and 2, produce commodities for a multi-market. In a particular year, industry 1 required 3000 tons of its own output and otherwise produced 9000 tons of which industry 2 required 4000. Industry 2 required 2000 tons of its own output but also produced 8000 tons, 6000 of which were consumed by industry 1. The only significant input was labour: industry 1 required 6000 and industry 2 required 20,000 man-hours.

	Requirements of industry 1	industry 2	Surplus	Total
Industry 1	3000	4000	5000	12,000
Industry 2	6000	2000	2000	10,000
Primary input	6000	20,000 (in man-hours)		

Table E5.1. The production (in tons) of the industries 1 and 2 and its disposal.

Table E5.1 gives the inter-industry requirements and the surplus output of each industry. The total output is the sum of all three. To compute the consumption matrix, we need the elements a_{ij}, i.e. the requirement of input i to produce unit quantity of output j. To get these, the two columns of Table E5.1 are divided by the total output of the corresponding industry. Thus the matrix A' is

$$\begin{bmatrix} 0.25 & 0.4 \\ 0.5 & 0.2 \end{bmatrix}$$

and A'' is

$$[0.5 \quad 2.0] .$$

The units of A'' are man-hours, and of A' are tons of input, per ton of output.

Obviously the matrix A' is productive. The matrix $(I - A')^{-1}$ is

$$\begin{bmatrix} 2.0 & 1.0 \\ 1.25 & 1.875 \end{bmatrix} .$$

Suppose in the following year the total man-hours of labour available increases to 27,000, i.e. $\mathbf{y}_2 = 27{,}000$. The final output vector $\mathbf{y}_1$ can be written $(y(1), y(2))$ and has to satisfy the constraint

$$3.5y(1) + 4.25y(2) \leqslant 27{,}000.$$

This constraint limits the total possible output. Thus suppose the nation wanted to increase the surplus output of industry 2 by 20%, i.e. 2400 tons: the surplus output of industry 1 would then be limited to $(27{,}000 - 11{,}200)/3.5$ tons.

The units in which the inputs and the outputs are measured only affects the elements of the consumption matrix (see EE5.8). Thus monetary units can be used to compute the consumption matrix: this makes for consistency within the matrix and eases the task of getting the empirical data.

EE5 EXERCISES

5.1 The production of a certain commodity requires two inputs. It can be produced by any of four activities, which have activity vectos (8, 1), (5, 2), (3, 4) and (1, 5). Draw the isoquants for the production of 1, 2 and 3 units of output.

5.2 In Exercise 5.1, find the combination of activities which produces 2 units of output and which minimizes the cost when the prices of unit amounts of the inputs are:

(i) equal at £10 each;
(ii) £10 for the first and £50 for the second.

5.3 A clothing factory produces jackets and trousers. Three machines (a cutter, a sewer and a dyer) are used in the production. The manufacture of one jacket requires 1 hour on the cutter, 3 hours on the sewer and one hour on the dyer, and one pair of trousers requires 1 hour on the cutter, 1 hour on the sewer and no time on the dyer. The dyer can only operate for 3 hours, the sewer for 12 hours and the cutter for 7 hours per day. Everything made in the factory is sold: a profit of £8 is made on each jacket and £5 on each pair of trousers. How should the machines be used in order to maximize the profit? Should the answer be in integers?

5.4 (A transportation problem) A foreign car manufacturer ships its cars to Britain to be distributed from central depots at Oxford and Derby. The cars arrive at one of three ports: Liverpool, Bristol and Harwich. Each month the supplies of cars to these ports are: Liverpool 5000; Bristol 8000; Harwich 6000. To meet their orders the Oxford depot requires 10,000 cars and the Derby depot 9000.

The transportation costs per car from each port are given as follows:

	to	Oxford	Derby
from			
Liverpool		£29	£25
Bristol		£27	£30
Harwich		£22	£27.

Determine how the manufacturer should direct its cars in order to minimize its transportation costs.
(Hint: formulate the problem in terms of six variables and then eliminate four of them.)

5.5 (A diet problem) Dietitians have determined that a healthy diet should contain a minimum of 0.5 kg of carbohydrate, 0.25 kg of protein and 30 mg of Vitamin C per day. In an underdeveloped country, the foods available are rice, beans and pineapples, and have the following nutritional properties per kilogram:

	kg carbohydrate	kg protein	mg of Vit. C	cost
rice	0.75	0.05	2.0	£0.05
beans	0.5	0.3	15.0	£0.15
pineapple	0.5	0.0	60.0	£0.1.

Find the amounts of these foods which satisfy the dietary requirements and cost the least. (Please note that the amounts quoted are fictional.)

5.6 Formulate the dual of the diet problem, Exercise 5.5, and give a realization.

5.7 Consider the following input–output table for three industries, A, B and C:

to	A	B	C	surplus
A	1	2	1	4
B	1	1	2	4
C	1	1	2	4
primary i/p	5	4	3	

Determine the production and primary input requirements of each industry in terms of general final demands.

5.8 In 1980, firm A produced 500 tonnes of steel, and this required 20 tonnes of steel products produced by firm B; they sold 80 tonnes of their production to firm B, who produced 80 tonnes of steel products. Thus firm A sold 420 tonnes of steel and firm B sold 60 tonnes of steel products to other customers. Assuming that firms A and B work in the same way, what must their production be if they want to sell 570 tonnes of steel and 95 tonnes of steel products on the open market in 1981?

If they both employed 50 people in 1980, how many people do they need to employ in 1981?

5.9 Show that the effect of changing the units in which the output of an industry is measured is to multiply the ith row and the ith column of the consumption matrix by the same factor.

How does this affect the intensity vector? Show that a productive matrix remains productive under this transformation.

5.10$^{(m)}$ Investigate the consequences of introducing money into an input–output model. Try a system with one industry which requires a certain percentage of its own output and an import as a primary input. Another input could be labour. The sale of the surplus production is as exports and as home goods, the exports paying (exactly) for the imports and the home goods being bought by the labour force, who spend all their wages on them.

(i) Can anything be learnt about wages and prices from this simple model?

(ii) Suppose the labour force is divided into two groups, managers and workers, with the managers being paid the profit of the industry. Is it possible to maximize this profit? What are the consequences.

CHAPTER E6

Afterthoughts

E6.1 FURTHER TOPICS

In this part of the book we have given an introduction to the basic theory of microeconomics. In E2 was presented the theory of demand, in E3 the theory of supply and in E4 we saw how the two came together in the market and how this determined the prices. Although these three topics form a self-contained whole, there is much more in microeconomics to study. On the one hand, each of the above topics can be elucidated further and special cases investigated more thoroughly, e.g. duopoly and dynamics. On the other hand, there are topics which have not even been mentioned, e.g. **welfare economics** and **optimization over time**.

To incorporate the facts that people probably tend to optimize over a period of time, which may be long in comparison with the unit of time used in the theory and that people have a memory, is extremely important, and might affect the whole theory. It is also important to incorporate time-delays into the theory; this is of special interest to mathematicians, for as we shall see in part P on populations, there are many problems when reactions are not instantaneous. All our microeconomic models have assumed instantaneous reactions on the parts of consumers, entrepreneurs and markets and that the people involved act to optimize their utility or their profits at each instant, not over a period of time.

E6.2 LIBERAL ECONOMICS

In E4.2 the ideal competitive market was introduced and in E4.5 it was compared with a monopolistic market as to the consequences for prices and supply.

The ideal market, in general, is more beneficial; it has other benefits because by definition (see point (4), E4.2) entrepreneurs can and do enter the market and hence consumers benefit by having their desires for consumption satisfied. Whether these consequences occur and whether the ideal market exists or can be made to exist are discussed briefly in E6.3. Nevertheless it is noteworthy that in the ideal competitive market, whether it exists or not, people are free to pursue their individual desires as hard as they can and the result is supposedly beneficial to all.

This is the philosophy of **liberal economics**, i.e. people should be free to and should maximize the attainment of their selfish desires and as a result the community will benefit – a comforting philosophy for the greedy. A more appropriate criticism should be made using the analysis of SM1 (see E6.3). Here we contrast it with the results of one of the 'games', known as the Prisoners' Dilemma, presented in part G. In it the participants pursue their own selfish ends and both suffer as a consequence, i.e. they get a result very much worse than if they had both acted selflessly. A fuller discussion of this is presented in G5.3.

E6.3 CRITIQUE

An important aspect of any mathematical model is the verification of its descriptive part, a careful criticism of any normative parts and a testing of any solutions to see if they are practical. Such a critique of microeconomic theory is a major task; there is only room in this book for the following few observations.

In microeconomics it is difficult to distinguish between the descriptive and normative aspects of the theory; for example, is an ideal competitive market meant to be a description of an actual market or a solution to the problem of finding the best possible way of organizing a market? It may be both.

The descriptive side

Are the theories of demand, supply and the market a valid description of the actual way consumers, suppliers and markets behave? Can these theories be used predictively?

In constructing the theory of demand, we have neglected brand names, the effects of packaging, advertising and fashion, problems of uncertain quality, the building-up of goodwill, the possibility of optimizing over a period of time, etc., all of which may have an effect on people's preferences. Even if these effects can be neglected, the theory of E2 is only valid for simple goods such as butter or toilet soap. That theory may give insights into the way people desire other commodities such as land, leisure or labour, but it is an assumption to believe the theory applies to all goods or, indeed, to the whole of life.

The theory of demand regards people as if they were lone individuals and as if they had no memory, i.e. the demand of each transaction is determined by the desires of one individual acting selfishly and as if he had no memory of any previous transactions. People sometimes act altruistically and often in groups, e.g. as families, clubs, or nations.† They also have memories of the standards of products and service, and this affects their preferences.

Thus there must be doubts as to the quantitative accuracy of demand theory. Qualitatively, however, it gives some useful concepts, and this justifies the trouble taken in its development. Except for predicting 'money illusion', it does not predict many results on its own.

The theory of supply is also questionable, as most suppliers probably fix their price in a way different from that of E3. The complexities of supply, with labour, the law, the wholesale and the retail trade, and storage to take into account cannot be covered accurately by a general theory. The meaningful content of the theory is small; it provides the concepts of a cost function and a supply function, but without quantitative cost functions there are hardly any predictions.

In market behaviour, general microeconomic theory has some significant meaning: it predicts that in general prices will increase (decrease) when demand (supply) increases, and that prices for a commodity tend to decrease the more suppliers there are. All of these results are borne out in practice, although we make no quantitative comparison of theoretical predictions with observation here.

The ideal market may occur for some simple commodities; the existence of near-substitutes makes markets behave more like an ideal market. On the other hand, the conditions for an ideal market are unlikely to occur in complex commodities; in particular the long-term conditions are unlikely to be satisfied; for example, it is difficult for new firms to start producing aeroplanes or automobiles because of the initial capital and expertise required. The monopolistic model is unlikely to be accurate because of the existence of near-substitutes. The latter requires a consideration of multi-markets, which are complicated enough if all the commodities obeyed the simple ideal market conditions; if, however, the other previously-mentioned factors need to be considered and some of the commodities are produced oligopolistically, the analysis is extremely difficult.

After this critique the reader may feel that mathematical microeconomic theory is a waste of time. Not so: it has produced some very useful concepts in a simple, clear and direct way and has shown up in a stark and straightforward manner the problems that the microeconomist has to face.

The normative side

The psychological assumptions, i.e. that consumers maximize their utility and entrepreneurs maximize their profit, act in the theory both as descriptions of

† Is it realistic to describe emotions and feelings in the same way as preferences, i.e. by using a utility function? Note that it is impossible to construct an individual utility function for someone who desires the success of others.

the way people behave and as **norms**. With the latter role it is the task of microeconomics to find the way(s) of arranging the economy to optimize the satisfaction of these norms.

For a given commodity, if unaffected by the market behaviour of other commodities and if no externalities are present, microeconomic theory shows that the ideal competitive market is the *optimal* solution. Is it a *practical* solution? Where the ideal market is a description of the actual market, it is obviously so; probably for some other commodities which are simple to make, it may be possible to change the actual market into an ideal market. For complex commodities, such as aeroplanes, it looks impractical.

In a multi-market situation, most demand comes from the desires of people who are paid for their labour. If labour costs are decreased, the work-force receives less money; then demand for consumer goods decreases, so that to maintain equilibrium their supply also decreases. As the multi-market is so interdependent, supply and demand decreases, thereby causing a recession. Thus decreasing labour costs may not be the optimal policy in a multi-market; so it may not be optimal to have an ideal market in labour.

The behavour of a multi-market is very complex, especially when the actual market in some commodities is monopolistic, oligopolistic or oligopsomistic, and there are externalities present; does trying to change one or two markets into ideal markets improve the satisfaction of these norms?

All this assumes the norms are satisfactory. For simple commodities such as butter they probably are; for labour they are not, because to consider labour as such a commodity ignores the individual labourer, his dignity, self-respect and his own wishes. Different norms are required for labour; as unemployment is so degrading and socially undesirable it may even be desirable to maximize the use (consumption) of labour. Labour plays an important role in any multi-market analysis, so that any normative discussion based on the previous norms alone can be misleading and dangerous.

Finally the norms should be questioned as to what they aim to achieve. If their aim is the happiness of mankind, it is doubtful if they are correct; to pursue selfish ends, as these norms require, is usually a recipe for misery; most religions and philosophies, particularly Christianity and Buddhism, suggest different ways for the pursuit of happiness. But that is another question!

Part G:
CONFLICT AND COOPERATION

CHAPTER G1

Introduction

Consider the situation in which a trade union and an employer negotiate wage rates, productivity, etc. Both the trade union and the employer have some desires; they enter negotiation aiming to maximize the achievement of these aims. To obtain some of these ends, the two sides may be in direct competition, e.g. over wage rates, whereas to obtain others it may be in their interests to cooperate, e.g. to improve the viability of the company. In this part of the book we want to try to analyse quantitatively situations in which competition and cooperation occur.

Let us return to the complex situation above. The model of it which we choose to make will depend on which aspects interest us. To identify the amounts of cooperation and competition between the employer and the trade union, we conceptually simplify the situation: let us assume that the employer has control over certain parts of the business, e.g. investment. Suppose that these parts can be represented by a variable x, i.e. the employer can choose a value of x within some range and this choice represents a decision on such parts of the business. Similarly the trade union has control over certain other parts of the business, e.g. the response of the work-force. We also suppose that the choice of the trade union can be represented by the choice of a different variable y. Suppose that the employer's desires and the trade union's desires can be represented by utility functions $f(x, y)$ and $g(x, y)$ respectively. Then the problem is that one person, the employer, wants to maximize $f(x, y)$ and is only able to control x, and another person, the trade union, wants to maximize $g(x, y)$ and is only able to control y.

Let us make some observations on the mathematics of this problem:

(i) this problem is different from the usual maximization problems in which calculus is used, as they involve only one person wanting to maximize one function;
(ii) the outcome, i.e. the value of $g(x, y)$ for one party, e.g. the trade union, depends not only on the choices he makes for y, but also on the choice of x made by the other party, i.e. the employer. The two parties are interdependent;
(iii) with the criteria so far provided there is no unique solution, i.e. the mathematical problem is not well-posed. To make the problem tractable and to find a 'solution' we must seek some other criteria.

This kind of mathematical problem occurs in models of other situations, e.g. duopoly. The archetype of this situation is the **game**: the players try to maximize the points they win but the outcome for each player depends not only on his own decisions but also on the decisions of others. In some situations the interests of the players may conflict but in others it may pay the players to cooperate.

The part of applied mathematics which has been developed to tackle such problems is known as **Game Theory**. This subject is a mixture of applications and abstract mathematics – a typical bit of mathematical modelling. The original theory was based on model versions of parlour games; it does not concern itself with physical games where skill, fitness, etc. are involved. The importance of Game Theory lies in the description and analysis of the systems it observes. It provides a way of analysing quantitatively some systems in which interdependence and hence conflict and cooperation are important, and of seeing how much conflict and how much cooperation there is or there can be in the system.

The techniques of Game Theory can be applied to any system involving interdependence; this includes not only parlour games but also other game-like systems which occur in economics, politics, psychology, sociology and even war. These systems, however, are usually very complex, so that a mathematical model of the conflict and cooperation in the system is not easy or straightforward; the analysis is usually only up to orders of magnitude, it being too much to expect exact numbers. In this book, most of our examples come from parlour games.

The theory sometimes provides 'solutions' but these have not proved very useful as they have not always corresponded to the reality of the situation. Game Theory is an example of a mathematical theory which has helped in the qualitative analysis of some systems without producing many quantitative results.

Before trying to construct a theory it is best to look at some examples of 'games' (see G2). From these examples we derive the essential characteristics of a **game**. Although some games are deterministic, i.e. a decision by all the players leads to a definite outcome, others are probabilistic, i.e. such a decision leads to several outcomes, each with its own probability. Examples of the latter occur when the result depends on the fall of a dice or the draw of a card; an example of the former is the children's game 'Scissors, Paper, Stone' in which two players each choose one of the titles and win, lose or draw according to which title they chose.

When we know what a 'game' is, we can develop the theory. Thus in G3 we look at utility again, so that 'risk' can be incorporated into it. For instance, if I am interested in buying a certain make of car, I cannot be certain that everything in the car will be perfect, e.g. the door-locks might be defective. If I know the probability that such things occur, then I can, with the help of the theory, calculate a new utility which takes this risk into account. This is an essential part of the theory for games of chance.

Once utility has been defined it is possible to identify conflict and cooperation within the theory. This is also done in G3. In G4 we look at two-person zero-sum games, where the theory is easiest and has made the most advances. As this book is designed to serve as an introduction, we usually only consider two-person games.

CHAPTER G2

Games of the Theory

G2.1 INTRODUCTION

In this chapter we provide some examples of 'games'. The aim is to examine these games and draw from them their characteristic features. These features can then be considered as the 'axioms' of Game Theory. The other aim is to try to achieve an understanding of the technical terms which occur in these axioms.

The first game is 'Scissors, Paper, Stone' in which each player has only one move. The second has exactly the same characteristics but is an example taken from a war situation. The third has several moves and the fourth, known as 'Rustic Poker', involves chance. All these four are games of pure conflict. The remaining games are different: 'Prisoners' Dilemma' illuminates many social and economic situations, and involves both conflict and cooperation, as do 'Duopoly' and 'Oligopoly'. The latter is the only game presented here which involves more than two players.

It is not necessary to study all these games at this point; it is only the first game which needs to be understood well for most of this part of the book but an appreciation of the role of chance, as in 'Rustic Poker', and the role of cooperation and conflict, as in the 'Prisoners' Dilemma' and in 'Duopoly', would make the reader appreciate Game Theory more.

G2.2 THE GAMES

'Scissors, Paper, Stone

This is a traditional children's game for two players. Each player chooses one of three objects, scissors, paper or stone, and the players simultaneously declare their choice. Now scissors are supposed to cut paper, paper is supposed to wrap stone and stone is supposed to blunt scissors. Thus a choice of scissors beats a choice of paper, which in turn beats a choice of stone, which in turns beats a choice of scissors. A draw results if both players choose the same object.

Each player has three choices as to how he is going to play the complete game. These choices are known in Game Theory as **strategies**. Suppose the winner gains one point, the loser loses one point and no points are awarded if a draw occurs. Then the resulting points gained by the players are a function of the strategies chosen by each of the players. The results, or **outcomes** as they are usually called, can be exhibited in a matrix form:

		B's strategies		
		scissors	paper	stone
	scissors	0	1	−1
A's strategies	paper	−1	0	1
	stone	1	−1	0

$$\begin{bmatrix} 0 & 1 & -1 \\ -1 & 0 & 1 \\ 1 & -1 & 0 \end{bmatrix}. \quad \text{(G2.2.1)}$$

The above matrix (G2.2.1), U say, is known as A's outcome matrix and represents the points gained in the game by A, the player whose strategies determine which row is to be considered. The other player B has strategies which determine the column. His outcomes are given by the matrix $-U$.

A problem for the guerillas' leader

Consider the following (fictional) problem: the city of Beirana is under attack from some guerillas and the government is sending reinforcements from Salvare, the capital, 40 miles away to the south. There is a lake between the two cities with roads joining them on both the east and the west sides. The western route takes 3 days whereas the eastern route takes only 2 days. Aratro, the guerilla leader, only has sufficient men to deploy on one of the routes. If he deploys them on the same route as the troops travel, his men can harass the troops for all the time they are on the road. If, however, he deploys them on the other route, the men will not have time to move around the lake and harass the troops at all.

Aratro and the government both have two strategies, i.e. to choose either the eastern road or the western road. The outcome matrix for Aratro is

		government's strategies	
		E	W
Aratro's	E	2	0
strategies	W	0	3

$$\begin{bmatrix} 2 & 0 \\ 0 & 3 \end{bmatrix} \quad \text{(G2.2.2)}$$

where the numbers refer to the number of days that the troops are harassed. The government's outcome matrix is the negative of Aratro's, as the government presumably does not want its troops harassed.

'Threepenny Nim'

This game for two players is played with three pennies; initially two of these pennies are 'heads' and one is 'tails'. Players make moves alternatively, and a move consists either of turning over any coin which is 'tails' or of removing any number of coins which are 'heads'. The loser is the player who takes the last coin.

The possible plays of the game can be represented by a tree diagram. The state of the game at any time depends on the coins left, and in Fig. G2.1 the states have been labelled by numbers. In many systems (see SM1) a state depends on its history, so that it is conventional to consider states such as (5) and (9) as distinct.

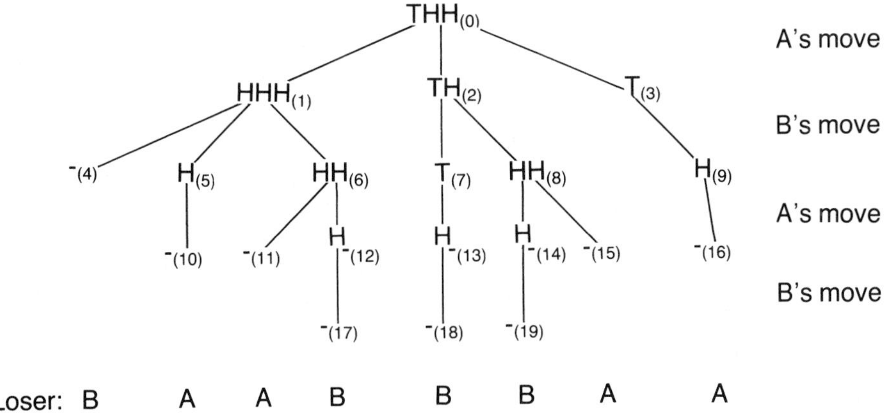

Fig. G2.1. Game-tree for 'Threepenny Nim'.

Suppose the winner gains a point and the loser loses a point. Then outcomes are determined by the moves of the players. It is possible, however, for each player to make more than one move; also any move may be affected by the opponent's previous move. In this game then we need to ask 'what do we mean by the "strategies"?' Only then can we construct an outcome matrix.

'Rustic Poker'

This game is sometimes known as 'Bluffing'. A hat contains two cards, marked W (for Win) and L (for Lose). The two players, A and B, stake themselves in by each placing £s in the kitty. Suppose A starts: he draws one of the two cards and looks at it without letting B see it. He then either folds, in which case B pockets the kitty and the game ends, or raises by an amoung £$(s' - s)$, thus making his total stake £s'. B can then either fold, in which case A gets the kitty, i.e. A gains

£s, or 'call', i.e. he puts £$(s' - s)$ more into the kitty. B then draws the remaining card. The winner is the player with W on his card.

Although a simple game, it is more complicated than 'Scissors, Paper, Stone' as it depends on chance, i.e. on what card A draws from the hat. We do not know what the strategies are nor how to measure the outcomes: if a course of action leads to several results, each with its own probability, how do we measure the player's desire to take that course? This leads us, in G3, to look at utility again.

'The Prisoner's Dilemma'

Two men, A and B again, are apprehended by the police and found to possess a quantity of forged bank-notes. The detective in charge of the investigation is convinced that the two men are the counterfeiters – but there is insufficient evidence for a conviction in court, unless at least one of the men confesses. The detective is a canny fellow. He puts the men into separate rooms for interrogation and separately makes the same proposition to each of them: 'Why not confess to being a counterfeiter? If you confess, and your mate does not, then you will get off with only a warning; but if you don't confess and your mate does, then you'll get at least 8 years. It's in your own interest to confess.' For the lesser crime of carrying forged bank-notes, the prisoners will both get 2 years in gaol, but if they both confess they will get 5 years. The prisoners are both aware of these penalties.

The strategy for each prisoner is obvious: either he confesses (C) or he refuses (R) to confess. The outcome matrix is also straightforward:

$$\begin{array}{lcc} & \multicolumn{2}{c}{B\text{'s strategies}} \\ & \text{C} & \text{R} \end{array}$$

$$A\text{'s strategies} \quad \begin{matrix} \text{C} \\ \text{R} \end{matrix} \begin{bmatrix} -5\,(-5) & 0\,(-8) \\ -8\,(0) & -2\,(-2) \end{bmatrix} \qquad \text{(G2.2.3)}$$

This is A's outcome matrix; B's outcomes are given in brackets.

What should the prisoners do?

'Duopoly'

Two firms A and B, assumed identical for simplicity, produce the same commodity (see E4.6). Because of their production methods, each firm is only able to produce 0, 2, 4, or 6 units. The cost to A of producing q_A units is

$$£(4 + (q_A^3 - 9q_A^2 + 27q_A)/2) \qquad \text{(G2.2.4)}$$

and firm B has an identical cost function. The revenue for firm A is £pq_A, where p is the price of a unit. The profit to firm A is thus

$$£(pq_A - (4 + (q_A^3 - 9q_A^2 + 27q_A)/2)). \qquad \text{(G2.2.5)}$$

The public demand for the commodity depends on the price p and is given by the demand function. Let us suppose that the demand function is given by

$$D(p) = (72 - p)/4. \qquad \text{(G2.2.6)}$$

The total production is

$$q_A + q_B. \qquad \text{(G2.2.7)}$$

We assume that the market is in equilibrium, i.e. demand equals supply; this determines the price if the supply is known, i.e.

$$q_A + q_B = D(p). \qquad \text{(G2.2.8)}$$

A's profit then is determined not only by A's decision on how much to produce but also by B's decision. Similarly B's profit is affected by both decisions.

The strategies for A and B are to produce 0, 2, 4 or 6 units. The outcomes are the profits of the firms; A's outcome matrix U, in £s per period, is

$$\begin{array}{lc} & \quad B\text{'s strategies} \\ & \begin{array}{cccc} 0 & 2 & 4 & 6 \end{array} \\ A\text{'strategies} \begin{array}{c} 0 \\ 2 \\ 4 \\ 6 \end{array} & \begin{bmatrix} -4 & -4 & -4 & -4 \\ 111 & 95 & 79 & 63 \\ 206 & 174 & 142 & 110 \\ 257 & 209 & 161 & 113 \end{bmatrix}. \end{array} \qquad \text{(G2.2.9)}$$

B's outcome matrix is U^{T}, the transpose of U; as A and B are identical, the game is said to be symmetrical (see G3.3). Note that

$$U + U^{\mathrm{T}} \neq 0. \qquad \text{(G2.2.10)}$$

*'Oligopoly'

In an oligopolistic market (see E4.6) the number of suppliers is finite but greater than two. We consider an example based on the preceding duopoly game, but with three suppliers, A, B and C with cost function (G2.2.4). As before they each produce 0, 2, 4, or 6 units. Suppose the demand function is changed to

$$D(p) = (66 - p)/3. \qquad \text{(G2.2.11)}$$

Assuming an equilibrium market, the price is determined from (G2.2.11):

$$p = 66 - 3\,(q_A + q_B + q_C). \qquad \text{(G2.2.12)}$$

The outcome matrix is now a 3*3*3 matrix. Many of the elements are the same because of the symmetry between the players. Thus we list in Table G2.1 many of the distinct elements, in units of £s per unit time. Given also are the sum of the profits and the price per unit.

ABC	*A*	*B*	*C*	Sum	*p*
006	–4	–4	257	249	48
024	–4	79	174	249	48
222	79	79	79	237	48
026	–4	67	221	284	42
044	–4	150	150	296	42
224	67	67	150	284	42
046	–4	126	185	307	36
226	55	55	185	295	36
244	55	126	126	307	36
066	–4	149	149	294	30
246	43	102	149	294	30
444	102	102	102	306	30
266	31	111	111	253	24
446	78	78	111	267	24
466	54	77	77	208	18
666	41	41	41	123	12

Table G2.1. The profits for the firms in 'Oligopoly'. The first column denotes the amounts produced by each firm.

G2.3 CHARACTERISTICS OF A GAME

Our 'games' have exhibited deterministic and probabilistic characteristics, and the ideas of strategy and outcome. A strategy is a course of action for a player, which together with the strategies of the other players leads to a complete play of the game. The outcome of a game, however, does not necessarily measure the desire of a player to pursue a particular line of play. This is measured by his pay-off (see G3) which is determined by his preferences.

The following 'axioms', then, incorporate chance, strategies, outcomes and preferences and are suggested as a foundation for our theory, i.e. a game in Game Theory is characterized as follows.

(1) Each player has a well-defined set of possible courses of action. These are called **pure strategies**.
(2) The outcome of the game or the probabilities of the outcomes are completely determined by a choice of strategies by each player.
(3) Each player has an order of preference among the possible outcomes of the game.
(4) Every player has complete knowledge of the strategies, their outcomes and the preferences of all the players.

We elucidate further the idea of strategy in G2.4, and the idea of preference in G3. Note here, however, that as preference is subjective, a game is different if the players are different, i.e. in Game Theory a game cannot be divorced from the preference of its players. A simple example of this is the difference between a game of draughts played between two players of the same age, and a game played between a father and his young son. In the former case the two players usually try their hardest to win, whereas in the latter it is in the interests of the father to lose (without of course letting the son know!).

G2.4 STRATEGIES

What is a strategy?

This often causes confusion. A choice of strategies by all the players leads to a complete **play** of the game. Thus a strategy for a player must lay down in advance a complete set of moves, so that in **all** circumstances which may occur the player knows what he is going to do. To clarify the concept we look at strategies in the games 'Threepenny Nim' and 'Rustic Poker'.

In 'Threepenny Nim', a move by a player can be described by the two states which are connected by the move; for example,

$$(1) \rightarrow (6) \qquad \text{(G2.4.1)}$$

would describe B's move from HHH to HH. It can be seen from Fig. G2.1 that each player has at most two moves.

The strategy for a player consists of a set of first moves and a set of second moves: each set must contain a move out of every state that may occur as a result of his own previous moves and his opponent's possible previous moves.

For his initial move, A has a free choice. He can choose one of three alternatives: $(0) \rightarrow (1)$, or $(0) \rightarrow (2)$, or $(0) \rightarrow (3)$. Suppose A chooses to turn over the T coin leaving the game in the state 'HHH', i.e. he chooses $(0) \rightarrow (1)$. For his second move, A has to take into account only those possibilities which relate to his first move and to any possible moves that B has made. Looking at the game-tree we see that he only has a choice if B has chosen HH, i.e. state (6). Suppose that if this has happened, A chooses H, i.e. state (12). Then this part of A's strategy reads 'if B has chosen "–" I have won; if B has chosen "H" I have to choose "–" and if B has chosen "HH" I choose "H".'

This particular strategy of A then is as follows: 'choose "HHH" for my first move. For my second move I choose "–" if B has chosen "H" and I choose "H" if B has chosen "HH"; in all other cases my move is already determined.'

B, however, has to prepare for all eventualities. Thus if A had chosen the state 'TH', i.e. (2), then B would have the choice between two moves, namely to change the state of the game to 'T', i.e. (7), or 'HH', i.e. (8). The part of B's strategy for this move might thus be: 'if the game is in state (1) then I choose "HH", i.e. (5); if in state (2) I choose "HH", i.e. (8); and if in state (3) I choose "H", i.e. (9).' We can write this as:

$$\begin{cases} (1) \rightarrow (5); \\ (2) \rightarrow (8); \\ (3) \rightarrow (9). \end{cases} \qquad \text{(G2.4.2)}$$

For his second move, if he has one, B always has to choose '(–)'.

To see all the strategies we make a table; see Table G2.2.

	A's strategies 1st move	2nd move	B's strategies	1st move
$A1$	$(0) \to (1)$	$(6) \to (11)$	$B1$	$\begin{cases}(1) \to (4)\\(2) \to (7)\end{cases}$
$A2$	$(0) \to (1)$	$(6) \to (12)$	$B2$	$\begin{cases}(1) \to (5)\\(2) \to (7)\end{cases}$
$A3$	$(0) \to (2)$	$(8) \to (14)$	$B3$	$\begin{cases}(1) \to (6)\\(2) \to (7)\end{cases}$
$A4$	$(0) \to (2)$	$(8) \to (15)$	$B4$	$\begin{cases}(1) \to (4)\\(2) \to (8)\end{cases}$
$A5$	$(0) \to (3)$		$B5$	$\begin{cases}(1) \to (5)\\(2) \to (8)\end{cases}$
			$B6$	$\begin{cases}(1) \to (6)\\(2) \to (8)\end{cases}$

Table G2.2. The strategies in 'Threepenny Nim'.

Note that a move is not mentioned in Table G2.2 if there is no choice about it; for example, $(3) \to (9)$ is not mentioned. This also means that B's second move is not mentioned. The reason that two moves are sometimes included in one strategy, as in $B1$, is that B's choice depends on the state of the game at that time.

From the strategies, an outcome matrix can be constructed:

$$\begin{array}{c c} & \text{B's strategies} \\ & \begin{array}{cccccc} B1 & B2 & B3 & B4 & B5 & B6 \end{array} \\ \begin{array}{c} A1 \\ A2 \\ A3 \\ A4 \\ A5 \end{array} & \begin{pmatrix} 1 & -1 & -1 & 1 & -1 & -1 \\ 1 & -1 & 1 & 1 & -1 & 1 \\ 1 & 1 & 1 & 1 & 1 & 1 \\ 1 & 1 & 1 & -1 & -1 & -1 \\ -1 & -1 & -1 & -1 & -1 & -1 \end{pmatrix} \end{array} . \quad \text{(G2.4.3)}$$

The strategies in games with several moves are very complicated. The aim of the players in deterministic games such as 'chess' or 'go' is to devise a winning strategy. Game Theory, however, aims to find all the possible strategies and to see what outcomes they lead to. This is a daunting task in most parlour games and is unlikely to help the reader become a better player.

'Rustic Poker' involves chance. A only has one move, but each strategy must take into account all eventualities, i.e. include the possibility of getting W and of getting L. Thus one of his strategies is: 'if I get L, I fold, but if I get W, I raise.' Let us write this symbolically as 'L → F; W → R'. Then A has four strategies:

$$\begin{array}{ll} A1 & \text{`L} \to \text{F; W} \to \text{F'} \\ A2 & \text{`L} \to \text{F; W} \to \text{R'} \\ A3 & \text{`L} \to \text{R; W} \to \text{F'} \\ A4 & \text{`L} \to \text{R; W} \to \text{R'}. \end{array} \qquad \text{G2.4.4)}$$

B's strategies are to fold ($B1$) or to raise ($B2$). The outcome matrix will be left to G3.3, until after we have learnt how to calculate utility when chance is present.

Pure and Mixed Strategies

The strategies so far discussed are decisions which lead to a definite play of the game, and are called **pure strategies**. Each pure strategy can be labelled by the name of the player and a number, e.g. $A1$ in Table G2.2. A player can, however, choose a set of pure strategies and use a lottery device, such as a coin or a dice, to decide which pure strategy of this set he uses in any particular play of the game. This way of choosing a strategy is known as a **mixed strategy**.

Suppose a player chooses a mixed strategy using the set of pure strategies ($A1, A2, A3, \ldots, Ak$). Then the lottery device determines the probability p_j that A will decide to use the strategy A_j in a play of the game. Obviously

$$\sum_{j=1} p_j = 1. \qquad \text{(G2.4.5)}$$

Vector representation of strategies

It is useful to form a geometrical representation of strategies. Suppose a player has k pure strategies. Then we associate with pure strategy j a point on the jth axis of R^k a unit distance from the origin. A mixed strategy is then associated with the point $(p_1, p_2, \ldots, p_j, \ldots, p_k)$ and all strategies lie on the hyperplane

$$p_1 + p_2 + p_3 + \ldots + p_j + \ldots + p_k = 1. \qquad \text{(G2.4.6)}$$

Suppose this is one of A's strategies. We write it in vector notation as $\mathbf{p}_A$. This lies in a space associated with player A. The strategies of other players lie in different spaces; for example, $\mathbf{p}_B$ is one of B's strategies but is in a different space from $\mathbf{p}_A$.

A complete play occurs when every player chooses a strategy. Such a choice is specified by a vector $(\mathbf{p}_A, \mathbf{p}_B, \ldots, \mathbf{p}_M)$ if there are M players, where $\mathbf{p}_L$ is a strategy chosen by player L. Such a vector can be called a **play** vector.

**** The convex set of strategies**

As p_j is a probability it satisfies

$$p_j \geqslant 0. \quad \text{(G2.4.7)}$$

This equation defines a *closed half-space*. Probabilities must also satisfy

$$p_j \leqslant 1. \quad \text{(G2.4.8)}$$

This equation defines another closed half-space. The intersection of all these half-spaces is a *polyhedral convex set* lying on the hyperplane (G2.4.6). Figure G2.2 shows this set when there are three pure strategies; it is an equilateral triangle.

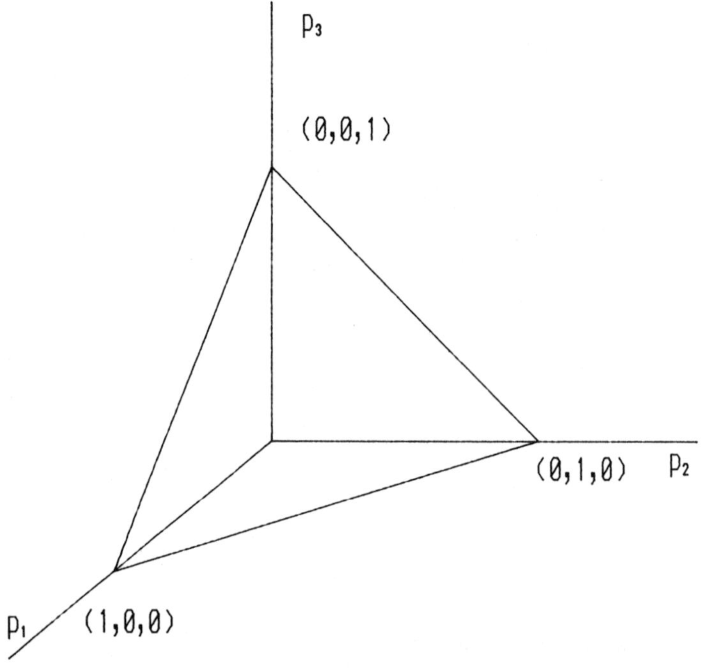

Fig. G2.2. The polyhedral convex set for the set of mixed strategies when there are three pure strategies. It is an equilateral triangle joining the points (1, 0, 0), (0, 1, 0) and (0, 0, 1).

G2.5 INFORMATION, STATES, ETC.

In the game 'Threepenny Nim', each player knows the state of the game at all times, i.e. each player has **perfect information**. This is not so in a game of chance such as Rustic Poker.

To classify such games as 'Scissors, Paper, Stone', 'Prisoners' Dilemma', and 'Duopoly', we make use of a **game-tree** as was done with 'Threepenny Nim' (see Fig. G2.1). A game-tree is an ordered set of vertices, with one initial vertex, and an arc joining a vertex and its subsequent vertices. There can be no closed loops made from the arcs. Each arc represents a move by one player or by a chance event, so that each vertex represents the **state** of the game at that stage of the game.

A game-tree for 'Scissors, Paper, Stone' can be got by letting one player (A say) go first. The state of the game after his move is not divulged to B, and this ensures that the game-tree is equivalent to the original game (see Fig. G2.2). The state after A's move may be either SCR, PPR or STN; the set of states is the **information set** for B after A's move. If the information set consists of only one member, the game is of perfect information. Obviously this game is not.

With a game of chance, the information set prior to a move contains the possible vertices together with the probability that a vertex is an actual state.

A game-tree is said to be the **extensive form** of a game, whereas the **normal form** is expressed in terms of strategies and an outcome matrix.

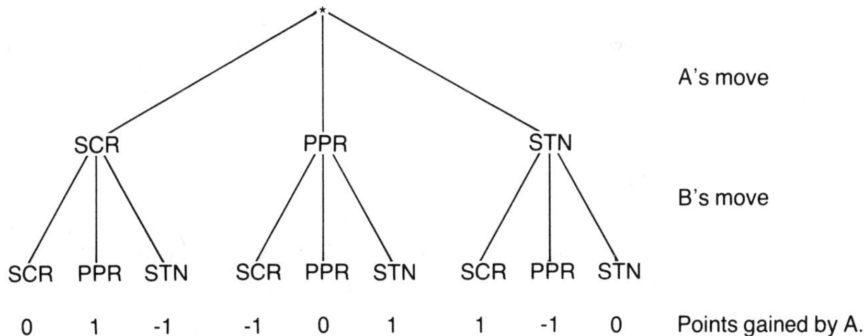

Fig. G2.3. Game-tree for 'Scissors, Paper, Stone'; the abbreviations stand for the respective objects.

'Prisoners' Dilemma', 'Duopoly' and 'Oligopoly' are of imperfect information. Indeed any game where players are required to make simultaneous 'moves' is, in general, one of imperfect information.

GE2 EXERCISES

2.1 In the two-player game of matching dice, each player chooses the number on a die: A wins if the sum of the numbers is even and B wins if the sum is odd. List the pure strategies and calculate the outcome matrices.

2.2 In a game for three players, each puts 1p into the kitty and chooses the number 1 or 2. If the sum of the numbers is divisible by 3, A wins; otherwise if the sum is even, B wins and if odd, C wins. Calculate the outcome matrices.

2.3 A game for two players, A and B, is played with four cards marked with the numbers 3, 3, 3 and 4. These cards are placed in a hat and each player stakes himself in with a £1 note. Each player draws one card and looks at it without allowing his opponent to see it. They then simultaneously raise the stakes by

£0 or £4. If a player's stake is higher than his opponent's, he wins and takes the complete kitty. If the stakes are equal, each player draws a further card; then the player with the larger sum on his two cards wins.

Draw a game-tree for this game, identify the information sets and find the pure strategies.

2.4 A game for two players, A and B, is played with a pack of three cards, two of which are blank and the other is a 'joker'. Initially each player puts 2p into the kitty. A is given a card which only he can see. He then puts either 1p or 3p into the kitty. B then must decide either to fold, or to 'see' for 2p. If he folds, all the kitty goes to A: if he 'sees', he is dealt a card face-upwards. The player with the 'joker' wins the kitty, but if both players have blank cards the kitty is divided equally.

Determine the pure strategies of both A and B.

2.5 A game consists of two consecutive plays of 'Prisoners' Dilemma'. What are the pure strategies of this new game? By adding the outcomes of the two plays together, calculate the outcome matrices of this game.

2.6(Morra) This is a two-player game. The players simultaneously show either one or two fingers and at the same time each one says a number. If A's or B's number is the same as the total of the number of fingers shown, then he wins that number of points from his opponent. Find the pure strategies and calculate the outcome matrices.

2.7(Goofspiel) Two players are each provided with three cards numbered 1, 2 and 3. On the first move, A and B simultaneously choose a card and the player with the higher number on his card wins a score of x, or $x/2$ if the cards are equal. The procedure on the next two moves is the same, but this time the winning player scores y and z on the second and third moves respectively. The player with the higher score wins an amount of money from his opponent equal to the difference in the scores.

Describe the game in extensive form. What are the pure strategies? Calculate the outcome matrices.

2.8 Two firms A and B are the only producers for a particular market. Their cost functions are $(q_A^3 - 3q_A^2 + 6q_A + 18)$ and $(q_B^3 - 6q_B^2 + 12q_B + 19)$, where q_A and q_B are the quantities manufactured by A and B respectively. The demand function is $(25 - p)$, where p is the price in the market. Each firm can only produce 1 or 3 units each. Assuming that profit is a suitable outcome, deduce an outcome matrix for both A and B.

2.9[(m)] Model the teaching of a child to be 'good' by the use of threats, bribes, punishments and rewards. How would you model the fact that repeated punishments have less effect?

CHAPTER G3

Outcomes, Pay-offs, Conflict and Cooperation

G3.1 OUTCOMES AND PAY-OFFS

In G2.3 we distinguished between outcomes and pay-offs: an outcome is the result of a game whereas a pay-off is a measure of the satisfaction of the player at the outcome of a particular play. Pay-offs differ from outcomes in several ways: (i) Even in the same game, outcomes may be in different units, e.g. one outcome might be a diamond and another might be a ruby, whereas pay-offs for a particular player should always be in the same units. (ii) Pay-offs are subjective, i.e. they depend on the preferences of the player. For example, the desire of a millionaire for an outcome of £100 is less than that of the average worker; recidivists like going to prison although most people dislike it. (iii) Pay-offs are functions of the play and hence of the strategies used. This is important in games of chance and when mixed strategies are used.

Pay-offs are got from utility theory (see E2): a player's preference between outcomes that are certain can be described by his utility function, i.e. for the respective utilities $U(x)$ and $U(y)$, outcome x is preferred to outcome y when $U(x) > U(y)$. This function is, for a given player, in the same units and takes into account the subjectivity of the pay-offs. In many instances the subjectivity is unimportant: for example, players' desires for money (or whatever the units in which the outcomes are measured) are often the same.

To take (iii) into account, utility theory must be extended (see G3.2).

G3.2 THE UTILITY THEORY OF VON NEUMANN AND MORGENSTERN

From the players' preferences between the outcomes, we need to construct pay-offs for mixed strategies and for games of chance. We first consider **deterministic** games in which a play of pure strategies determines a particular outcome.

Pay-offs in deterministic games

Suppose $\mathbf{x}$ $(= (\mathbf{x}_A, \mathbf{x}_B, \ldots))$ and $\mathbf{y}$ $(= (\mathbf{y}_A, \mathbf{y}_B, \ldots))$ are play-vectors involving pure strategies only and leading to outcomes which player A likes best and least respectively. Assign utility values $U(\mathbf{x})$ and $U(\mathbf{y})$ to these outcomes. The values of these utilities are arbitrary, except that $U(\mathbf{x}) > U(\mathbf{y}) > 0$.

A play which involves mixed strategies is given by

$$\lambda\mathbf{x} + (1 - \lambda)\mathbf{y}, \qquad \text{(G3.2.1)}$$

where $0 < \lambda < 1$. Such a mixed play can be obtained by using suitable lottery devices. Von Neumann and Morgenstern (VNM for short) assert that the expected utility of the outcome of the game for A when this play-vector is used is

$$\lambda U(\mathbf{x}) + (1 - \lambda)\, U(\mathbf{y}). \qquad \text{(G3.2.2)}$$

The whole range of utility values for player A can in principle be obtained by using lottery devices which give different values of λ. To find the utility value of any outcome from a different play-vector, say $\mathbf{p}$ $(= (\mathbf{p}_A, \mathbf{p}_B, \ldots))$ we vary λ until A feels indifferent between the outcome of strategy $\mathbf{p}$ and the outcome of $(\lambda\mathbf{x} + (1 - \lambda)\mathbf{y})$. The utility value of the outcome is then (G3.2.2) with that value of λ.

VNM assert that the relationship between the strategy (G3.2.1) and the utility (G3.2.2) is true for all plays $\mathbf{p}, \mathbf{p}'$, i.e.

$$U(\lambda\mathbf{p} + (1 - \lambda)\mathbf{p}') = \lambda U(\mathbf{p}) + (1 - \lambda)U(\mathbf{p}') \qquad \text{(G3.2.3)}$$

for all λ such that $0 \leqslant \lambda \leqslant 1$.

Games of chance

In these games in particular choice of strategies leads to several outcomes, each with a well-defined probability. If a play-vector gives rise to outcomes 1, 2, 3, etc., with probabilities $p_1, p_2, p_3, \ldots$, player A assigns utility values U_1, U_2, etc. to these outcomes in the usual way, and his expected utility is

$$\sum_j p_j U_j. \qquad \text{(G3.2.4)}$$

Each play-vector thus gives rise to an expectation value over the outcomes. The pay-offs can now be measured in exactly the same way as previously, but with the expectation values replacing the actual outcomes in (G3.2.2).

Definition of pay-off

To each play-vector, in any type of game, whether deterministic or probabilistic, is associated a utility for each player. This is called the player's **pay-off** for that play-vector. The pay-off is dependent on the player through his ordering of the outcomes. The **pay-off matrix** is the matrix of pay-offs given by the different strategies of the players, as with the outcome matrix.

Indeterminancy of the VNM pay-offs

All the pay-offs depend on the two utilities $U(\mathrm{x})$ and $U(\mathrm{y})$, which are arbitrary in general. Thus, in general, all the pay-offs for a player are only determined to within a linear transformation, i.e. if

$$U(\mathrm{x}_A) \to U'(\mathrm{x}_A) \quad \text{and} \quad U(\mathrm{y}_A) \to U'(\mathrm{y})$$

then

$$\begin{aligned} \lambda U(\mathrm{x}) + (1-\lambda)U(\mathrm{y}) &\to \lambda U'(\mathrm{x}) + (1-\lambda)U'(\mathrm{y}) \\ &= s(\lambda U(\mathrm{x}) + (1-\lambda)U(\mathrm{y})) + t, \end{aligned} \tag{G3.2.5}$$

where

$$s = (U'(\mathrm{x}) - U'(\mathrm{y}))/(U(\mathrm{x}) - U(\mathrm{y})), \tag{G3.2.6}$$

and

$$t = (U'(\mathrm{x})U(\mathrm{y}) - U'(\mathrm{y})U(\mathrm{x}))/(U(\mathrm{x}) - U(\mathrm{y})). \tag{G3.2.7}$$

Thus the VNM pay-offs have slightly different transformation properties from the original utility functions (see E2): they can only be transformed by a monotically increasing linear function. Nevertheless because of these properties interpersonal comparisons of utility are still, in general, not possible.

Content of the VNM theory

The VNM utility theory is derived from certain axioms; this is the reason the result (G3.2.3) is logically reasonable. These axioms can be found in several books, e.g. see Reading List, EHQ, GO, GB. The important question from a scientific point of view is 'are these axioms and their results in accord with a player's actual preferences?'

The VNM theory of utility is making an assertion about the preferences of a player. This assertion does not hold for every person: for example, there are those who derive satisfaction from the very act of gambling, preferring some mixed strategies to any pure strategies, in contradiction to (G3.2.3).

Thus reality and the VNM theory of utility do not always agree. It is sometimes argued (see Reading list, GB, for example) that the Theory of Games is not a theory about the way people actually play 'games' but is a theory about the way people *should* play games†, i.e. the way a perfectly rational man (often inappropriately called 'Homo Economicus') would behave; this approach does not make the theory useless as a mathematical model because it can still be used to determine what strategies to adopt in order to achieve certain ends in given situations. This argument, however, does not apply to the pay-offs, as they are an integral part of the game and should represent the real situation. The

† i.e. the theory is normative (see SM1).

argument that the 'rational man' *should* use a particular set of pay-offs is one for the discipline of ethics, not of science: for Game Theory to be useful, the 'games', and this includes the pay-offs, should be realistic models of the actual situations.

The justification of VNM utility theory is that, although a simplification of reality, it is as yet the only 'realistic' theory that allows us to construct a tractable theory of conflict and cooperation.

G3.3 THE COMPARISON OF UTILITIES

Players' utilities are subjective and not uniquely determined. These difficulties can be overcome in particular cases and/or by making special assumptions. We investigate these possibilities now.

Two-person zero-sum games

When a game is such that the interests of the two players are diametrically opposed, the preferences of the players are completely opposite; that is, if player A prefers outcome x to outcome y, then player B prefers y to x, i.e.

$$\text{if} \quad x \succ_A y, \quad \text{then} \quad y \succ_B x. \tag{G3.3.1}$$

The utilities can then be chosen so that

$$U_A + U_B = 0 \tag{G3.3.2}$$

for any outcome of the game; the pay-off matrices sum to zero, and the game is called a **zero-sum** game.

Such games are usually arranged to satisfy (G3.3.2). The utilities may, however, by VNM utilities and not satisfy (G3.3.2). To transform the pay-off matrices into the zero-sum form, we use a linear transformation as described in G3.2). We look for numbers s and t such that

$$U_A' = sU_A + 6,$$
$$U_B' = U_B, \tag{G3.3.3}$$

so that the utilities U' satisfy (G3.3.2). The number s has to be strictly positive (i.e. it cannot be zero), but t may be negative.

This technique can also be used to test whether a game is zero-sum.

Outcomes again

When all the outcomes of a game are in the same units, e.g. points or money, we can define the outcome when probability is involved, by the expected outcome; this would be the usual procedure and corresponds exactly with the procedure which determined the VNM pay-offs. Using such outcomes to measure pay-offs has the advantages that they are objective and that they are easily measurable or calculable, in contrast to VNM utilities.

Because of the difficulty of measuring actual pay-offs, in this book we only discuss games in which the outcomes are all in the same units and use outcomes to measure pay-offs unless otherwise stated.

We shall use the more general terms 'pay-off' and 'pay-off matrix' when in fact we are using outcomes and outcome matrices. Unless otherwise stated the pay-offs are not transformable by a linear transformation.

Such outcomes can be compared and can be classified as follows:

(i) **transferable** pay-offs, such as money;

(ii) **non-transferable** pay-offs, such as years in prison.

'Rustic Poker'

We now find the pay-offs in this game by calculating the expectation values of the outcomes. If A plays strategy $A1$ he always loses £s. For the play $(A1, B1)$ there is a probability of $\frac{1}{2}$ that A will get L, in which case he loses £s, and a probability of $\frac{1}{2}$ that he gets W, in which case he wins £s. Thus the pay-off in this case to A is £0. For the play $(A2, B2)$ the probabilities for getting the cards remain the same, but A now wins £s' if he has W on his card. Thus A's expected gain is £$\frac{1}{2}(s' - s)$. The other pay-offs can be similarly computed to give the following pay-off matrix for A:

$$\begin{array}{ll} & \quad B\text{'s strategies} \\ & \quad\; B1 \qquad\quad B2 \\ A\text{'s strategies} \quad \begin{array}{c} A1 \\ A2 \\ A3 \\ A4 \end{array} & \begin{pmatrix} -s & -s \\ 0 & \frac{1}{2}(s' - s) \\ 0 & -\frac{1}{2}(s' + s) \\ s & 0 \end{pmatrix} . \end{array} \qquad \text{G3.3.4)}$$

The reader should verify these pay-offs. What is B's pay-off matrix?

Symmetric games

When the outcomes are comparable, it is possible to make the following definition: a game is said to be **symmetric** for two players A and B if their strategies are the same and a swap of the strategies leads to a swap in the outcomes.

G3.4 COMMUNICATION: CONFLICT AND COOPERATION

Communication

In some games the players are allowed to communicate and in others they are not. For example, the government may make it illegal for duopolists to cooperate as it might not be in the consumers' interests. We call the first type **communicative** games and the second **non-communicative.**

Conflict and cooperation

To demonstrate these effects we consider three separate two-player games: suppose the players A and B have strategies $A1, A2$ and $B1, B2$ respectively. The pay-off matrices are as follows:

for game 1

$$\begin{array}{cc} & \begin{array}{cc} B1 & B2 \end{array} \\ \begin{array}{c} A1 \\ A2 \end{array} & \begin{pmatrix} 3(3) & 0\,(0) \\ 0\,(0) & 3\,(3) \end{pmatrix}; \end{array} \qquad \text{G3.4.1)}$$

for game 2

$$\begin{array}{c} A1 \\ A2 \end{array} \begin{pmatrix} 3\,(-3) & 0\,(0) \\ 0\,(0) & -3\,(3) \end{pmatrix}; \qquad \text{(G3.4.2)}$$

for game 3 (cf. the 'Prisoner's Dilemma')

$$\begin{array}{c} A1 \\ A2 \end{array} \begin{pmatrix} -5\,(-5) & 0\,(-8) \\ -8\,(0) & -2\,(-2) \end{pmatrix}. \qquad \text{(G3.4.3)}$$

These are A's pay-off matrices; B's pay-offs are given in brackets. These games exhibit three very different types of pay-off and we now discuss them.

Cooperation

In game 1, if the game is communicative, it pays the two players to cooperate, i.e. by either choosing the play $(A1, B1)$ or choosing the play $(A2, B2)$ they can gain more, on average, than if they did not cooperate.

Pure conflict

In game 2, A's gains are matched by B's losses and vice versa. Thus in game 2, the two players are in total conflict. This is a **zero-sum** game. In such games there is no reason for the two players to collaborate, as they cannot improve their collective pay-off by such action. 'Scissors, Paper, Stone', 'Threepenny Nim' and 'Rustic Poker' are all zero-sum games.

There is in general no need to specify zero-sum games as communicative or non-communicative. Care needs to be taken, however, if the pay-offs of the two players are specified in units of VNM utility because of the possibility of linear transformations. In this case, the pay-off matrices may not add to zero, so that it may seem as if cooperation is possible. The utilities should in this case be transformed to zero-sum form, as discussed in G3.3.

Simultaneous Conflict and cooperation

In the traditional form of the 'Prisoners' Dilemma' (see G2.2) the players are not allowed to communicate as they are in separate rooms. Suppose, however, that communication is allowed: there is scope for cooperation, as the prisoners may feel that they don't want to go together to prison for 5 years, and they can avoid this if they both choose not to confess, i.e. if they choose their second strategies. There is also competition between the players as A may think that he can get away scot-free if he confesses and B does not. Thus game 3 involves both conflict and cooperation. We shall analyse the 'Prisoners' Dilemma' game more fully in G5.

In a communicative game for two or more players, some or all of them may form a **coalition**: before making their choices of strategy they communicate with each other and decide which strategies will benefit the coalition. Obviously a **rational** player will only join the coalition if he gains more utility out of the coalition's share-out than he would get if he played on his own. In the share-out a player may get more than he would expect to get from the outcome of the game: this means that he has received a **side-payment**. This may be beneficial to the coalition to ensure that this player makes a particular choice of strategy. This is only possible if the pay-offs are transferable. Coalitions and side-payments are two of the more fascinating aspects of communicative games.

G3.5 DOMINATION

Consider a game for two players, A and B. Suppose that u_{ij} is the pay-off for A when A and B play strategies Ai and Bj respectively, i.e. u_{ij} is the ijth element of A's payoff matrix. If there exists a row k with elements u_{kj} and a row i with elements u_{ij} such that

$$u_{kj} \leqslant u_{ij} \quad \text{for all values of } j$$

except that at least one value of j is such that

$$u_{kj} < u_{ij}, \tag{G3.5.1}$$

then we say that strategy Ak is dominated by strategy Ai. Alternatively it can be said that strategy Ai dominates strategy Ak.

It seems obvious that player A will never play strategy Ak, so that strategy Ak should be eliminated from the game. This is true in zero-sum games but may not be so in other games which are repeated, as we shall see in G5.

We have already had two examples of dominated strategies: the first one is in the 'Prisoners' Dilemma', where the strategy 'Confess' dominates 'Refuse' for either player; in 'Rustic Poker', strategies $A1$ and $A3$ are dominated.

G3.6 EQUILIBRIUM

In non-communicative games which are played once, there may be play-vectors in which a player may not want to alter his own strategy, because the pay-offs become worse if he changes his strategy. Thus in a non-communicative game we find the following definition is of use:

a play-vector $\mathbf{p}^e = (\mathbf{p}_A^e, \mathbf{p}_B^e, \ldots, \mathbf{p}_J^e, \ldots)$ is called an **equilibrium play-vector** if, for all J, the pay-off U_J for player J is such that

$$U_J(\mathbf{p}_A^e, \mathbf{p}_B^e, \ldots, \mathbf{p}_J, \ldots) \leqslant U_J(\mathbf{p}_A^e, \mathbf{p}_B^e, \ldots, \mathbf{p}_J^e, \ldots) \qquad \text{(G3.6.1)}$$

for all strategy vectors $\mathbf{p}_J$.

GE3 EXERCISES

3.1 Show that the game of 'Duopoly' described in G2.2 cannot be transformed into a zero-sum game.

3.2 In a game for two players, they have the following pay-off matrices

$$\begin{pmatrix} 8 & -2 & 4 & 6 \\ 8 & 12 & 6 & 14 \\ 2 & 4 & -4 & 8 \end{pmatrix} \quad \begin{pmatrix} -2 & 13 & 4 & 1 \\ -2 & -8 & 1 & -11 \\ 7 & 4 & 16 & -2 \end{pmatrix}.$$

Transform these matrices to a zero-sum form.

3.3 Find the pay-off matrices in the game of GE2.3.

3.4 Find the pay-off matrices in the game of GE2.4.

3.5 A non-cooperative game between two players A and B is played with two coins. When a head is thrown on the toss of a coin, a score of 2 is made and when a tail is thrown only 1 is scored. Each player puts 60p into the kitty. The first move is made by A: he can choose to throw one coin, in which case he takes 40p from the kitty and registers his score, or two coins, in which case he scores the average of the two numbers if they are different or the sum if they are the same. B can also choose to throw one coin, in which case he scores the number on the coin plus $\frac{1}{2}$, or two coins, in which case he scores in the same way as A. The winner, the player with the higher score, takes the rest of the kitty but if the scores are equal, the kitty is divided equally. Calculate the pay-off matrices for A and B.

3.6 Show that in the game of 'Threepenny Nim', each player has a strategy which dominates all the other strategies.

3.7 Show that in the game 'A Problem for Aratro', play-vectors involving pure strategies only are not equilibrium play-vectors.

3.8 What conditions on the pay-off matrices make a game fair for all the players? If the game is a two-player zero-sum game, what kind of pay-off matrix does each player have?

3.9 In a game which favours A, the two players A and B have m and n strategies, and pay-off matrices U_A and U_B respectively. To ensure fairness, a new game is invented, in which a coin is tossed and the winner has A's strategies and pay-off matrix, and the loser has to take B's place. What are the pure strategies in this new game and how are the pay-off matrices related to U_A and U_B?

3.10 Suppose the original game in Exercise 3.9 is a zero-sum game. Construct the normal form of a game consisting of two simultaneous plays of the original game and where in the second A and B exchange strategies and pay-off matrices. How is the normal form related to the normal form of the fair game found in Exercise 3.9?

3.11$^{(m)}$ Model income-tax payments and gathering as a game for many individuals and the government. Note that for the government, increasing the number of tax inspectors increases the costs in salaries but may increase the tax revenue, as the probability of catching tax evaders and cutting down on tax avoidance is increased. Consider only a finite number of strategies for the individual and for the government.

(i) At first consider all individuals as similar; write out carefully all the pure strategies and calculate the pay-off matrix for an individual. Are any strategies dominated? What form does the government's pay-off matrix take and how can it be calculated? How should the government decide how to gather the taxes?

(ii) Consider a more complicated situation with three types of individual:

(a) one who does casual work;
(b) one who works for a big employer;
(c) one rich enough that he employs a tax accountant.

CHAPTER G4

Two-person Zero-sum Games

G4.1 THE PAY-OFF MATRICES

In this chapter, we investigate the decisions made by rational players as to what strategies to play in a zero-sum game. Throughout the chapter the players are called A and B. The pay-off matrix for A is written U_A so that its ijth element is A's pay-off when the strategies (Ai), (Bj) are played. We write the pay-off matrix for B as U_B which is constructed so that its ijth element is the pay-off for B when the play-vector is (Ai, Bj). Suppose that A and B have m and n pure strategies respectively. Then U_A and U_B are both $(m * n)$ matrices.

Unless otherwise stated the pay-off matrices are in zero-sum form:

$$U_A + U_B = 0. \qquad \text{(G4.1.1)}$$

For convenience, U_A is often written as U with elements u_{ij}; U_B has elements $-u_{ij}$.

G4.2 THE RATIONAL MAN'S CHOICE OF STRATEGY

Each person plays a game in his own way. It would be a difficult statistical exercise to find out how a game is played on average so that a descriptive discussion is not worth attempting. A normative discussion is possible and more useful. We thus ask the question: how *should* a person play?

It might be argued that a rational man will want to maximize his utility, but this is not in general an attainable aim as the outcome of a game depends not only on his actions but also on the choices of his opponents. The usual norm assumed in this branch of Game Theory is that *the rational man adopts a strategy which minimizes the losses he could possibly incur.*

It is now our task to discover the implications of this norm, i.e. is it possible to find a strategy which satisfies the norm? Such a strategy is called a **solution.** We also need to see whether the norm and the solutions are **practical.**

It is easiest at first to assume that a solution exists and that it consists of pure strategies. Other possibilities are investigated later.

G4.3 GAMES WITH SADDLE-POINTS

Let us suppose that a solution occurs at a pure strategy for both A and B. Such a solution is easy to find and shows clearly the implications of the norm. Afterwards we find the criterion for the occurrence of such a solution. In G4.4 we show that a solution can always be found, although often it is in mixed strategies.

Security level

For each of A's pure strategies, there is a minimum pay-off. This is called the **security level** of that pure strategy. Thus

$$\min_j (u_{ij}) \tag{G4.3.1}$$

is the security level for the pure strategy Ai. Then the rational player, if he is only using pure strategies, wants to find the strategy Ai which gives the maximum of the security levels. Then A is assured of the pay-off

$$\max_i (\min_j (u_{ij})). \tag{G4.3.2}$$

This is usually written as α, and is known as the pure strategy **maximin** of U_A.

U_B has elements $(-u_{ij})$. B's security level for pure strategy Bj is

$$\min_i (-u_{ij}). \tag{G4.3.3}$$

He then is looking for the pure strategy Bj which maximizes his security levels. He is then assured of the pay-off

$$\max_j (\min_i (-u_{ij})). \tag{G4.3.4}$$

This amount is usually written as β.

This is equivalent to finding the pure strategy Bj which minimizes the set

$$(\max_i (u_{ij})), \tag{G4.3.5}$$

ensuring B the pay-off

$$\beta = -\min_j (\max_i (u_{ij})) \tag{G4.3.6}$$

at least. $-\beta$ is usually called the pure strategy **minimax** of U_A. To avoid having to calculate B's pay-off matrix, it is usualy to calculate β using (G4.3.5) and (G4.3.6)..

As an example, consider the pay-off matrix for A:

$$\begin{pmatrix} -4 & 12 & -6 \\ -5 & -8 & 6 \\ -4 & -3 & -4 \\ -3 & 3 & -1 \end{pmatrix} \quad \begin{matrix} -6 & (1,3) \\ -8 & (2,2) \\ -4 & (3,1) \text{ and } (3,3) \\ -3 & (4,1). \end{matrix} \tag{G4.3.7}$$

The security levels for A are shown at the right, together with the element where they occur. Then A wants to find the maximum of the set

$$(-6, -8, -4, -3) \tag{G4.3.8}$$

so that he can minimize his losses to -3 by choosing the pure strategy $A4$, i.e.

$$\alpha = -3. \tag{G4.3.9}$$

Player B has pay-off matrix

$$\begin{pmatrix} 4 & -12 & 6 \\ 5 & 8 & -6 \\ 4 & 3 & 4 \\ 3 & -3 & 1 \end{pmatrix}. \tag{G4.3.10}$$

The security levels are

$$3 \quad -12 \quad -6$$

at positions

$$(4,1) \quad (1,2) \quad (2,3).$$

Then B wants to find the maximum of the set

$$(3, -12, -6). \tag{G4.3.11}$$

Thus B chooses the pure strategy $B1$, giving

$$\beta = 3. \tag{G4.3.12}$$

It is more usual to find the minimax, i.e. the minimum of the set $(-3, 12, 6)$, and hence get the result

$$-\beta = -3. \tag{G4.3.13}$$

In a zero-sum game the total of the pay-offs to the players is zero. Thus if A is assured of α, and B is assured of β, then

$$\alpha + \beta \leqslant 0. \tag{G4.3.14}$$

Saddle-points

Suppose that U's maximin and minimax occur at the same play-vector, (Ar, Bs) say. Then

$$\alpha + \beta = 0. \tag{G4.3.15}$$

It can also be seen that

$$u_{rs} = \max_i (\min_j (u_{ij})) = \min_j (\max_i (u_{ij})). \tag{G4.3.16}$$

This means that for the particular row r, u_{rs} is the minimum in that row: it also means that for a particular column s, u_{rs} is the maximum in that column. The element (Ar, Bs) is then called a **saddle-point**.

In the example above, the play $(A4, B1)$ is a saddle-point. Saddle-points are significant, as will become clearer after the following two theorems:

Theorem G4.3.1. A two-person zero-sum game has a saddle-point if and only if $\alpha + \beta = 0$.

Suppose $\alpha + \beta = 0$. Then consider the play (Ar, Bs) such that $u_{rs} = \alpha = \max_i (\min_j (u_{ij}))$. Then, as $\beta = -\min_j (\max_i (u_{ij})) = -\alpha = -u_{rs}$, the element (Ar, Bs) is a saddle-point. (There can be more than one saddle-point, but they all have the same value of α, as the maxima and minima are absolute, not just local as in calculus.) Conversely, if u_{rs} is a saddle-point, then

$$\alpha = \max_i (\min_j (u_{ij})) > u_{rs},$$

$$-\beta = \min_j (\max_i (u_{ij})) < u_{rs}$$

so that

$$\alpha + \beta \geqslant 0.$$

Thus from (G4.3.14),

$$\alpha + \beta = 0.$$

**Theorem G4.3.2. Any finite two-person zero-sum game of perfect information has a saddle-point.*

We give no proof of this theorem.

A saddle-point is an **equilibrium solution** of the game, as it is desired by both players; to put it in terms analogous to mechanics, the psychological forces acting on the two players are equal and opposite at the saddle-point. The reader should verify this against the definition of equilibrium play-vector (see G3.5).

Note also that even if A knows that B has chosen the strategy (Bs), A still chooses the strategy (Ar), i.e. he gains nothing from knowing B's choice. This is not surprising if the game is one of perfect information.

G4.4 GAMES WITHOUT A SADDLE-POINT

The need for mixed strategies

When $\alpha + \beta \neq 0$, there is not a saddle-point and the pure strategy that gives a maximin does not lead to equilibrium; consider the following example:

$$\begin{pmatrix} 4 & -3 \\ -4 & 3 \end{pmatrix} \qquad \begin{matrix} \text{row minimum} \\ -3 \\ -4 \end{matrix}$$

column maximum:

$$4 \quad 3. \tag{G4.4.1}$$

In this game

$$\alpha + \beta = -6, \tag{G4.4.2}$$

and there is no saddle-point: how should A play?

If the game had a saddle-point, A should choose strategy $A1$, according to the method developed in G4.3. His pay-off cannot be worse than -3. If B also uses this method of choosing, he chooses strategy $B2$, so that his pay-off is no worse than -3. The play-vector is then $(A1, B2)$ and A gets -3. This suits B but not A, but if A knows that B is going to choose strategy $B2$, he will choose $A2$ and gain $+3$. This is nice for A but not so nice for B. If B guesses that A is going to choose $A2$, he will choose $B1$, and claim $+4$! Maybe A should double-bluff B by choosing $A1$ after all; if it worked, A would win $+4$, but could he be sure that B would . . . ?

This vicious circle, with each player trying to outguess the other, reflects the fact that this game has no stable pure strategy solution: whatever solution we consider, at least one player will want to alter his choice of pure strategy.

The situation is one where information is at a premium: if one of the players knows the pure strategy that his opponent is going to choose then he can use that information to maximize his pay-off. Thus there can be no rule which determines the precise pure strategy that a player chooses, for if there were it would become known to his opponent who could then take advantage of it. What each player needs is a rule which determines how often a pure strategy should be chosen but does not determine the actual strategy at each play. i.e. he needs to know the probability that a particular pure strategy should be chosen and the actual choice is then left to a lottery device giving that probability. Thus the players need a prescription for choosing mixed strategies.

The problem

In finding a mixed strategy, each player is still using the criterion suggested in G4.3, i.e. each player is trying to minimize any losses he might make. Player A is trying to find the values p_i^e of the probabilities p_i such that

$$\underset{j}{\text{minimum}} \left(\sum_i p_i \, u_{ij} \right) \tag{G4.4.3}$$

is a maximum. Player B is searching for the values q_j^e of the probabilities q_j such that

$$\underset{i}{\text{maximum}} \left(\sum_j u_{ij} \, q_j \right) \tag{G4.4.}$$

is a minimum. In vector notation we want vectors **p** and **q** such that

$$\min_j (\mathbf{p}.U)_j \quad \text{and} \quad \max_i (U.\mathbf{q})_i \tag{G4.4.5}$$

are a maximum and a minimum respectively. We write α' and $(-\beta')$ respectively for these quantities; they are called the **maximin** and **minimax** of U.

Finding the optimal mixed strategies is not easy. It is equivalent to the problem of linear programming, as we shall show in G4.5; it is only in simple cases that either problem can be easily solved. One of these cases is now presented.

2*2 pay-off matrices: a graphical method

To demonstrate this, let us consider the pay-off matrix (G4.4.1). Suppose that A chooses strategies $A1$ and $A2$ with probabilities p and $(1 - p)$ respectively. Then the pay-off matrix becomes

$$\big((4p - 4(1 - p)) \quad (-3p + 3(1 - p))\big). \tag{G4.4.6}$$

To find the maximin, let us draw the graphs of these two functions for $0 \leqslant p \leqslant 1$ (see Fig. G4.1). They are straight lines which meet when

$$(8p - 4) = (-6p + 3). \tag{G4.4.7}$$

One line lies below the other, except at the point at which they meet. Thus the maximum value of A's minimum gains occurs when the two lines meet, in this case at $p = \frac{1}{2}$. In this case the pay-offs are both zero.

How should B play? Suppose B chooses strategies $B1$ and $B2$ with probabilities q and $(1 - q)$ respectively. Then the outcomes for B are

$$\begin{bmatrix} (-4q + 3(1 - q)) \\ (4q - 3(1 - q)) \end{bmatrix}. \tag{G4.4.8}$$

Let us again draw the graphs of these functions (see Fig. G4.2). They are straight lines and the minimax occurs when the two lines meet, i.e. when

$$(3 - 7q) = (7q - 3). \tag{G4.4.9}$$

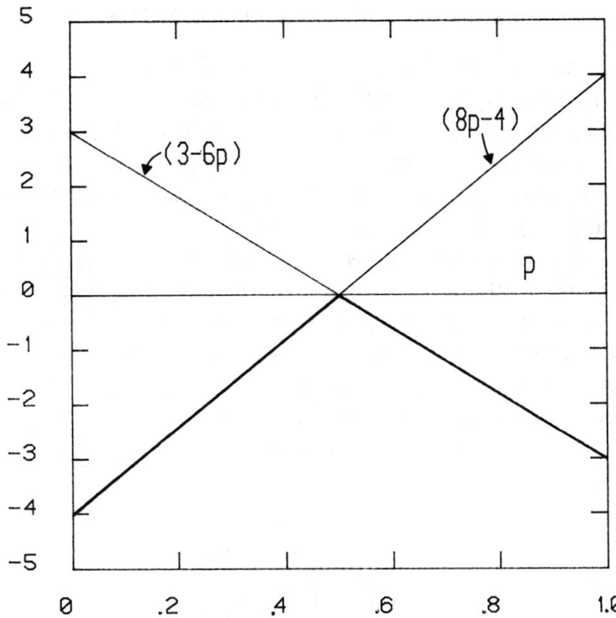

Fig. G4.1. The expected pay-offs $(8p - 4)$ and $(3 - 6p)$ for A. The minimum of these is shown as a thick line.

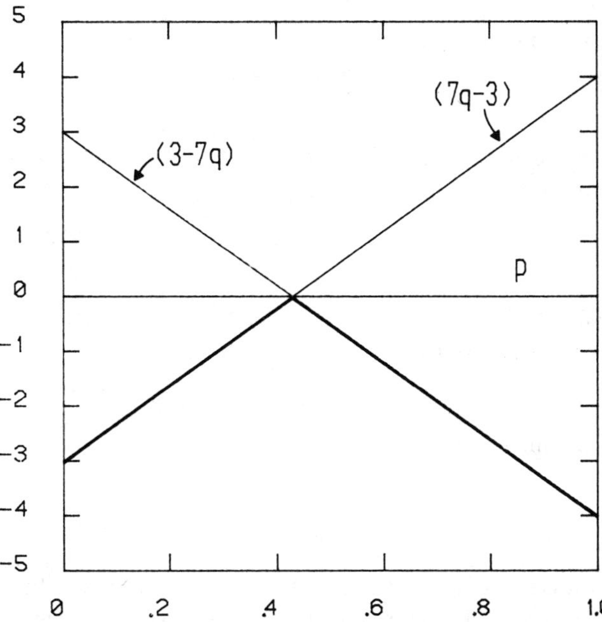

Fig. G4.2. The expected pay-offs $(3 - 7q)$ and $(7q - 3)$ for B. The minimum of these is shown as a thick line.

*G4.5 EQUIVALENCE WITH LINEAR PROGRAMMING

To show that the problem posed in (G4.4.3) is equivalent to the problem of linear programming is of great help, because the results and methods learnt there can be applied in this branch of Game Theory. Of course these can be derived separately and in G4.6 and G4.7 this is done, with only a passing reference to linear programming. Nevertheless the reader will gain a better understanding if he can appreciate fully these connections.

To make the connection it is necessary for α' and $(-\beta')$ to be positive. These numbers are finite, as the elements a_{ij} are finite; they can be made positive by adding a suitably large and positive number λ to all the elements of U_A. This does not alter the probabilities $\mathbf{p}^e$ and $\mathbf{q}^e$ that are required to give the minimax and maximin respectively; it just adds λ to α' and $(-\beta')$. When the probabilities have been derived, the original values of α and $(-\beta)$ can be got by subtracting λ.

As α' and $(-\beta')$ are now positive, we can transform A's problem by defining some new variables z_i and d:

$$z_i = p_i/d;$$

$$d = \min_j \left(\sum_i p_i u_{ij} \right). \qquad \text{(G4.5.1)}$$

These variables are non-negative, i.e.

$$z_i \geqslant 0. \qquad \text{(G4.5.2)}$$

Then by definition

$$\sum_i z_i u_{ij} \geqslant 1. \qquad \text{(G4.5.3)}$$

Let us write $\mathbf{J}_m$ and $\mathbf{J}_n$ for the vectors (1, 1, 1, . . .) with m and n components respectively. Now

$$\sum_i z_i = 1/d. \qquad \text{(G4.5.4)}$$

We want the maximum value of d, i.e. we are seeking a vector $\mathbf{z}$ with components z_i such that

$$\mathbf{J}_m \,.\, \mathbf{z}, \qquad \text{(G4.5.5)}$$

is a minimum. The constraints are

$$U^{\mathrm{T}} . \mathbf{z} \geqslant \mathbf{J}_n \qquad \text{(G4.5.6)}$$

$$\mathbf{z} \geqslant \mathbf{0}. \qquad \text{(G4.5.7)}$$

This problem is of the same form as the l.p. problem (see (E5.3.7), (E5.3.8) and (E5.3.9)). (Note, however, that U^{T} and $\mathbf{J}_m$ replace A and $\mathbf{p}$ in (E5.3.7) and (E5.3.8).)

For player B, we define variables r_j and e where

$$r_j = q_j/e$$

$$e = \max_i \left(\sum_j u_{ij}\, q_j \right). \tag{G4.5.8}$$

Thus

$$\sum_j u_{ij}\, r_j \leqslant 1 \tag{G4.5.9}$$

and

$$\sum_j r_j = 1/e, \tag{G4.5.10}$$

so that B is seeking a vector $\mathbf{r}$ with components r_j such that

$$\mathbf{r} \,.\, \mathbf{J}_n \tag{G4.5.11}$$

is a maximum subject to the constraints

$$\mathbf{r} \,.\, U^{\mathrm{T}} \leqslant \mathbf{J}_m \tag{G4.5.12}$$

$$\mathbf{r} \geqslant \mathbf{0}. \tag{G4.5.13}$$

This problem is of the same form as the l.p. problem (E5.4.1)–(E5.4.3). B's problem is thus the dual of A's.

The pure strategies are feasible solutions to these problems, so that both l.p. problems are feasible. Thus the result of the Fundamental Duality Theorem (Theorem E5.4.3) is applicable. In Game Theory this result is known as the Minimax Theorem, and shows that

$$\alpha' = -\beta'. \tag{G4.5.14}$$

The other important consequence of showing the equivalence with linear programming is that the methods developed for finding solutions of l.p. problems can also be used for these Game Theory problems. This means that for large games the Simplex method can be used (see Reading List, GJ or GO).

In passing, we note that the problem (G4.5.11–G4.5.13) is exactly the same one we met when determining linear production functions in E5.2.

G4.6 THE MINIMAX THEOREM

In the graphical method of solution we found that $\alpha' = -\beta'$. This result is always true for games with a finite number of pure strategies and was originally proved by Von Neumann. The theorem, known usually as the Minimax Theorem, states that the maximum of ($\underset{j}{\text{minimum}}$ $(p_i\, u_{ij})$) over the set of probabilities p_i is equal to the minimum of ($\underset{j}{\text{maximum}}$ $(u_{ij}\, q_j)$) over the set of probabilities q_j, i.e.

$$\alpha' = -\beta'. \tag{G4.6.1}$$

The common value of these two quantities is called the **value** of the game.

This result is equivalent to the Fundamental Duality Theorem (Theorem E5.4.3) of linear programming. Like that, it is difficult to prove; the proof can be found in the books GJ and GO (see the Reading List). We can prove a preliminary result, equivalent to (G4.3.14):

Theorem G4.6.1. $\alpha' + \beta' \leqslant 0$.

As α' is a minimum value of $\sum_i u_{ij} p_i^e$,

$$\sum_i u_{ij} p_i^e \geqslant \alpha \quad \text{for all } j. \tag{G4.6.2}$$

As $-\beta'$ is a maximum value of $\sum_j u_{ij} q_j^e$,

$$\sum_j u_{ij} q_j^e \leqslant -\beta' \quad \text{for all } i. \tag{G4.6.3}$$

Thus

$$\sum_i \sum_j p_i^e u_{ij} q_j^e \leqslant \sum_i -p_i^e \beta' = -\beta' \tag{G4.6.4}$$

and

$$\sum_i \sum_j p_i^e u_{ij} q_j^e \geqslant \sum_j \alpha' q_j^e = \alpha'. \tag{G4.6.5}$$

Hence the theorem.

Three results which are useful in finding the solutions of games and which follow from the Minimax Theorem are the following:

Theorem G4.6.2. The optimal probabilities p_i^e *and* q_j^e *satisfy the following conditions:*

$$p_i^e = 0 \quad \text{whenever} \quad \sum_j u_{ij} q_j^e < \alpha'; \tag{G4.6.6}$$

$$q_j^e = 0 \quad \text{whenever} \quad \sum_i p_i^e u_{ij} > \alpha'. \tag{G4.6.7}$$

This is easily proved: let $I = \sum_i \sum_j p_i^e u_{ij} q_j^e$. Then

$$I = \sum_j q_j^e \left(\sum_i u_{ij} p_i^e \right) \geqslant \sum_j q_j^e \alpha' = \alpha', \tag{G4.6.8}$$

and

$$I = \sum_i p_i^e \left(\sum_j u_{ij} q_j^e \right) \leqslant \sum_i p_i^e \alpha' = \alpha'. \tag{G4.6.9}$$

Thus

$$\alpha' \leqslant I \leqslant \alpha'$$

$$\Rightarrow \qquad I = \alpha'. \qquad \text{(G4.6.10)}$$

But $\mathbf{p}^e, \mathbf{q}^e \geqslant \mathbf{0}$. Thus if $\sum_i u_{ij} p_i^e \geqslant \alpha'$, $I > \alpha'$, unless $q_j^e = 0$. The result (G4.6.7) is obtained in a similar way.

Theorem G4.6.3. The optimal probabilities also obey the conditions: when $p_i^e \neq 0$,

$$\sum_j u_{ij} q_j^e = \alpha'; \qquad \text{(G4.6.11)}$$

when $q_j^e \neq 0$,

$$\sum_i p_i^e u_{ij} = \alpha'. \qquad \text{(G4.6.12)}$$

This theorem follows immediately from Theorem G4.6.2.

The Minimax Theorem also allows us to prove the following result:

Theorem G4.6.4. If the best strategy for either player is a pure strategy, then the best strategy for the other player is also a pure strategy and the game is a saddle-point game.

Suppose without loss of generality that A's best strategy is a pure strategy, (Ui'). Then the maximin occurs at the $\underset{j}{\text{minimum}}\,(u_{i'j})$, j' say, and the value of the game is $u_{i'j'}$. By the Minimax Theorem the 'best' result that B can achieve is $(-u_{i'j'})$, which occurs at the pure strategy (Bj'). Thus B should also play a pure strategy, and so the play (Ai', Bj') gives a saddle-point.

Equilibrium

The reader should verify that $(\mathbf{p}^e, \mathbf{q}^e)$ is an equilibrium play-vector.

G4.7 SOLUTIONS OF SIMPLE GAMES

Preliminaries

When trying to find the solution of any two-person zero-sum game the following two preliminaries can make the task easier:

(a) search for dominated rows and columns and remove them (remember that a row may become dominated after a dominated column has been removed, and vice versa);

(b) see if the game has a saddle-point. If so, the solution is obtained by the methods of G4.2. If not, we have to find a mixed strategy solution.

Mixed strategy solutions

The standard way of solving large games is to turn the problem into an l.p. problem and use the Simplex method. For (2 × 2) games, however, the graphical method is easier, and for other small games the probabilities q_j^e can be got by solving the simultaneous equations (see Theorems G4.6.2–G4.6.4)

$$\sum_j u_{ij} q_j^e = \sum_j u_{i'j} q_j^e \tag{G4.7.1}$$

$$\text{for all } i, i' \text{ such that } p_i^e \neq 0,\ p_{i'}^e \neq 0. \tag{G4.7.2}$$

The values of p_i^e can be obtained in a similar way. The difficulty lies in finding the values of i, i' which satisfy (G4.7.2). Once $\mathbf{q}^e$ has been got, this method can easily be used to get $\mathbf{p}^e$. For large games this involves a large amount of computation, which the Simplex method avoids, but it is suitable for use in small games. It will now be used to get solutions in two of them: (i) a (2 × 3) game; (ii) a (3 × 3) game.

(2 × 3) games

Consider the game with the matrix

$$\begin{pmatrix} 2 & 4 & 3 \\ 4 & 1 & 2 \end{pmatrix}. \qquad \text{G4.7.3)}$$

First we note that there are no dominated rows or columns. The difficulty is in finding B's best strategy. A's best strategy can be found by the graphical method and this is done first. It can be seen that the maximin occurs when

$$2p_1^e + 4(1 - p_1^e) = 3p_1^e + 2(1 - p_1^e), \tag{G4.7.4}$$

i.e. when

$$p_1^e = \tfrac{2}{3} \quad \text{and} \quad p_2^e = \tfrac{1}{3}. \tag{G4.7.5}$$

B then gets $(-2^2/3, -3, -2^2/3)$. Thus $q_2^e = 0$. The game can now be treated as a (2 × 2) game and B's strategies found by the graphical method. Alternatively it can be found by looking at A's expected pay-offs when B plays strategy $B1$ with probability q_1^e and strategy $B2$ with probability $(1 - q_1^e)$. The pay-off matrix for A is then

$$\begin{bmatrix} 2q_1^e + 3(1 - q_1^e) \\ 4q_1^e + 2(1 - q_1^e) \end{bmatrix}. \tag{G4.7.6}$$

To find q_1^e Theorem G4.6.3 tells us to equalize these two pay-offs, giving $q_1^e = \frac{1}{3}$. Then $\beta' = 2\frac{2}{3}$, which is equal to $(-\alpha')$, in accordance with the Minimax Theorem.

*** (3 X 3) games**

In this case we use the equivalent l.p. method, and in particular the problem given by (G4.5.11)–(G4.5.13). First, to ensure that the l.p. problem is soluble, a positive constant may need to be added to U (see G4.5). We are seeking a vector $\mathbf{r}$ such that $(r_1 + r_2 + r_3)$ is a maximum subject to the conditions $r_j \geqslant 0$, $\sum_j u_{ij} r_j \leqslant 1$. The probabilities p_i^e and the value of the game can be found from $\mathbf{r}$:

$$\alpha' = 1/r_j, \quad q_j = \alpha' r_j. \tag{G4.7.7}$$

The maximum of an l.p. problem occurs at a vertex of the feasible region (see E5.3). It cannot occur at a pure strategy as there is no saddle-point, so that in (3 X 3) games there are only four vertices to consider: one where no values of r_j are zero and the other three with just one r_j zero. The first is found from the three equations

$$\sum_j a_{ij} r_j = 1, \quad i = 1, 2, 3. \tag{G4.7.8}$$

It is best to use a graphical method to find the other three vertices: that is, to find the vertex when $r_3 = 0$, draw the lines

$$a_{i1} r_1 + a_{i2} r_2 = 1, \quad i = 1, 2, 3 \tag{G4.7.9}$$

in a space with coordinates (r_1, r_2). The vertices can then be seen by inspection.

Having found the vertices, the sum of the components is computed, and the maximum chosen, thereby giving the value and the probabilities using (G4.7.7). The probabilities p_i^e can now be found directly: if $q_j^e = 0$,

$$\sum_i a_{ij} p_i^e = \alpha'. \tag{G4.7.10}$$

There are at least two of these equations which, together with the equation

$$p_1^e + p_2^e + p_3^e = 1 \tag{G4.7.11}$$

which expresses conservation of probability, are sufficient to determine $\mathbf{p}^e$.

As an example, consider the game with pay-off matrix

$$\begin{pmatrix} 2 & 6 & 3 \\ 5 & 1 & 2 \\ 3 & 3 & 5 \end{pmatrix}. \tag{G4.7.12}$$

No rows or columns dominate, and there is no saddle-point. All the elements of A are positive. The constraint equations are

$$\begin{aligned} 2r_1 + 6r_2 + 3r_3 &= 1 \\ 5r_1 + r_2 + 2r_3 &= 1 \\ 3r_1 + 3r_2 + 5r_3 &= 1\,. \end{aligned} \qquad \text{G4.7.13)}$$

The vertex where they meet is $(\frac{13}{80}, \frac{7}{80}, \frac{1}{20})$. To find the vertex in the $r_3 = 0$ plane we draw the straight lines in that plane of the constraint equations. From Fig. G4.3 we see that the appropriate vertex is the meet of the first two constraint equations, i.e. at $(\frac{5}{28}, \frac{3}{28}, 0)$. The other two vertices are $(\frac{3}{19}, 0, \frac{2}{19})$ and $(0, \frac{2}{21}, \frac{1}{7})$. The sum r_j at these vertices is $(\frac{24}{80}), (\frac{8}{28}), (\frac{5}{19}), (\frac{5}{21})$, so that the maximum occurs at the first vertex. The value of the game is $\frac{10}{3}$, so that the probabilities are $(\frac{13}{24}, \frac{7}{24}, \frac{1}{6})$.

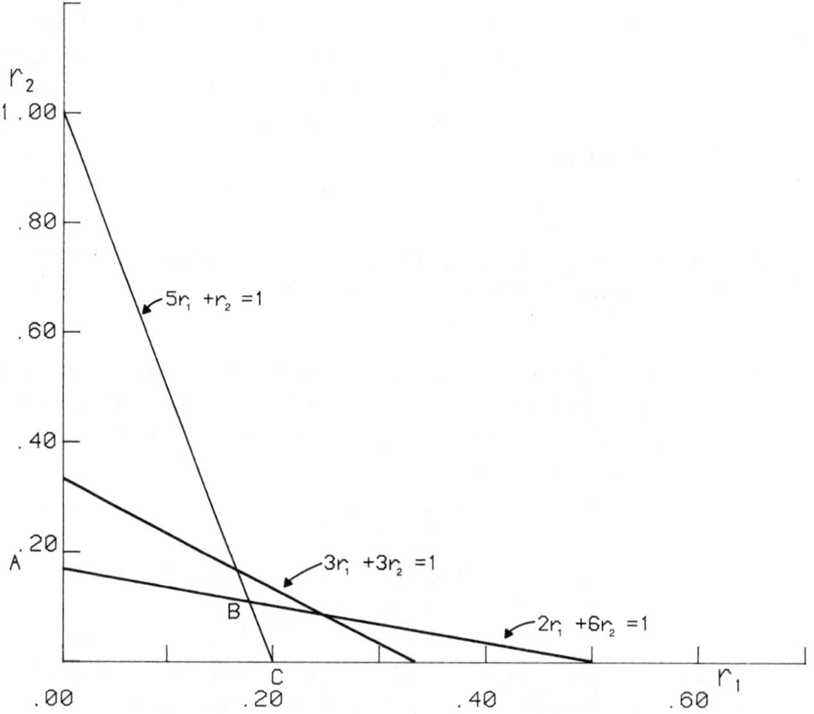

Fig. G4.3. The straight lines given by the constraint equation (G4.7.13) in the plane $r_3 = 0$. The part of the feasible region in this plane is the quadrilateral nearest the origin, i.e. $CABC$, and the required vertex is B.

To find $\mathbf{p}^e$ we solve the equations

$$\begin{aligned} 2p_1^e + 5p_2^e + 3p_3^e &= \tfrac{10}{3} \\ 6p_1^e + p_2^e + 3p_3^e &= \tfrac{10}{3} \\ 3p_1^e + 2p_2^e + 5p_3^e &= \tfrac{10}{3}. \end{aligned} \tag{G4.7.14}$$

The equation (G4.7.11) is automatically satisfied. The result is $(\frac{1}{3}, \frac{1}{3}, \frac{1}{3})$.

* G4.8 INFINITE GAMES

All the games so far have had pay-off matrices with a finite number of elements. There are games in which the pay-off matrix is infinite. These usually occur when at least one of the players has strategies which depend on a continuous variable, e.g. the size of a bet or the direction of a gun. One delivery in cricket or in baseball can be viewed as such a game: the bowler (or pitcher) can vary his direction and his speed in infinitely many ways; the batsman can vary the position of his bat in infinitely many ways so that both the bowler and the batsman have an infinite number of strategies. At the present there is a lot of research into 'pursuit' games, e.g. how one missile can catch another.

Such situations are complicated. Here we look at a simple mathematical game: the players, A and B, choose numbers x and y such that $0 < x, y < 2$ so that the point (x, y) lies within the square with vertices $(0, 0)$, $(2, 0)$, $(0, 2)$ and $(2, 2)$. The pay-offs depend on which of four triangles (x, y) lies in, each triangle having one vertex at $(1, 1)$ and two other vertices at the corners of the square. The pay-offs are shown in Fig. G4.4, with a zero pay-off if (x, y) lies on any diagonal of the square. It can be seen that this game has an infinity of strategies for A and B.

There are many other interesting infinite games: the reader may like to see how 'Rustic Poker' can be modified to include bets of any size in a particular range. The detailed consideration of such games is beyond the scope of this book.

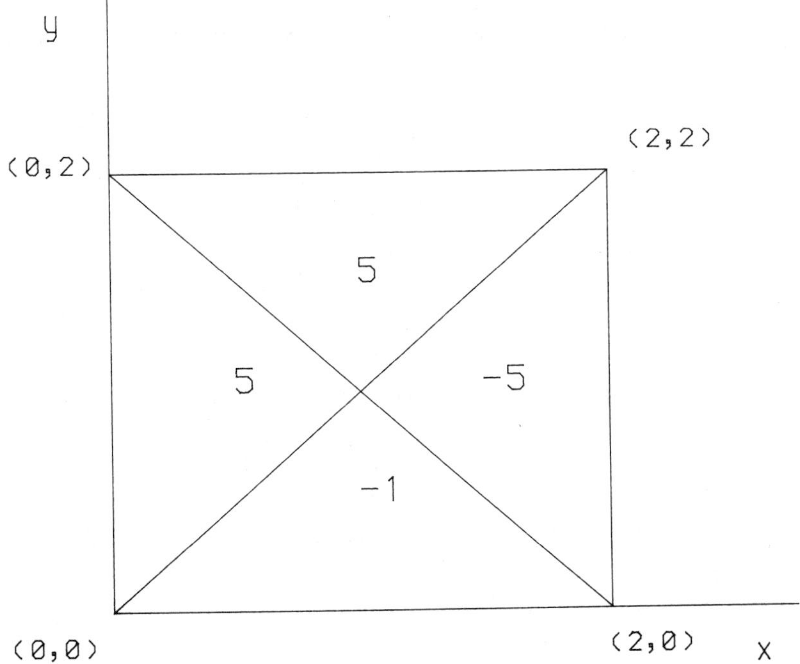

Fig. G.4.4. The pay-offs in the infinite game of G4.8.

G4.9 PRACTICALITY

We have shown that solutions exist for zero-sum games when the norm is the one proposed in G4.2. Are these solutions practical?

If the game is a saddle-point game, the solution is a pure strategy solution which can obviously be put into practice. If the game is not, the solution is a mixed-strategy one. Let us assume that a lottery device which generates the required probabilities can be made. Is using the mixed-strategy solution going to lead to the results that we want? In any single play of a game, a pure strategy has to be chosen; if that strategy is chosen by a lottery device it may give a pay-off which is worse than one chosen in a different way. For example, in (G4.7.12) if the device chose ($A2$), the security level is only 1 whereas for ($A3$) it is 3.

If the game is repeated many times, however, this difficulty disappears and the player expects to get the expectation value associated with the chosen mixed strategy. Thus for such repeated games, the norm of G4.2 and the soltuions we have found are practical. For games which are only played once, the mixed strategy solution may be impractical or even dangerous: should Aratro (see G2.1) decide the route for his guerillas by tossing a coin? Should the use of a nuclear weapon be decided by the throw of a dice? This is a controversial issue and may demand a fresh look at the norm we have used.

GE4 EXERCISES

4.1 Find the solutions of the following zero-sum games where the pay-off matrices are:

(i) $\begin{pmatrix} 4 & -1 & 2 & 3 \\ 4 & 6 & 3 & 7 \\ 1 & 2 & -2 & 4 \end{pmatrix}$; (ii) $\begin{pmatrix} 1 & -3 & -2 & 0 & 3 \\ 4 & 2 & 3 & 2 & 6 \\ 3 & -1 & 5 & -4 & 0 \\ 7 & 2 & 8 & 2 & 2 \\ 0 & 1 & -3 & -2 & -1 \\ 5 & -4 & 1 & -1 & 3 \end{pmatrix}$.

4.2 Find the solutions of the following zero-sum games with pay-off matrices:

(i) $\begin{pmatrix} -1 & 1 \\ 1 & -2 \\ 0 & -1 \end{pmatrix}$; (ii) $\begin{pmatrix} 1 & 2 & 1 \\ 2 & 2 & 2 \\ 0 & 1 & 3 \end{pmatrix}$; (iii) $\begin{pmatrix} 1 & 2 & 1 \\ 2 & 1 & -1 \\ 3 & 0 & 4 \end{pmatrix}$;

(iv) $\begin{pmatrix} 1 & 2 & 1 \\ 2 & 1 & -1 \\ 1 & 0 & 4 \end{pmatrix}$.

4.3 Find the best strategy for both players in the following zero-sum games:

(i) $\begin{pmatrix} 2 & 3 & 1 \\ 5 & -2 & -1 \\ -1 & 4 & 0 \end{pmatrix}$; (ii) $\begin{pmatrix} 2 & 3 & 1 \\ -3 & -2 & -1 \\ -1 & 4 & 3 \end{pmatrix}$; (iii) $\begin{pmatrix} 2 & 3 & 1 \\ 5 & -2 & 2 \\ -1 & 4 & 3 \end{pmatrix}$;

(iv) $\begin{pmatrix} 2 & 3 & 3 \\ 5 & -2 & 2 \\ -1 & 4 & 3 \end{pmatrix}$.

4.4 Find the best strategies for both players in the zero-sum games with the following pay-off matrices:

(i) $\begin{pmatrix} 3 & 5 & 2 \\ 1 & 6 & 2 \\ 6 & -3 & -1 \end{pmatrix}$; (ii) $\begin{pmatrix} 3 & 5 & 2 \\ 1 & 6 & 3 \\ 0 & -3 & 3 \end{pmatrix}$; (iii) $\begin{pmatrix} 3 & 5 & 4 \\ 1 & 4 & 1 \\ 10 & 4 & 7 \end{pmatrix}$;

(iv) $\begin{pmatrix} 3 & 5 & 2 \\ 1 & 6 & 3 \\ 6 & -3 & 3 \end{pmatrix}$.

4.5 Each of the following is a pay-off matrix for A in a zero-sum game:

(i) $\begin{pmatrix} 1 & 4 \\ 7 & 6 \end{pmatrix}$; (ii) $\begin{pmatrix} 3 & -2 \\ -1 & 2 \end{pmatrix}$; (iii) $\begin{pmatrix} 1 & 4 & 0 & 0 \\ 7 & 6 & 0 & 0 \\ 0 & 0 & 3 & -2 \\ 0 & 0 & -1 & 2 \end{pmatrix}$.

In (i) and (ii) find the optimal strategies for both players and the values of the games. Find the optimal strategies in (iii) and show that the value of this game is $\frac{6}{13}$.

4.6 A duel between two players(?) is fought with silent pistols: each pistol has only one shot. They start a distance $2a$ apart and walk slowly towards each other at the same speed. Player A has a probability of $p_A(x)$ and player B $p_B(x)$ of hitting his opponent if A or B respectively shoots when a distance x apart. Both $p_A(x)$ and $p_B(x)$ are monotonically decreasing functions of x such that they are always non-negative and are equal to 1 when $x = 0$. Once a player has been shot he cannot fire his pistol. Calculate the pay-off matrices for A and B.

4.7[(m)] Whist is too complicated to analyse using Game Theory. Try to build a game-theoretic model of a card game which is a bit like whist. Suggested is a version with two players with three cards each in which the pack consists of eight cards and two suits.

(i) First study Goofspiel (GE2.7) to see how it can be modified to include two suits with the players not playing simultaneously. Always determine carefully the pure strategies first; a game-tree is often helpful.

(ii) Extend the model to the case with two cards left in the pack.

CHAPTER G5

Further Games

G5.1 TWO-PERSON, NON-SERO-SUM, NON-COMMUNICATIVE GAMES

There are many non-communicative games for two players which are not zero-sum. Two of them are presented in G2.2, i.e. 'Duopoly' and the 'Prisoners' Dilemma'.

If the norm of G4.2 is adopted, the mathematical analysis for finite games is similar to the one presented in G4 for two-person zero-sum games. Consider a two-person game with two players A and B with m and n strategies respectively, so that their pay-off matrices can be defined as in G4.1 and satisfy

$$U_A + U_B \neq 0. \tag{G5.1.1}$$

Then A wants to find probability values p_i^e such that $\min_j \left(\sum_i p_i^e (u_A)_{ij}\right)$ is a maximum of $\min_j \left(\sum_i p_i (u_A)_{ij}\right)$. The problem for A is exactly the same problem as in the zero-sum case (see G4.4) and so is equivalent to the linear programming problem (see G4.5). Thus a solution exists for A and indeed for B. There is, however, a difference with the case of the zero-sum game as B's equivalent l.p. problem is not the dual of A's l.p. problem. Consequently there are several results in G4 which do not generalize, e.g. the Minimax Theorem and Theorem G4.6.4.

One important difference is that the play-vector(s) which give the maximin strategies are not necessarily equilibrium points. This can be seen with an example: consider the pay-off matrices

$$U_A = \begin{pmatrix} -3 & 1 \\ -2 & 1 \end{pmatrix} \qquad U_B = \begin{pmatrix} -3 & -2 \\ 2 & 1 \end{pmatrix}. \qquad \text{G5.1.2)}$$

$(A2, B2)$ is the play-vector with the maximin strategies, but is not an equilibrium point. There is little point in A choosing to play a maximin strategy if it is not part of an equilibrium play-vector, because B may choose a different strategy and A then gets less than his due. The norm of G4.2 is not always satisfactory in these games.

Should we search for a norm based on equilibrium play? To find the equilibrium is usually straightforward: if A plays $(A1)$ with probability p, and B plays $(B2)$ with probability q, the expected pay-offs are

$$U_A = (1 - 3q + p - 2pq) \quad U_B = (1 - 3p + q - 2pq) \qquad \text{(G5.1.3)}$$

with $0 < p < 1$ and $0 < q < 1$. Thus the minima of U_A w.r.t. p and of U_B w.r.t. q occur when (p, q) have values $(0, 1)$, $(\frac{1}{2}, \frac{1}{2})$ and $(1, 0)$. There are thus three equilibrium points. Which should be chosen? If A chooses the one which gives him the maximum pay-off, and B does the same, the resulting pay-offs gives the worst possible result, i.e. the play-vector is $(A1, B1)$. Thus the use of equilibrium as a norm is also rather unsatisfactory.

Another problem in these games is the meaning of mixed strategies. In a zero-sum game a player learnt nothing about the game from the play of any previous game, so that a mixed strategy could be interpreted as the ratio of the number of times the pure strategies were used when the game is repeated many times; in such a game there is no reason to modify the choice of pure strategy because of the choices made in previous plays. In non-zero sum games there may well be, i.e. the choice on the third play, say, may depend on the strategies chosen on the first and second plays; this will be seen in the 'Prisoners' Dilemma' game. If this is the case, using a mixed strategy may lead to worse results than using a pure strategy if the game is played once, and if played many times, it may be wise to learn from the strategies used previously.

** G5.2 'DUOPOLY' AND 'OLIGOPOLY'

'Duopoly'

This game illustrates some of the difficulties discussed in G5.1. From the outcome matrix for the duopoly game of G2.2, we see that the strategy of producing 6 units dominates all other, so that the play (6, 6) is an equilibrium solution. It is in fact the Cournot solution mentioned in E4.6.

There are, however, other plays which produce greater total profit. These all lie in the Pareto Optimal Set (POS) (see E4.6). This set is (6, 0), (6, 2), (6, 4), (4, 2), (4, 4), (4, 6), (2, 4), (2, 6), (0, 6). The one which produces the maximum profit is (4, 4) and this is the **collusion** solution. Notice that the Cournot solution is not Pareto optimal.

Actual duopoly, as in E4.6, can be considered as a game, but a difficulty arises because the number of strategies available to each player is infinite. This also occurs in the Edgeworth Box bargaining scheme (see E2.7), which can also be viewed as a game. The ideas of Pareto optimality etc., however, are not altered by the infinite number of strategies.

'Oligopoly'

In the oligopoly game of G2.2, the strategy of producing 6 units does not dominate the other strategies, as the play (4, 6, 6) gives a bigger profit to A than (6, 6, 6). Pareto optimality can again be defined, i.e. a play is Pareto optimal if a change to any other play results in a loss of utility for one of the players. In this game the POS consists of the plays (0, 0, 6), (0, 2, 6),), 4, 6), (2, 2, 6), (2, 4, 6), (2, 4, 4), (4, 4, 4).

G5.3 'THE PRISONERS' DILEMMA'

The dominating solution

From the outcome matrices in G2.2 we see that the 'confess' strategy dominates the 'refuse' strategy for both A and B. Thus it is in the 'best' interests of both A and B to confess; then both A and B are sentenced to spend 5 years in prison. If, however, they had both adopted the 'refuse' strategy they would have only been sentenced to 2 years gaol. Thus by pursuing their separate selfish desires they are both worse off. This result should be compared with the doctrince of liberal economics (see E6.2).

Dilemmas for three or more players

The game of 'Prisoners' Dilemma' may be played by more than two players. As an example of a similar game for three players, consider the game of 'Oligopoly' presented in G2 with the demand function modified to

$$D(p) = (75 - p)/3. \tag{G5.3.1}$$

Most of the outcome matrix is shown in Fig. G5.1.

ABC	A	B	C	sum	p
004	–4	186	186	368	51
224	85	85	186	356	51
046	–4	162	239	397	45
226	73	73	239	385	45
244	73	162	162	397	45
066	–4	203	203	402	39
246	61	138	203	402	39
444	138	138	138	404	39
266	49	167	167	383	33
446	114	114	167	395	33
466	90	131	131	354	27
666	95	95	95	285	21

Fig. G5.1. Some of the outcomes of the modified oligopoly game.

We assume that communication is forbidden. The strategy of choosing to produce 6 lots of the commodity dominates all other possible strategies. If each player does, however, produce 6 lots, their profit is less than if they each produced 4.

Real examples of the 'Prisoners' Dilemma'

There are numerous real examples of this, of which one type comes from the over-exploitation of a common finite resource and another from economic situations.

A representative example of the first type is of a piece of common land which can be used for grazing. If every farmer in the vicinity lets his cattle use the common, then the land is over-grazed, the common becomes a waste land and the cattle do not get sufficient sustenance. Nevertheless it does not pay any farmer to exclude his cattle from the common as this only benefits the other farmers' cattle.

A similar example, with particular relevance to the present day, is whaling. If every country continues to hunt certain species of whale, the species will become extinct; however, for any country to withdraw from hunting these whales only benefits those other countries which continue hunting them. Pollution of the environment by factories etc. can also be analysed in these terms; it is also claimed that the nuclear-arms race between the Eastern and Western blocs is an example of the game.

There are numerous examples from economics. The duopoly game in G2 is one: the strategy of producing 6 lots dominates the other strategies but if all the players do this, the profit to each is much less than if they produced 4 lots.

Trade unions submitting independent wage claims is another example. To see this, consider an economy with two unions, A and B, who can submit either a high (C) or a low (R) wage claim and in all cases these claims are met. If both submit high claims, inflation increases considerably with (supposedly) resulting unemployment for the workers of both unions. If both submit a low wage claim, the economy thrives: if one puts in a low wage claim and the other a high one, there is some inflation which hurts everyone equally but the workers who gained a big increase in money wages do better than when both unions submit low claims.

Other economic examples occur when foreign goods are bought or there is massive investment overseas. For example, suppose it is better value to purchase a foreign car. Then it pays the individual to buy a foreign car; however, if everyone in a nation buys foreign cars, the national car manufacturers go bankrupt and everyone suffers the social and financial effects and the taxes to pay for the unemployment.

The effect of communication

Suppose that the two prisoners had some means of communication, i.e. suppose they could cooperate, before they had to confess. Would it make any difference?

The answer is no, because unless they can completely trust each other, it is in a prisoner's interests to double-cross his colleague and confess.

Thus the results of allowing communication depend on the characters of the individuals, making it impossible for any general theory to provide meaningful solutions. Game Theory has tended to by-pass this problem by only studying **cooperative** games in which *absolutely binding* agrreements on the strategies used by the players are entered into before the play begins.

Overcoming the Dilemma

'The Prisoners' Dilemma' presents a depressing outlook for all those situations to which the game is applicable. Will the world eventually be devoid of whales, full of pollution, inflation, and going backrupt because of the arms race?

There are at least two ways out of the dilemma. The first one is to create some external agent which changes the outcomes and/or forces the players to forego their selfish desires and seek a collective good. Such an agent might be like the International Whaling Commision, or the United Nations, but able to impose sanctions on anyone who adopted a C strategy. For example, suppose the prisoners belonged to a crime syndicate such as the Mafia. If it shot anyone who confessed, the pay-offs would become:

$$\begin{array}{cc} & \begin{array}{cc} \text{C} & \text{R} \end{array} \\ \begin{array}{c} \text{C} \\ \text{R} \end{array} & \begin{pmatrix} -\infty\,(-\infty) & -\infty\,(-9) \\ -9\,(-\infty) & -2\,(-2) \end{pmatrix} \end{array}. \tag{G5.3.2}$$

The R strategy suddenly becomes more attractive!

The other solution to the dilemma is to play the game many times.

Repeated dilemmas

If the game is repeated n times, where n is large, the game changes its nature. There are $2^{2^{(n-1)}}$ strategies for the nth game, because of the possible choices made in earlier games. It is thus possible in the course of the games for player A to tell B about his choices of strategy and vice versa; player A can reward and/or punish B for unselfish or selfish choices.

A plan for player A, if he wants to ensure a play of (R, R) in most of the games, is to choose R until B chooses C, and then play C until B chooses R. Then A chooses R until B chooses C again, with a minimum of usually two games. This can be interpreted as A trusting B until B swindles A; then A punishes B until B behaves well. When the game has been played many times on the computer, this (moral?) plan has so far been shown to be the most successful. Even when played twice consecutively with the outcome matrix of a single game as in G2.2, the C–C (confess twice) strategies are not immediately dominating: it is only when player B eliminates his dominated strategies that player A finds C–C dominates the other strategies (see GE5.3). This suggests that if played many times, equilibrium plays other than 'always confess' will occur.

Morality rewarded? Maybe, but it should be pointed out that such a plan may work for two-player games, but where many players are present, the rewards and punishments that one player can give are small and have little effect.

G5.4 CRITIQUE

A sensible critique of Game Theory along the lines suggested in SM1 is difficult, because Game Theory as such does not model any specific real situation. From our point of view, any criticism of Game Tehory should be about its applicability, about how well it identifies and quantifies conflict and cooperation, and about the suitability of the norms and the practicality of the solutions. Obviously the success or failure of Game Theory depends on the situation to which it is applied.

The obvious applications to which Game Theory can be applied are parlour games. Most of these games are much too complicated to be amenable to our analysis; if they were not, the games would be boring. Nevertheless the ideas which Game Theory has brought into prominence, and in particular the ideas about the conditions for the formation of coalitions, have helped to clarify the nature of some of these games and to develop new games.

There are a variety of other applications (see G1). In political studies the use has been mainly qualitative, but political scientists are increasingly interested in Game Theory. An unexpected subject in which Game Theory has made an impact is evolution: here a 'game' involving a genetic strategy and/or a behavioural strategy is played many times and the optimal choice is likely to survive. This topic will be discussed further in P4.8.

The original aim of Game Theory was to clarify some of the problems in economics, but whether it has been successful or not is the subject of controversy among economists (what topic isn't?). It has helped to clarify ideas, but quantitatively it has not, in general, led to any conclusions.

It is in decision-making that it has been significantly helpful in a quantitative way. In using game-theoretic methods, quantitative assessments, even if only approximate ones, have had to be made and then used in conjunction with theoretical methods of solution to give some idea what decisions are optimal. This way of making decisions is more precise than relying on hunches and prejudices.

GE5 EXERCISES

5.1 In the game 'Duopoly' of G2.2, show that if the game is played twice in succession there are 4^3 pure strategies for each player. Show also that if played n times, there are $4^{(2n-1)}$ pure strategies for each player.

5.2 Is the game of 'Prisoners' Dilemma' fair between the two players? Show that the game (suggested in GE2.5) of two consecutive plays of 'Prisoners' Dilemma' is different from the game of two simultaneous plays (see GE3.10). What can you deduce about the differences between zero-sum and non-zero-sum games for two players?

5.3 In the two-play game (see GE2.5 and the preceding exercise) of 'Prisoners' Dilemma', are there any dominated or dominating strategies? Is this game another example of 'Prisoners' Dilemma'?

5.4$^{(m)}$ Two factories are situated by a lake and use fresh water from it. They also can pour their contaminated water into the lake. Construct a game of the 'Prisoners' Dilemma' type for the cost to the factory owners of choosing to decontaminate their used water or not.

5.5$^{(m)}$ Consider the way a large business or city council makes decisions on how it spends money. There may be several ways: should a new factory be built, or new machinery be bought, or dividends be given to the shareholders? There may be several imponderables, e.g. the future state of the economy, future government policy. Can all this be modelled using Game Theory? If so, what are the pure strategies? Does a mixed strategy have any meaning? How do you think decisions could be made in this way?

Part P:
POPULATION DYNAMICS

CHAPTER P1

Introduction

Population dynamics is the study of changes in the populations of systems and how the population of one system can affect the population of another. To get a clearer idea of the subject let us list some of the types of object that interest us:

(i) **microbes**, e.g. the spread of infection in a community, the growth of bacteria in a wound, or the growth of culture in a laboratory test tube.

(ii) **animals**, e.g. the population of herrings in the North Sea or the number of rats in a large city.

(iii) **plants**, e.g. the population of a particular type of weed or tree.

(iv) **molecules in a chemical or biochemical reaction**; for example, how long does it take for a reaction to be *99%* complete?

(v) **elementary particles**, e.g. the population of neutrons in a nuclear reactor.

(vi) **business systems**, e.g. the numbers of treasury bills in circulation or of word-processors.

(vii) **proportions** of a given animal or microbe population which have particular characteristics, e.g. the ratio of the numbers of a given bacteria immune to a particular antibiotic to those not immune.

Population changes may have important economic and social consequences; for example, the farmer wants to know how large the pest population is when his crop is most vulnerable and what effects pesticide spraying will have: the surgeon wants to know the rate at which bacteria will increase if a certain surgical operation is undertaken: and the fisherman wants to know what effect fishing quotas will have on fishing stocks and consequently on fishing catches.

A wide variety of systems is studied in population dynamics. Terminology, however, varies between the real systems; for simplicity the description in this book is in terms of animal behaviour unless otherwise stated. Thus we use words such as species, birth, death, etc. The same model may have other realizations, which the reader should try to discover: for instance, most of these words can also be used for the study of microbes and plants: they are also relevant with careful translation to the study of the population behaviour of molecules and elementary particles. Business systems may be very different, so that in general such applications are not discussed in this book. The mathematical techniques used, e.g. stability of equilibria and Markov chain theory, are, however, useful in most of these other topics, including microeconomics and Game Theory.

In general, population dynamics studies the variation in populations of various systems with position and time. Let us express this mathematically: consider a region of area $D_{\mathbf{r}}$ around a point $\mathbf{r}$. It should be small enough for there to be no change in the habitat but large enough for there to be a significant number of systems in it. Suppose the number of systems of type i in $D_{\mathbf{r}}$ is $D_{\mathbf{r}}n_i(\mathbf{r}, t)$ at time t; $n_i(\mathbf{r}, t)$ is a number density. Our aim is to discover how $n_i(\mathbf{r}, t)$ varies with $\mathbf{r}$ and t.

Many species have their own pecularities; for example, some plants need a particular species of insect to fertilize their flowers. Nevertheless most of them have some important characteristics in common; the ones that are readily observable are: (a) **birth**; (b) **natural death**; (c) **food**; (d) **interaction** between different species; (e) **migration**; (f) **perturbations** caused by the randomness of their environment.

Let us look at these characteristics in more detail.

(a) **Birth**. This increases the number density $n(\mathbf{r}, t)$. The birth-rate depends on many factors, e.g. the amount of food available and the number of fertile adults. This in turn depends on the age distribution of the species. For animals with a short gestation–maturity period, T, the birth-rate at $(\mathbf{r}, t)$ can be considered as a function of the density $n(\mathbf{r}, t)$ of fertile adults at $(\mathbf{r}, t)$, but for animals with a long T, the birth-rate depends on the number density at time $(t - T)$ and at places other than $\mathbf{r}$.

(b) **Natural death**, i.e. from age or starvation. The death-rate depends on the food available and the number of animals liable to die, which in turn depends on the age distribution of the species.

(c) **Food**. This affects both the birth-rate and the death-rate. It is important to remember that the amount of food available at any given time is finite.

(d) **Interaction**. There are three main ways what animals of two different species can interact. They can help each other's population growth, or can hinder such growth or one can help and the other can hinder. These are respectively known as the **symbiotic**, the **competitive species** and the **predator–prey** systems. In the last-mentioned, one species, the predator, feeds on the other, the prey; for example, foxes catch and kill rabbits. Hence the presence of foxes increases the death-rate of rabbits and the presence of rabbits increases the food supply, and hence the birth-rate, of foxes. In the competitive-species system, the two species compete for the same resource, usually food. In this and the predator–prey system it is not clear how the populations of the species vary and a mathematical model may help us find out.

With animals, interactions are in general binary, but in chemical and biochemical reactions, interactions sometimes occur between more than two 'species'; for example, the rate of a particular reaction between two chemicals may depend on the presence of catalysts and enzymes; these help to increase the reaction-rates so that the rate at which the compound increases depends not only on the amounts of the two chemicals present but also on the amounts of catalyst etc. present.

(e) **Migration**. The movement of animals has an effect on $n(\mathbf{r}, t)$. Such movement may be purposive, as in the migration of birds, or it may be random, as in the diffusion of a chemical. In both cases it has important consequences.

(f) **Perturbations**. The environment of most real systems, particularly animal systems, is constantly changing, so that the actual populations are always subject to fluctuations. When populations are large, these fluctuations are in general unimportant, but when populations are small, these fluctations are significant, for example, there is a sizable probability that the species will die out in such circumstances. As these perturbations are difficult to take into account, most mathematical models tend to neglect them so that these models only have validity if the populations are never small, i.e. of comparable size to the size of the fluctuations. This is an important point to note when evaluating any model.

With a mathematical model, it is important to check the predictions of the model against real data. In population dynamics, the systems are often so complex that it is difficult to model them except in a simplified manner. This is particularly true of animal behaviour. Hence it is very difficult to know whether the predictions of any model are valid even when they do agree with experimental data. Good data on animal behaviour is difficult to get, although what is available is interesting. Data on chemical reactions is more readily accessible and reliable; the data on microbes is also better as they can be studied in laboratory conditions.

In a short introduction to the subject it is difficult to take migration into account, particularly as it would involve mathematical techniques of a difficulty beyond the scope of this book. We thus confine ourselves to a study of systems which are independent of $\mathbf{r}$, the position. Such systems could be homogeneous systems (where migration is unimportant) or systems confined to a fixed region, e.g. animals on an island or chemicals in a beaker.

Population behaviour can be modelled using deterministic or probabilistic assumptions. P2 and P3 use the former and P4 the latter. In P2 we model one-species behaviour, when its effect on the environment is small and can be neglected. In P3 we look at models for the populations of two interacting species. P4 looks briefly at the effect of stochastic birth-rates and fluctuating environments; in particular it develops the mathematical theory of Markov chains and shows how it is useful in modelling the populations of genes. It also includes a brief look at the application of the Theory of Games to population dynamics.

CHAPTER P2

Single-Species Behaviour

P2.1 INTRODUCTION

The way the environment affects the population of a species depends in general not only on the number $n(t)$ of the given species but also on many other factors. In certain circumstances it is possible to ignore these other factors and consider the effect of the environment on $n(t)$ as a function of n only. A simple example of this is where a particular species is unaffected by the environment except for the provision of food.

In this chapter we study the population dynamics of a species in circumstances of this kind. We want to find out how the number density $n(t + \Delta t)$ at the time $(t + \Delta t)$ depends on n at previous times; this leads to equations of the form

$$(n(t+\Delta t) - n(t))/\Delta t = f[n], \qquad \text{(P2.1.1)}$$

where $f[n]$ depends on n at times $t' \leqslant t$. The modelling process aims to determine the exact form, and in particular the form of $f[n]$, of equation (P2.1.1). For example, when the increments Δt can be considered as negligible in comparison with the other time constants of the model, time can be considered as a continuous variable and equation (P2.1.1) becomes a differential equation

$$\mathrm{d}n/\mathrm{d}t = f[n]. \qquad \text{(P2.1.2)}$$

These, (i.e. (P2.1.1) and (P2.1.2)) are causal equations.

This chapter begins with a description of the simplest models of population dynamics, i.e. we take time as a continuous variable and study the exponential growth and logistic models. Both models lead to equations of the form (P2.1.2) with $f[n]$ depending only on the number density $n(t)$ at time t. In P2.4 and P2.5 we see that simple models for chemical reactions and fish populations lead to more complex equations of the same form. The remainder of the chapter is devoted to an introduction to the complexities brought in by consideration of age-structures, gestation periods and breeding seasons. These necessitate the introduction of discrete time intervals and time-delays into the equations. Note also that in this chapter and the next we assume that the environment is constant, and neglect any environmental fluctuations.

P2.2 EXPONENTIAL GROWTH

The rate of increase in the population of a system is known as the **birth-rate**. As this increases monotonically with $n(t)$, let us assume that it can be written as $bn(t)$. The rate of decrease is the **death-rate**; let us similarly assume that this is $dn(t)$. This suggests, from (P2.1.2), that the equation

$$\frac{\mathrm{d}n}{\mathrm{d}t} = (b-d)\,n(t) \qquad \text{(P2.2.1)}$$

describes the population dynamics of the system.

This equation (P2.2.1) is easily solved:

$$n(t) = A \exp\,[(b-d)t]\,, \qquad \text{(P2.2.2)}$$

where A is the value of n at time $t = 0$. The predictions of this solution are that if $b > d$ the population increases exponentially and without limit; it increases by a factor e every τ units of time, where

$$\tau = 1/(b-d). \qquad \text{(P2.2.3)}$$

The constant τ is known as the **relaxation time** of the system. If, however, $d > b$, the population decreases by a factor e every $|\tau|$ units of time.

Before we compare the predictions with the data, we ought to examine the conditions under which we derive the equation (P2.2.1). First of all we have ignored the age distribution of the species, i.e. we have assumed that all members of the population are fertile and all are equally likely to die. We have also ignored the periods of gestation and of growth to adulthood because we have assumed both a continuous variation of n and that the increase in $n(t)$ depends only on n at the time t. Is this last assumption reasonable if τ is much longer than the above periods?

Fig. P2.1(a) shows the growth of *Paramecium* population grazing a vegetation renewed at a constant rate, and Fig. P2.1(b) shows the growth of yeast in a culture. Each graph shows approximately the same behaviour: as time increases, each population tends to a constant amount N. This is in contradiction to the prediction of unlimited growth. Nevertheless when $n(t)$ is small in comparison with N, the growth is exponential. Thus the exponential-growth model is valid for n much smaller than N, but is invalid for $n \sim N$. We thus need a modified model which has the characteristics of the exponential growth model at small n, but tends to an equilibrium value at large t. Such a model is the **logistic** or Verhulst model.

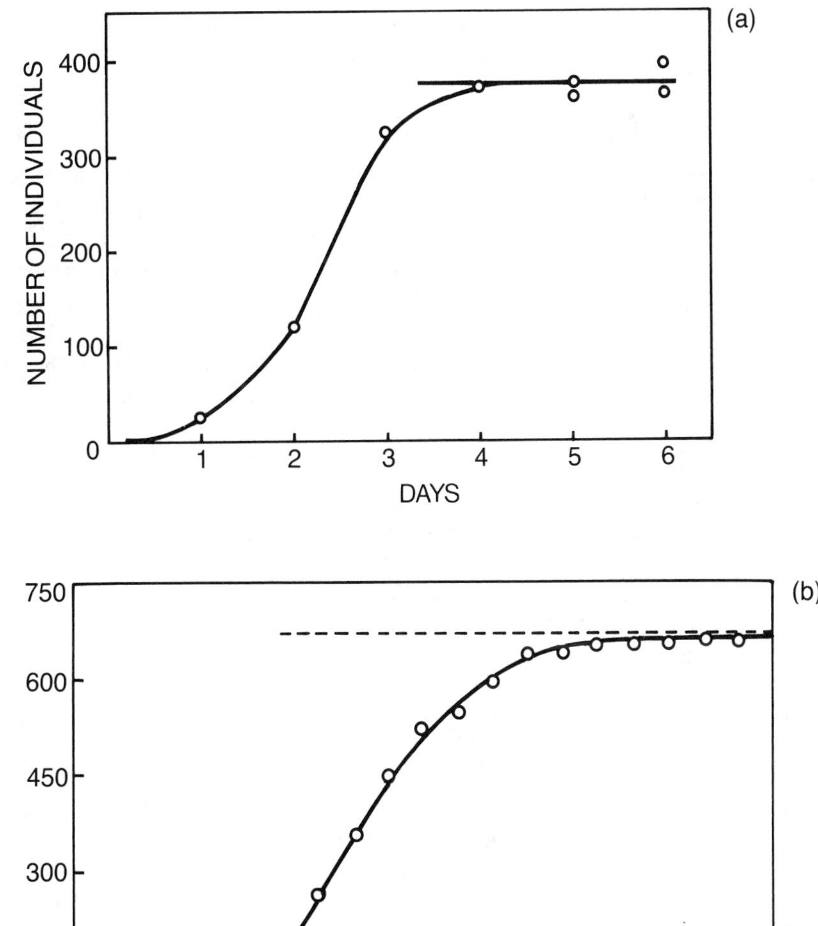

Fig. P2.1. (a) The growth of a laboratory population of *Paramecium caudatum* fitted to the logistic equation. Circles are observed counts; line is the fitted curve. (From Gause.) (b) The logistic growth of a laboratory population of yeast cells. (From Pearl.) (Reproduced, with permission, from *Principles of Animal Ecology*, W.C. Allee, A.E. Emerson, O. Park, T. Park and K.P. Schmidt, W.B. Saunders Co., Philalplina, 1949.

To improve a model, we must ask ourselves the question: what factors have we not taken into account? To answer this question we might reason as follows: for small n, the population has enough to eat and our model is satisfactory: for large n, however, because of the finiteness of the food supply, there is not enough for every member to eat, so that then our model is unsatisfactory. We see how to include this effect in the next section.

P2.3 THE LOGISTIC MODEL

As we saw in P2.2, when n is large there is less than the required food for each member of the species. This has the effect of increasing the death-rate, because of the increased probability of disease and starvation, and of decreasing the birth-rate because the offspring are less healthy and hence have less chance of survival.

A simple model of this effect is to assume that $(b-d)$, the birth-rate minus the death-rate, decreases linearly with n. Equation (P2.2.1) then becomes

$$\frac{\mathrm{d}n}{\mathrm{d}t} = \frac{n}{\tau}\left(1 - \frac{n}{\nu}\right) \tag{P2.3.1}$$

where ν is a constant. This equation is the **logistic** equation.

To solve (P2.3.1) we separate the variables:

$$\frac{\mathrm{d}n}{n(1-n/\nu)} = \frac{\mathrm{d}t}{\tau}; \tag{P2.3.2}$$

the L.H.S. is integrated by using partial fractions

$$\frac{1}{n(1-n/\nu)} = \frac{1}{n} + \frac{1/\nu}{1-n/\nu}. \tag{P2.3.3}$$

Two possibilities have to be considered: (i) $A < \nu$; (ii) $A > \nu$, where $A = n(0)$. In case (i) we can integrate (P2.3.2) immediately to get

$$\ln(n/A) - \ln\{(1-n/\nu)/(1-A/\nu)\} = t/\tau \tag{P2.3.4}$$

and hence

$$\frac{n(\nu - A)}{A(\nu - n)} = \exp[t/\tau] \tag{P2.3.5}$$

which gives, after some manipulation,

$$n = \nu A/(A + (\nu - A)\exp[-t/\tau]). \tag{P2.3.6}$$

In case (ii) we write the R.H.S. of (P2.3.3) as

$$\frac{1}{n} - \frac{1/\nu}{n/\nu - 1} \tag{P2.3.7}$$

and then we integrate (P2.3.2) to get

$$\ln(n/A) - \ln\{(n/\nu - 1)/(A/\nu - 1)\} = t/\tau \tag{P2.3.8}$$

which again gives the result (P2.3.5) after some manipulation.

The graphs of the two solutions are shown in Fig. P2.2. In both cases, $n \to \nu$ as $t \to \infty$. We can thus identify ν with N, the constant, introduced in P2.2. From the logistic equation itself we see that when $n = N$, $dn/dt = 0$; we thus call N an **equilibrium** value.

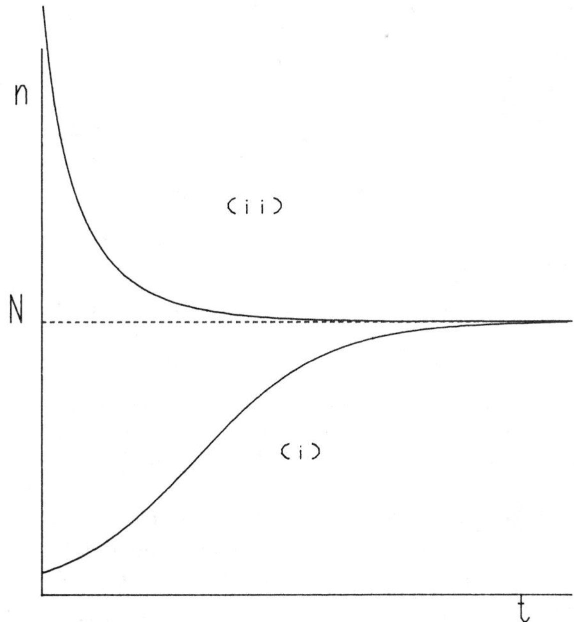

Fig. P2.2. Solutions of the logistic equation.

When $A > N$ (case (ii), Fig. P2.2)), n decreases monotonically until it reaches the equilibrium value. When $A < N$, n never becomes greater than N, but is monotonically increasing. We confine our discussion to this more usual case, (i), to see if it agrees with experiment.

We have already shown that $n \to N$ at $t \to \infty$. We also need to show that when n is small, the result (P2.3.6) reduces to (P2.2.2), i.e. exponential growth. (P2.3.6) can be written

$$n = A \exp[t/\tau] \Big/ \left(1 + \frac{A}{N}(\exp[t/\tau] - 1)\right). \tag{P2.3.9}$$

For $n/N \ll 1$, $A \exp(t/\tau)/N \ll 1$, which for $t > 0$ implies $A/N \ll 1$. In that case the second term in the denominator in (P2.3.9) only gives a second-order contribution and can be ignored. (P2.3.9) then becomes the result (P2.2.2).

The curve has a sigmoid shape and satisfies the criteria suggested in P2.2. As can be seen from Fig. P2.1, it fits the data well for the growth of *Paramecium* and of yeast. The logistic equation thus seems a reasonable model for populations under the assumptions made.

Is the logistic equation the full story? In Fig. P2.3 is shown the growth of water fleas in culture, which does not conform to the logistic curve. The reasons for this discrepancy must lie in the assumptions, such as neglect of life-span and age-structure, that we have made in deriving the logistic equation.

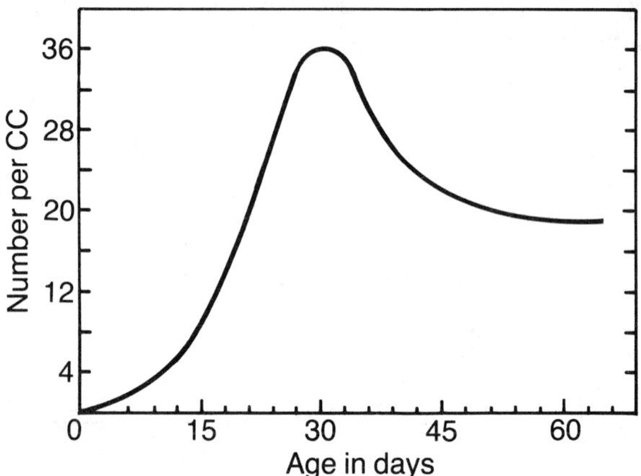

Fig. P2.3. Growth of water fleas (*Daphnia*) in culture. This shows a deviation from the logistic model. (Reproduced, with perimission, from *Fundamental Ecology* by A.S. Boughey, Intertext Books, Scranton, N.J.)

It is interesting to note that the logistic model was originally proposed by Verhulst in 1837 to explain the behaviour of the population of the U.S.A. It was 3.9×10^6 in 1790 and by taking $N = 197 \times 10^6$ and $\tau = 3.191$ years, a reasonable fit to the data is obtained until 1930†. This should not, however, be considered as a triumph for the logistic model, because the U.S.A. population does not conform to its assumptions: for example, there has been substantial immigration into the U.S.A., and the food supply has increased dramatically owing to increased land use and better agriculture. Such a model thus has no predictive value.

P2.4 CHEMICAL REACTIONS

At first sight it might appear difficult to cast the equations which govern such reactions into the form (P2.1.2) because each reaction rate depends on the number densities‡ of the various constituents (and there may be several of these). Nevertheless because of the conservation laws, these number densities are not independent and it is often possible to obtain an equation like (P2.1.2) for each constituent.

Let us give a simple example. Consider a reaction in which constituents A and B go to the compound AB. Let n_A, n_B and n_{AB} be the number densities of

† See MBB.

‡ 'number density' means the number of atoms (or molecules) of a particular constituent in a unit volume.

constituents A, B and AB respectively. Then if all the other parameters, e.g. temperature, are kept constant the rate of increase of n_{AB} is a function of n_A, n_B and n_{AB}:

$$\mathrm{d}n_{AB}/\mathrm{d}t = f(n_A, n_B, n_{AB}). \tag{P2.4.1}$$

Now one A molecule and one B molecule go to one AB molecule, so that every time an AB molecule is formed there is one less A and one less B. Thus

$$n_A = N_A - n_{AB}, \quad n_B = N_B - n_{AB} \tag{P2.4.2}$$

where N_A and N_B are the original number densities of A and B atoms respectively. Thus

$$\mathrm{d}n_{AB}/\mathrm{d}t = f(N_A - n_{AB}, N_B - n_{AB}, n_{AB}) \tag{P2.4.3}$$

which is of the form (P2.1.2).

To get an explicit form for the function f, we might argue as follows: for the compound AB to be formed, an A 'atom' must collide with a B 'atom', so that the rate at which AB is formed is proportional to the probability of A and B colliding. This probability in turn is proportional to $n_A\, n_B$ so that

$$\mathrm{d}n_{AB}/\mathrm{d}t = kn_A\, n_B \tag{P2.4.4}$$

where k is the proportionality coefficient and is in units of volume/time. Equation (P2.4.3) then becomes

$$\mathrm{d}n_{AB}/\mathrm{d}t = k(N_A - n_{AB})(N_B - n_{AB}). \tag{P2.4.5}$$

The coefficient k might be a function of n_{AB}. Let us assume, however, that it is constant. Then (P2.4.5) is easily solved: first we separate the variables

$$\int_0^{n_{AB}} \frac{\mathrm{d}n_{AB}}{(N_A - n_{AB})(N_B - n_{AB})} = kt. \tag{P2.4.6}$$

If $N_A = N_B$ we can immediately integrate the L.H.S. to get

$$n_{AB} = N_A^2\, kt/(1 + N_A\, kt). \tag{P2.4.7}$$

If $N_A \neq N_B$, we use partial fractions: the L.H.S. is

$$\int_0^{n_{AB}} \frac{\mathrm{d}n_{AB}}{(N_B - N_A)} \left\{ \frac{1}{N_A - n_{AB}} - \frac{1}{N_B - n_{AB}} \right\} \tag{P2.4.8}$$

so that

$$n_{AB} = N_A\, N_B \left\{ \frac{\exp\,[(N_B - N_A)kt] - 1}{N_B \exp\,[(N_B - N_A)kt] - N_A} \right\}. \tag{P2.4.9}$$

Thus as $t \to \infty$

$$N_{AB} \begin{array}{ll} \to N_A & \text{if } N_B > N_A \\ \to N_B & \text{if } N_A > N_B \end{array}.$$

This simple model is verified in various simple reactions, e.g. $H_2 + I_2 \rightarrow 2HI$. Another simple reaction agreeing with this model is where n-propyl bromide reacts with the thiosulphate ion

$$RBr + S_2O_3^{-2} = RSSO_3^- + Br^-. \tag{P2.4.10}$$

In Fig. P2.4 is plotted ln $[(N_B - n_A)/(N_A - n_A)]$ against time, where n_A is the concentration of the n-propyl bromide.

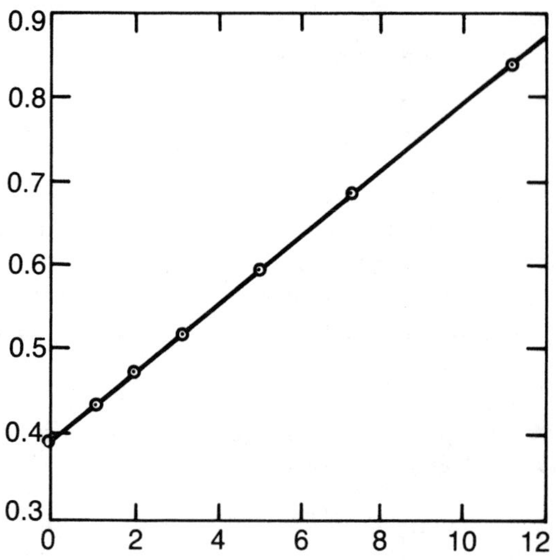

Fig. P2.4. Second-order plot for the reaction of n-propyl bromide with sodium thiosulphate (data from Crowell and Hammett). (Reproduced, with permission, from A.A. Frost and R.G. Pearson.)

It is easy to generalize the above arguments to simple reactions involving three or more constituents. Of more interest are catalytic reactions where the presence of a particular constituent helps the reaction. A simple example occurs when a molecule A decays into two constituents B and C and the rate of reaction depends on the amount of B present, i.e.

$$dn_B/dt = kn_B\, n_A\,. \tag{P2.4.11}$$

The conservation laws give

$$n_A + n_B = N_A + N_B \tag{P2.4.12}$$

so that (P2.4.11) becomes

$$dn_B/dt = kn_B\,(N_A + N_B - n_B) \tag{P2.4.13}$$

which is the logistic equation. Fig. P2.5 shows a graph of the trypsin concentration in the reaction of trypsinogen into trypsin: it has a typical sigmoid shape.

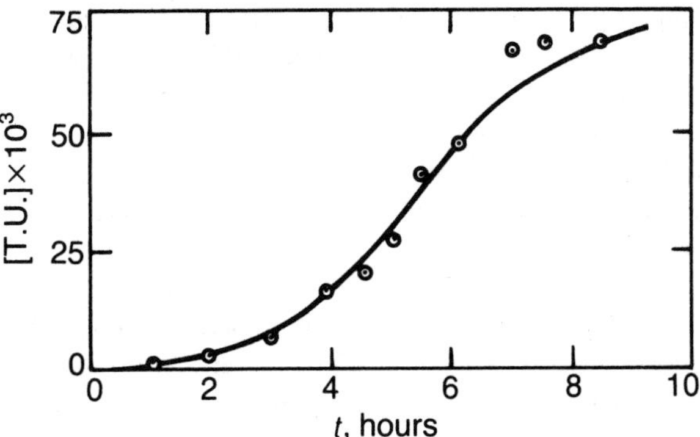

Fig. P2.5. Autocatalytic conversion of trypsinogen into trypsin (Kunitz and Northrop). (Reproduced, with permission, from A. A. Frost and R. G. Pearson, *Kinetics and Mechanism*, John Wiley.)

Catalytic reactions are of great interest in biochemistry, when one type of molecule may act as a template for the formation of other molecules. Such reactions are often very complicated, with one reaction using the molecules formed by another reaction. Even a seemingly simple reaction such as $H_2 + Br_2 \to 2HBr$ is complicated because it involves first the dissociation of the bromine molecules into atoms followed by various reactions between atoms and molecules. For further details about these reactions, the reader should consult other books, e.g. *Kinetics and Mechanism* by A. A. Frost and R. G. Pearson (John Wiley and Sons) and *Self-Organisation in Nonequilibrium Systems* by G. Nicolis and I. Prigogine (John Wiley and Sons).

P2.5 GENERAL ONE-SYSTEM EQUATIONS

More complex systems can sometimes be modelled by equations of the form (P2.1.2). An example of this occurs when there is predation by Man. The amount of predation by an animal species usually depends on the population size of that species (see P3.6) so that the number of prey depends on the number of predators and vice versa. Predation by Man, however, is different in that the human population is almost independent of the number of any given species of prey. For example, the decrease in the rabbit population caused by the disease myxamatosis and the decrease in the population of certain types of whale have had little or no effect on the size of the human population.

Thus we might consider the equation

$$dn/dt = \frac{n}{\tau}\left(1 - \frac{n}{N}\right) + g(n) \qquad \text{(P2.5.1)}$$

as a possible description of the population of a species whose most important predator is Man, e.g. herrings or whales. In (P2.5.1) the first term on the R.H.S. is the usual term that occurs in the logistic equation and is considered as describing the behaviour of n in the absence of predation. The function $g(n)$ represents the effects of Man's predation. Strictly speaking, $g(n)$ should be dependent on the time, because of the variation in the size of the human population and changes in predation-techniques, laws, etc. Here, however, we assume that $g(n)$ is independent of t.

When the predation is commercial fishing, a typical form for $g(n)$ might be

$$g(n) = -\alpha_1 n^2 N/(N^2 + \alpha_2 n^2)\tau \qquad \text{(P2.5.2)}$$

where α_1 and α_2 are constants and $(\alpha_1/\alpha_2)N/\tau$ represents the maximum possible rate of fishing. As $n \to 0$, $g(n) \to 0$, reflecting the fact that, because of economic factors, fishing decreases when the supply of fish decreases.

Qualitative 'Solutions'

In this section we want to show how useful information about the solutions of equations such as (P2.1.2) and (P2.5.1) can be obtained without actually solving the equations. By studying the equation itself we can get a qualitative description of how $n(t)$ changes with time. This kind of information turns out to be very useful as we often want to understand how the behaviour of the solution alters when circumstances alter. For example, what happens to $n(t)$ when the parameters (τ, N, α_1, α_2) in the equations (P2.5.1) and (P2.5.2) and/or the initial value $n(0)$ change? This could happen in commercial fishing when fishing quotas are imposed and α_1/α_2 changes. It should also be remembered that the exact values of these parameters and even the form of the equations are rarely known well because of observational difficulties, so that it is always wise to see how $n(t)$ alters even for small variations in the parameters. The qualitative descriptions mentioned above allow us to do this.

Of course it is always possible to solve the equations to a high degree of accuracy either by analytical means or by using a computer. Sometimes this is desirable, but sometimes it does not give us what we want, because the results are difficult to analyse and to comprehend†. A single result does not tell us how $n(t)$ alters when the parameters alter, and it is not always easy to get this information from 'exact' results.

Let us consider an equation of the form (P2.1.2). In our earlier example

$$f(n) = \frac{n}{\tau}\left(1 - \frac{n}{N}\right) + g(n). \qquad \text{(P2.5.3)}$$

The way to a qualitative understanding of the solutions is to find the zeros of $f(n)$, i.e. where

$$f(n) = 0 \qquad \text{(P2.5.4)}$$

and to examine the sign of $f(n)$ between each pair of zeros. At a zero of $f(n)$, all the derivatives‡ of n w.r.t. t are zero, so that n is stationary at such a value, i.e.

† There are few things more confusing than a sheet of computer paper covered with numbers!

‡ We have assumed that $f(n)$ is differentiable an infinite number of times.

if n reaches such a value it stays at that value. So the zeros of $f(n)$ are points of equilibrium. Thus if n_1 is a zero of $f(n)$, and $n(t_0) > n_1$ for some time t_0, then $n(t) \geqslant n_1$ for all time. Similarly if $n(t_0) < n_2$, where n_2 is another zero of $f(n)$, then $n(t) \leqslant n_2$. So if n_1, n_2 are adjacent zeros of $f(n)$ such that $n_1 < n(t_0) < n_2$, then

$$n_1 \leqslant n(t) \leqslant n_2 \qquad \text{for } t > t_0. \tag{P2.5.5}$$

Suppose also that $f(n) > 0$ for $n_1 < n < n_2$. Then $\mathrm{d}n/\mathrm{d}t > 0$ and n is always increasing. Thus as $t \to \infty$, $n(t) \to n_2$. Similarly if $f(n) < 0$, then $\mathrm{d}n/\mathrm{d}t < 0$ and as $t \to \infty$, $n(t) \to n_1$.

We thus have a qualitative description of the behaviour of $n(t)$. To find the actual time it takes for $n(t)$ to get to a value close to n_1 (say) it is only necessary to evaluate the integral

$$\int (1/f(n))\,\mathrm{d}n.$$

between the relevant units.

The above discussion is related to the 'stability' of the zeros of $f(n)$. If n_1 is a zero of $f(n)$, and is such that $f(n_1 + \epsilon) > 0$ and $f(n_1 - \epsilon) < 0$, where ϵ is small and positive, then n_1 is said to be an 'unstable' point of equilibrium. Similarly if $f(n_1 + \epsilon) < 0$ and $f(n_1 - \epsilon) > 0$, then n_1 is an 'asymptotically stable' point of equilibrium. If $f(n)$ has the same sign on both sides of n_1, then n_1 is said to be 'semi-stable'. These considerations can be linked to thebehaviour of $\mathrm{d}f/\mathrm{d}n$ at $n = n_1$, provided it is non-zero (see PE2.7).

Examples

Let us illustrate this with two examples: (i) the logistic equation and (ii) the equation got from (P2.5.2).

(i) The logistic equation

The graph of $f(n)$ for the logistic equation is given in Fig. P2.6. It is parabolic. There are two equilibrium points, i.e. zeros of $f(n)$: these are $n = 0$ and $n = N$. The former is unstable and the latter is stable, with $f(n)$ positive for $0 < n < N$ and negative for $n > N$. Thus $n \to N$ as $t \to \infty$, no matter what the initial value A. The direction of n is indicated by the arrows.

(ii) Commercial fishing†

In this case we write

$$f(n) = (n(N^2 + \alpha_2 n^2) - n^2(N + \alpha_1 N + \alpha_2 n^2/N))/\,\tau(N^2 + \alpha_2 n^2). \tag{P2.5.6}$$

There are no zeros of $f(n)$ for $n < 0$: $n = 0$ is a zero so that there are either two or four non-negative real roots. Note also that $f(n) \to -\infty$ as $n \to \infty$, and $\mathrm{d}f/\mathrm{d}n > 0$ at $n = 0$. Taking $\alpha_2 = 100$ the graph of $f(n)$ must have one of the

† The equations presented here may be unrealistic. The aim of this section, however, is to demonstrate how qualitative 'solutions' can be obtained, and how they can be interpreted, so in this context the reality of the model is not important.

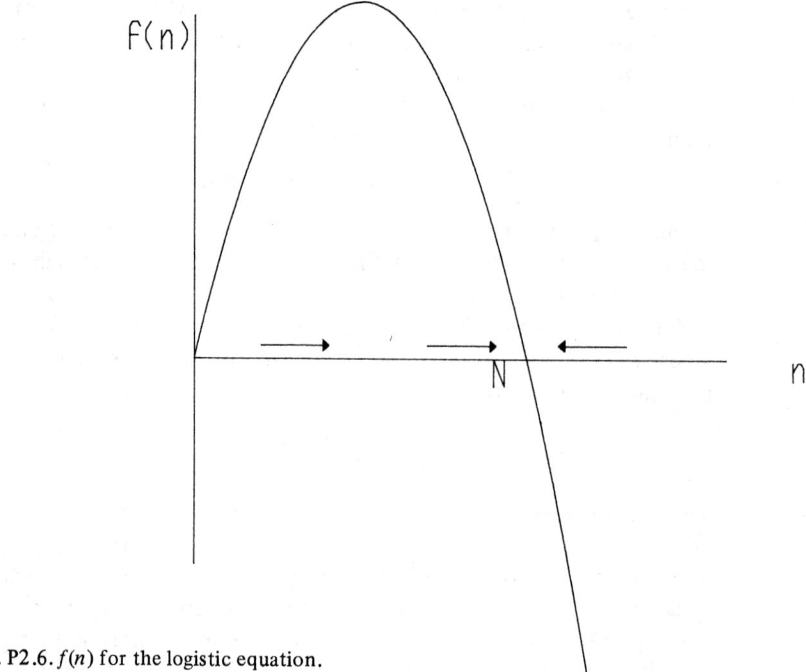

Fig. P2.6. $f(n)$ for the logistic equation.

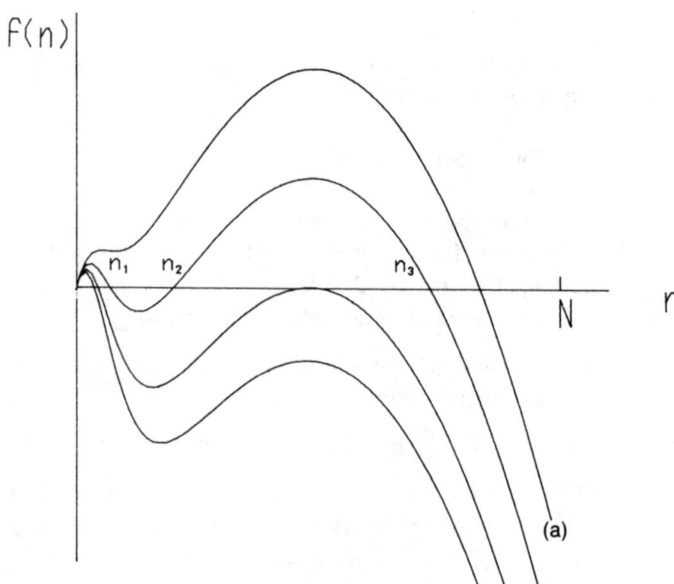

Fig. P2.7. The function $f(n)$ for equation (P2.5.6), the 'commercial fishing' example.

shapes sketched in Fig. P2.7 with $\alpha_1 \sim 14$ in (a), ~ 20 in (b), ~ 26 in (c) and 30 in (d). We label the other roots of $f(n)$ as n_1, n_2 and n_3 in increasing order of magnitude.

In case (a) there are two roots n_0 and n_3: as t increases $n \to n_3$ so that n_3 is the asymptotically stable solution. In case (b) there are four roots n_0, n_1, n_2, n_3. If $0 < n < n_2$, $n \to n_1$ as t increases whereas if $n > n_2$, $n \to n_3$. Thus n_1 and n_3 are asymptotically stable equilibrium values and n_0 and n_2 are unstable. In case (c), the n-axis touches $f(n)$ at $n = n_2$. If $0 < n < n_2$, $n \to n_1$ as t increases, whereas if $n > n_2$, $n \to n_2$. Thus n_1 is an asymptotically stable equilibrium value, but n_2 is semi-stable. In case (d), $f(n)$ has only two roots, n_0 and n_1. As t increases, $n \to n_1$, and n_1 is the asymptotically stable solution. In all cases, n_0 is unstable.

Interpretation of the solutions to (ii)

Suppose equations (P2.5.1) and (P2.5.2) are a model for the effect of fishing on the population of a certain type of fish. What are the implications of our 'solutions'? The public in general, whether they be fishermen or consumers of fish, wish to see the average rate of fishing maximized, where 'average' means over a long period of time. We assume that the constant α_1 can be varied in order to achieve this aim, i.e. by chaning the number of fishermen, or some other way, we can alter α_1. In mathematical terms, then, we want to maximize F with respect to α_1, where

$$F = \frac{1}{T} \int_0^T \left(-g(n(t))\right) \mathrm{d}t \quad \text{for large } T. \tag{P2.5.7}$$

What value of α_1 should be chosen?

To answer this question we assume that T is sufficiently large that F is obtained by substituting the equilibrium value of $n(t)$ into F. We again give a qualitative argument. In case (d), the equilibrium value n_1 is so small that the catches (in the long run) are small. In case (c) the fish population is unlikely to be n_2, because accidental perturbations such as disease or unsuitable weather conditions would ensure that at some time $n(t) < n_2$; thus the equilibrium fish population is n_1 and again the catches are small. In case (b), $(-g(n))$ has decreased, from cases (d) and (c), but the equilibrium fish population has increased dramatically to n_3. Thus the catches are much greater than in cases (c) and (d). In case (a) the equilibrium value is always n_3 but $(-g(n))$ has decreased, so that the catches are smaller than in case (b).

Thus it would seem that case (b) gives the best value of α_1. This is, of course, subject to proviso that the difference $(n_3 - n_2)$ is larger than natural fluctuations in the fish population†. Having done this qualitative analysis, it is then appropriate to do some calculations to verify it.

† Why?

P2.6 AGE-STRUCTURE AND BREEDING SEASONS: 1

In Britain and America for a few years after World War II there was a baby boom. Approximately 20 years later the birth-rate again increased in those countries because the original children had reached maturity and were themselves having babies. This is an example of a time-delay due to the age-structure of a species, i.e. the birth-rate depends on the number of births at a finite time previously.

In human populations the age-structure is important in the prediction of future populations; the birth-rate and the death-rate depend on the number of fertile adults and on the number of old people respectively. Most humans under 18 and above 45 years of age can be considered as infertile and the death-rate of those over 70 is higher than those aged between 20 and 40†.

There are several mathematical ways of modelling such situations. One of these is to consider only the number $x(t)$ of fertile adults. Then if we assume that all adults die before they reach infertility (as happens with most species in the wild), and that adults of all ages are equally likely to die, the population of adults is given by an equation of the form

$$\frac{\mathrm{d}x}{\mathrm{d}t} = f(x(t), x(t-T)), \qquad \text{(P2.6.1)}$$

where T is the time it takes between fertilization and adulthood: there is a **time-delay**. Another way of treating such situations mathematically is to divide the population into different age-groups and examine the dynamics of each group.

A species may breed only at a particular time, e.g. in the spring. With some species of insects and with 'annual' plants, the adults die off every autumn, so that the population of adults in the spring of year $(m + 1)$ depends on the number of adults in year m, i.e.

$$n(m+1) = n(m) + \Delta t \ f(n(m)) \qquad \text{(P2.6.2)}$$

where the time interval Δt is one year. Thus this model has time as a discrete variable. Such a model is suitable even when a few of the adults survive from one breeding season to the next. Nevertheless some species have breeding seasons but live for many years and produce only a few young every year; then as can be seen from equation (P2.2.3) the 'relaxation time' τ is large and the time increment Δt short in comparison with τ, so that a continuous equation without time-delay is more appropriate than equation (P2.6.1).

For the previous cases however we are led to a study of equations with discrete time variation both for simple systems (P2.7) and for those with an age-structure (P2.8), and to equations involving time-delays (P2.9).

† Do you think that the gestation period of 9 months is significant in the way human populations change?

P2.7 DISCRETE TIME MODELS

The simplest model of this type corresponds to exponential growth, i.e. has constant birth- and death-rates. Suppose that the time Δt between two breeding seasons be T, so that the number of animals existing at time $(m+1)T$ (where m is an integer) is $(b-d)Tn(mT)$ more than at time mT, where $n(mT)$ is the number of animals at time mT. Thus

$$n((m+1)T) = \left(1 + \frac{T}{\tau}\right) n(mT). \tag{P2.7.2}$$

which can be easily solved to give

$$n(mT) = \left(1 + \frac{T}{\tau}\right)^m n(0). \tag{P2.7.3}$$

This result can be written

$$n(mT) = n(0) \exp(m\gamma) \tag{P2.7.4}$$

where

$$\gamma = \ln\left(1 + \frac{T}{\tau}\right). \tag{P2.7.5}$$

Thus the solution (P2.7.3) has the same exponential growth as (P2.2.2), the result of the continous time model, and obviously has the same defects as that model.

The arguments presented in P2.3 suggest a discrete logistic model

$$\frac{n((m+1)T) - n(mT)}{T} = \frac{n(mT)}{\tau}\left(1 - \frac{n(mT)}{N}\right). \tag{P2.7.6}$$

It is not possible to solve this equation analytically, but it is possible to discover the form of the solution. For simplicity we assume that $n(0)$ is small in comparison with N. Then $n(T) > n(0)$, and n increases until it is greater than or equal to N. If $n(mT) > N$, then $n((m+1)T) < n(mT)$; thus n does not increase monotonically. Suppose for some value of m, $n(mT)$ has a value close to N, i.e.

$$n(mT) = N + y(mT) \tag{P2.7.7}$$

where $y(mT)$ is small. Then equation (P2.7.6) becomes

$$y((m+1)T) - y(mT) = -\frac{T}{\tau}(N + y(mT))\, y(mT)/N. \tag{P2.7.8}$$

As $y(mT)$ is small, neglect of the term in $(y(mT))^2$ shows that

$$y((m+1)T) \approx \left(1 - \frac{T}{\tau}\right) y(mT). \tag{P2.7.9}$$

Thus when

$$T/\tau < 1, \tag{P2.7.10}$$

y decreases monotonically to zero as m increases, and the behaviour of $n(mT)$ is similar to the behaviour in the continous case (see Fig. P2.2(i)). This is not surprising as condition (P2.7.10) allows time to be considered as continous. When

$$1 < T/\tau < 2$$

$|y|$ decreases to zero but y oscillates in sign, i.e. n oscillates about the value N before converging to it. For $T/\tau = 2$, the linearized equation (P2.7.9) suggests that the oscillations continue indefinitely, but according to the actual equation (P2.7.6) the oscillations slowly die out. For $T/\tau > 2$, the oscillations grow until the linearized equation (P2.7.8) is no longer valid. The actual behaviour is then very complicated (see PE2.12) and for $T/\tau > 3$, negative values of n can occur.

When adult fish are removed from an aquarium once they have laid their eggs, the generations are kept strictly apart. Then the fish population sometimes exhibits the oscillatory behaviour of the regime $1 < T/\tau < 2$. Of greater interest however, is the mathematical behaviour of equation (P2.7.6) for larger values of T/τ. The solutions exhibit **'chaotic'** behaviour, in which the solutions for values of T/τ infinitesimally close are totally different from each other.

* P2.8 AGE-STRUCTURE: 2

The provision of maternity hospitals, secondary schools, universities, homes for the elderly, etc. is an important task, so that if too few or too many are provided, the economic and social costs may be enormous. The planners must therefore have a good estimate of the numbers in each age group of the human population. For example, the planners in America and in the U.K. have had to cope with the baby boom mentioned in P2.6 and are now having to cope with the drop in the birth-rate which has occurred in recent years.

One model which gives some reasonable predictions is to divide the population into sets classified by their age and to use a discrete time interval of one year. Thus we write $n_i(m)$ as the number of individuals who are i years of age on a fixed day, 1 January say, in the year m. Suppose $d_i(m)n_i(m)$ and $b_i(m)n_i(m)$ of these die and give birth respectively in the year m. Then

$$n_0(m+1) = \sum_i b_i(m)n_i(m) \tag{P2.8.1}$$

$$n_1(m+1) = (1 - d_0(m))n_0(m) \tag{P2.8.2}$$

and in general

$$n_{i+1}(m+1) = (1 - d_i(m))n_i(m). \tag{P2.8.3}$$

Let us write these equations in matrix–vector form:

$$\mathbf{n}(m) \equiv \begin{bmatrix} n_0(m) \\ n_1(m) \\ \vdots \\ \vdots \end{bmatrix}; \tag{P2.8.4}$$

$$\mathbf{A}(m) \equiv \begin{bmatrix} b_0 & b_1 & b_2 & b_3 & \cdot & \cdot \\ 1-d_0(m) & 0 & 0 & 0 & \cdot & \cdot \\ 0 & 1-d_1(m) & 0 & 0 & \cdot & \cdot \\ 0 & 0 & 1-d_2(m) & 0 & \cdot & \cdot \\ 0 & 0 & 0 & 1-d_3(m) & \cdot & \cdot \\ \cdot & \cdot & \cdot & \cdot & \cdot & \cdot \\ \cdot & \cdot & \cdot & \cdot & \cdot & \cdot \end{bmatrix}. \tag{P2.8.5}$$

Then these equations can be written

$$\mathbf{n}(m+1) = \mathbf{A}(m) \,.\, \mathbf{n}(m). \tag{P2.8.6}$$

Matrix methods for these types of problem were introduced by Leslie in 1945. The matrix $\mathbf{A}(m)$ is often known as a **Leslie matrix.**

This model can be simplified by grouping some of the age groups together. The simplest grouping might be to choose three groups, writing p_1 for the children aged between zero and 17 years inclusive, p_2 for the number of fertile adults aged between 18 and 42 inclusive, and p_3 for the older group of 43 years or more. The mathematics is simplified if we consider these groups as homogeneous, with no deaths among the children or adults, and all older people living until 69 years of age. Then we get

$$\begin{aligned} p_1(m+1) &= 16p_1(m)/17 + bp_2(m) \\ p_2(m+1) &= p_1(m)/17 + 23\,p_2(m)/24 \\ p_3(m+1) &= p_2(m)/24 + 26\,p_3(m)/27 \end{aligned} \tag{P2.8.7}$$

where b is the birth-rate. These equations can be written in vector–matrix form with

$$\mathbf{p}(m) = \begin{pmatrix} p_1(m) \\ p_2(m) \\ p_3(m) \end{pmatrix} \qquad \mathbf{A} = \begin{bmatrix} \frac{16}{17} & b & 0 \\ \frac{1}{17} & \frac{23}{24} & 0 \\ 0 & \frac{1}{24} & \frac{26}{27} \end{bmatrix} \tag{P2.8.8}$$

giving

$$\mathbf{p}(m+1) = \mathbf{A}\,.\,\mathbf{p}(m). \tag{P2.8.9}$$

Solving the equations

When the Leslie matrix $\mathbf{A}(m)$ depends on m, the only way to determine the vectors $\mathbf{n}(m)$ (or $\mathbf{p}(m)$) from a given initial value $\mathbf{n}(0)$ is by calculation. When, however, $\mathbf{A}(m)$ is constant, it is possible to use eigenvalue–eigenvector techniques to discover the general time variation of $\mathbf{n}(m)$.

For simplicity let us assume that all the eigenvalues of $\mathbf{A}$ are real and distinct. Then all the eigenvectors are linearly independent and any vector can be expressed in terms of them. In particular, the initial vector $\mathbf{n}(0)$ can be written

$$\mathbf{n}(0) = \sum_{\alpha} c_{\alpha}\, \mathbf{N}_{\alpha} \tag{P2.8.10}$$

where $\mathbf{N}_{\alpha}$ is the eigenvector corresponding to the eigenvector λ_{α}, and c_{α} is the coefficient in the expansion. Then

$$\mathbf{n}(1) = \mathbf{A}\,.\left(\sum_{\alpha} c_{\alpha}\, \mathbf{N}_{\alpha}\right) = \sum_{\alpha} \lambda_{\alpha}\, c_{\alpha}\, \mathbf{N}_{\alpha} \tag{P2.8.11}$$

and in general

$$\mathbf{n}(m) = \sum_{\alpha} (\lambda_{\alpha})^{m}\, c_{\alpha}\, \mathbf{N}_{\alpha}. \tag{P2.8.12}$$

Thus if for some β, $|\lambda_{\beta}| < 1$, then the coefficient of $\mathbf{N}_{\beta}$ in $\mathbf{n}(m)$ for large m is negligible. If $|\lambda_{\gamma}|$ is the maximum value of $|\lambda_{\alpha}|$ then, provided c_{γ} is non-zero,

$$\mathbf{n}(m) \underset{m \text{ large}}{\longrightarrow} (\lambda_{\gamma})^{m}\, c_{\gamma}\, N_{\gamma}, \tag{P2.8.13}$$

i.e. the age distribution becomes dominated by the one eigenvalue.

* P2.9 TIME-DELAYS

We have already seen how age-structure and breeding seasons may give rise to a time-delay in the equation for $n(t)$. Another reason for a time-delay may be that the food supply takes time to develop. For example, an animal may feed on a plant which is an annual, so that the total food available depends on the number of plants in the previous year, and this in turn is a function of the number of animals present in the previous year. Thus the logistic equation (P2.3.1) should be replaced by a time-delay equation of the form

$$\mathrm{d}n(t)/\mathrm{d}t = \frac{n(t)}{\tau}\left(1 - \frac{n(t-T)}{N}\right) \tag{P2.9.1}$$

where T is the appropriate time-delay.

The solution of this equation is beyond the scope of this book and the reader is referred to the book PS1 for further details. The reader will also find there a model of the blow-fly population in which the time-delay is due to the age-structure. The resulting equation is similar to (P2.9.1).

The presence of a delay in the system usually introduces large amplitude oscillations if the delay time is longer than or of the same size as the relaxation time of the system. This can be seen in a simple discrete time model: consider the equation

$$\frac{n((m+1)T)-n(mT)}{T}=\frac{n(mT)}{\tau}\left(1-\frac{n((m-1)T)}{N}\right) \tag{P2.9.2}$$

which is the discrete logistic equation (P2.7.6) with a delay of one period, equal to T units of time. The equilibrium value of $n(mT)$ is N and to find out how $n(mT)$ behaves when it has a value near N we use the expression (P2.7.7) and get, for small y,

$$y((m+1)T)-y(mT)\approx -y((m-1)T)\,T/\tau \tag{P2.9.3}$$

where we have neglected the quadratic term in y.

The general solution of an equation of the form (P2.9.3), which is called a recurrence relation, is

$$y(mT)=Az_1^m+Bz_2^m \tag{P2.9.4}$$

where z_1, z_2 are the roots of the quadratic equation

$$z^2-z+T/\tau=0 \tag{P2.9.5}$$

and A and B are constants determined by the initial conditions†. Equation (P2.9.5) has roots

$$z=\tfrac{1}{2}\left(1\pm\sqrt{(1-4T/\tau)}\right) \tag{P2.9.6}$$

which are both real if

$$T/\tau\leqslant\tfrac{1}{4} \tag{P2.9.7}$$

when the usual logistic behaviour occurs‡. When

$$T/\tau>\tfrac{1}{4} \tag{P2.9.8}$$

the two roots are complex conjugates, and can be written $re^{\pm i\theta}$ where

$$r=\sqrt{\frac{T}{\tau}},\quad \cos\theta=\sqrt{\frac{\tau}{4T}}\quad\left(0\leqslant\theta\leqslant\frac{\pi}{2}\right). \tag{P2.9.9}$$

Then the solution (P2.9.4) can be written

$$y(mT)=Cr^m\sin(m\theta+D) \tag{P2.9.10}$$

where C and D are constants which are determined by the initial conditions in the same way as A and B. In these conditions $n(mT)$ oscillates about its equili-

† Note that two initial values, for instance $y(1)$ and $y(0)$, are required to determine A and B.

‡ Note that when $T/\tau=\frac{1}{4}$, the solution for $y(mT)$ is different from (P2.9.4). See PE2.12.

brium value with a period $2\pi T/\theta$. When $T/\tau > 1$ the oscillations get larger with m, so that (P2.9.3) is not valid; when $T/\tau < 1$ the oscillations get smaller, so that $n(m)$ converges to its equilibrium value N.

Although the behaviour in the two versions of the logistic equation, one with and one without a time-delay, is similar there are considerable differences. These are listed in Table P2.1. This shows that a time-delay makes the population less stable.

	(i)	(ii)
No oscillations	$T<\tau$	$T<\frac{\tau}{4}$
Convergent oscillations	$\tau<T<2\tau$	$\frac{\tau}{4}<T<\tau$
Divergent oscillations	$T>2\tau$	$T>\tau$
Period of oscillations	$2T$	$2\pi T/\theta$

Table P2.1. Conditions determining the behaviour of populations obeying the discrete logistic equation: (i) without a time-delay; (ii) with a time-delay.

PE2 EXERCISES

2.1 The density x of bacteria in a culture satisfies the exponential growth equation with a relaxation time τ that varies with the density x, i.e. $\tau = (0.4 + 10^{-7}x)$ minutes where x is the density in cells/ml. How long does it take for the density to increase from 10^8 cells/ml to 10^9 cells/ml.?

2.2 The logistic equation $dn/dt = \beta n - \sigma n^2$ models the growth of yeast in a culture. A suggestion for an improved equation is

$$dn/dt = n(a_1 - a_2 n)^{1/2}$$

where a_1 and a_2 are constants.

(i) Identify a_1 and a_2 in terms of β and σ by requiring that the two equations have the same form for the smallest values of n and also the same equilibirum values of n.

(ii) Let $n_0 < \beta/\sigma$ be the initial value of n. Show that the solution of the improved equation satisfies

$$(a_1 - a_2 n)^{1/2} = \beta[A \exp(-\beta t) - 1]/[A \exp(-\beta t) + 1],$$

where A depends on β, σ and n_0.

(iii) Deduce that n reaches its equilibrium value in a finite time which, for $n_0 \ll \beta/\sigma$, is approximately $\ln(4\beta/\sigma n_0)/\beta$.

2.3 It has been suggested that some species which would have a constant birth-rate b if the supply of food were unlimited, have a birth-rate which decreases by a factor $N/(N + n)$ as n increases while the death-rate d remains constant. Show that n satisfies the equation

$$\mathrm{d}n/\mathrm{d}t = \frac{n((b-d)N - dn)}{(n+N)} .$$

If $b = 2d$ show that

$$(N-n)^2/n = ((N-n_0)^2/n_0)\exp(-dt)$$

where n_0 is the initial value of n.

2.4 Suppose there is a large number N of sites in which a plant of a certain species can grow. Let the number of plants at time t be $n(t)$ $(<N)$. Suppose further that each plant produces seeds at a given rate and that the probability of a seed finding a vacant site is proportional to the number of vacant sites. Assuming that a seed on a vacant site grows quickly to an adult plant, show that $n(t)$ obeys a logistic equation.

2.5 Two molecules A, B combine to form a product AB (one of each) at a rate proportional to the number density (i.e. concentration) of each molecule. Suppose there are N of A and $2N$ of B initially, and that at time t, the number of independent As is n. Show that $\mathrm{d}n/\mathrm{d}t = -cn(N+n)$ where $c > 0$, and find n as a function of t.

2.6 Two types, A and B, of atom will form a molecule AB_2 under certain conditions (i.e. one atom of A and two atoms of B form one molecule AB_2). In a fixed volume, the rate of formation is $(n_1 n_2^2/kT(k+n_3))$ where n_1, n_2, n_3 are respectively the population densities of the atoms A, B and the molecule, and k and T are constants. Initially $n_1 = n_2 = k$ and $n_3 = 0$. Show that

$$\ln\left(\frac{k-2n_3}{k-n_3}\right) + \frac{3k}{4(k-2n_3)} = \frac{t}{2T} + \frac{3}{4} .$$

2.7 The derivative $\mathrm{d}f/\mathrm{d}n$ at a point $n = n_0$ can be defined by expanding $f(n)$ in a power series in $(n - n_0)$, i.e.

$$f(n) = f(n_0) + (n-n_0)(\mathrm{d}f/\mathrm{d}n) + O((n-n_0)^2).$$

Let n_0 be an equilibrium point where $\mathrm{d}f/\mathrm{d}n$ is non-zero. Show that the sign of $\mathrm{d}f/\mathrm{d}n$ determines the stability of the equilibrium.

2.8 The E.E.C. commissioner wants a simple mathematical model to describe the effect of fishing on the total herring population x in the North Sea. He is advised that the equation

$$\frac{dx}{dt} = \frac{x}{\tau}\left(1 - \frac{x}{N}\right) - NC(x),$$

where $NC(x)$ represents the number of herring caught per unit time, is a reasonable approximation. $C(x)$ is approximately $(y_1 - y_2N/x)/\tau$ for $x > y_2/y_1$ where $y_2 < 0.002$. The legal limit on the rate of fishing is Ny_1/τ and $(y_2/x)N^2/\tau$ is the decrease in this rate of fishing when x is small and fishing becomes less economic.

Two functions f and g are defined for $x > 0$. The function f is defined by $f(x) = -x(x^2/N - x + y_1N)$ and $g(x) = f(x) + y_2N^2$. Sketch the graphs of $f(x)$ and $g(x)$ for the cases: (i) $y_1 = \frac{1}{3}$; (ii) $y_1 = \frac{1}{4}$; (iii) $y_1 = \frac{4}{25}$. Discuss also the stability of the equilibrium points and the behaviour of the solutions $x(t)$ of the equation $x(dx/dt) = g(x)$ $(x > 0)$ for these values of y_1.

The commissioner has to decide on a value for y_1 which the fishermen should, but may not exactly, obey. Discuss the effects of fishing on the herring stocks in the North Sea and suggest, with reasons, a value of y_1 which the commissioner should adopt.

2.9 The population $n(m)$ of a certain species after the mth breeding season is related to $n(m - 1)$ by $n(m) = N\alpha n(m - 1)/(N + n(m - 1))$ where α is a number greater than one, and N is constant. Find the equilibrium value of n and show that n approaches this value monotonically.

2.10 Describe how the evolution of the population of a single species with an age distribution may be modelled by the matrix equation

$$N(t + T) = \mathbf{A}N(t).$$

Identify the elements of the column matrices $N(t)$ and $N(t + T)$ and of the Leslie matrix $\mathbf{A}$.

In a particular case the birth-rates of individuals whose ages are 0, 1, 2 and 3 years are 0, 5, 0 and $\frac{16}{3}$. The corresponding death-rates are $\frac{1}{4}$, $\frac{1}{2}$, $\frac{1}{2}$ and 1 (the individuals never survive beyond age 3). Show that the eigenvalues of the Leslie matrix satisfy the equation

$$\lambda^4 - a\lambda^2 - 1 = 0$$

and obtain the value of a. Find an eigenvector of A with maximum real eigenvalue. Describe the evolution in time of a population which has initially 128, 48, 12 and 3 individuals of ages 0, 1, 2 and 3 years, respectively.

2.11 Consider an animal species which breeds once every six months but which feeds on a plant which is annual. Justify the equation

$$n(m + 1) - n(m) = \frac{T}{\tau}\, n(m)\left(1 - \frac{n(m-2)}{N}\right) \qquad (m \text{ an integer})$$

as a suitable equation for the behaviour of the animal's population. What is the equilibrium population? Find the equation that describes small deviations from this equilibrium and when $T/\tau = \frac{3}{8}$, find the periods of oscillation of these deviations.

2.12 Consider the discrete 'logistic' difference equation (P2.7.6).

(i) Show, when $T/\tau < 1$, that if $n(T) < N$, then $y(mT) < N$ for all m, and how the solution of the above equation models the growth of yeast in a culture.

(ii) Suppose $2 < T/\tau < \sqrt{8}$. Express $n((m+1)T)$ in terms of $n((m-1)T)$, i.e. write

$$n((m+1)T) = F_2(n((m-1)T)).$$

The transformation F_2 has four equilibria: $n = 0, N$ are unstable, the others are asymptotically stable. Find them and describe the behaviour of $n(mT)$ for large m.

2.13 Show that when $T/\tau = \frac{1}{4}$, the solution of equation (P2.9.3) is

$$y(mT) = (\tfrac{1}{2})^m \quad (Am + B)$$

and that $n(mT) \to N$ monotically as $m \to \infty$.

2.14 A herd consists of a large (fixed) number of cows. Each cow can move freely between two fields A and B. The probability per unit time that any particular cow in A will migrate to B is a constant W. The grazing in A is better than in B, so that the corresponding probability for migration from B to A is $11W$. Write down differential equations which describe the change with time of the cow populations n_A, n_B in A and B respectively and show that at equilibrium $n_A/n_B = 11$.

When food is placed in a trough in B, the net number of migrations from A to B is increased by an amount $bW(4n_B^2 - 3n_B^3/N)/N$ where b is a positive constant (< 11) depending on the amount of food. Obtain a differential equation of the form $dx/dt = Wf(x)$ where $x = n_B/N$. Sketch $f(x)$ in the cases: (i) $b = 1$; (ii) $b = 9$; (iii) $b = 11$, indicating the approximate position of any equilibrium points. Determine their stability. Comment briefly on your results.

2.15$^{(m)}$ Consider the population behaviour of a species of small bird, e.g. a sparrow. They breed during the spring and summer; there is a lot of predation of the young birds in the summer and autumn, and many birds die during the winter owing to the cold and the lack of food. What is the maximum age of the species in the wild? Model the age-structure of the population as the seasons vary. Start with a simple linear model. The total number does not vary much year by year: can you develop a model which ensured that the population returned to its equilibrium value after a large fluctuation caused, for example, by a hard winter?

2.16$^{(m)}$ It takes time for a fish to reach maturity. Consider what effects this has on the fishing model of P2.5; include the effect of arranging net sizes so that only mature fish are caught.

2.17$^{(m)}$ Some interesting effects on the age distribution of the human population have occurred recently in industrialized countries:

(i) older industrial cities have declined and new 'garden' towns have been constructed. Model the age distribution in these places and see how it varies in time. What effects are important for the planners?

(ii) owing to advances in health, people are living longer and owing to the pill, the birth-rate has dropped. Model these effects and see if the age distribution ever becomes stable again? People are also having children later, i.e. when aged over 30; also include this effect in your model.

CHAPTER P3

Interacting Species

P3.1 INTRODUCTION

As an example of the way two species can interact, let us consider a simplified model of the population behaviour of foxes and rabbits, in which it is assumed that the foxes eat nothing but rabbits. Let $x_1(t)$ and $x_2(t)$ denote the populations of rabbits and foxes respectively at time t. Then the food available to the foxes is proportional to $x_1(t)$, so that the rate at which the foxes increase is also proportional to $x_1(t)$. It is thus plausible that

$$\mathrm{d}x_2/\mathrm{d}t = -x_2/\tau_2 + a_2 x_1 x_2, \tag{P3.1.1}$$

where the term $a_2 x_1 x_2$ represents the rate of increase of foxes due to eating the rabbit population and the term $(-x_2/\tau_2)$ represents the rate at which the foxes would die out if there were no rabbits available.

Suppose the rabbits have an unlimited food supply and that the only reason for their population to remain finite is predation by foxes. The rate of predation may be presumed proportional to the number of times that rabbits and foxes meet, which is linearly proportional to both x_1 and x_2 in a first approximation. We thus write

$$\mathrm{d}x_1/\mathrm{d}t = x_1/\tau_1 - a_1 x_1 x_2. \tag{P3.1.2}$$

The two equations (P31.1) and (P31.2) are known as the Lotka–Volterra equations after the two men who first discussed them. They represent a typical **'predator–prey'** system and we shall analyse them more fully later in this chapter. Here we observe that the two equations form a closed, state-determined system (see SM1) in which the variables x_1 and x_2 are interrelated.

In this chapter we study systems of interacting populations. In most real situations there are many species, n say, interacting with each other. If time is considered as a continuous variable, and time-delays, breeding seasons and age-structure are neglected, the equations governing the populations sizes $x_1, \ldots, x_n$ have the form

$$\mathrm{d}x_i/\mathrm{d}t = f_i(x_1(t), x_2(t), \ldots, x_n(t), t) \quad i = 1, \ldots, n, \tag{P3.1.3}$$

where the functions f_i are real-valued functions. If the interaction with the environment is constant, the functions f_i do not explicitly depend on time and the system can be considered as closed. Then the equations (P3.1.3) become

$$\mathrm{d}x_i/\mathrm{d}t = f_i(x_1(t), x_2(t), \ldots, x_n(t)). \tag{P3.1.4}$$

Such a set of equations is said in mathematics to be **autonomous**.

In this chapter we mainly discuss systems where $n = 2$, because the mathematics when $n > 2$ is too complicated. None the less there is much of interest in two-species systems. Besides the predator–prey system there are two others: the **competing-species** system in which two species compete for the same food and the **symbiotic** system in which the two species help each other's reproduction.

The study of the equations (P3.1.3) is of great interest because they occur in many contexts. For instance, nth-order differential equations can often be transformed into the form (P3.1.3). As an example, consider the equation

$$\mathrm{d}^2y/\mathrm{d}t^2 = f_1(\mathrm{d}y/\mathrm{d}t, y). \tag{P3.1.5}$$

By writing

$$\mathrm{d}y/\mathrm{d}t = x_1, \quad y = x_2, \tag{P3.1.6}$$

we get equations of the form (P3.1.4):

$$\mathrm{d}x_1/\mathrm{d}t = f_1(x_1, x_2), \quad \mathrm{d}x_2/\mathrm{d}t = x_1. \tag{P3.1.7}$$

As population systems have many mathematical techniques in common we study the mathematics of the equations (P3.1.4) first (see P3.2 and P3.3). We then look at the real systems: in P3.4 we examine the competing-species system and in P3.5 the symbiotic system. P3.6, P3.7 and P3.8 are devoted to the predator–prey system, introducing a new mathematical concept, the **limit cycle**. In P3.9 we look at two-species behaviour from a general point of view.

P3.2 MATHEMATICAL TECHNIQUES: 1. TRAJECTORIES

In the next two sections we examine the mathematics of the equations (P3.1.4).

What do we want to get from these equations? The solutions perhaps? In general it is not possible to solve for x_i as an analytic function of t, and we have to use numerical methods, two of which are given at the end of this section.

Such solutions, however, are of limited use; we really need an overall picture of the shape of all the possible solutions and of how they depend on the initial conditions and the parameters of the equations. Thus we aim first to learn as much as possible about the solutions without actually finding them.

Trajectories

The space of points with coordinates $(x_1, x_2, \ldots, x_n)$ is known as **phase-space**, or when $n = 2$, the **phase-plane**. Consider a particular solution of (P3.1.4). For each value of t, it defines a point in phase-space, so that as t varies, this point traces out a **trajectory**, known sometimes as an **orbit** or **path**. The equation of the trajectory is found by eliminating t from (P3.1.4). When $n = 2$, we get

$$dx_2/dx_1 = f_2(x_1, x_2)/f_1(x_1, x_2). \qquad \text{(P3.2.1)}$$

The trajectories in our study are continuous and possess a direction for increasing t. We require these properties for any realistic model; they can also be proved mathematically under general conditions. The gradient of the trajectory at any given point is determined by its equation, e.g. by (P3.2.1). Thus trajectories cannot cross or touch, except where the gradient is not defined, i.e. at points where the functions f_i are all zero.

Such points are known as **equilibrium** points (or **critical** points). At them

$$f_i(x_1, x_2, \ldots, x_n) = 0 \quad i = 1, 2, \ldots, n. \qquad \text{(P3.2.2)}$$

Near such points, trajectory directions may change sharply. The behaviour of trajectories then needs special consideration and this is given in section P3.3.

Away from equilibrium points the trajectories undergo no sharp changes of direction. It is then possible to sketch the trajectories. This is best done by the method of **isoclines**: an isocline is a curve in phase-space on which the trajectory has a fixed gradient. On each isocline, some dashes with the correct gradient are drawn. These **lineal elements** are the tangents to the trajectories at the point where the trajectory and the isocline meet. If sufficient isoclines and lineal elements are drawn, some of them can be joined to form parts of the trajectories. A trajectory's direction has, however, to be got from the original equations (P3.1.4).

When there are only two variables, we call the curve $f_2 = 0$ the **zero isocline** and the curve $f_1 = 0$ the **infinite isocline**, as the gradient of the trajectories at these isoclines is zero and infinite respectively. It is also convenient to fix the **direction** by the angle between the positive direction of the trajectory's tangent and the positive direction of the x_1-axis. This angle lies between $-\pi$ and π.

Let us illustrate the isocline method by using the equations of our 'foxes and rabbits' model. Equation (P3.2.1) becomes

$$dx_2/dx_1 = (-x_2/\tau_2 + a_2x_1x_2)/(x_1/\tau_1 - a_1x_1x_2). \qquad \text{(P3.2.3)}$$

For an example put $2\tau_1 = \tau_2 = 1$ and $a_1 = a_2 = \frac{1}{300}$. The zero and infinite isoclines are the straight lines $x_1 = 300$ and $x_2 = 300$ respectively; for $dx_2/dx_1 = -\frac{1}{2}$ the isocline is the line $x_2 = x_1$ and for $dx_2/dx_1 = 1$, it is the rectangular hyperbola

$$x_1x_2 - 100x_1 - 100x_2 = 0. \qquad \text{(P3.2.4)}$$

These isoclines and some of their lineal elements are shown in Fig. P3.1. They should be compared with the actual trajectories, which are shown in Fig. P3.9.

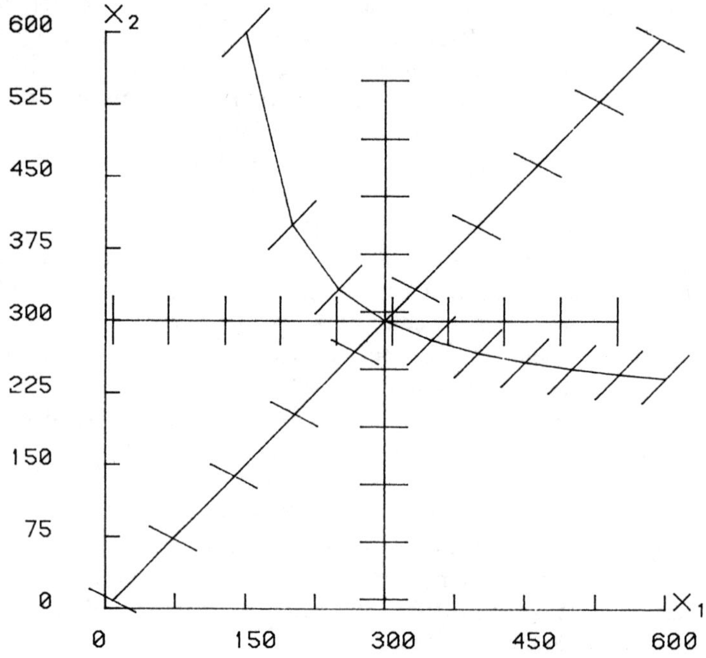

Fig. P3.1. Isoclines and lineal elements for equation (P3.2.3).

Numerical methods

If we want more exact pictures of the trajectories and/or the dependence of the populations on time we usually have to use numerical methods. We briefly describe two such methods here; for fuller details the reader is referred to specialist books on numerical analysis. We restrict discussion to systems with $n = 2$.

It is easiest to work with the equations (P3.1.4): we can then also find the variation of the populations with t. The time is divided up into a set of discrete intervals, such that the time is t_m at the end of the mth interval. We write

$$h_m = t_m - t_{m-1}, \quad x_i(m) = x_i(t_m),$$
$$f_i(m) = f_i(x_1(t_m), x_2(t_m)). \qquad \text{(P3.2.5)}$$

A crude estimate of $x_i(m)$ is $y_i^{(m)}$, where

$$y_i(m) = x_i(m-1) + h_m f_i(m-1). \tag{P3.2.6}$$

The **improved Euler method** gives a better estimate of $x_i(m)$: we write the differential equations (P3.1.4) as integral equations:

$$x_i(m) = x_i(m-1) + \int f_i(x_1, x_2)\, \mathrm{d}t. \tag{P3.2.7}$$

The integral cannot be obtained analytically, so that we use the trapezoidal rule:

$$x_i(m) = x_i(m-1) + h_m (f_i(m-1) + f_i(m))/2. \tag{P3.2.8}$$

This equation is called an *implicit* equation because $x_i(m)$, the required result, appears on the R.H.S. If this equation is solved exactly the result may, in certain circumstances, be very inaccurate. The approximate solution got by putting the estimate $y_i(m)$ in the R.H.S. of (P3.2.8) does not suffer in this way:

$$x_i(m) = x_i(m-1) + \tfrac{1}{2}h_m (f_i(m-1) + f_i(y_1(m), y_2(m))). \tag{P3.2.9}$$

This gives an *explicit* formula for $x_i(m)$ which can be evaluated immediately. The local truncation error in this method is of order h_m^2.

The Runge–Kutta Method

To get a more accurate value of $x_i(m)$, the integral in (P3.2.7) needs to be evaluated by a better method. This can be done by taking a weighted average of values of f_i at different points in the interval. The method has the same advantages over the improved Euler method that Simpson's rule has over the trapezoidal rule in numerical integration. Like Simpson's rule, the method requires two equal intervals and hence determines $x_i(m+1)$. We therefore write

$$\begin{aligned}
h_{m+1} &= h_m, & f_i^{(y)}(m) &= f_i(y_1(m), y_2(m)),\\
z_i(m) &= x_i(m-1) + h_m f_i^{(y)}(m), & f_i^{(z)}(m) &= f_i(z_1(m), x_2(m)),\\
u_i(m) &= x_i(m-1) + 2h_m f_i^{(z)}(m), & f_i^{(u)}(m) &= f_i(u_1(m), u_2(m)).
\end{aligned} \tag{P3.2.10}$$

Then the Runge–Kutta formula for $x_i(m+1)$ is

$$x_i(m+1) = x_i(m-1) + h_m(f_i(m-1) + 2f_i^{(y)}(m) + 2f_i^{(z)}(m) + f_i^{(u)}(m))/3. \tag{P3.2.11}$$

P3.3 MATHEMATICAL TECHNIQUES: 2. EQUILIBRIA

Trajectories often travel towards or away from equilibrium points, or change direction sharply near them. Thus to get an overall picture of the trajectories, their behaviour near the equilibrium points needs to be well understood. We look first at the equations (P3.1.4) for any n and then specialize to $n = 2$.

We adopt a vector notation, denoting a point $(x_1(t), x_2(t), \ldots, x_n(t))$ by $\mathbf{x}(t)$. Equations (P3.1.4) can then be written

$$\mathrm{d}\mathbf{x}(t)/\mathrm{d}t = \mathbf{f}(\mathbf{x}(t)). \tag{P3.3.1}$$

A vector function, like $\mathbf{f}(\mathbf{x})$, of a vector is known as a **vector field**. The equilibrium points are the solutions of the equations

$$\mathbf{f}(\mathbf{x}) = \mathbf{0}. \tag{P3.3.2}$$

Suppose $\mathbf{x}^{\mathrm{e}}$ is such an equilibrium point. Points $\mathbf{x}$ near $\mathbf{x}^{\mathrm{e}}$ can be written

$$\mathbf{x} = \mathbf{x}^{\mathrm{e}} + \epsilon(t), \tag{P3.3.3}$$

where the sizes of the components of ϵ are small in comparison with the sizes of the components of $(\mathbf{x}' - \mathbf{x}^{\mathrm{e}})$ where $\mathbf{x}'$ is any other equilibrium point.

To find how the trajectories behave, we substitute (P3.3.3) into (P3.3.1):

$$\mathrm{d}\epsilon(t)/\mathrm{d}t = \mathbf{f}(\mathbf{x}^{\mathrm{e}} + \epsilon(t)) \tag{P3.3.4}$$

$$= \mathbf{f}(\mathbf{x}^{\mathrm{e}}) + (\epsilon\,.\,\nabla)\,\mathbf{f}(\mathbf{x}^{\mathrm{e}}) + \mathbf{O}(\epsilon^2), \tag{P3.3.5}$$

using the Taylor expansion of $\mathbf{f}$. From (P3.3.2), to first order in ϵ,

$$\mathrm{d}\epsilon(t)/\mathrm{d}t = (\epsilon\,.\,\nabla)\,\mathbf{f}(\mathbf{x}^{\mathrm{e}}), \tag{P3.3.6}$$

or in suffix notation

$$\mathrm{d}\epsilon_i(t)/\mathrm{d}t = \sum_j (\partial f_i/\partial x_j)\,\epsilon_j(t), \tag{P3.3.7}$$

where $\partial f_i/\partial x_j$ is evaluated at $\mathbf{x} = \mathbf{x}^{\mathrm{e}}$. The **community matrix**, A, has its ijth element, a_{ij}, as $\partial f_i/\partial x_j$ so that (P3.3.6) becomes

$$\mathrm{d}\epsilon/\mathrm{d}t = A\,.\,\epsilon. \tag{P3.3.8}$$

Neglecting terms of $\mathbf{O}(\epsilon^2)$ in (P3.3.5) is known as **linearizing** the equations near $\mathbf{x}^{\mathrm{e}}$, and the solution of (P3.3.8) as the **linearized** solution. To solve (P3.3.8) put

$$\epsilon(t) = \eta\,\exp(\lambda t), \tag{P3.3.9}$$

where η is independent of t. To satisfy (P3.3.8),

$$(A - \lambda I)\,.\,\eta = \mathbf{0}, \tag{P3.3.10}$$

where I is the unit $(n{*}n)$ matrix. Thus λ must be an eigenvalue of A.

There are n eigenvalues of A, some of which may be complex, as A, although real, is not necessarily symmetric. For a particular eigenvalue λ, ϵ grows or diminishes in size if the real part of λ is positive or negative respectively, so that correspondingly $\mathbf{x}(t)$ moves away from or closer to $\mathbf{x}^{\mathrm{e}}$.

To discover the actual motion, not only do we need the values of λ, but also the eigenvectors η. If all the eigenvalues are different, each eigenvalue λ has a correspondingly eigenvector η_λ, where

$$(A - \lambda I)\,.\,\eta_\lambda = \mathbf{0}. \tag{P3.3.11}$$

Then the actual solution of (P3.3.8) is a linear combination of the solutions (P3.3.9):

$$\epsilon(t) = \sum_{\lambda} b_\lambda \, \eta_\lambda \exp(\lambda t), \tag{P3.3.12}$$

where the coefficients b_λ depend on the initial conditons. Thus if any of the eigenvalues λ have positive real parts, $\epsilon(t)$ in general grows larger and the equilibrium point is said to be **unstable**. If all of the eigenvalues λ have negative real parts, then $\epsilon(t)$ grows smaller, $\mathbf{x}(t)$ moves towards $\mathbf{x}^{\mathrm{e}}$ and the equilibrium point is said to be **asymptotically stable.**

The opposite to being unstable is being **stable**. An equilibrium point where the real parts of the eigenvalues are all zero may not be unstable, in which case it is stable. It does not, however, have to be asymptotically stable.

The initial conditions determine the parameters b_λ so that $\epsilon(t)$ is known for $t > 0$. To draw general pictures of trajectories, however, t can be given any value, even a negative one, and several different sets of initial conditions can be used.

Stability of equilibria

We now investigate the behaviour of trajectories near equilibrium points and hence their stability. We only consider the case $n = 2$.

The matrix A is 2*2 and has two eigenvalues λ_1 and λ_2. These are either both real or both complex conjugates, as the characteristic equation is real. Except when the eigenvalues are equal, the general linearized solution near $\mathbf{x}^{\mathrm{e}}$ is

$$\mathbf{x}(t) = \mathbf{x}^{\mathrm{e}} + b_1 \, \eta_1 \exp(\lambda_1 t) + b_2 \, \eta_2 \exp(\lambda_2 t). \tag{P3.3.13}$$

Let us investigate the possible cases:

(i) *both real*: $\lambda_1 > \lambda_2 > 0$.
The equilibirum point is unstable. For $t < 0$, $\exp(\lambda_1 t) < \exp(\lambda_2 t)$ so that by taking $t \to -\infty$ we see that all the trajectories except one have a tangent at $\mathbf{x}^{\mathrm{e}}$ parallel to η_2; one trajectory, which occurs when $b_2 = 0$, has a tangent parallel to η_1. This type of equilibrium is called an **improper node.**

The point (1, 1) is an equilibrium point for the set of equations

$$\mathrm{d}x_1/\mathrm{d}t = x_1(2x_1 + x_2 - 3), \quad \mathrm{d}x_2/\mathrm{d}t = x_2(x_1 + 2x_2 - 3). \tag{P3.3.14}$$

Then

$$A = \begin{bmatrix} 2 & 1 \\ 1 & 2 \end{bmatrix}, \tag{P3.3.15}$$

and has eigenvalues $\lambda_1 = 3, \lambda_2 = 1$. Thus this is an unstable improper node; it is illustrated in Fig. P3.2. The eigenvectors η_1 and η_2 are (1, 1) and (1, −1) respectively.

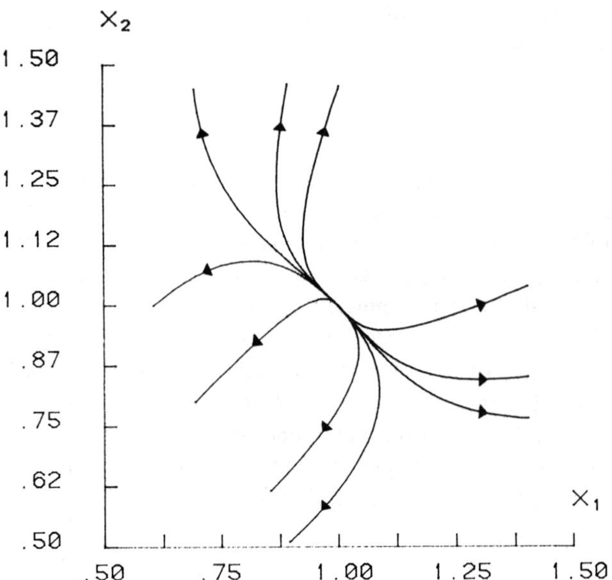

Fig. P3.2. Trajectories near the unstable improper node (1, 1) for equations (P3.3.14).

(ii) *both real*: $0 > \lambda_2 > \lambda_1$.
This is very similar to case (i) but is asymptotically stable. The substitution of $(-t)$ for t does not alter the trajectories but reverses their direction. The eigenvalues are also altered in sign: thus Fig. P3.2 with arrows reversed is a typical example of this behaviour. This type of equilibrium point is also called an improper node.

** (iii) *both real and equal*: $\lambda_1 = \lambda_2$.
If $a_{12} = a_{21} = 0$, then $a_{11} = a_{22}$ and the solutions are

$$\epsilon_i = X_i \exp(-a_{11}t), \tag{P3.3.16}$$

where the numbers X_i are independent of each other and depend only on the initial conditions. The equilibrium point is called a **proper node** because the trajectories approach (if $a_{11} < 0$) or recede (if $a_{11} > 0$) from it in all possible directions.

When at least one of a_{12}, a_{21} is non-zero, the linearized solution is

$$\mathbf{x} - \mathbf{x}^e = (\mathbf{X} + b_1\ \mathbf{Y}t)\exp(\lambda t), \tag{P3.3.17}$$

where **Y** is the eigenvector corresponding to λ, and **X** satisfies

$$\mathbf{X} + b_1\mathbf{Y} = A\ .\mathbf{X}. \tag{P3.3.18}$$

This equation (P3.3.18) with the initial conditions determines **X** and b_1. By letting $t \to \pm\infty$ according as $\lambda \gtrless 0$, we see that the trajectories are tangential to **Y**. Thus this point is another example of an improper node.

(iv) *both real*: $\lambda_1 > 0 > \lambda_2$.
This equilibrium point is unstable. By taking t large and both positive and negative, it can be seen that the trajectories tend to be tangential to both eigenvectors. The direction in which they travel is towards the eigenvector with the positive eigenvalue. This equilibrium is called a **saddle-point**.

The point (1, 1) is a saddle-point for the equations

$$dx_1/dt = x_1(x_1 + 4x_2 - 5), \quad dx_2/dt = x_2(x_1 + x_2 - 2). \tag{P3.3.19}$$

Then

$$A = \begin{bmatrix} 1 & 4 \\ 1 & 1 \end{bmatrix} \tag{P3.3.20}$$

and has eigenvalues 3, −1 and corresponding eigenvectors (2, 1) and (2, −1). The trajectories near (1, 1) are shown in Fig. P3.3.

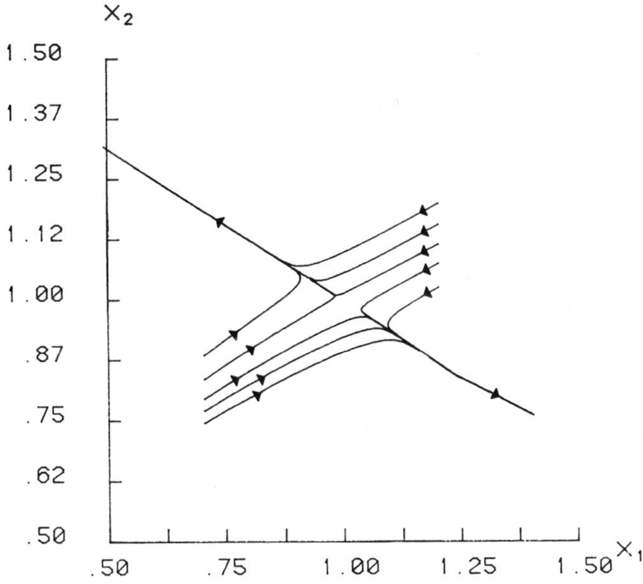

Fig. P3.3. Trajectories near the saddle-point (1, 1) of the equations (P3.3.19). Note how the lines through (1, 1) with gradients $\pm \frac{1}{2}$ are tangents. The trajectories travelling away from (1, 1) are separate, but by very small amounts.

(v) *Pure imaginary*: $\lambda_{1,2} = + i\mu$.
The general linearized solution is

$$\mathbf{x}(t) - \mathbf{x}^e = (X_1 \xi_1 + X_2 \xi_2)\cos(\mu t) + (X_2 \xi_1 - X_1 \xi_2)\sin(\mu t), \tag{P3.3.21}$$

where $(\xi_1 \pm i\xi_2)$ are the eigenvectors, and X_1, X_2 are real parameters determined by the initial conditions. The trajectory (P3.3.21) is an ellipse; it does not move away from or towards $\mathbf{x}^e$; it is stable, not asymptotically stable. The equilibrium point is a **centre**. The meet (300, 300) of the zero and infinite isoclines in equations (P3.1.1–P3.1.2) is a centre (see Fig. P3.1). The trajectories are shown in Fig. P3.9.

(vi) *Complex conjugates*: $\lambda_{1,2} = \lambda \pm i\mu \ (\lambda \neq 0)$.
The general linearized solution is similar to (P3.3.21):

$$\mathbf{x}(t) = \mathbf{x}^e + \exp(\lambda t)\left((X_1\, \xi_1 + X_2\, \xi_2)\cos(\mu t) + (X_2\, \xi_1 - X_1\, \xi_2)\sin(\mu t)\right). \qquad \text{(P3.3.22)}$$

If $\lambda < 0$, $|\mathbf{x}(t) \to \mathbf{x}^e| \to 0$ as $t \to \infty$ and $\mathbf{x}^e$ is asymptotically stable. If $\lambda > 0$, $\mathbf{x}^e$ is unstable.

The trajectories would be ellipses, if $\lambda = 0$. For $\lambda \neq 0$, the trajectories spiral away from or towards $\mathbf{x}^e$. The equilibrium point is known as a **spiral point**.

The behaviour of the trajectories can be shown more rigorously using polar coordinates (see below). Here we look at a simple example: consider the equations

$$\mathrm{d}x_1/\mathrm{d}t = x_1 - 2x_2 + 1, \quad \mathrm{d}x_2/\mathrm{d}t = 2x_1 + x_2 - 3, \qquad \text{(P3.3.23)}$$

which have an equilibrium point at (1, 1). The eigenvalues are (1 + 2i) with

$$\xi_1 = (1, 0), \quad \xi_2 = (0, -1). \qquad \text{(P3.3.24)}$$

Thus the solutions are

$$x_1 - 1 = \exp(t)\,(X_1 \cos(2t) + X_2 \sin(2t)),$$
$$x_2 - 1 = \exp(t)\,(X_1 \sin(2t) - X_2 \cos(2t)), \qquad \text{(P3.3.25)}$$

so that

$$(x_1 - 1)^2 + (x_2 - 1)^2 = \exp(2t)\,(X_1^2 + X_2^2). \qquad \text{(P3.3.26)}$$

Some trajectories are sketched in Fig. P3.4.

Summary

A summary of our results obtained by a first-order analysis is given in Table P3.1

Eigenvalues		Type of equilibrium point	Stability
$\lambda_1 > \lambda_2 > 0$		Improper node	Unstable
$\lambda_1 < \lambda_2 < 0$		Improper node	Asymptotically stable
$\lambda_2 < 0 < \lambda_1$		Saddle-point	Unstable
$\lambda_1 = \lambda_2 > 0$		Proper or improper node	Unstable
$\lambda_1 = \lambda_2 > 0$		Proper or improper node	Asymptotically stable
$\lambda_{1,2} = \pm i\mu$		Centre	Stable
$\lambda_{1,2} = \lambda \pm i\mu$		Spiral point	
	$\lambda > 0$		Unstable
	$\lambda < 0$		Asymptotically stable

Table P3.1. Summary of behaviour near equilibrium points.

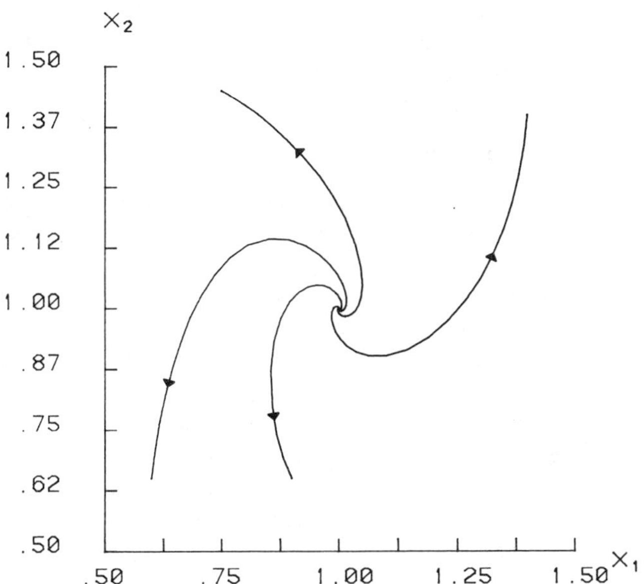

Fig. P3.4. Trajectories near the spiral point (1, 1) of the equations (P3.3.23).

* Polar coordinates

These are coordinates r, θ satisfying

$$x_1 = r\cos(\theta) \qquad x_2 = r\sin(\theta). \tag{P3.3.27}$$

The distance between the origin and the point (x_1, x_2) is r, and θ is the angle between the x_1-axis and the line joining the origin to (x_1, x_2). Differentiation gives

$$\mathrm{d}r/\mathrm{d}t = (x_1\,\mathrm{d}x_1/\mathrm{d}t + x_2\,\mathrm{d}x_2/\mathrm{d}t)/(x_1^2 + x_2^2)^{1/2}, \tag{P3.3.28}$$

$$\mathrm{d}\theta/\mathrm{d}t = (x_1\,\mathrm{d}x_2/\mathrm{d}t - x_2\,\mathrm{d}x_1/\mathrm{d}t)/(x_1^2 + x_2^2). \tag{P3.3.29}$$

To use polar coordinates for the behaviour near an equilibrium point $\mathbf{x}^e$, we shift the origin to $\mathbf{x}^e$ and write

$$\epsilon_1 = r\cos(\theta) \qquad \epsilon_2 = r\sin(\theta). \tag{P3.3.27a}$$

Then from (P3.3.8) and (P3.3.29),

$$\begin{aligned}\mathrm{d}\theta/\mathrm{d}t &= (a_{21}\,\epsilon_1^2 + (a_{22} - a_{11}) - a_{12}\,\epsilon_2^2)/(\epsilon_1^2 + \epsilon_2^2)\\ &= ((2a_{21}(\epsilon_1 + (a_{22} - a_{11})\,\epsilon_2/2a_{21}))^2 - ((a_{22} - a_{11})^2 + 4a_{12}\,a_{21})\,\epsilon_2^2)/4a_{21}.\end{aligned} \tag{P3.3.30}$$

In case (iv) the condition for complex roots is

$$(a_{22} - a_{11})^2 + 4a_{12}\,a_{21} < 0, \tag{P3.3.31}$$

so that the numerator in (P3.3.30) is always positive. Then $d\theta/dt$ has a constant sign, that of a_{21}. Thus if $a_{21} > 0$, θ always increases and the spiral travels anti-clockwise, and if $a_{21} < 0$, it travels clockwise.

** Second-order terms

In our discussion we have only included first-order terms; is this valid? Does the inclusion of second-order terms have any effect on the type of equilibrium point?

In most cases the first-order approximation is valid. It is only when there is a possibility of the first-order terms cancelling each other that second-order terms have to be considered in the determination of the type of equilibrium. This can happen when the two eigenvalues are equal, giving the possibility that the equilibrium may also be a spiral point, and, more importantly, when the two eigenvalues are pure imaginary. In this case the inclusion of the non-linear terms can change the predicted stability. The equilibrium can now be either a spiral point, which is either unstable or asymptotically stable, or a stable centre.

Consider the example

$$dx_1/dt = -x_2 + x_1(x_1^2 + x_2^2)^{1/2},$$
$$dx_2/dt = x_1 + x_2(x_1^2 + x_2^2)^{1/2}. \qquad \text{(P3.3.32)}$$

The linear approximation predicts that the origin is a centre. Taking the non-linear terms into account using (P3.3.28)

$$dr/dt = x_1^2 + x_2^2 = r^2, \qquad \text{(P3.3.33)}$$

so that r is always increasing. Thus the origin is an unstable spiral point. Note that in (P3.3.33) there are no linear terms, i.e. they have cancelled each other out.

A centre is thus said to be **structurally unstable**, i.e. any small disturbance is likely to change such an equilibrium point to some totally different type. We shall observe this in the predator–prey system.

The analysis of equilibrium points using first-order theory does not cover all possibilities. What happens when there are no first-order terms? There can be a variety of behaviours: for example, at the point (a, b) the equations

$$dx_1/dt = x_1((x_1 - a)^2 - (x_2 - b)^2)$$
$$dx_2/dt = x_2(x_1 - a)^3\,(x_2 - b)^2 \qquad \text{(P3.3.34)}$$

are in equilibrium but the trajectories there are not like those near any first-order equilibrium points. These types rarely, if ever, occur in studies of animal populations.

* Relation between equilibria and the gradients of isoclines

The isoclines $f_i = 0$ meet at the equilibrium point and there have the gradient of

$$-(\partial f_i/\partial x_1)/(\partial f_i/\partial x_2) \qquad \text{(P3.3.35)}$$

$$= -a_{i1}/a_{i2}. \qquad \text{(P3.3.36)}$$

These gradients are thus related to the conditions which determine the type of equilibrium. For example, when the roots are real, a necessary and sufficient condition for the roots to have opposite signs, i.e. for a saddle-point, is that

$$(a_{11}+a_{22})^2 < (a_{22}-a_{11})^2 + 4a_{12}\,a_{21}, \qquad \text{(P3.3.37)}$$

i.e.

$$a_{11}\,a_{22} < a_{12}\,a_{21}, \qquad \text{(P3.3.38)}$$

which is the same as

$$(\partial f_1/\partial x_2)\,(\partial f_2/\partial x_1) > (\partial f_1/\partial x_1)\,(\partial f_2/\partial x_2). \qquad \text{(P3.3.39)}$$

This can be related to the gradients in certain circumstances.

P3.4 TWO COMPETING SPECIES

In this and most of the following sections, i.e. P3.5, 3.6, 3.7 and 3.9, we look at mathematical models of the population dynamics of two interacting species. We only discuss models in which time is taken to be a continuous variable, and we neglect effects due to age-structure, breeding seasons, time-delays, etc. In P3.9, we adopt a general approach but in the other sections we develop specific models. In this section we look at a specific model which seeks to describe the population changes of two species which compete for the same food.

If only one species were present its population changes can be described in most circumstances by the logistic equation

$$\mathrm{d}x_i/\mathrm{d}t = (x_i/\tau_i)\,(1-x_i/N_i). \qquad \text{(P3.4.1)}$$

The effect of species j is to decrease the food supply to species i by an amount proportional to x_j. Thus the equations

$$\mathrm{d}x_i/\mathrm{d}t = (x_i/\tau_i)\,(1-x_i/N_i-\sigma_i x_j/N_j) \quad (j\neq i) \qquad \text{(P3.4.2)}$$

are a reasonable model for two competing species in the same circumstances in which the logistic equation is reasonable. In (P3.4.2) the parameters σ_i are positive numbers whose significance we shall see later. The populations N_i are called the **isolated equilibrium populations.**

These equations cannot be solved analytically; to get some results we need a picture of the trajectories. For this we look at the equilibria, which are given by:

$$x_i(1-x_i/N_i-\sigma_i x_j/N_j)=0 \quad (i\neq j). \qquad \text{(P3.4.3)}$$

There are thus four equilibrium points: we label them O, P, Q and R:

$$O\,(0,0),\quad P\,(0,N_2);\quad Q\,(N_1,0);$$

$$R\,((N_1(1-\sigma_1),\quad N_2(1-\sigma_2))/(1-\sigma_1\sigma_2)). \qquad \text{(P3.4.4)}$$

The origin O is an unstable, improper node; the stability of the other points depends on the size of the parameters σ_i.

As a specific example, let $N_1 = N_2 = 600$, $\sigma_1 = \sigma_2 = 2$, with $\tau_1 = \frac{1}{2}$ and $\tau_2 = 1$ year. The isolated equilibrium populations are both 600. Equations (P3.4.2) are now

$$dx_1/dt = 2x_1(1 - (x_1 + 2x_2)/600)$$

$$dx_2/dt = x_2(1 - (2x_1 + x_2)/600). \quad \text{(P3.4.5)}$$

The equilibrium points O, P, Q and R of these equations are

$$(0, 0), \quad (0, 600), \quad (600, 0), \quad (200, 200). \quad \text{(P3.4.6)}$$

Near the origin the community matrix A is

$$A = \begin{bmatrix} 2 & 0 \\ 0 & 1 \end{bmatrix}. \quad \text{(P3.4.7)}$$

The eigenvalues are 2 and 1 with corresponding eigenvectors (1, 0) and (0, 1). Thus the trajectories are tangential to the x_2-axis at the origin and O is an unstable improper node. A sketch of the trajectory behaviour near O is given in Fig. P3.5.

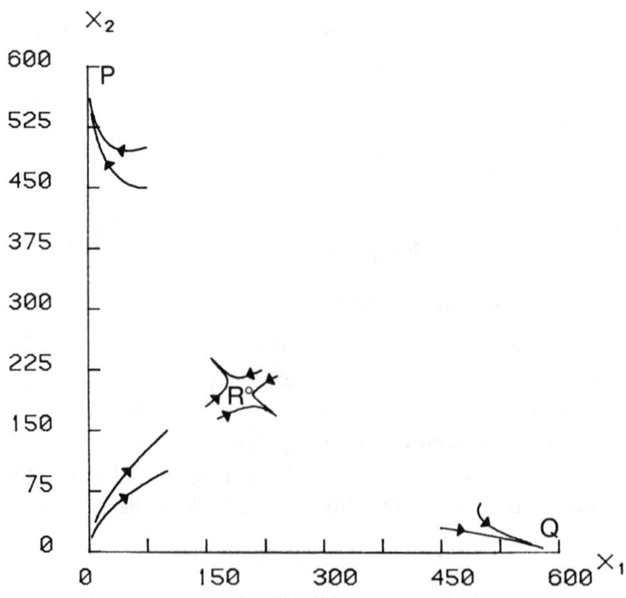

Fig. P3.5. Trajectories near the equilibrium points O, P, Q, R of the competing-species equations (P3.4.5).

To linearize around Q we write

$$x_1 = 600 + \epsilon_1, \quad x_2 = \epsilon_2. \tag{P3.4.8}$$

Thus

$$d\epsilon_1/dt = 1200\,(-\epsilon_1 - 2\epsilon_2)/600$$

$$d\epsilon_2/dt = -\epsilon_2. \tag{P3.4.9}$$

and

$$A = \begin{bmatrix} -2 & -4 \\ 0 & -1 \end{bmatrix}, \tag{P3.4.10}$$

and has eigenvalues -2, -1. The corresponding eigenvectors are $(1, 0)$ and $(-4, 1)$. This is an asymptotically stable improper node with the trajectories tangential to a line through Q with direction $(-4, 1)$.

Similarly the point P, $(0, 600)$, is an asymptotically stable improper node, with eigenvalues -2 and -1 and corresponding eigenvectors $(1, 2)$ and $(0, 1)$. Most of the trajectories are tangential to the x_2-axis at P.

To linearize about R, $(200, 200)$, we write

$$x_1 = 200 + \epsilon_1, \quad x_2 = 200 + \epsilon_2, \tag{P3.4.11}$$

giving

$$d\epsilon_1/dt = 400\,(-\epsilon_1/600 - 2\epsilon_2/600)$$

$$d\epsilon_2/dt = 200\,(-\epsilon_2/600 - 2\epsilon_1/600) \tag{P3.4.12}$$

and

$$A = \begin{bmatrix} -\frac{2}{3} & -\frac{4}{3} \\ -\frac{2}{3} & -\frac{1}{3} \end{bmatrix}. \tag{P3.4.13}$$

The eigenvalues are $(-1 \pm \sqrt{11/3})/2$, and R is a saddle-point. The corresponding eigenvectors are approximately $(1, -0.843)$ and $(1, 0.593)$. The behaviour of the trajectories near this point is also shown in Fig. P3.5.

To draw the trajectories, we need to find some isoclines. The zero and infinite isoclines are the straight lines QR, PR respectively. The direction of the trajectories changes sign along both lines when the point R is crossed. Another straight line which is an isocline is the line OR (this line is always an isocline for the equations (P3.4.2)). The isoclines are drawn in Fig. P3.6.

When this information is pieced together we get a general picture of the trajectories. In Fig. P3.7 are shown some trajectories got by numerical integration; note how well the qualitative arguments have predicted the actual results.

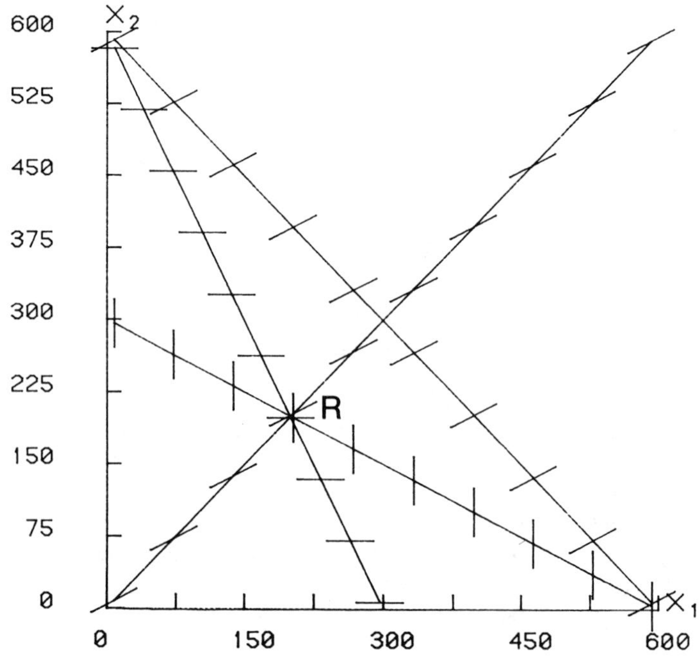

Fig. P3.6. Isoclines and lineal elements for the competing-species equations (P3.4.5).

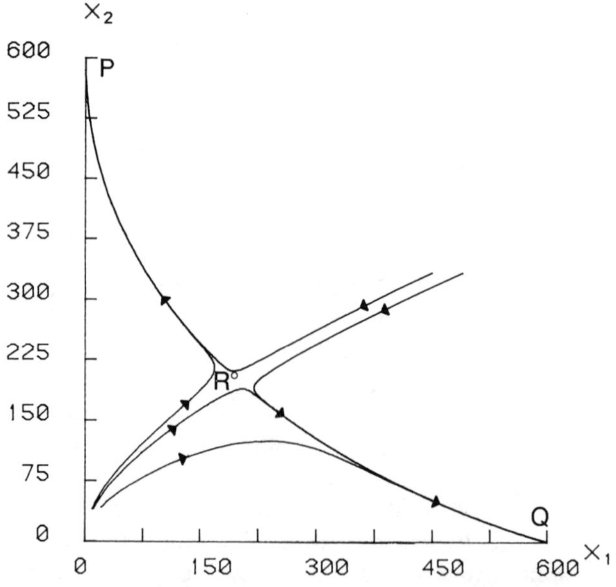

Fig. P3.7. Trajectories for the competing-species equations (P3.4.5).

Interpretation

How do we interpret the behaviour of these trajectories in terms of the actual populations? Consider an initial population of (20, 50). This is on a trajectory close to the origin and travels towards R, i.e. both populations increase to almost (200, 200). When close to R, the trajectory veers away towards Q, i.e. the population of the second species declines and eventually dies out, while x_1 reaches its isolated equilibrium value of 600. On the other hand, consider initial populations of (20, 70). Again the trajectory lies close to the origin and travels towards R, i.e. both populations increase to almost 200. When close to R the trajectory veers away towards P, i.e. the population of the first species declines and eventually dies out while x_2 increases to its isolated equilibrium value of 600. The behaviour of the populations with time is shown in Fig. P3.8.

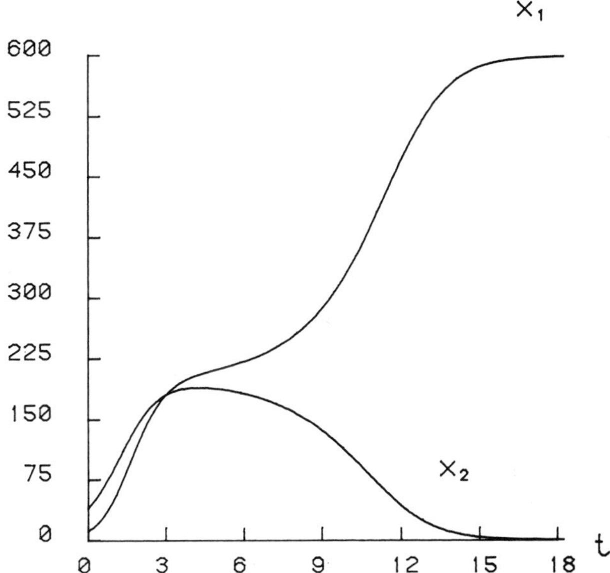

Fig. P3.8. The behaviour, with time, of the populations x_1, x_2 along the trajectory which ends at Q in Fig. P3.7.

As can be seen from Fig. P3.7, for almost all initial populations, one or other of the species dies out eventually. This result is the basis for 'Gause's principle': '*two species with identical requirements cannot co-exist in a habitat.*' There are several observations that seem to agree with this principle; for example, the mountain hare in Scotland has died out in lowland areas and been replaced by the common hare.

In our example, the parameters σ_1 and σ_2 are greater than one, and R is a saddle-point. When both σ_1 and σ_2 are less than one, the point R becomes an asymptotically stable improper node, and the points $(N_1, 0)$ and $(0, N_2)$ become saddle-points. Thus the trajectories travel towards R, which means that the two species co-exist. When $\sigma_1 < 1$ and $\sigma_2 > 1$, the point R is not in the first quadrant, and the point P, $(0, N_2)$, is a saddle-point. The point Q, $(N_1, 0)$, is the only asymptotically stable improper node, so that all the trajectories travel towards Q. This means that the second species always dies out. We leave the reader (see PE3.3 and PE3.4) to work out the details of these various situations.

The parameter σ_1 measures the number of requirements (food, habitat, etc.) of species 1 which can be consumed by species 2, relative to the total number of requirements of species 1; and it measures the relative abilities of the two species to acquire them. A more precise, more quantitative, definition is not possible.

The implications of our further results are obvious: if two species have identical requirements, one will die out, but if each has some separate requirements, they can co-exist. It thus 'pays' a species either to eat a variety of foods, or to find some ecological niche, e.g. different food or habitat, not used by any other species. Thus the actual size of the parameters σ_i is an important practical question.

In passing, the reader may like to note the unusual mathematical result we have obtained in Fig. P3.7: although (20, 50) and (20, 70) are points that are very close together, the trajectories through these points end at the points P and Q which are distant from each other.

P3.5 SYMBIOTIC BEHAVIOUR

There are numerous examples where the presence of one species helps the population growth of another and vice versa. For instance, a species of animal and a species of plant may help each other: the plant provides food for the animal and the animal helps in the reproduction processes of the plant, as with bees and flowers. Dairy farming, e.g. cows, is an example of a symbiotic relationship between cow and man, in which each species provides food for the other.

Consider a situation in which two species interact symbiotically. Each species may be able to exist independently of the other, or one or both may die out if the other is not present. Here we consider the model for the population behaviour of two species, one of which can exist independently whereas the other would die out if the first were not present. We might expect that a suitable set of equations for the population behaviour without the other's presence would be

$$\mathrm{d}x_1/\mathrm{d}t = (x_1/\tau_1)(1 - x_1/N_1),$$

$$\mathrm{d}x_2/\mathrm{d}t = -x_2/\tau_2. \tag{P3.5.1}$$

The effect of the presence of either species is to increase the birth-rate of the other species by an amount proportional to its population. This affects the relaxation times; does it affect the logistic effect, i.e. the value of N_1, for the first species? Let us assume at first that it does not. The equations then are

$$\mathrm{d}x_1/\mathrm{d}t = (x_1/\tau_1)(1 - x_1/N_1 + \sigma_1 x_2/N_2), \tag{P3.5.2a}$$

$$\mathrm{d}x_2/\mathrm{d}t = (x_1/\tau_2)(-1 + \sigma_2 x_1/N_1), \tag{P3.5.2b}$$

where all the parameters are positive. The two parameters σ_1 and N_2 have been introduced, but here only the quotient σ_1/N_2 is used.

These equations do not 'work': for the second species to survive, $\sigma_2 > 1$ but then x_2 can grow without limit. To overcome this problem, we include a logistic term for the second species, and then the equations become

$$\mathrm{d}x_1/\mathrm{d}t = (x_1/\tau_1)(1 - x_1/N_1 + \sigma_1 x_2/N_2), \quad \text{(P3.5.3a)}$$

$$\mathrm{d}x_2/\mathrm{d}t = (x_2/\tau_2)(-1 - x_2/N_2 + \sigma_2 x_1/N_1). \quad \text{(P3.5.3b)}$$

These equations still have problems: nevertheless it is instructive to analyse them. Note that σ_1 and N_2 are now separate parameters.

There are three equilibrium points, O, Q and R, with respective coordinates

$$(0, 0),\ (N_1, 0),\ ((N_1(1-\sigma_1)/(1-\sigma_1\sigma_2)),\quad (N_2(\sigma_2 - 1)/(1-\sigma_1\sigma_2))). \quad \text{(P3.5.4)}$$

For R to be in the first quadrant, σ_1 and σ_2 have to satisfy either of the following sets of conditions:

$$\sigma_1\sigma_2 < 1, \quad \sigma_1 < 1, \quad \sigma_2 > 1. \quad \text{(P3.5.5)}$$

$$\sigma_1\sigma_2 > 1, \quad \sigma_1 > 1, \quad \sigma_2 < 1. \quad \text{(P3.5.6)}$$

Under condition (P3.5.6), the point Q is asymptotically stable and R is a saddle-point, whereas under (P3.5.5), Q is a saddle-point and R is asymptotically stable. So with condition (P3.5.6) the second species dies out. It is only with condition (P3.5.5) that symbiosis occurs, because then all trajectories travel towards R. Then the presence of the second species increases the population of the first, as

$$N_1(1-\sigma_1)/(1-\sigma_1\sigma_2) > N_1. \quad \text{(P3.5.7)}$$

The parameters σ_i measure the amount that species i gains from the presence of the other. The requirement $\sigma_2 > 1$ shows that the second species must gain a considerable amount from the first species for it to survive. The requirement $\sigma_1 < 1$ acts to limit the populations: this condition is artificial, i.e. is not in accord with any real situation. In reality the population of the first species would be limited by logistic effects; thus we should have included in our equations an effect of symbiosis on the logistic term. This requires the introduction of another parameter, the equation for x_1 becoming

$$\mathrm{d}x_1/\mathrm{d}t = (x_1/\tau_2)(1 - x_1/N_1 + \sigma_1 x_2/N_2 - \rho_1 x_1 x_2/N_1 N_2). \quad \text{(P3.5.8)}$$

The mathematics is now more complicated, but the reader might like to investigate the case when $\rho_1 = 1$ and see that there are now no restrictions on σ_1.

The other situations in which symbiosis can occur can be analysed in a similar way. The interesting case is when both species would die out if the other were not present. Using equations of the form (P3.5.3b) leads to the origin being an asymptotically stable equilibrium point. The point R is usually a saddle-point, but can be a centre. Then the trajectories either travel towards the origin, in which cases both species die out, or travel towards infinity, i.e. both species increase without limit. This, then, is not a suitable model: to improve it, extra terms, as in (P3.5.8) for example, have to be included. This is discussed further in P3.9.

When both species can exist independently, equations such as (P3.5.2a) can 'work', provided the zero and infinite isoclines meet. We leave the reader to investigate this further (see PE3.10). A better model would, however, incorporate extra terms as in (P3.5.8).

P3.6 PREDATOR–PREY SYSTEMS

In P3.1 we introduced the Lotka–Volterra equations (P3.1.1–P3.2.1) as a model for the population behaviour of predator–prey systems. Let us now 'solve' them to see if the results are reasonable and in accord with the available experimental evidence.

There are two equilibrium points, the origin O and the point R at $(1/a_1\tau_1, 1/a_2\tau_2)$. The former is a saddle-point with the axes as eigenvectors. R is a centre, where the equations (P3.3.7) become

$$\mathrm{d}\epsilon_1/\mathrm{d}t = -a_1\epsilon_2/a_2\tau_2, \quad \mathrm{d}\epsilon_2/\mathrm{d}t = a_2\epsilon_1/a_1\tau_1. \tag{P3.6.1}$$

Thus near R, the trajectories are circles with centre R: it takes a time $2\pi\sqrt{\tau_1\tau_2}$ for the system to travel round one of these circles.

An analysis using the methods of P3.2 and P3.3 is unnecessary as the trajectories can be found analytically. Their equation is separable: we write it as

$$\mathrm{d}x_1(a_2x_1 - 1/\tau_2)/x_1 = \mathrm{d}x_2(1/\tau_2 - a_1x_2)/x_2, \tag{P3.6.2}$$

which can be integrated to give

$$Cx_1^{\tau_1}\,x_2^{\tau_2} = \exp(\tau_1\,\tau_2(a_2x_1 + a_1x_2)) \tag{P3.6.3}$$

where C is a constant of integration. For given x_1, there are zero or 2 solutions for x_2, and vice versa, so that the trajectories (P3.6.3) are closed curves (see Fig. 3.9), which become circles near R (see PE3.12).

Another way (see PE3.12) of solving (P3.1.1–P3.1.2) is to show that the expression

$$\ln(C(t)) = \tau_1\tau_2(a_2x_1 + a_1x_2) - \ln((x_1)^{\tau_1}\,(x_2)^{\tau_2}) \tag{P3.6.4}$$

is a constant of the motion.

The Lotka–Volterra equations thus predict oscillatory behaviour for both populations. It is not possible to solve analytically for the populations in terms of the time t, so that it is not easy to see how the period T of oscillation varies with the particular trajectory under consideration. Nevertheless it can be seen that the trough in the prey population precedes that of the predator population by at least $\pi\sqrt{\tau_1\tau_2}/2$. The average population over a period can be found easily: integrating (P3.1.1) from a time t_0 to a time $(t_0 + T)$, i.e. over a period, we get

$$\ln(x_2(t_0 + T)/x_2(t_0)) = -T/\tau_2 + a_2\int_0^T x_2(t)\mathrm{d}t. \tag{P3.6.5}$$

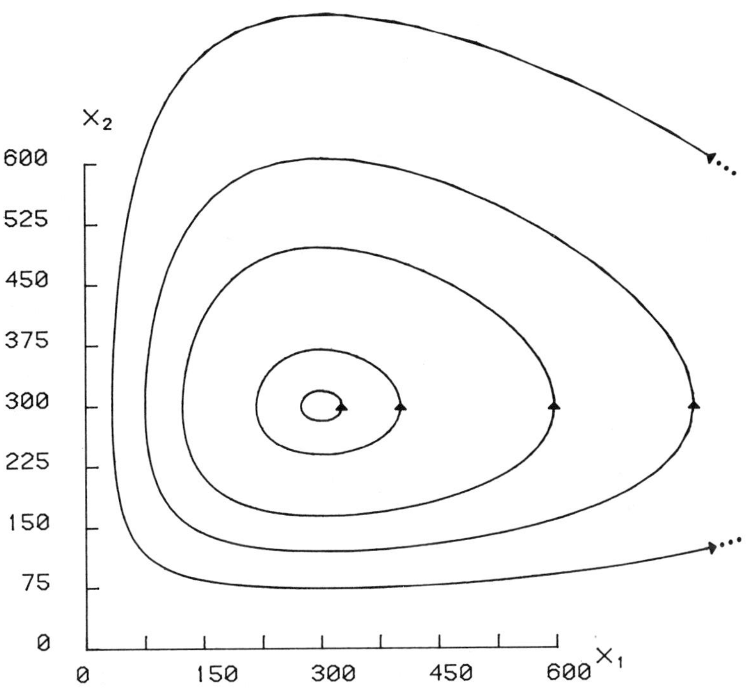

Fig. P3.9. Trajectories for the Lotka–Volterra equations of (P3.2.3).

The left-hand side is zero so that

$$(1/T)\int_0^T x_2(t)\mathrm{d}t = -1/a_2\tau_2, \tag{P3.6.6}$$

i.e. the average predator population is the same as it would be if the populations were at the equilibrium point R, no matter which trajectory is being considered.

There are several biological systems which show the kind of oscillations shown by the solutions of the Lotka–Volterra equations. The populations of sharks and fish in the Adriatic Sea is one, and this behaviour was the original reason for Volterra's interest. Another example is the populations of lynx and snowshoe hare in Canada (see Fig. P3.10). This shows a fairly consistent periodic cycle with a period of between 9 and 10 years. The peak populations vary in size, but this variation has little effect on the period of oscillations. The troughs in the lynx population occur simultaneously or just after the troughs in the hare population.

At first sight this looks like a triumph for the model. There are, however, some disturbing features. Besides the systems that show oscillations there are many real predator–prey systems that seem to show no oscillatory behaviour. The (Lotka–Volterra) model cannot explain both types of behaviour satisfactorily. There are also discrepancies in the agreement with experiment: for example, the model cannot predict the closeness in time between the troughs of the two populations. More worrying is the lack of stability of the model's

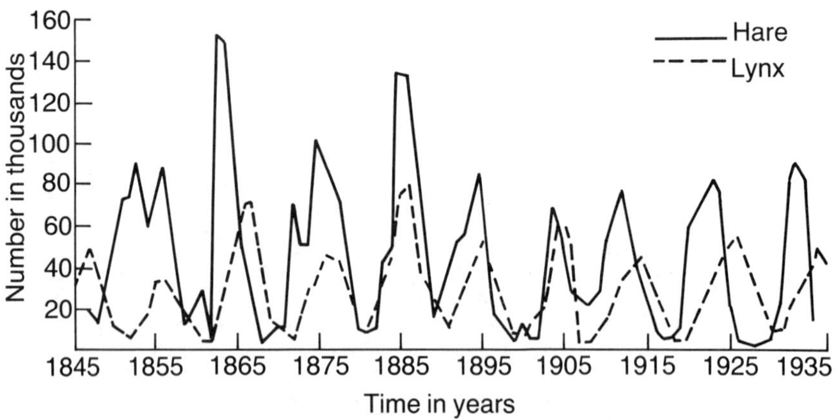

Fig. P3.10. Population cycles in the lynx and its principal prey, the snowshoe hare, in Canada. The vertical axis gives the number of pelts received by the Hudson Bay Company. (After D. A. MacLulich (1937), 'Fluctuations in the numbers of the varying hare (*Lepus americanus*), University of Toronto Studies, Biol. Ser., No. 43.)

behaviour: once on a trajectory the system stays on that trajectory but, if disturbed, the system moves to another trajectory on which it stays, i.e. there is no stabilizing force restoring the system to the original trajectory. A real system experiences many disturbances (owing to the weather, food supply, etc.) and yet the lynx–hare system shows remarkable stability in its oscillatory behaviour.

Another worrying aspect of the L–V model is its structural instability: as we remarked in P3.3, any small additional term in the equations with a centre may change the centre to another type of equilibrium point, without oscillatory behaviour. This is illustrated when we try to improve the model by the inclusion of logistic effects. The equations become

$$\mathrm{d}x_1/\mathrm{d}t = (x_1/\tau_1)(1 - x_1/N_1 - \sigma_1 x_2/N_2), \tag{P3.6.7}$$

$$\mathrm{d}x_2/\mathrm{d}t = (x_2/\tau_2)(-1 - x_2/N_2 + \sigma_2 x_1/N_1), \tag{P3.6.8}$$

where we have written $a_1 = \sigma_1/N_2\tau_1$, $a_2 = \sigma_2/N_1\tau_2$ to conform with previous notation. There are now three equilibrium points, O, Q and R, with coordinates $(0, 0)$, $(N_1, 0)$ and $((N_1(1 + \sigma_1)/(1 + \sigma_1\sigma_2)), (N_2(\sigma_2 - 1)/(1 + \sigma_1\sigma_2)))$ respectively. To stop the predators dying out, we require $\sigma_1 > 1$. Then O and Q are saddle-points and R is an asymptotically stable spiral point for realistic values of the parameters. A trajectory is shown in Fig. P3.11.

In this case the oscillations are damped, dying off with a relaxation rate

$$(1 + \sigma_1\sigma_2)\tau_1\tau_2/((1 + \sigma_1)\tau_2 + \tau_1(\sigma_2 - 1)), \tag{P3.6.9}$$

which is quite rapid.

Such a prediction is in accord with those real systems which show no oscillations. The equations (P3.6.7–P3.6.8) are a more realistic version of the L–V equations; however, they need modification if they are also to model those

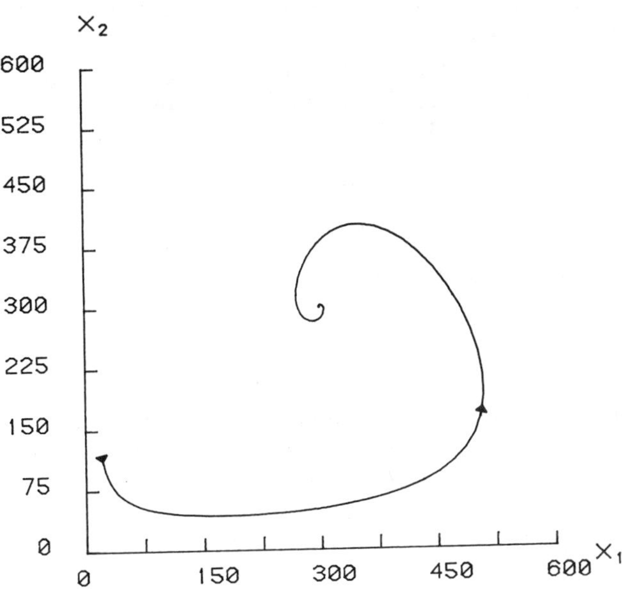

Fig. P3.11. A spiral trajectory for the Lotka–Volterra equations with logistic terms (see equations (P3.6.7–P3.6.8)).

systems which exhibit stable oscillations. To do this, how should we proceed? There are two questions to be asked: the first is 'have we a mathematical concept which gives stable oscillations for a system like the predator–prey system?' and the second is 'what is the specific mechanism which leads to these oscillations?' The former question is tackled in the next section, P3.7, and the latter in P3.8.

** P3.7 LIMIT CYCLES

The experimental evidence suggests that some predator–prey systems show stable oscillatory behaviour. Because of the fluctuating environment, this behaviour must be asymptotically stable. Thus we need a mathematical concept which provides asymptotically stable closed trajectories; also only a few such trajectories should exist. The set of trajectories around a centre is not a suitable candidate for such a concept as there is no asymptotic stability, there are an infinite number of closed trajectories and the system is structurally unstable.

The concept with the required behaviour is a **limit cycle**. This is a closed path to which neighbouring trajectories travel either as $t \to \infty$ or as $t \to -\infty$.

The idea is best illustrated by an example. Consider the equations

$$\mathrm{d}x_1/\mathrm{d}t = x_1 + x_2 - x_1 r^2, \quad \mathrm{d}x_2/\mathrm{d}t = -x_1 + x_2 - x_2 r^2, \tag{P3.7.1}$$

which are defined for all values of x_1, x_2, positive and negative. The only equilibrium point is the origin, and this is an unstable spiral point. We might expect all trajectories to spiral outwards from the origin, but this does not happen because the cubic terms in (P3.7.1) drive them back towards the origin.

To see this more clearly, we introduce polar coordinates. From (P3.3.38)

$$r\,\mathrm{d}r/\mathrm{d}t = r^2\,(1 - r^2), \tag{P3.7.2}$$

$$\mathrm{d}\theta/\mathrm{d}t = -1, \tag{P3.7.3}$$

both of which can be integrated:

$$\theta = -t + C, \tag{P3.7.4}$$

$$r = (D/(D + \exp(-2t))^{1/2}). \tag{P3.7.5}$$

C and D are constants of integration. Some trajectories are sketched in Fig. P3.12. It can be seen that as $t \to \infty$, all the trajectories tend to the unit circle whose centre is O. Thus this circle is a limit cycle.

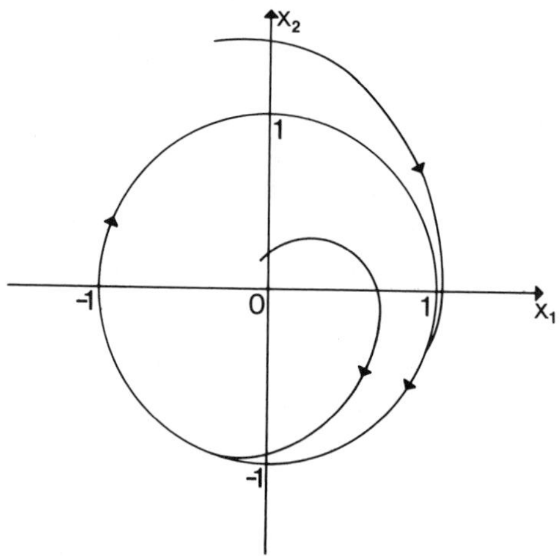

Fig. P3.12. Sketch of two trajectories and the limit cycle ($x_1^2 + x_2^2 = 1$) for the equations (P3.7.1).

A limit cycle divides its neighbourhood into two regions, an *inside* and an *outside*: it is said to be **stable** if the trajectories travel towards it on both sides, **semi-stable** if they only travel towards it on one side, and **unstable** if they go away from it on both sides. Our example is stable.

When making mathematical models it is useful to know when limit cycles occur and what mathematical effects cause them. Two theorems are useful in this respect; we state but do not prove them.

Theorem P3.7.1. Suppose the functions f_1, f_2 in equations (P3.1.4) for two variables have continuous partial derivatives in a domain D. *Any close trajectory in* D *must enclose at least one equilibrium point. If it encloses only one, the equilibrium point cannot be a saddle-point.*

This theorem helps us to form a typical picture of how a stable limit cycle with only one equilibrium point within it occurs. The equilibrium point, R say, is unstable and all the trajectories travel away from it, but are prevented from moving completely away by some non-linear restoring terms. In our example (P3.7.1), these restoring terms are the cubic terms.

Theorem P3.7.2 (The Poincaré–Bendixson theorem). Suppose the functions f_1, f_2 are well-behaved in a finite domain D$'$ *which does not contain an equilibrium point. If a trajectory stays in* D$'$ *for all t greater than some value t_0, then that trajectory either is a closed curve or tends towards a closed curve as $t \to \infty$.*

The closed curve in this theorem is either a limit cycle or a trajectory around a centre. In either case it contains an equilibrium point showing, from Theorem P3.7.1, that D' must have a hole in it. The theorem shows that, if a finite domain D contains only unstable equilibrium points in it but there are restoring terms in the equations which confine the trajectories to D, then a limit cycle must occur. This is a convenient way of constructing a limit cycle.

** P3.8 MORE PREDATOR–PREY MODELS

There are many predator–prey systems and they vary enormously in size and in other characteristics. In some, the predators may be small in comparison with the size of the hosts, e.g. parasites, and in others they may be large, e.g. lions. Not all these systems show oscillatory behaviour, and in those that do there may be many mechanisms causing such behaviour.

In this chapter we describe one particular mechanism which can cause limit cycles and show how the values of the parameters are chosen in this model.

In deriving equations (P3.6.7–P3.6.8) we assumed that the rate at which predators caught prey was proportional to x_1. This cannot be true for large x_1 because predators take time to kill and digest their prey – even lions can feel full up! To take this affect into account, equations (P3.6.7–P3.6.8) can be modified:

$$\mathrm{d}x_1/\mathrm{d}t = (x_1/\tau_1)(1 - x_1/N_1) - x_2\,\phi(x_1)/N_2, \tag{P3.8.1}$$

$$\mathrm{d}x_2/\mathrm{d}t = (x_2/\tau_2)(-1 - x_2/N_2) + kx_2\,\phi(x_1)/N_2, \tag{P3.8.2}$$

where $\phi(x_1)$ is called the **functional response** of the predators to the prey. If the predators take a constant time to catch and digest a prey, then $\phi(x_1)$ has the form

$$\phi(x_1) = \sigma_1(x_1/N_1\tau_1)/(1 + bx_1/N_1), \tag{P3.8.3}$$

where b is a positive constant.

By writing

$$\sigma_1/N_2\tau_2 = k\sigma_1/N_1\tau_1, \tag{P3.8.4}$$

we see that the only difference between the new equations and (P3.6.7–P3.6.8) is the presence of the denominator $(1 + bx_1/N_1)$ in (P3.8.3). The mathematical effect of this is to change the coordinates of the equilibrium point R and to make it less stable. In the original equations (P3.6.7–P3.6.8), a_{11} and a_{22} are negative, so that provided the roots are complex, R is asymptotically stable. The term a_{11} is now:

$$a_{11} = (\partial f_1/\partial x_1) = (x_1/\tau_1)((-1/N_1) + \sigma_1 x_2 b/(N_1 N_2(1 + bx_1/N_1)) \tag{P3.8.5}$$

at R. If the last term in (P3.8.5) is large enough, the sign of a_{11} can be changed and R can be made unstable.

In this way a limit cycle containing the point R can be constructed. Let the coordinates of R be (r_1, r_2). The restoring forces which operate when the trajectory becomes distant from R are the logistic effects. For a limit cycle to occur these effects must be small at R, requiring

$$r_1 \ll N_1, \quad r_2 \ll N_2. \tag{P3.8.6}$$

The effect of the denominator in $\phi(x_1)$ must also be significant if the equations are to behave differently from the original ones. Thus

$$br_1/N_1 > 1. \tag{P3.8.7}$$

This means that b must be larger than one.

To show that these requirements do lead to a limit cycle, let us take the following values for the parameters:

$$N_1 = N_2 = 1000, \quad b = 7.5, \quad \sigma_1 = 10, \quad \sigma_2 = 15, \quad \tau_1 = \tau_2 = 1, \tag{P3.8.8}$$

to get the equations

$$\mathrm{d}x_1/\mathrm{d}t = x_1(1 - x_1/1000 - 0.010x_2/(1 + 7.5x_1/1000)), \tag{P3.8.9}$$

$$\mathrm{d}x_2/\mathrm{d}t = x_2(-1 - x_2/1000 + 0.015x_1/(1 + 7.5x_1/1000)). \tag{P3.8.10}$$

The point R with coordinates (200, 200) is an unstable spiral point. Trajectories can be drawn using numerical techniques, and the limit cycle found. Fig. P3.13 shows the limit cycle sandwiched between two trajectories, both travelling towards it. In Fig. P3.14 is shown the behaviour of the populations with time, as the limit cycle is traversed. The populations undergo periodic oscillations as expected.

Does this model explain the periodic behaviour of certain predator–prey systems? To decide this we have to judge our results against experimental evidence. This is difficult as the available measurements show large statistical fluctuations and probably include the effects of migration; nevertheless our populations vary too sinusoidally whereas the experimental results exhibit several harmonics. We also note that at R, $a_{11} < 0$ in our model, so that $f_1(x_1, r_2)$ is negative for $x_1 < r_1$. It can be argued (see P3.9) that this is unrealistic. For example, the reason foı introducing the denominator in the functional response ϕ is to remove the linearity of ϕ when x_1 is large; but to get a limit cycle we require the denominator to have an effect when x_1 is much less than N_1..

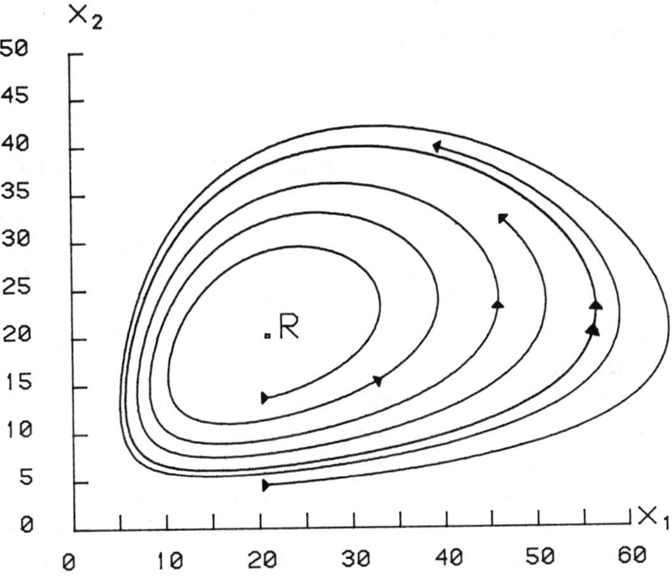

Fig. P3.13. The limit cycle (marked with two arrows) sandwiched between two trajectories, all satisfying equations (P3.8.9–P3.8.10).

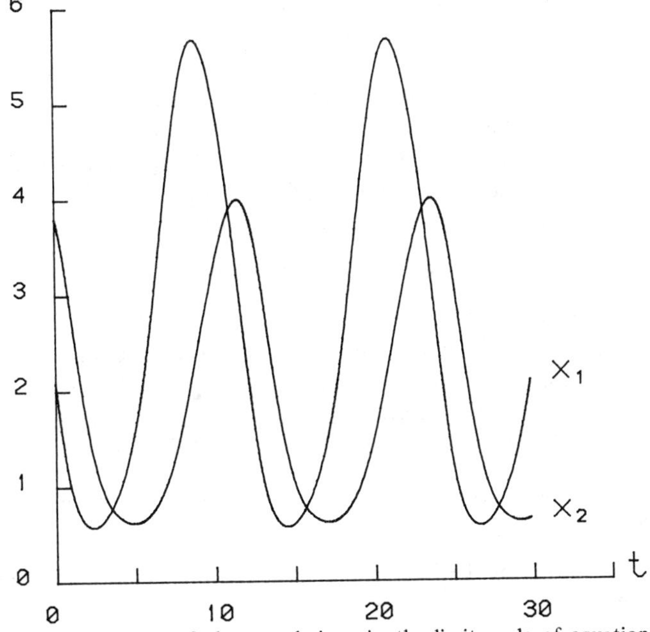

Fig. P3.14. The behaviour of the populations in the limit cycle of equations (P3.8.9–P3.8.10).

What, then, is a better explanation for the occurrence of limit cycles in predator–prey systems? Although effects such as digestion time may play some role, the main cause seems to be time-delays, probably due to breeding seasons and gestation periods. As we saw in P2, time-delays have a tendency to destabilize. Unfortunately, the mathematics of these effects is too complicated for us to go into here.

** P3.9 TWO INTERACTING SPECIES: A GENERAL APPROACH

In the previous sections, we looked at specific mathematical models of the population dynamics of two interacting species. In P3.8, however, we saw how a change in the functional response of the predators changed the predicted behaviour by introducing the possibility of a limit cycle. How can we be sure that the results of our models are general, i.e. occur because of the type of interaction and not because of the particular functions we have use? For example, is Gause's principle valid for all competing species, or is it just an artifact of the linear interaction we used in the equations (P3.4.2)? In this section we try to see what general conditions a model has to satisfy, and look briefly at what results can be got from such a general approach. We only consider models satisfying the same conditions as previously, i.e. time is a continuous variable etc. For notational convenience, we often denote the species by i and j, where $i \neq j$.

We assume that the environment is constant, so that the populations are described by two autonomous equations:

$$\mathrm{d}x_1/\mathrm{d}t = f_1(x_1(t), x_2(t)), \quad \mathrm{d}x_2/\mathrm{d}t = f_2(x_1(t), x_2(t)). \tag{P3.9.1}$$

We assume that f_1, f_2 are continuous and differentiable.

What are the general conditions that must be imposed on f_1, f_2 to make them suitable for use in equations that describe changes in populations?

The first conditions are straightforward. If one species has zero-population, then it cannot reproduce. The **zero conditions** are thus:

$$\textit{if } x_i = 0, \quad \textit{then } f_i(x_i, x_j) = 0. \tag{P3.9.2}$$

The second condition we need is one that ensures that there is a constraint on the growth of any population because resources are finite. In specific models this task is usually performed by a logistic term (see P2.3). In a general approach our requirement is that $\mathrm{d}x_i/\mathrm{d}t$ must be negative for large x_i. This can usually be ensured by the following constraint, which we shall call the **logistic constraint**:

For any given, finite value of x_j, there exists a positive value x_i^0 such that for all $x_i > x_i^0$, $f_i(x_i, x_j) < 0$. (P3.9.3)

This condition (P3.9.3) can in most circumstances be satisfied by the requirement that

$$\partial^2 f_i/\partial x_i^2 < 0 \quad \textit{everywhere}. \tag{P3.9.4}$$

Although these conditions ensure finite values for the competing-species and predator–prey systems, it is not always sufficient for the symbiotic system; we return to that difficulty later.

Let us now look at the conditions needed to specify a particular type of interaction between two species. Such interactions can be categorized for a system containing more than two species, but nevertheless are nearly always binary in animal interactions. For species i to predate on, or to compete with, species j,

$$\partial f_j/\partial x_i < 0 \quad \text{for } x_j > 0. \tag{P3.9.5}$$

To get a general term to cover both predation and competition, let us say that species j **loses** to species i in this interaction. Similarly when species j is helped by species i

$$\partial f_j/\partial x_i > 0 \quad \text{for } x_j > 0 \tag{P3.9.6}$$

and we say that species j **gains** from species i in this interaction.

When there are only two species involved we can describe these interactions by giving each species a title, e.g. the predator becomes a **gainer** and the prey becomes a **loser**. Then the competitive-species system is the loser–loser system, i.e.

$$\partial f_1/\partial x_2 < 0, \quad \partial f_2/\partial x_1 < 0: \tag{P3.9.7}$$

the predator–prey system becomes the gainer–loser system:

$$\partial f_1/\partial x_2 < 0, \quad \partial f_2/\partial x_1 > 0: \tag{P3.9.8}$$

and the symbiotic system becomes the gainer–gainer system:

$$\partial f_1/\partial x_2 > 0, \quad \partial f_2/\partial x_1 > 0. \tag{P3.9.9}$$

These conditions are applicable for all $x_1 > 0, x_2 > 0$.

There is one other condition that is required: for a species to survive, there must be an increase in its population for some values of the populations. Thus:

There exists at least one region in which f_i is positive. (P3.9.10)

** Consequences

We only consider two-species sytems. One consequence of (P3.9.4) is immediate:

Theorem P3.9.1. For a given value of x_j, $x_j^{(0)}$ say, there is at most one positive value of x_i, $x_i^{(0)}$ say, at which f_i is zero.

With at most one value of x_i where $\partial f_i/\partial x_i$ is zero, there can be at most two values of x_i at which f_i is zero. As $f_i = 0$ when $x_i = 0$, the theorem follows.

Theorem P3.9.2. $f_i(x_i, x_j^{(0)}) > 0$ for all x_i such that $0 < x_i < x_i^{(0)}$.

This follows from Theorem P3.9.1 and from the logistic constraint. There is a simple corollary:

Theorem P3.9.3. $\partial f_i/\partial x_i < 0$ *on the isocline* $f_i = 0$.

Theorem P3.9.4. For any $x_i > 0$, *there is at most one value of* $x_j > 0$ *such that* $f_i(x_i, x_j) = 0$.

This follows from the definitions of the interactions.

The isocline $f_i = 0$ is continuous and divides the positive quadrant into two regions, as can be seen from the above theorems. The region where $f_i > 0$ touches the x_j-axis. If the species is a loser, this region must also be adjacent to the origin.

Theorem P3.9.5. The gradient of the isocline $f_i = 0$ *is positive or negative according as the species is a gainer or a loser.*

This follows from the expression $(-\partial f_i/\partial x_1)/(\partial f_i/\partial x_2)$ for the gradient of the isocline.

The logistic and the zero conditions should confine the trajectories to a finite region of the first quadrant; they cannot escape across the axes, or off to infinity. As trajectories are continuous and cannot cross except at equilibrium points, each trajectory must, according to the Poincaré–Bendixson theorem, travel towards an equilibrium point or eventually become a closed curve (see P3.8).

What equilibrium points are there? The origin is always an equilibrium point. Are there any on the axes? If the species i is a loser, then the isocline $f_i = 0$ crosses the ith-axis at a positive value, N_i, the isolated equilibrium population. If the species j is a gainer, then there is no requirement for its zero isocline to cross the jth-axis at a positive value; indeed, if the only food for species j comes from species i, then species j cannot exist independently of species i and there is no equilibrium point on the positive jth-axis. At an equilibrium point $(N_1, 0)$,

$$a_{11} < 0; \quad a_{21} = 0. \tag{P3.9.11}$$

(See P3.3.) Thus the nature of $(N_1, 0)$ depends on the sign of a_{22}. Similarly the nature of $(0, N_2)$ depends on the sign of a_{11}.

To discuss the other equilibrium points we look at the specific systems.

Loser–loser systems: consider the region S with points (x_1, x_2) where $f_1 < 0$, $f_2 < 0$; S has the property that all points (x_1', x_2') with $x_1' < x_1$ and $x_2' < x_2$ also belong to S. The boundary of S consists of parts of the axes and parts of the isoclines $f_i = 0$, both of which have negative gradients. For a trajectory to enter S, either it goes from left to right across $f_2 = 0$ with its direction zero or it goes upwards across $f_1 = 0$ with its direction as $\pi/2$. However, every trajectory in S has a direction between $-\pi$ and $-\pi/2$. Hence

Theorem P3.9.6. No trajectory enters S.

Note also that if the point $(N_1, 0)$ (or $(0, N_2)$) lies on the boundary of S, then it is asymptotically stable.

There can be any number of equilibrium points, including zero, in the positive quadrant. If there are none, one of the points $(N_1, 0)$, $(0, N_2)$ lies on the boundary of S and then the other species dies out. If there is an equilibrium point R, the gradients at R of the isoclines $f_1 = 0, f_2 = 0$ determine whether R is a saddle-point or not.

Theorem P3.9.7. There are no limit cycles in a loser–loser system and hence there cannot be any stable oscillatory behaviour.

The equilibrium points lie on the boundary of S and are either saddle-points or stable improper nodes. If there were a limit cycle, it would have to contain an equilibrium point and hence have to enter S. This would contradict Theorem P3.9.6.

It would be unusual for there to be more than one positive equilibrium point and so it is natural to assume that there is only one. Then the loser–loser system is necessarily like the model proposed in P3.4, with the only significant difference being that the isoclines $f_i = 0$ do not have to be straight lines. The gradients of the zero and infinite isoclines play the role of the parameters σ_1, σ_2. The implications of P3.4 are thus still valid provided we adopt this new interpretation of σ_i.

The gainer–gainer system: as we saw in P3.5 there are problems in finding a suitable logistic constraint to ensure that this system has finite populations. Neither condition (P3.9.4) nor condition (P3.9.3) always suffices. This can be overcome by assuming (P3.9.4) and requiring that the gradient of $f_1 = 0$ is increasing and the gradient of $f_2 = 0$ is decreasing, i.e. that on the respective isoclines

$$\partial/\partial x_1(-\partial f_1/\partial x_2/\partial f_1/\partial x_1) > 0$$

$$1/x_2(-\partial f_2/\partial x_2/\partial f_2/\partial x_1) < 0. \qquad \text{(P3.9.12)}$$

From (P3.9.12) there is one positive equilibrium point if both species can exist independently; if only one species can independently exist, there may be no such point, in which case the other species dies out, or one such point, which is asymptotically stable.

If neither species can independently exist, (P3.9.12) ensures that there are, besides the origin, either zero or two equilibrium points. The origin is asymptotically stable, so that both species die out if there are no points; if there are two, the one nearer the origin is a saddle-point and the other is asymptotically stable, to which most trajectories travel. The species then co-exist and there is symbiosis. This can be seen from the directions of the lineal elements on the isoclines $f_i = 0$.

Gainer–loser system: the isoclines $f_i = 0$ can meet at most once, as their gradients have the opposite sign. If they do not meet, the gainer system dies out. If they meet, we have, at the equilibrium point R,

$$a_{11} < 0 \quad a_{22} < 0 \tag{P3.9.13}$$

and

$$a_{12} < 0 \quad a_{21} > 0 \quad a_{12}a_{21} < 0. \tag{P3.9.14}$$

R is thus always asymptotically stable. (Note the difference with the equations (P3.8.9–P3.8.10): why is this?) Usually, $a_{12}a_{21}$ is large, as it represents the interaction between the systems. The eigenvalues at R are then complex and so, from (P3.9.13), R is a spiral point.

Can there be any limit cycles around R? If there is only one, it cannot be stable, because R is asymptotically stable. Thus for this system to exhibit stable periodic behaviour, there must be at least two limit cycles; the system would then be very complicated and the mechanism causing periodic behaviour would be complex. This seems unlikely.

Is it possible for state-determined systems to show stable periodic behaviour without becoming very complicated? It should be remembered that we are assuming a two-species system, whereas in reality, the system might depend on other species and factors. If, however, this assumption is realistic, the answer would seem to be 'no'. Nevertheless our arguments all depend on the results (P3.9.13), which follow from (P3.9.4). It could be argued that (P3.9.4) should not be taken as a global property; we leave the reader to argue over this point. The author thinks that the most likely cause of periodic behaviour is the various time-delays in real systems, and that state-determined equations are not the right model.

P3.10 AFTERTHOUGHTS

This chapter has shown how state-determined equations can model successfully some but not all situations in which two species interact. We have not considered systems in which there are time-delays or where time should be considered as a discrete variable. There are some interesting results to be got from such analyses, but space and difficulty unfortunately preclude us from investigating them here. here.

PE3 EXERCISES

3.1 Draw isoclines and lineal elements for the following sets of equations:

(i) $dx_1/dt = 4x_1(1 - x_1/2 - x_2/4)$; $dx_2/dt = 5x_2(1 - x_1 - x_2/5)$;
(ii) $dx_1/dt = 4x_1(1 - x_1/2 - x_2/4)$; $dx_2/dt = 5x_2(-1 + x_1 + x_2/5)$,
(iii) $dx_1/dt = 4x_1(1 - x_1 + x_2/4)$; $dx_2/dt = 5x_2(1 - x_1/4 - x_2)$.

Use them to sketch trajectories starting at the points $(\frac{1}{5}, \frac{1}{4})$, $(4, 5)$, $(4, \frac{1}{4})$.

3.2 Draw isoclines, lineal elements and some trajectories for the equations

$$dx_1/dt = x_1(-1 - x_1 + 6x_2 - x_1x_2),$$

$$dx_2/dt = x_2(-1 + 6x_1 - x_2 - x_1x_2).$$

3.3 Classify the equilibrium points for the 'competitive-species' equations

$$dx_1/dt = 2x_1(1 - (x_1 + x_2/5)/600),$$

$$dx_2/dt = x_2(1 - (x_1/5 + x_2)/600),$$

and draw some trajectories starting near the points (0, 0), (500, 50), (50, 500). Show that the species can co-exist. What terms in the equations cause them to give results qualitatively different from those of equations (P3.4.5)?

3.4 Find and classify the equilibrium points of the equations

$$dx_1/dt = 2x_1(1 - (x_1 + 2x_2)/600),$$

$$dx_2/dt = x_2(1 - (x_1/2 + x_2)/600).$$

Sketch trajectories starting at points (400, 10) and (400, 200).

3.5 Find and classify the equilibrium points of the equations

$$dx_1/dt = 2x_1(1 - (x_1 + x_2)/1200),$$

$$dx_2/dt = x_2(1 - (x_2 - x_1)/600).$$

Sketch trajectories starting at points (2000, 10) and (10, 200).

3.6 Find and classify the equilibrium points of the equations

$$dx_1/dt = 15x_1(1 - (x_1 - x_2/5)/600),$$

$$dx_2/dt = 5x_2(1 + (x_1 - 3x_2/5)/600).$$

Sketch trajectories starting at points (1200, 10) and (10, 20).

3.7 In Exercises 3.4, 3.5, 3.6 consider the variables x_1, x_2 as representing the number densities of two interacting species. Explain in each case the meaning of the terms in the equations in terms of their interactions with each other and with their environment.

3.8 The equations

$$dx_1/dt = x_1(1 - x_1/N_1 - x_2/N_2),$$

$$dx_2/dt = 2x_2(1 - x_1/N_1 - x_2/N_2)$$

describe the populations x_1, x_2 of two species. What is the interaction between them? What do you expect to happen as $t \to \infty$? What are the equilibrium points?

Suppose $N_1 = N_2$. Find analytic solutions when initially:
(i) $x_2 = 2x_1 = N/100$; (ii) $x_2 = 12x_1 = N/100$; (iii) $x_2 = 24x_1 = N/100$. Draw the corresponding trajectories.

3.9 The equations

$$x(r+1) = 2x(r) - x(r)y(r), \quad y(r+1) = -y(r)/2 + x(r)y(r)$$

describe how the populations $x(r)$ and $y(r)$ of two species at year r change with time. What kind of interaction occurs between the species? How do the various terms in the equation arise?

Find the positive equilibrium point of the equations. Linearize the equations about this point and hence discuss its stability. Interpret your result.

3.10 Write down equations describing the population changes of two species which can exist independently and which are in a symbiotic relationship. Show that the zero and infinite isoclines must meet if the equations are to 'work'.

Draw some trajectories for the equations

$$\mathrm{d}x_1/\mathrm{d}t = x_1(1 - x_1/N + x_2/2N), \quad \mathrm{d}x_2/\mathrm{d}t = 2x_2(1 - x_2/N + x_1/2N)$$

and describe the population growth when the initial populations are $(N/2, N/20)$.

3.11 When $ah > bk$, show that the function H, where

$$H = (ah - bk)\ln(y) + hk\ln(x) - hcy - h^2 x,$$

has a maximum at an equilibrium point of the predator–prey equations

$$\mathrm{d}x/\mathrm{d}t = ax - bx^2 - cxy, \quad \mathrm{d}y/\mathrm{d}t = -ky + hxy.$$

Show further that $\mathrm{d}H/\mathrm{d}t > 0$ except when $x = k/h$. What can you conclude from this?

3.12 The equations for a predator–prey system are

$$\mathrm{d}x/\mathrm{d}t = x(1-y), \quad \mathrm{d}y/\mathrm{d}t = y(-1+x).$$

Find the equilibrium points and classify them. Show that the function

$$C = (x - \ln(x)) + (y - \ln(y)) \qquad (x, y > 0)$$

is a positive constant. By expanding C in powers of $(x - 1)$ and $(y - 1)$ show that the trajectories near the point $(1, 1)$ are circles.

Consider the equations

$$\mathrm{d}x/\mathrm{d}t = x(1 - y + (1-4C)/400(x-1)),$$

$$\mathrm{d}y/\mathrm{d}t = y(-1 + x + (1-4C)/400(y-1)).$$

Find now the equation of motion of C. Show that the trajectory

$$C(x, y) = \tfrac{1}{4}$$

is a limit cycle.

3.13 The population densities x, y of two species X, Y satisfy the equations

$$\mathrm{d}x/\mathrm{d}t = 6x(1 - (x + y)/200), \quad \mathrm{d}y/\mathrm{d}t = -6y(1 - x/300).$$

Explain the significance of the terms in these equations. Find the equilibrium values, classify them and give their stability. Draw a trajectory which starts at (10,600) and describe the populations as this trajectory is followed.

3.14 The following equations describe how the departures x, y and z from equilibrium of the populations of three species change with time t close to their equilibrium values:

$$\mathrm{d}x/\mathrm{d}t = 15x - 32y + 25z, \quad \mathrm{d}y/\mathrm{d}t = 8x - 17y + 14z,$$
$$\mathrm{d}z/\mathrm{d}t = 2x - 4y + 4z.$$

Write the equations in a matrix form: $\mathrm{d}\mathbf{x}/\mathrm{d}t = A \,.\, \mathbf{x}$. Find the eigenvalues and eigenvectors of A. By expressing $\mathbf{x}$ in terms of the eigenvectors, find the general solution of the above equations. Is the equilibrium point stable?

3.15 Derive the periodic solutions, if any, of the two coupled equations

$$\mathrm{d}x/\mathrm{d}t = -y + x(r^2 - 1)(r^2 - 4)(r^2 - 9)/r,$$
$$\mathrm{d}y/\mathrm{d}t = x + y(r^2 - 1)(r^2 - 4)(r^2 - 9)/r$$

and discuss their stability.

3.16 Investigate how the survival of a species A which competes with another species B depends on the relaxation rates τ_A, τ_B, and on the equilibrium populations N_A, N_B and the parameters σ_A, σ_B (both greater than one). At first, take the initial populations to be $(N_A/10, N_B/10)$, but later vary them to see how the survival depends on the initial conditions. Does survival depend on the absolute values or the ratios of the terms τ_A, N_B, etc.?

3.17 Treat the deviations of demand and supply from their equilibrium values as two 'populations' and derive equations for them assuming that $\mathrm{d}p/\mathrm{d}t = f(D - D_\mathrm{e}, S - S_\mathrm{e})$, where f is some function. Derive, using P3.3, conditions on the gradients of f, D, and S which make p_e a stable equilibrium; compare with the results of E4.10.

3.18$^{(\mathrm{m})}$ Model a symbiotic system of two species A and C, such that the birth-rate of A is increased by the presence of C but that A has to provide food for C. By deriving some equations, finding the equilibrium points, and drawing some trajectories, draw some general conclusions about the system.

3.19$^{(m)}$ Model a system of three species A, B and C in which A and B are in competition and A and C are in symbiosis. Suppose the relaxation rate of B is greater than C's and the relation between A and C is as described in Exercise E18. Use the results of Exercise 3.16 and Exercise 3.18 to see whether it 'pays' A to have the symbiotic relationship with C.

3.20$^{(m)}$ Is it possible to model the changes in size of two firms by the equations used to model the populations of two species? Assume that there are only two firms in existence. Can any implications, e.g. Gause's principle, or that symbiosis is worth while, be drawn from your models?

CHAPTER P4

The Probabilistic Approach

P4.1 INTRODUCTION

So far in our study of population behaviour we have ignored the effects of probability. This is unrealistic. Probability enters our study in two ways: **demographic stochasticity** arises because the actual number of offspring of a member of a species may vary, i.e. even if the environment is constant the number of births by a member of a species is not fixed, only its probability is determined; **environmental stochasticity** is more important and arises because the environment is always fluctuating; relaxation times, interaction parameters, etc. do not have fixed values and the most we can know about them is their probability distribution.

The incorporation of probabilistic effects into our models makes them more realistic. The reason why we studied deterministic models first was that they are easier to understand and their mathematics is easier. The mathematical problems involved in probabilistic models are usually very difficult: more progress can be made with deterministic models, but we have to be sure that their use is justified. Thus one of our tasks is to look at simple probabilistic models and see under what circumstances the corresponding deterministic models give the same results. In P4.2, then, we study the simple exponential growth model which incorporates demographic stochasticity and compare it with the model of P2.2.

There is one class of probabilistic models whose mathematics is reasonably simple. These are ones in which time can be taken as a discrete variable and the probabilities for the populations at the end of each period depend in a constant linear way on the probabilities of the populations at the beginning of each period. These models involve the mathematics of **stationary finite Markov chains**: this is discussed in P4.3, P4.4 and P4.5. Such models arise in many situations and in every type of population study. The most obvious application is in genetics.

When there is environmental stochasticity, the parameters in the models are fluctuating with time, in contrast to the systems with demographic stochasticity. The mathematics of models for such systems is very difficult; indeed it is difficult to construct equations which correspond to deterministic equations such as the logistic and interacting-species equations and it is virtually impossible to solve them. We only give a short review of such models and this is done in P4.6.

Finally in P4.7 and P4.8 we look at the phenomenon of evolution and at how it may possibly be caused. In P4.7 we introduce a simple model in which evolutionary effects on genetics are manifest and in P4.8 we show the relevance of Game Theory: this has become important in recent years and is a subject in which the ideas of Game Theory have been tested against experiment.

P4.2 EXPONENTIAL GROWTH

We consider a model of exponential growth involving demographic stochasticity, in which a birth-event in a particular time interval is only probable, not certain. We first consider a model in which time is considered as a continuous variable. Take a unit δt of time so small that only one offspring at most is born to a member during δt: the probability of this is then $r\delta t$, and the probability that there is no birth is

$$1 - r\delta t. \qquad \text{(P4.2.1)}$$

Let $P(n, t)$ be the probability that the population is n at time t. Then

$$P(n, t+\delta t) = \sum_{j=0}^{n} \sigma_j P(n-j, t) \qquad \text{(P4.2.2)}$$

where σ_j is the probability that j births occur in the time δt; this is proportional to $(\delta t)^j$. Retaining only first-order terms in δt in (P4.2.2), we get the equation

$$P(n, t+\delta t) = \sigma_0 P(n, t) + \sigma_1 P(n-1, t). \qquad \text{(P4.2.3)}$$

Now

$$\sigma_0 = (1 - r\delta t)^n \qquad \text{(P4.2.4)}$$

$$= 1 - nr\delta t \qquad \text{(P4.2.5)}$$

to first order in δt. Similarly,

$$\sigma_1 = (n-1)\, r\delta t. \qquad \text{(P4.2.6)}$$

Thus the equation that determines $P(n, t)$ is

$$\mathrm{d}P(n, t)/\mathrm{d}t = -nrP(n, t) + (n-1)rP(n-1, t). \qquad \text{(P4.2.7)}$$

It is easily solved. Suppose that at time $t = 0$ the population is exactly n_0:

$$P(n, 0) = 0, \quad n \neq n_0, \quad P(n_0, 0) = 1. \tag{P4.2.8}$$

Let us also suppose that $r > 0$, so that the population never decreases. Thus

$$P(n, t) = 0, \quad n < n_0. \tag{P4.2.9}$$

Then

$$\mathrm{d}P(n_0, t)/\mathrm{d}t = -n_0\, rP(n_0, t) \tag{P4.2.10}$$

$$P(n_0, t) = \exp(-n_0 rt). \tag{P4.2.11}$$

From this we can deduce that

$$P(n_0 + 1, t) = n_0 \exp(-n_0 rt)(1 - \exp(-rt)), \tag{P4.2.12}$$

$$P(n_0 + j, t) = ((n_0 + j - 1)!/((j!)(n_0 - 1)!)) \exp(-n_0 rt)(1 - \exp(-rt))^j. \tag{P4.2.13}$$

This last result can be proved by induction.

Compare this result with the deterministic one, (P2.2.2). The important quantities in a probabilistic model are the **average** (or **expectation value**) of the population, and its **variance**. The former is the population we expect to find and the latter is a measure of the deviation of actual observations from this average.

The expected value of the population is written $<n>$ (or $E(n)$ in statistics' books) and is defined as

$$<n> = \sum_n nP(n, t). \tag{P4.2.14}$$

It is a function of t. Then

$$<n> = n_0 \exp(rt), \tag{P4.2.15}$$

i.e. the expectation value gives the same result as the deterministic model, if we identify r as $(b - d)$, i.e. birth-rate minus death-rate. The variance, $<(n - <n>)^2>$, is

$$n_0 \exp(2rt)(1 - \exp(-rt)). \tag{P4.2.16}$$

The **statistical root-mean-square relative fluctuation** is defined as $(<(n - <n>)^2>)^{1/2}/<n>$, which in this model is

$$n_0^{-1/2}(1 - \exp(-rt))^{1/2} \tag{P4.2.17}$$

which is less than $n_0^{-1/2}$. Thus for *large* populations, the statistical fluctuations caused by demographic stochasticity in the exponential growth model are small and the deterministic model is adequate. This is a general result for models incorporating demographic stochasticity, so that, provided the populations are large, the deterministic equations are adequate. The probabilistic model gives more information about the system but at the expense of a harder calculation.

A simple model incorporating demographic stochasticity can be developed for systems in which time is discrete (see P2.7). Suppose an individual has a probability rT of giving birth to one offspring and probability $(1 - rT)$ of not giving birth in the interval T. Then the probability that j births occur to n animals in T is

$$_nC_j\,(1-rT)^{n-j}\,(rT)^j. \tag{P4.2.18}$$

Let $P(n, m)$ be the probability that the population is n at time mT. A relation between $P(n, m + 1)$ and $P(n, m)$ can be easily obtained (see PE4.2).

P4.3 STATIONARY FINITE MARKOV CHAINS: 1. SOME MODELS

In the exponential growth model of P4.2 with discrete time, the probabilities $P(n, m + 1)$ at time $(m + 1)T$ are linearly related to the probabilities $P(n', m)$ at time mT. If we view a species as a system, the size n of the population can be viewed as the state of the system. This view leads to a generalization of probabilistic population dynamics by investigating other possible states of the system: we thus want to investigate the behaviour of $p_j(m)$, which is the probability that at time mT the system is in state j.

In certain circumstances the mathematics of this is relatively easy. Suppose the set of states of a system is finite. Let us label these states with integers $1, 2, 3, \ldots, k$ and remember that time is a discrete variable. Then if $p_i(m)$ is linearly related to the probabilities $p_j(m - 1)$, i.e.

$$p_j(m) = \sum_i w_{ij}\,p_i(m-1), \tag{P4.3.1}$$

with

$$w_{ij} \geqslant 0, \tag{P4.3.2}$$

then we are said to have a **Markov chain**. If, further, the numbers w_{ij} are independent of time, then the chain is said to be **stationary**.

Let us look at a few examples. Consider the way an animal responds to a certain stimulus, e.g. a dog when it is told to 'sit'. Suppose it has two responses, a 'correct' response and an 'incorrect' one. Suppose that the animal's response to the $(m + 1)$th stimulus depends linearly on its response to the mth stimulus, but not on its response to any previous stimuli, i.e. the animal remembers only the immediate past. This assumption is known as the **Markov hypothesis**. We write $p_1(m)$, $p_2(m)$ for the probability that the animal responds correctly, incorrectly to the mth stimulus. Then, using our assumption,

$$p_1(m+1) = p_1(m)w_{11}(m) + p_2(m)w_{21}(m),$$

$$p_2(m+1) = p_1(m)w_{12}(m) + p_2(m)w_{22}(m). \tag{P4.3.3}$$

The coefficients w are conditional probabilities; for example, $w_{12}(m)$ is the probability that the animal gives a correct response at time $(m + 1)T$, given that it has made an incorrect response at time mT. We write (P4.3.3) in vector form:

$$\mathbf{p}(m) = (p_1(m), p_2(m)), \tag{P4.3.4}$$

$$W(m) = \begin{bmatrix} w_{11}(m) & w_{12}(m) \\ w_{21}(m) & w_{22}(m) \end{bmatrix}; \tag{P4.3.5}$$

equations (P4.3.3) become

$$\mathbf{p}(m + 1) = \mathbf{p}(m) \,.\, W(m). \tag{P4.3.6}$$

Note that the vectors $\mathbf{p}(m)$ are row vectors and that $\mathbf{p}(m)$ pre-multiplies the matrix $W(m)$ in (P4.3.6); this arrangement is conventional in the theory of Markov chains.

With **stationary** Markov chains, the conditional probabilities w are independent of time. Then the vector $\mathbf{p}(m)$ can be expressed in terms of $\mathbf{p}(0)$:

$$\mathbf{p}(m) = \mathbf{p}(0)\, W^m. \tag{P4.3.7}$$

This tells us how quickly, if ever, the animal learns the correct response.

The matrix W is the **transition** matrix: its elements are **transition** probabilities. The elements of a row form a complete set of probabilities:

$$\sum_{j=1} w_{ij} = 1. \tag{P4.3.8}$$

The actual state of the system is, in general, given by a mixed state, which is a probability distribution over the pure states.

Let us now look at two models more directly relevant to population problems. The first is a **random walk** model: consider the movement of a 'drunkard' at a party. Suppose the party takes place in five adjacent rooms (see Fig. P4.1). The aim of our model is to determine how long the drunkard spends in each room.

Fig. P4.1. The rooms at the party.

There are five pure states in this model – the drunkard being in room 1, 2, 3, 4 or 5. Suppose the drunkard decides to spend T minutes in a room before deciding whether to move to an adjoining room or not. Suppose also that the drunkard, inebriated as he is, has no memory about which rooms he has visited, so that the probability that he visits a room at time $(m + 1)T$ depends only on which room he is in at time mT. Suppose also that his state does not change significantly during the party, so that these probabilities do not vary with time.

The movements of the drunkard between the rooms obey the conditions of the theory of stationary finite Markov chains. To apply this theory we want to know the transition matrix. To find the elements we suppose the drunkard to be in a particular room i; then when he makes a decision he can either stay in room

i with probability $w_{i,i}$ or move to the adjoining rooms, $i + 1$ or $i - 1$ (if they exist), with corresponding probabilities $w_{i,i+1}$ and $w_{i,i-1}$. The transition matrix is

$$\begin{matrix} w_{11} & w_{12} & 0 & 0 & 0 \\ w_{21} & w_{22} & w_{23} & 0 & 0 \\ 0 & w_{32} & w_{33} & w_{34} & 0 \\ 0 & 0 & w_{43} & w_{44} & w_{45} \\ 0 & 0 & 0 & w_{54} & w_{55} \end{matrix} \quad . \tag{P4.3.9}$$

The actual transition probabilities w depend on the feelings of the drunkard and the contents of each room. Suppose one room, 1 say, is so attractive that, if he ever reached it, he would not want to leave it, e.g. the drinks room. Then

$$w_{12} = 0: \quad w_{11} = 1. \tag{P4.3.10}$$

Such a pure state is known as an **absorbing state**. Suppose also that the other transition probabilities in a row are equal: then W becomes

$$\begin{matrix} 1 & 0 & 0 & 0 & 0 \\ \frac{1}{3} & \frac{1}{3} & \frac{1}{3} & 0 & 0 \\ 0 & \frac{1}{3} & \frac{1}{3} & \frac{1}{3} & 0 \\ 0 & 0 & \frac{1}{3} & \frac{1}{3} & \frac{1}{3} \\ 0 & 0 & 0 & \frac{1}{2} & \frac{1}{2} \end{matrix} \quad . \tag{P4.3.11}$$

Absorbing states occur in general whenever one of the diagonal transition probabilities w_{rr} is unity. Then, because of the conditions (P4.3.2) and (P4.3.8),

$$w_{rj} = 0 \quad j \neq r. \tag{P4.3.12}$$

Thus once the state r is entered, the system never leaves it.

In general, Markov chain theory tells us what the proportions in the pure states are expected to be. This is useful if we want to calculate the ratio of the number of animals with a particular characteristic, e.g. the ratio of the number of people with brown eyes to those with blue eyes. The behaviour of the total population is only obtainable if the states are a function of the number of animals. If this can be infinite the number of states is infinite, which makes the theory of Markov chains more complicated.

An example from genetics

Suppose at one position in the chromosomes the gene can be either a or b. The heritable characteristics are determined by a pair of genes so that this position is designated by (aa), (bb) or (ab), the order of the genes not being significant. To produce offspring, two parents are required, so that the genes of the offspring are determined by the genes of the parent paris. The order of the parents is, in general, not significant so that there are six possibilities for the set of genes of the parent pairs at this position in the chromosomes:

$$(aa, aa) \quad (bb, bb) \quad (aa, ab) \quad (aa, bb) \quad (ab, ab) \quad (ab, bb). \qquad \text{(P4.3.13)}$$

From the offspring, suppose two are chosen as parents and the process repeated. The system of genes at a particular position for such parent pairs is a stationary finite Markov chain. There are a finite number of pure states (see (P4.3.13)), and each state depends only on the previous state; the transition probabilities are also supposedly independent of time. Evolutionary effects such as the effect of the environment and fertility are important in most systems but not in this one.

We can determine the probabilities of genes of the parent pairs if we can determine the transition probabilities between each generation. These can be calculated if we assume that an offspring takes genes from each parent with equal probability. The resulting transition matrix is as follows:

	(aa, aa)	(bb, bb)	(aa, ab)	(aa, bb)	(ab, ab)	(ab, bb)
(aa, aa)	1	0	0	0	0	0
(bb, bb)	0	1	0	0	0	0
(aa, ab)	$\frac{1}{4}$	0	$\frac{1}{2}$	0	$\frac{1}{4}$	0
(aa, bb)	0	0	0	0	1	0
(ab, ab)	$\frac{1}{16}$	$\frac{1}{16}$	$\frac{1}{4}$	$\frac{1}{8}$	$\frac{1}{4}$	$\frac{1}{4}$
(ab, bb)	0	$\frac{1}{4}$	0	0	$\frac{1}{4}$	$\frac{1}{2}$.

(P4.3.14)

The reader should try to calculate this for himself. As an example we show how the fifth row is calculated. A parent pair with genes (ab, ab) gives rise to offspring with genes (aa) or (bb) with probabilities $\frac{1}{4}$ each and to offspring with genes (ab) with probability $\frac{1}{2}$, as it occurs twice, i.e. (ab) and (ba) are equivalent. Then the probability of choosing a pair of parents from these offspring with genes (aa, aa) is $\frac{1}{16}$. The probability of choosing (aa, ab) is $2(\frac{1}{4})(\frac{1}{2})$, the factor 2 arising because (aa, ab) and (ab, aa) are equivalent.

P4.4 STATIONARY FINITE MARKOV CHAINS: 2. MATHEMATICS

If the size of the transition matrix W is small then it is possible to evaluate $\mathbf{p}(m)$ for all m using (P4.3.7); however, if there are many pure states, calculation of $\mathbf{p}(m)$ is complicated. In either case it is useful to know how $\mathbf{p}(m)$ behaves for large m. There are several different types of behaviour for $\mathbf{p}(m)$ depending on the nature of W, so that we need to classify these different types of transition matrix. We do this formally later, but let us first exhibit the different behaviours in a simpler way.

Let us write $w_{ij}^{(m)}$ for the ijth element of W^m. Then we say that the state i **communicates** with state j if there exists an integer n such that $w_{ij}^{(n)}$ is non-zero.

It means that if the system starts in pure state i then there is a finite probability that at some time in the future it will be in state j. The states i and j, where $i \neq j$, are said to **intercommunicate** if there exist an n and an m such that $w_{ij}^{(n)}$ and $w_{ji}^{(m)}$ are both non-zero. This is symbolically written

$$i \leftrightarrow j. \tag{P4.4.1}$$

For convenience we write for all states i,

$$i \leftrightarrow i. \tag{P4.4.2}$$

Then the relation $\leftrightarrow$ is an equivalence relation (the proof is left to the reader) and so partitions the set of pure states into equivalence classes.

These equivalence classes can be easily identified by drawing a **transition diagram**. If $w_{ij} \neq 0$, we write

$$i \rightarrow j. \tag{P4.4.3}$$

The diagram is got by representing the pure states by points and putting the relations (P4.4.3) between the points. If a closed arc occurs, the points on the arc form part of or the whole of an equivalence class. In Fig. P4.2 are drawn the relations '$\rightarrow$' for the states in the chain (P4.3.11). Thus states 2, 3, 4 and 5 are in one equivalence class and state 1 is in a separate class. There is no intercommunication between states 1 and 2.

Fig. P4.2. A transition diagram for the transition matrix (P4.3.11).

It is useful to classify these classes when there is more than one of them. Let us label them $a, b, c, \ldots$. We say that class a communicates with class b if there exist states i_a in a and i_b in b such that $i_a \rightarrow i_b$; we write this symbolically as

$$a \rightarrow b. \tag{P4.4.4}$$

Being in separate equivalence classes, a and b cannot intercommunicate. A class a is called a **closed** set if for every state i_a of a and every state j_b not belonging to a,

$$w_{i_a j_b} = 0. \tag{P4.4.5}$$

As

$$(W^n)_{i_a j_b} = \sum_k w_{i_a k} (W^{(n-1)})_{k j_b}, \tag{P4.4.6}$$

it can be shown by induction that a closed set a does not communicate with other states.

An absorbing state is an example of a closed set consisting of one state. With finite Markov chains, closed sets have the ergodic property (the value of a measurement after an infinite time has elapsed is equal to its expectation value) so that they are also known as **ergodic** sets and their states as **ergodic** states.

It may be possible to separate the pure states into two or more sets which have no communication with each other. The system is then **separable** and the sets themselves are Markov chains. We always assume that the system is **non-separable**.

The relation '→' (i.e. communicates with) partially orders the equivalence classes. Thus to identify the classes we choose a positive integer m and, if required, a Greek letter, in such a way that $m > n$ if there are classes $(m\alpha)$ and $(n\beta)$ with $(n\beta) \to (m\alpha)$. The Greek letter is used only when it is required to distinguish between classes with the same integer. Closed sets have

$$m = 1. \tag{P4.4.7}$$

States in classes with $m > 1$ are called **transient** states.

Canonical form for the transition matrix

This enables us to give the transition matrix a simple structure. We put the states in their equivalence classes and order them according to the integer m describing the class. The transition matrix then has the form

	1α	1β	2α	2β	2γ	3	4	.....
1α	$P_{1\alpha}$	0	0	0	0	0	0	...
1β	0	$P_{1\beta}$	0	0	0	0	0	...
2α	$R_{2\alpha\,1\alpha}$	$R_{2\alpha\,1\beta}$	$P_{2\alpha}$	0	0	0	0	...
2β	$R_{2\beta\,1\alpha}$	$R_{2\beta\,1\beta}$	0	$P_{2\beta}$	0	0	0	...
2γ	$R_{2\gamma\,1\alpha}$	$R_{2\gamma\,1\beta}$	0	0	$P_{2\gamma}$	0	0	...
3	$R_{3\,1\alpha}$	$R_{3\,1\beta}$	$R_{3\,2\alpha}$	$R_{3\,2\beta}$	$R_{3\,2\gamma}$	P_3	0	...
..	....	....	....	....	....	....	....	

(P4.4.8)

where the entries are, in general, matrices, the P matrices being square and the 0s standing for matrices with every element zero. One element of one of the R matrices in a row of (P4.4.8) must be non-zero.

The nth power of such a canonical matrix retains the same canonical form, i.e. zero-matrices in the upper right triangle and square matrices, $(P_m)^n$, in the diagonal position (m). Note that, for $m > 1$,

$$\lim_{n\to\infty} (P_m)^n = 0. \tag{P4.4.9}$$

Classification of the transition matrices

A transition matrix is said to be **reducible** if it can be put in the canonical form with at least one zero-matrix in the upper right triangle. Otherwise it is **irreducible**. If the transition matrix is reducible, there exists at least one transient and one closed set and, if irreducible, there are no transient states and the whole set of states is closed. In the latter case we distinguish two cases: a transition matrix is called **regular** if there exists a finite positive integer n such that the elements of $(W)^n$ are all positive, i.e. non-zero. An irreducible transition matrix that is not regular is called **periodic**. An example of a periodic transition matrix is

$$\begin{bmatrix} 0 & 1 & 0 \\ 0 & 0 & 1 \\ 1 & 0 & 0 \end{bmatrix}. \tag{P4.4.10}$$

In this book we shall not consider periodic matrices, but only those that are regular or reducible.

Algebraic results

Theorem P4.4.1. All transition matrices have 'one' as an eigenvalue.

The characteristic equation which determines the eigenvalues is

$$|W - \lambda I| = 0. \tag{P4.4.11}$$

In the determinant, add all the rows and replace the entries in the first column by the sum. The determinant's value is unaltered and from (P4.3.8) the first column entries are all $(1 - \lambda)$. Thus $(1 - \lambda)$ is a factor of the characteristic equation.

Theorem P4.4.2. No eigenvalue has modulus greater than one.

Consider an eigenvalue $\lambda \neq 1$, with corresponding right eigenvector s. Let s_m be the component of s satisfying

$$|s_m| = \max_i (|s_i|). \tag{P4.4.12}$$

Now

$$\sum_i w_{mi} s_i = \lambda s_m \Rightarrow \sum_i w_{mi} |s_i| \geqslant |\lambda| |s_m|. \tag{P4.4.13}$$

By definition $|s_i| < |s_m|$, so that

$$\sum_i w_{mi} |s_m| = |s_m| \geqslant |\lambda| |s_m|, \tag{P4.4.14}$$

and the theorem follows.

There follow two theorems due to Perron and Frobenius. The proofs of these theorems are difficult and are not given here. The theorems are important and are not restricted to transition matrices – they apply to all finite square matrices with non-negative elements. Such matrices may occur elsewhere in population studies, e.g. Leslie matrices, so that here we give the theorems in their more general form.

Theorem P4.4.3. Suppose A is a finite square matrix with non-negative elements. Then:

(i) A has a positive eigenvalue λ_1 such that all other eigenvalues λ satisfy $|\lambda| \leqslant \lambda_1$;
(ii) the corresponding left eigenvector $\mathbf{x}^1$ is non-negative and non-zero;
(iii) if λ is an eigenvalue of A such that $|\lambda| = \lambda_1$ then (λ/λ_1) is a root of unity and $(\lambda/\lambda_1)^n \lambda_1$, where n is an integer, is also an eigenvalue of A.

Theorem P4.4.4. Suppose A is a finite square matrix with non-negative elements. Suppose also that A^n has all positive entries for some integer n. Then:

(i) A has a positive eigenvalue λ_1 such that all other eigenvalues λ satisfy $|\lambda| < \lambda_1$;
(ii) the corresponding left eigenvector $\mathbf{x}^1$ is positive;
(iii) λ_1 has multiplicity one.

For transition matrices these two theorems show that the eigenvalue $\lambda = 1$ has a corresponding left eigenvector which is non-negative and real.

For regular transition matrices there is only one eigenvalue with $\lambda = 1$. Note also that if $\mathbf{x}$ is a left eigenvector

$$\sum_i x_i w_{ij} = \lambda' x_j \tag{P4.4.15}$$

so that

$$\sum_j \sum_i x_i w_{ij} = \sum_i x_i = \lambda' \sum_j x_j \tag{P4.4.16}$$

implying, if $\lambda' \neq 1$,

$$\sum_i x_i = 0. \tag{P4.4.17}$$

The diagonal part of a transition matrix for a closed set is written (see (P4.4.8)) as P_1, so that P_1 can also be characterized as a transition matrix. Thus it has an eigenvalue 1 and the complete transition matrix W has at least as many eigenvalues 1 as there are closed sets.

P4.5 STATIONARY FINITE MARKOV CHAINS: 3. RESULTS

In this section we show how to derive the state and in particular its long-run behaviour. We start from the equation (P4.3.7).

We first consider those chains which have regular transition matrices. Suppose there are n pure states, so that W is an $n*n$ matrix. Suppose also that there are n linearly independent left eigenvectors $\mathbf{x}^\lambda$, where λ is the corresponding eigenvalue. Then the initial state can be written in terms of these eigenvectors:

$$\mathbf{p}(0) = \sum_\lambda a_\lambda \mathbf{x}_\lambda . \tag{P4.5.1}$$

Then

$$\mathbf{p}(m) = \sum_\lambda \lambda^m a_\lambda \mathbf{x}_\lambda . \tag{P4.5.2}$$

In this case it is easy to evaluate $\mathbf{p}(m)$; the long-run behaviour is also very simple. For all eigenvalues less than 1, $\lambda^m \to 0$ as m gets large, so that

$$\mathbf{p}(m) \to a_1 \mathbf{x}^1 . \tag{P4.5.3}$$

Let us normalize $\mathbf{x}^1$ as follows:

$$\sum_i x_i^1 = 1. \tag{P4.5.4}$$

Then, from (P4.5.1) and (P4.4.16),

$$\sum_i p_i(0) = 1 = a_1 . \tag{P4.5.5}$$

Thus

$$\mathbf{p}(m) \to \mathbf{x}^1 , \tag{P4.5.6}$$

irrespective of the initial state $\mathbf{p}(0)$.

The result that, with a regular transition matrix, the state tends in the long run towards $\mathbf{x}^1$, whatever the initial state, is true in all cases.

Let us examine our model of the learning process in an animal (see P4.3). For convenience we write the transition matrix (P4.3.5) as

$$\begin{bmatrix} a & (1-a) \\ (1-b) & b \end{bmatrix} \tag{P4.5.7}$$

where a, b are non-zero and not equal to one. This transition matrix has eigenvalues 1 and $(a + b - 1)$, with corresponding left eigenvectors

$$((1-b), (1-a))/(2-a-b), \quad (1, -1), \tag{P4.5.8}$$

where $\mathbf{x}^1$ has been normalized according to (P4.5.4). Our result (P4.5.6) shows that in the long run the animal gives the correct response with a probability

$$(1-b)/(2-a-b). \tag{P4.5.9}$$

The probabilities after m goes are given by the state vector $\mathbf{p}(m)$:

$$\mathbf{p}(m) = ((1-b), (1-a))/(2-a-b) + a_2(a+b-1)^m (1, -1) \tag{P4.5.10}$$

where the coefficient a_2 is determined by the initial state $\mathbf{p}(0)$:

$$a_2(1, -1) + ((1-b), (1-a))/(2-a-b) = \mathbf{p}(0). \tag{P4.5.11}$$

Another way of deriving $\mathbf{p}(m)$ is to see that the equation,

$$\mathbf{p}(m+1) - \mathbf{p}(m) \,.\, W = \mathbf{0}, \tag{P4.5.12}$$

is just a set of coupled difference equations. These can be solved for the individual components of $\mathbf{p}(m)$. For example, in our learning theory example we can write

$$\mathbf{p}(m) = (p_1(m), (1 - p_1(m))). \tag{P4.5.13}$$

Then equation (P4.5.12) becomes

$$\begin{aligned} p_1(m+1) &= p_1(m)a + (1-p_1(m))\,(1-b) \\ &= p_1(m)\,(a+b-1) + (1-b). \end{aligned} \tag{P4.5.14}$$

This is like a differential equation, with a particular integral and a general solution; the solution of (P4.5.14) is thus

$$p_1(m) = a_2(a+b-1)^m + (1-b)/(2-a-b) \tag{P4.5.15}$$

which is exactly the result (P4.5.10).

The state denoted by the eigenvector $\mathbf{x}^1$ is called the **equilibrium** state of the system. The rate at which the system approaches equilibrium (i.e. the relaxation rate) is given, in units of the interval T, by the logarithm of the largest modulus of those eigenvalues not equal to one. In our example (see (P4.5.10)) this is

$$1/\ln|a+b-1|. \tag{P4.5.16}$$

Absorption problems

Let us now consider Markov chains with reducible transition matrices. The canonical form of a non-separable transition matrix can be written

$$\begin{bmatrix} P & 0 \\ R & Q \end{bmatrix} \tag{P4.5.17}$$

where P and Q are square matrices. We write the space of pure states, which are members of closed sets, as π, and the space of transient states as θ. If there are l_1 closed and l_2 transient states, P is $l_1 \times l_1$ and Q is $l_2 \times l_2$. The matrix Q is a productive matrix (see E5.5.); the proof in the general case is complicated, but in the simple case where $\sum_l Q_{il} < 1$ for all i, it can be seen quite simply by taking $\mathbf{z}'$ as the vector with unit components, i.e. $\mathbf{z}' = (1, 1, 1, 1, \ldots)$.

Suppose the system starts in the transient pure state i. The probability that on the nth go, the system is in the pure state j, belonging to θ, is $(Q^n)_{ij}$. Thus the average number of visits made to state j is

$$\delta_{ij} + Q_{ij} + (q^2)_{ij} + (Q^3)_{ij} + \ldots + (Q^n)_{ij} + \ldots$$

$$= \delta_{ij} + \sum_{n=1} (Q^n)_{ij} \equiv N_{ij}. \qquad \text{(P4.5.18)}^\dagger$$

N is the **characteristic** matrix. The series is convergent so that the $l_2 \times l_2$ matrix

$$N = (1 - Q)^{-1}. \qquad \text{(P4.5.19)}$$

The number of visits made to the transient states is equal to the length of time spent there. This is the **mean absorption time** and, for the initial state $\mathbf{p}(0)$, is

$$T \sum_{i,j} p_i(0) N_{ij}. \qquad \text{(P4.5.20)}$$

The probability of being absorbed in state k of π, after n periods, is

$$\sum_{j \epsilon \theta} (Q^n)_{ij} R_{jk} \qquad \text{(P4.5.21)}$$

so that the total probability of being absorbed in this state is

$$\sum_{n=0} \sum_{j \epsilon \theta} (Q^n)_{ij} R_{jk} = \sum_{j \epsilon \theta} N_{ij} R_{jk} = (NR)_{ik}. \qquad \text{(P4.5.22)}$$

In the random walk with the transition matrix (P4.3.11), $\pi = (1)$ and $\theta = (2, 3, 4, 5)$. Then

$$Q = \begin{bmatrix} \frac{1}{3} & \frac{1}{3} & 0 & 0 \\ \frac{1}{3} & \frac{1}{3} & \frac{1}{3} & 0 \\ 0 & \frac{1}{3} & \frac{1}{3} & \frac{1}{3} \\ 0 & 0 & \frac{1}{2} & \frac{1}{2} \end{bmatrix}, \qquad R = \begin{bmatrix} \frac{1}{3} \\ 0 \\ 0 \\ 0 \end{bmatrix}, \qquad \text{(P4.5.23)}$$

so that

$$N = \begin{bmatrix} 3 & 3 & 3 & 2 \\ 3 & 6 & 6 & 4 \\ 3 & 6 & 9 & 6 \\ 3 & 6 & 9 & 8 \end{bmatrix}. \qquad \text{(P4.5.24)}$$

If the drunkard enters at room 3 his initial state has coordinates (0, 1, 0, 0) in θ. Thus we expect him to spend (3, 6, 6, 4) periods in rooms 2, 3, 4 and 5 respectively before entering room 1. His mean absorption time is 21 periods. Suppose, however, that he enters, with equal probability, room 4 or room 5. Then the initial state is $(0, 0, \frac{1}{2}, \frac{1}{2})$ and we expect him to spend (3, 6, 9, 7) periods in rooms 2, 3, 4 and 5 respectively; his mean absorption time is 25 periods.

In the genetics example (*aa, ab*), (*aa, bb*), (*ab, ab*), (*ab, bb*) are transient states, so that

† δ_{ij} is the Kronecker delta, i.e. $\delta_{ij} = 0$ if $i \neq j$ and $\delta_{ij} = 1$ if $i = j$.

$$N = \begin{bmatrix} \frac{8}{3} & \frac{1}{6} & \frac{4}{3} & \frac{2}{3} \\ \frac{4}{3} & \frac{4}{3} & \frac{8}{3} & \frac{4}{3} \\ \frac{4}{3} & \frac{1}{3} & \frac{8}{3} & \frac{4}{3} \\ \frac{2}{3} & \frac{1}{6} & \frac{4}{3} & \frac{8}{3} \end{bmatrix}. \tag{P4.5.25}$$

$$R = \begin{bmatrix} \frac{1}{4} & 0 \\ 0 & 0 \\ \frac{1}{16} & \frac{1}{16} \\ 0 & \frac{1}{4} \end{bmatrix}; \qquad NR = \begin{bmatrix} \frac{3}{4} & \frac{1}{4} \\ \frac{1}{2} & \frac{1}{2} \\ \frac{1}{2} & \frac{1}{2} \\ \frac{1}{4} & \frac{3}{4} \end{bmatrix}. \tag{P4.5.26}$$

If initially the state of the parent-pair is (ab, ab), i.e. $(0, 0, 1, 0)$ in θ, the parent-pairs spend an average $(\frac{4}{3}, \frac{1}{3}, \frac{8}{3}, \frac{4}{3})$ periods in states (aa, ab), (aa, bb), (ab, ab), (ab, bb) respectively so that the mean absorption time is $\frac{17}{3}$ generations. The probability of being absorbed in states (aa, aa) and (bb, bb) is then $\frac{1}{2}$ and $\frac{1}{2}$ respectively. If there were an equal probability of starting with parent-pairs (aa, ab) and (aa, bb), i.e. the state $(\frac{1}{2}, \frac{1}{2}, 0, 0)$, then the parent-pairs spend an average $(2, \frac{3}{4}, 2, 1)$ periods in these states so that the mean absorption time is $5\frac{3}{4}$ generations. The probability of being absorbed is then $\frac{5}{8}$ and $\frac{3}{8}$ in (aa, aa) and (bb, bb) respectively.

P4.6 ENVIRONMENTAL EFFECTS

In this section we consider the effect of the fluctuations of the environment on the population of a species. Any non-random fluctuations, e.g. seasonal variations, should be taken into account in the model itself, so that here we only consider the effect of random fluctuations.

In a real situation the population $n(t)$ of a species at time t is a measurable quantity but, because of environmental stochasticity, $n(t)$ cannot be calculated by a theoretical model. What can such a model calculate? It would incorporate the distribution of the random fluctuations which is assumed known; then if all the mathematical problems can be solved, the model would determine the distribution function $P(n, t)$, i.e. the probability that the population is n at time t. When there are several populations $n_1, n_2, \ldots,$ the distribution function is $P(n_1, n_2, \ldots, t)$.

In practice the calculation of $P(n, t)$ is very difficult; qualitatively speaking, the motion of $P(n, t)$ is influenced by two opposing tendencies. There is a **drift** or **frictional** effect which seeks to prevent P from becoming diffuse and there is a **diffusional** effect which does the opposite. An example of the former is the dynamical effect in the corresponding deterministic equation, whereas the latter arises mainly from the random fluctuations. Both these effects are seen in the Fokker–Planck equation which determines the dynamics of $P(n, t)$; this equation is beyond the scope of this book.

Equilibrium in these models means that $P(n, t)$ is independent of time; the actual populations $n(t)$ are not independent of time because of the fluctuating environment but the probability distribution is. Many animal populations are in such an equilibrium, so that we can learn a lot about their populations from a knowledge of the equilibrium distribution $P_e(n)$. For example, consider the effect of environmental stochasticity on a population which, if modelled by a deterministic model, would have an asymptotically stable equilibrium n_e, as in, for example, the logistic model. At equilibrium we might expect that $P_e(n)$ would have a maximum at n_e and would decrease as the value of n deviated from n_e. We can determine the validity of this picture by seeing what happens when the distribution is disturbed from $P_e(n)$.

If the drift effect is much stronger than the diffusional, $P_e(n)$ decreases rapidly with the deviation of n from n_e. Then the deterministic model is reasonable near n_e. If, however, the diffusional effect is stronger, $P_e(n)$ may not exist and if it does it will be very spread out. The deterministic model is then incorrect.

We can say that $P_e(n)$ is asymptotically stable if the distribution returns to $P_e(n)$ when disturbed. This requires, however, the corresponding deterministic model to be asymptotically stable for a finite region around n_e, so that the drift effect is stronger than the diffusional effect for all n such that $P_e(n)$ is non-zero.

What is the connection between $P_e(n)$ and the measurable population which varies with time because of the random fluctuations? These variations are of no interest except that they tell us about the random fluctuations: we are more interested in the time average of the populations over a period long in comparison with any fluctuations. Let us suppose that this average is large in comparison with the size of the fluctuations. Then it is usual to invoke the ergodic hypothesis which is that this time average is equal to the expectation value calculated from $P_e(n)$ because over a long time, $n(t)$ takes on all possible values with the same frequency as $P_e(n)$. This allows us to use $P_e(n)$ in further calculations.

The effect of random fluctuations on the time variation of populations when the distribution is far from equilibrium is an important but difficult topic. The reader is referred to the book by R. M. May for fuller details. One point that needs to be made here is that as populations never increase from zero, if $P(n, t)$ makes the probability that n is zero finite at some time t, then there is a finite probability that the population will become extinct. This means that any deterministic model that predicts a small population which does not die out is likely to be unrealistic. For example, if a predator–prey model predicts a limit cycle in which one of the populations becomes small at some point of the cycle, then every time the cycle is traversed, there is a finite probability that this population becomes extinct owing to the random fluctuations; thus in the long run it will become extinct.

** P4.7 EVOLUTION AND GENETICS

This is a large topic; we give here a brief illustration. In P4.5 we saw how the proportion of parent-pairs evolved in a particular situation. In the natural state, environmental effects and fertility are important. We modify the model of P4.5 to show how such effects modify the population growth.

We consider only the effects of a pair of genes with the individual genes being either a or b. Let $n_{aa}(m)$, $n_{ab}(m)$ and $n_{bb}(m)$ be the expected number of adult animals in the mth generation with genes (aa), (ab) and (bb) respectively. Our aim is to find how the quantities $n_{aa}(m+1)$ etc. are related to $n_{aa}(m)$ etc.

An animal with a particular set of genes is called a **genotype**. Let us suppose that there are equal numbers of male and female genotypes and that each female mates only once. Let us also suppose that males can mate as many times as opportunity presents itself and that mating takes a neglible time. Thus any female's mate has probabilities in the ratios $n_{aa}: n_{ab}: n_{bb}$ of having (aa), (ab) or (bb) genes respectively. Then the proportion of (aa, aa) parent-pairs is $k{n_{aa}}^2$ and the proportion of (aa, ab) parent-pairs is $k^2 n_{aa}n_{ab}$, where the number k is determined by the total number of parent-pairs. Thus

$$k = 1/2n(m), \tag{P4.7.1}$$

where

$$n(m) = n_{aa}(m) + n_{ab}(m) + n_{bb}(m). \tag{P4.7.2}$$

Let us write $x_{aa}(m)$ etc. for the number of offspring with genes (aa) etc. in the mth generation. Such offspring come from several types of parent-pairs. Thus

$$\begin{aligned} x_{aa}(m) = (f_{aa,aa}n_{aa}(m)\, n_{aa}(m) + f_{aa,ab}n_{aa}(m)\, n_{ab}(m) \\ + f_{ab,ab}{n_{ab}}^2(m)/4)/2n(m) \end{aligned} \tag{P4.7.3}$$

where $f_{aa,aa}$ represents the **fertility** of an (aa, aa) mating. Let us assume that parent-pairs have a common fertility f. Then

$$\begin{aligned} x_{aa}(m) &= (n_{aa}(m) + \tfrac{1}{2} n_{ab}(m))^2\, f/2n(m) \\ &= ((n(m) + y(m))/2)^2\, f/2n(m), \end{aligned} \tag{P4.7.4}$$

where

$$y(m) = n_{aa}(m) - n_{bb}(m). \tag{P4.7.5}$$

Similarly

$$x_{bb}(m) = ((n(m) - y(m))/2)^2\, f/2n(m): \tag{P4.7.6}$$

$$x_{ab}(m) = (4n^2(m) - (n(m) + y(m))^2 - (n(m) - y(m))^2)\, f/8n(m). \tag{P4.7.7}$$

How many offspring survive to become adults capable of mating? This depends on many factors, e.g. the numbers of predators and the ability to withstand cold: these are taken into account by a **fitness** function $W_{aa}(x_{aa}(m), x_{bb}(m), x_{ab}(m))$:

$$n_{aa}(m+1) = W_{aa}(x_{aa}(m), x_{bb}(m), x_{ab}(m)). \tag{P4.7.8}$$

The functions W are not known exactly but they are zero when there are no offspring; they are also likely to depend mainly on their own variable, i.e. W_{aa} on x_{aa}, and on the total number of offspring through a logistic factor. Now

$$x_{aa}(m) + x_{bb}(m) + x_{ab}(m) = fn(m)/2. \tag{P4.7.9}$$

Taking first-order terms and the logistic factor into account only, we get

$$n_{aa}(m+1) = w_{aa}x_{aa}(m)\,(1 - fn(m)/2N), \tag{P4.7.10}$$

where w_{aa} and N are constants, and we have ignored the explicit dependence of W_{aa} on $x_{ab}(m)$ and $x_{bb}(m)$. The final equations are

$$n_{aa}(m+1) = w_{aa}f(n(m)+y(m))^2\,(1 - fn(m)/2N)/8n(m),$$

$$n_{bb}(m+1) = w_{bb}f(n(m)-y(m))^2\,(1 - fn(m))2N)/8n(m),$$

$$n_{ab}(m+1) = w_{ab}\,f(n^2(m) - y^2(m))\,(1 - fn(m)/2N)/4n(m).$$

(P4.7.11)

Our aim is to find how these equations behave with two slightly different sets of values for (w_{aa}, w_{bb}, w_{ab}), which correspond to slightly different environments. This gives some insight into the working of evolution on genetics.

We first note that the equations (P4.7.11) can be expressed in terms of two variables, $n(m)$ and $y(m)$, only. When $w_{aa} = w_{bb}$,

$$y(m+1) = w_{aa}fy(m)\,(1 - fn(m)/2N)/2: \tag{P4.7.12}$$

$$n(m+1) = f(1 - fn(m)/2N)\,(w_{aa}(n^2(m) + y^2(m)) + w_{ab}(n^2(m) - y^2(m)))/4n(m). \tag{P4.7.13}$$

When

$$w_{aa}f(1 - fn(m)/2N)/2 < 1, \tag{P4.7.14}$$

y decreases and if this condition is true for all m, y ultimately becomes zero.

Equilibrium for equation (P4.7.12) requires

$$y = 0 \quad \text{or} \quad n = 2N(1 - 2/w_{aa}f)/f. \tag{P4.7.15}$$

Putting these results into (P4.7.13) gives one equilibrium at

$$y = 0, \quad n = 2N(1 - 4/f(w_{aa} + w_{ab}))/f \tag{P4.7.16}$$

and the other at

$$y = \pm n, \quad n = 2N(1 - 2/w_{aa}f)/f. \tag{P4.7.17}$$

The first is stable (unstable) and the second unstable (stable) if

$$w_{ab} > (<)\, w_{aa}. \tag{P4.7.18}$$

Thus if $w_{ab} > w_{aa}$, all genotypes, in general, survive. If, however, $w_{ab} < w_{aa}$, n_{ab} and either n_{aa} or n_{bb} tend to zero and only one of the genotypes (aa) or (*bb*) survives. Thus in our model, two very different types of population are the survivors in two situations which can differ by quite small amounts. Note that our model is not meant to be a model of any particular real situation and so is not verifiable.

In the real world, evolution depends on many characteristics, determined partly by all the gene-pairs. Thus it is difficult to develop realistic models and it is difficult to verify them, as most models explain past events, and do not predict the future. Experimental evidence is also rare as we do not know much about genotypes that do not survive. Note that one gene of a pair may **dominate** its partner, so that animals with the same characteristics (known as **phenotypes**) may be different genotypes. It is the phenotypes that are usually affected by the environment.

There is one species of moth, the melanic, about which there is some information: the phenotypes are of a light and a dark colour; in country areas the light-coloured phenotype is predominant as birds cannot see it against the background of lichen, and in polluted city areas the dark-coloured phenotype is more common, as the background is dark. As smoke pollution decreases in the city areas, the ratio of dark to light phenotypes has decreased in these areas and models have been able to explain the measurements quantitatively.

** P4.8 EVOLUTION AND THE THEORY OF GAMES

When defining the fitness function in P4.7, we assumed, except for the random fluctuations, a deterministic environment. Individual animals, however, react to each other's behaviour so that the behaviour, and hence the fitness, of one animal may depend on the behaviour of another and vice versa. This is the type of situation met in the Theory of Games; but before we use that theory we must look carefully at the terms involved and at our aims. What is meant by game, strategy and pay-off in the context of evolution and animal behaviour?

The aim is to understand the behaviour of a species and how it evolved. For example, in some species the adult males fight each other and inflict horrible, even fatal, wounds; in others, only a display of aggression occurs, why?

In a first attempt at a model incorporating Game Theory, we might think of two individual animals of the same species contesting to see which of them procreates. The pay-off to an individual is the probability that its genes will be transmitted to the next generation, i.e. that it will have some offspring. The strategies are the different types of behaviour adopted by an individual animal in the contest. These types of behaviour may be determined by the animal's genes, or by its early development, or by both.

Such individual contests may occur many times in an animal's lifetime. Suppose that an animal has just experienced such a contest; does this affect its behaviour at the next contest? If it meets a different animal, there is unlikely to be a correlation between the contests. Let us assume that this is so. Then we can construct a **total pay-off** matrix, the pay-offs representing the total surviving offspring of an animal if it adopts a certain behavioural strategy.

Let us look at an archetypal model called the Hawk–Dove model, developed by Maynard Smith who pioneered the application of Game Theory to evolution. In this model there are two behavioural strategies, the Hawk's (H) behaviour, which means fighting, and the Dove's (D) behaviour, which means putting on a display but retreating if the situation warrants it. Let us consider the consequences when two individuals A and B meet. If both A and B play strategy H, they fight with the consequence that one of them wins but one or both may be hurt. If A plays H, and B plays D then A wins but if A plays D, and B plays H then B wins. If they both play D then one of them wins but a lot of time is wasted by both players.

Injury means that the contestants cannot take part in future contests for a time so that their chances of procreation are diminished. Similarly the wasting of time also diminishes the chances of procreation. Thus the total pay-off matrix, for a series of contests over the lifetime of an animal, takes the form:

$$\begin{array}{cc} & \begin{array}{cc} \mathrm{H} & \mathrm{D} \end{array} \\ \begin{array}{c} \mathrm{H} \\ \mathrm{D} \end{array} & \begin{bmatrix} (w/2-i) & w \\ 0 & (w/2-t) \end{bmatrix} \end{array}, \tag{P4.8.1}$$

where w is the total number of offspring that survive to a player who wins, i represents the number of offspring lost due to injury, and t the number lost due to time wasted in display. The game is assumed to be symmetric, i.e. an exchange of strategies leads to the exchange of pay-offs. Thus the diagonal pay-offs have terms $w/2$ in them because there is an equal probability of either player winning.

Different members of a species may adopt different strategies. Individual animals do not have to adopt the same strategy all the time. To make the theory of use for understanding evolution we require that the pay-offs of a strategy are reflected in the behaviour of the next generation. We thus define a 'mixed' strategy such that the proportion of strategies adopted by the 'average' animal is given by the mixed strategy, and this determines through the total pay-off matrix the proportion of the strategies adopted by the next generation. For example, in the Hawk–Dove model, if the proportion of H strategies adopted is $p(m)$ in the mth generation then the pay-off to Hawks is

$$(w/2-i)\,p(m)+w(1-p(m)) \tag{P4.8.2}$$

so that the proportion of Hawkish to Dovish behaviour in the $(m+1)$th generation is

$$p(m)\,(p(m)\,(w/2-i)+w(1-p(m)))/((1-p(m))^2\,(w/2-t)). \tag{P4.8.3}$$

From this we develop the dynamics of the model:

$$\begin{aligned} p(m+1)/(1-p(m+1)) &= p(m)\,((w/2-i)\,p(m) \\ &\quad + w(1-p(m)))/(1-p(m))^2\,(w/2-t). \end{aligned} \tag{P4.8.4}$$

It is easy to see what the equilibrium proportions are. As $0 \leqslant p \leqslant 1$, they are given by

$$p = 0, \quad \text{or} \quad p = 1,$$

$$\text{or} \quad p(w/2 - i) + w(1 - p) = (1 - p)(w/2 - t). \qquad \text{(P4.8.5)}$$

We find that there is a mixed strategy equilibrium

$$p = (w/2 + t)/(i + t) \qquad \text{(P4.8.6)}$$

provided $w/2 < i$.

The equilibrium behaviour which evolves is the one which is asymptotically stable and is known as the **Evolutionary Stable Strategy** or **ESS**. In the Hawk–Dove model above, the mixed equilibrium strategy, if it exists, is usually the ESS. Thus if the risk of injury is greater there is a proportion of 'doves' in the population.

This result cannot be taken as pertaining to any real situation as we have made too many assumptions and neglected too many factors; for instance we have neglected the presence of males and females in the population.

Let us now look at a general contest with strategies $1, 2, \ldots, n$, and a total pay-off matrix with elements u_{ij}. For simplicity let us assume that the game is symmetric. Suppose the proportions of strategies played by the mth generation are $p_1(m): p_2(m): p_3(m): \ldots : p_n(m)$. Then the pay-off to players of strategy i is

$$\sum_{j=1} u_{ij}\, p_j(m) \qquad \text{(P4.8.7)}$$

so that

$$p_1(m+1): p_2(m+1): \ldots : p_n(m+1)$$

$$= \sum_{j=1} p_1(m) u_{1j}\, p_j(m): \sum_{j=1} p_2(m) u_{2j}\, p_j(m): \ldots . \qquad \text{(P4.8.8)}$$

As proportions must sum to one, we get

$$p_i(m+1) = \sum_j p_i(m) u_{ij}\, p_j(m) \Big/ \sum_i \sum_j p_i(m) u_{ij}\, p_j(m). \qquad \text{(P4.8.9)}$$

The equilibrium strategies are got by putting $p_i(m+1)$ equal to $p_i(m)$ for all m, so that they are given by the solutions of the equations

$$p_i = 0 \quad \text{or} \quad \sum_{j=1} u_{ij}\, p_j = \sum_i \sum_j p_i\, u_{ij}\, p_j. \qquad \text{(P4.8.10)}$$

These are the conditions which determine the stationary points of the quadratic expression

$$\sum_{i,j} p_i\, u_{ij}\, p_j, \qquad \text{(P4.8.11)}$$

subject to the constraint of conservation of proportion. Note that the game here is, in general, not a zero-sum game, and that the ESS is, in general, neither a maximin nor an equilibrium strategy in the Game Theory sense.

The equilibrium strategies have to be tested for stability to see which of them are ESSs. This is done by perturbing the systems from equilibrium, linearizing equation (P4.8.9) and then investigating the motion – the usual procedure. Let

$$p_i(m) = p_i^e + \epsilon_i(m) \tag{P4.8.12}$$

where p_i^e is the ith component of the equilibrium proportions. Then

$$\sum_i \epsilon_i(m) = 0 \tag{P4.8.13}$$

to conserve the total proportionality. As it is stationary, (P4.8.11) is unchanged to first order when none of p_i^e is zero. In this case

$$\epsilon_i(m+1) = \epsilon_i(m) + \sum_j p_i^e u_{ij} \epsilon_j(m) \sum_{i,j} p_i^e u_{ij} p_j^e. \tag{P4.8.14}$$

When one or more of $p_i^e = 0$, the analysis is more complicated.

There may, in general, be two or more ESSs (see PE4.13); then the population may evolve to any of them. There may be no ESSs, in which case the dynamics is like a limit cycle.

The applications of Game Theory to evolution are rapidly growing, and the verification of the results is more successful than in the application to economics, probably because fitness is a more measurable and objective quantity than utility. The reader is referred to Maynard Smith's book (PS2) for further details.

PE4. EXERCISES

4.1 Obtain the equation

$$dP(n, t)/dt = (n+1)\, sP(n+1, t) - (r+s)\, nP(n, t) + (n-1)\, rP(n-1, t)$$

for the probability distribution for a model similar to that of P4.2 but in which a member can also die, the probability of which is s in time t. Solve these equations when $r = 0$ and the initial population is N.

4.2 Obtain the relation

$$P(n, m+1) = \sum_{j=0} {}_{n-j}C_j (1 - rT)^{n-2j} (rT)^j P(n-j, m)$$

for the discrete time model discussed in P4.2. Calculate $P(n_0, m)$ for all m.

4.3 Draw transition diagrams for the following Markov chain matrices:

(i) $\begin{bmatrix} \frac{1}{4} & 0 & \frac{3}{4} \\ \frac{1}{2} & \frac{1}{2} & 0 \\ \frac{1}{2} & 0 & \frac{1}{2} \end{bmatrix}$; (ii) $\begin{bmatrix} \frac{1}{2} & 0 & 0 & \frac{1}{2} \\ \frac{1}{3} & \frac{1}{3} & \frac{1}{3} & 0 \\ 0 & \frac{1}{4} & \frac{1}{2} & \frac{1}{4} \\ \frac{1}{4} & 0 & 0 & \frac{3}{4} \end{bmatrix}$.

Identify the classes and put the matrices into canonical form.

4.4 Determine the behaviour for all time of the following transition matrices:

(i) $\begin{bmatrix} \frac{1}{2} & \frac{1}{2} \\ \frac{2}{3} & \frac{1}{3} \end{bmatrix}$; (ii) $\begin{bmatrix} 1 & 0 \\ \frac{2}{3} & \frac{1}{3} \end{bmatrix}$.

Does the long-time behaviour agree with the theoretical predictions?

4.5 A betting machine has four lights, one red, one green, one blue and one white. The winning light comes on at the end of a play, and the probability that a particular colour wins depends only on the colour of the previous winner. Write r, g, b and w for the probabilities for the red, green, blue and white lights respectively winning. If the previous winner was red, $r = g = b = w$: if it was green, then $g = 0$ and $r = b = w$: if it was blue, $b = w = 0$ and $r = g$: and if it was white, $g = \frac{1}{2}$, $b = \frac{1}{3}$, $w = \frac{1}{6}$, $r = 0$. Find the transition matrix. Assuming that it is regular, show that in the long run, $b = 7w/6$ and $g = 23w/16$.

A player can place a bet for a particular winning colour: if his stake is on blue or white he gets back three times his stake but if on red or green only two times his stake. If the player places 1p randomly between the colours, how much on average does he lose per bet?

4.6 A red bag initially contains four red balls and a white bag four white balls. At each go, one ball is taken from the red bag and one from the white bag at random; the two balls are then put back into the bags at random, one in each. Identify the states of the system and the long-run behaviour.

4.7 An office consists of three people, A, B and C, with C the boss, B the senior clerk and A the junior clerk. The office deals with incoming letters; all start in A's in-tray and it always takes a day for letters to move from one in-tray to another. C has two in-trays, one for letters which he must read and reply to, and the other which acts as a file to which all letters go after replies have been written.

Any letter in A's or B's in-trays has a probability $\frac{1}{2}$ that it will receive an immediate reply and be sent to C for filing. Otherwise a letter in A's in-tray has a probability $\frac{3}{8}$ and $\frac{1}{8}$ of being passed to B and C respectively: a letter in B's in-tray has probabilities of $\frac{1}{3}$ and $\frac{1}{6}$ of being passed respectively to A and C. Show that the proportion of letters to which A, B and C reply is $\frac{4}{7}:\frac{3}{14}:\frac{3}{14}$. Find the average length of time before a letter reaches the file.

4.8 A game of 'table cricket' is played with two identical coins. The score which a batsman gets off the nth ball he receives is I_n which is the nearest integer to $(I_{n-1} + u_n)/3$, and u_n is determined by the throw of the coins. For two tails, u_n is zero, for a head and a tail, u_n is two and for two heads, u_n is four. When $I_0 = 1$ show that the batsman cannot score more than two off any ball.

The batsman is 'out' if $I_n = 0$, and then does not receive another ball. Find the transition matrix for the probabilities of scoring I_{n+1} when I_n is known. Calculate the average number of balls and the average score of a batsman before he is out.

4.9 In the country of Scongland, the weather is never the same on two consecutive days. If it is fine one day, it always rains the next day. If it rains one day, there is an equal probability of it being fine or snowing on the next day, and if it snows, next day it will, with equal probability, be either fine or rain. Writing $f(n)$, $r(n)$, $s(n)$ for the probabilities that on the nth day it is fine, it rains or it snows, find the transition matrix which expresses $f(n)$, $r(n)$, $s(n)$ in terms of $f(n-1)$ etc.

The probabilities $f(0)$, $r(0)$, $s(0)$ are known.

(i) By considering P^4, or otherwise, show that P is regular. Find the long-run values of $f(n)$, $r(n)$ and $s(n)$.

(ii) Obtain an equation relating $f(n)$ to $f(n-1)$ and find $f(n)$ in terms of $f(0)$. Get an equation for $r(n)$ in terms of $r(n-1)$ and $f(n-1)$ and hence find $r(n)$.

(iii) Similarly find $s(n)$ and compare them with the results from (i).

4.10 (i) Use the Perron–Frobenius theorem to derive the result (P2.8.13) for Leslie matrices that are regular.

(ii) Consider the Leslie matrix

$$A = \begin{bmatrix} \frac{16}{17} & b & \frac{1}{27} \\ \frac{1}{17} & \frac{23}{24} - b & 0 \\ 0 & \frac{1}{24} & \frac{26}{27} \end{bmatrix}$$

and its use in (P2.8.9). Show that the total population is constant. Show also that A has an eigenvalue of one. What is the population distribution after many years?

4.11 Verify the stability conditions for the equilibria in the model of evolution and genetics in P4.7. Does it make any difference if the logistic term is absent?

4.12 In a general two-player symmetric game with two strategies find the condition(s) which make a mixed strategy the ESS. Check your results in the Hawk–Dove model.

4.13 In the Hawk–Dove model, with $w/2 - i > 0$, are the pure strategies ESSs?

4.14 In a two-player symmetric game with three strategies (1, 2, 3) the behaviour is given by a point (p_1, p_2, p_3) in the equilateral triangle shown in Fig. G2.2.

(i) Show that the perpendicular distance from P to the side 23 of the triangle is proportional to p_1.

(ii) Consider the Hawk–Dove Retaliator game with the pay-off matrix

$$\begin{array}{c} \\ H \\ D \\ R \end{array} \begin{array}{c} \begin{array}{ccc} H & D & R \end{array} \\ \begin{bmatrix} -1 & 2 & -1 \\ 0 & 1 & 0.9 \\ -1 & 1.1 & 1 \end{bmatrix} \end{array} .$$

Show that there are two ESSs and investigate the 'trajectories' in the triangle.

(iii) Consider the 'Scissors, Paper, Stone', game see G2.2 with a small reward for a draw:

$$\begin{array}{c} \\ Sc \\ P \\ St \end{array} \begin{array}{c} \begin{array}{ccc} Sc & P & St \end{array} \\ \begin{bmatrix} 0.1 & 1 & -1 \\ -1 & 0.1 & 1 \\ 1 & -1 & 0.1 \end{bmatrix} \end{array} .$$

Show that there are no ESSs.

4.15$^{(m)}$ Develop a model of evolution and genetics along the lines of P4.7, in which time is considered as a continuous variable. This occurs when the animals have an adult life which is long in comparison with the time between breeding seasons and with the time to reach maturity.

4.16$^{(m)}$ Model a three-animal contest in which the strategies are Hawk, Dove and Sneak.

Hints and Answers

EE2.2 (i) $\text{RCS} = (3U - 2x)/(2y - U)$.
(ii) $(2x - 3U)(2y - U) = 4U^2$.

2.3 $D(x_1) = p_2^2 y/p_1(p_2^2 + 27p_1^2)$: $D(x_2) = 27p_1^2 y/(p_2^2 + 27p_1^2)p_2$.

2.5 $10/7\sqrt{2}$ units of sugar, costing $180/7\sqrt{2}$ units of money.

2.6 $\epsilon_{11} = -(p_2^{1/2} + 2(2p_1)^{1/2})/2(p_2^{1/2} + (2p_1)^{1/2})$,
$\epsilon_{12} = -p_2^{1/2}/2(p_2^{1/2} + (2p_1)^{1/2})$: $\eta_1 = 1$, $\eta_2 = 1$, etc.

2.7 $4bp_y/p_x(p_x + 4p_y)$: $p_x/(p_x + 4p_y)$.

2.8 Let $f(u(x, y))$ be the new utility function. Then $\partial U/\partial x = (\mathrm{d}f/\mathrm{d}u)\,\partial u/\partial x = 4y^4x(\mathrm{d}f/\mathrm{d}u)/(2y^2 + x^2)^2$. The term $(\mathrm{d}f/\mathrm{d}u)$ cancels out in the maximization process. $D(x) = 2zp_1^{1/3}/(2p_1^{2/3} + (2p_2)^{2/3}) = \frac{9}{2}$ pence. $\mathrm{d}(p_1x)/\mathrm{d}t = 264/(17)(2^{1/3})$ pence per week.

2.9 (a) $(3/7)(B/M)^{1/2}$: (b) $49/67$: (c) the parameters are 0.3 and 0.7. Write them as b and m; calculate the demand for M in terms of m, b, p_B and p_M and calculate $\mathrm{d}/\mathrm{d}t(Mp_M/y)$.

2.10 Find dx_2/dx_1 in terms of x_1, x_2 and hence find d^2x_2/dx_1^2.

2.11 (i) Put $\lambda = \frac{1}{2}$, $\mathbf{q}^{1,2} = (x_1 + \delta x_1, x_2 \mp ((\partial U/\partial x_1)/(\partial U/\partial x_2))\,\delta x_1)$ in the condition for concavity, and demonstrate graphically the proof by drawing the indifference curve through $\mathbf{q}^1$ and $\mathbf{q}^2$:

(ii) find d^2x_2/dx_1^2 along an indifference curve in terms of $(\partial U/\partial x_1)$, $(\partial^2 U/\partial x_1^2)$, etc.

(iii) use (i) and the definitions of derivatives to show $d^2x_2/dx_1^2 < 0$, remembering that $\partial U/\partial x_{1,2} > 0$, and that only terms to second order are required.

2.12 $U_2 = (U_1)^2 + 4$.

2.14 Put equation (E2.6.14) and the derivative of (E2.4.4) in terms of differentials dp_i, dq_i and $d\lambda$, and obtain a symmetric matrix.

EE3.2 (i) $ax_2/(1-a)x_1$.

3.5 (iii) $4(1 - x^2/2(6 - x^2)) \sim 4(1 - q^{1/2}/12)$ for small q.

3.6 Expansion path is $x_1 r_1(1-\alpha) = \alpha r_2 x_2$.

$$q = A(C - b)\,(\alpha/r_1)^\alpha\,((1-\alpha)/r_2)^{1-\alpha}. \qquad (1).$$

The tangent to the isoquant at $x_1 = x_2 = 15$ is the isocost $C = x_1/3 + 2x_2/3 + 15$ when $C = 30$ units, so that 30 is the minimum cost. Putting $C = 30$ into (1) gives $q = 15$, showing that minimizing the cost and maximizing the output lead to the same results.

3.8 (i) is unrealistic, because its MC is negative at $q = \frac{10}{3}$.
$MC = 3q^2 - 20q + 33$.

3.9 (i) $AVC = q^2 - 10q + 33$ which has a minimum at $q = 5$. Thus the entrepreneur ceases production for $p = MC\ (q = 5) = 8$ units.
$3q^2 - 20q + 33 = p$ implies $q = (10 + (1 + 3p)^{1/2})/3$: hence
$S(p) = (10 + (1 + 3p)^{1/2})/3$ for $p \geqslant 8$; $S(p) = 0$ for $p < 8$.

3.10 $S(p) = \frac{17}{3}$ units; profits $= (17/3)(16) - C(17/3)$.

3.11 Suppose the entrepreneur needs q units per unit time. Then for (Nq/q_2) units of time he produces at rate q_2 and for $N(1 - q/q_2)$ units of time he ceases production, thereby giving the cost function described. In the ideal market, the entrepreneur does not use this part of the cost function curve.

EE4.1 $100(6p-6) = -300p + 3000$ gives $p = 4$ units. With the tax, the supply $= 100(6(p-1)-6)$ giving $p = 4\frac{2}{3}$ units. The increase in price is less than 1, but this is because the supply to the market is reduced.

4.2 $p = 30$ units ($q = 10$).

4.3 $p = \frac{49}{11}$.

4.4 (i) $p = 14.11$: (ii) $p = 8$: (iii) no supply.
(i) $q = 5.16, p = 14.84$: (ii) $q = 4.53, p = 8.47$:
(iii) $q = 4.41, p = 7.59$.

4.5 $p = 8$, profit $= 2$ units. In a monopoly, $p = (29-(19)^{1/2})/3$.

4.6 $S(p) = (7 + (1 + 3p)^{1/2})/3$ for $p \geqslant \frac{15}{4}$; $= 0$ for $p < \frac{15}{4}$.
(i) $p = \frac{35}{3}$, $q = 13N/3$; (ii) no supply.

4.7 $q = 12.5$, $p = 87.5$, profit $= 681.25$. If $p_1 = p_2$, the aggregate demand $D_1(p) + D_2(p) = D(p)$, so that the decomposition is possible. The answers are: $p_1 = 125$, $q_1 = 5$, $p_2 = 75$, $q_2 = \frac{15}{2}$, profit $= 775$. The monopolist and the second group of consumers prefer the new arrangement, whereas the first group does not.

4.8 $\mathrm{d}p/\mathrm{d}t = (k/3)(p-1)(p-2)$. Hence $p = (2 - A\exp(kt/3)))/(1 - A \exp(kt/3))$.

4.9 $p_e = 1$. (i) $E(p) = 3 - p - (6p^2/(1+2p^2))$; $E'(p_e) = -\frac{7}{3} < 0$.
(ii) $F(q) = 3 - q - (q/(6-2q))^{1/2}$; $F'(q_e) = -1\frac{3}{4} < 0$.
(iii) $S'(p_e) = \frac{4}{3}$, $D'(p_e) = -1$.

4.11 $p_e = 125$. $k_1, k_2 > 0$; $p = 125 - A\exp(-2k_1 t/5)$; p is stable in accord with Walras' stability condition, but Marshall's criterion predicts instability. The solution of the difference equation is $p_t = 125 + A(1 - 2k_2/5)^t$, which is stable if $k_2 < 5$.

4.12 Adam's excess demand function A_f for figs is $x_f - 6$, and A_a for apples is x_a. His budget constraint is $p_f A_f + p_a A_a = 0$. Similarly $E_f = y_f$, $E_a = y_a - 18$, and $p_f E_f + p_a E_a = 0$. $U_A = (A_f + 6)A_a/(9(A_f + 6) + A_a)$. Maximizing we get $p_f/p_a = A_a^2/(9(A_f + 6)^2) = (E_a + 18)^2/E_f^2$. Hence $(3 + (p_f/p_a)^{1/2})A_f = -18$ and $E_f(p_f/p_a)^{1/2}(1 + (p_f/p_a)^{1/2}) = 18$. The equilibrium conditions are $E_f + A_f = 0$, $E_a + A_a = 0$. Whence $p_f/p_a = 3$, $A_f = -18/(3 + 3^{1/2})$, $x_a = 54/(3 + 3^{1/2})$, etc..

EE5.1 Note that the third activity is dominated.

5.2 Let the intensity vector be $(z_1, z_2, 0, z_4)$. Then $z_1 + z_2 + z_4 = 2$.
(i) Cost $= £10(8z_1 + z_1 + 5z_2 + 2z_2 + z_4 + 5z_4) = £10(9z_1 + 7z_2 + 6z_4)$. The minimum occurs when $z_2 = z_4 = 0$, $z_4 = 2$: cost $= £120$.
(ii) Cost $= £10(8z_1 + 5z_1 + 5z_2 + 10z_2 + z_4 + 25z_4) = £10(13z_1 + 15z_2 + 26z_4)$. The minimum occurs when $z_2 = z_4 = 0$, $z_1 = 2$; cost $= £260$.

5.3 $2\frac{1}{2}$ jackets, $4\frac{1}{2}$ trousers, profit £$42\frac{1}{2}$. The answer is not necessarily in integers, as jackets and trousers not finished on one day can be finished on the next.

5.4 Let l, b, h be the number (in·thousands) of cars from Liverpool, Bristol and Harwich respectively, and l_o, l_d, and so on, be the numbers going to Oxford and Derby from Liverpool. Then $l_o + l_d = 5$, $b_o + b_d = 8$, $h_o + h_d = 6$, $l_o + b_o + h_o = 10$.
Cost $= 29l_o + 25l_d + 27b_o + 30b_d + 22h_o + 27h_d$. Eliminate l_d, b_d, h_d and h_o to give cost in terms of l_o and b_o. The constraints are $l_o \leqslant 5$, $b_o \leqslant 8$, $l_o + b_o \leqslant 10$: also $h_o \leqslant 6$, so that $l_o + b_o \geqslant 4$. Maximum occurs when $l_o = 0$, $b_o = 4$, cost $=$ £485,000.

5.5 Take axes 1, 2, 3 as rice, beans and pineapples. The feasible region has vertices $(0, \frac{5}{6}, \frac{7}{24})$, $(0, 2, 0)$, $(5, 0, \frac{1}{3})$, $(15, 0, 0)$. The minimum occurs at $(0, \frac{5}{6}, \frac{7}{24})$ kg.

5.7 If industries A, B, C wish to produce y_A, y_B, y_C units of output, they must produce $(40y_A + 13y_B + 11y_C)/32$, $(8y_A + 41y_B + 15y_C)/64$, $(8y_A + 9y_B + 47y_C)/32$ units respectively. The primary inputs are: $5(40y_A + 13y_B + 11y_C)/256$, $(8y_A + 41y_B + 15y_C)/64$, $3(8y_A + 9y_B + 47y_C)/256$.

GE2.1 The pure strategies for both A and B are to choose a number between 1 and 6 inclusive. A's outcome matrix is the following: (B's is $-A$'s).

		B's choice					
		1	2	3	4	5	6
A's choice	1	1	−1	1	−1	1	−1
	2	−1	1	−1	1	−1	1
	3	1	−1	1	−1	1	−1
	4	−1	1	−1	1	−1	1
	5	1	−1	1	−1	1	−1
	6	−1	1	−1	1	−1	1

2.2 The pay-offs are as follows, for (A, B, C) respectively:

		C's choice	*B*'s choice 1	*B*'s choice 2
A's choice	1	1	$(3,-1,-1)$	$(-1,3,-1)$
		2	$(-1,3,-1)$	$(-1,-1,3)$
	2	1	$(-1,3,-1)$	$(-1,-1,3)$
		2	$(-1,-1,3)$	$(3,-1,-1)$.

2.3

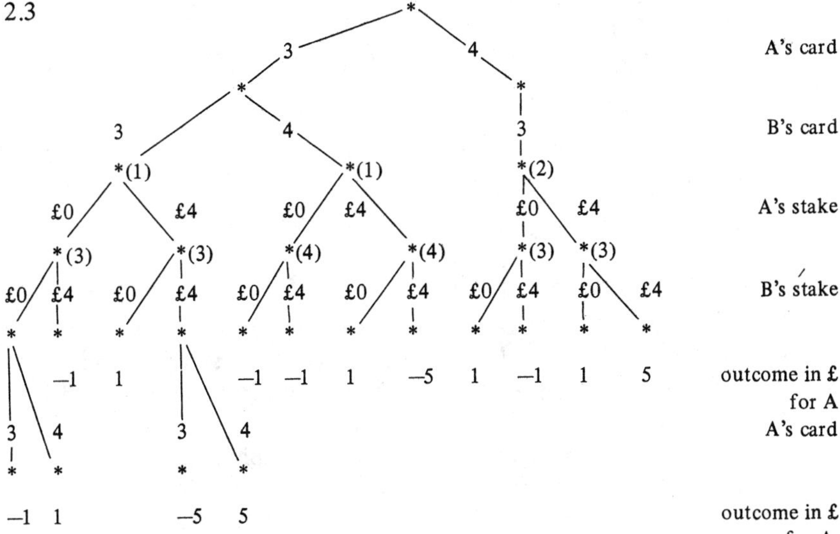

A typical strategy for A is: if my card is 3, I stake £0, but if it is 4, I stake £0. Write this symbolically as (3, £0; 4, £0); his other strategies are (3, £0; 4, £4), (3, £4; 4, £0), (3, £4; 4, £4). Call these 1, 2, 3, 4. B has the same strategies. States in the same information set have the same bracketed number.

2.4 We write W for the blank card and J for the joker. One strategy for A is: if the card is blank, put 1p into the kitty, but if the card is the joker, put 1p in. Write this symbolically as (W → 1; J → 1). His other strategies are: (W → 1; J → 3), (W → 3; J → 1), (W → 3; J → 3). One strategy for B is: if A puts in 1p, fold, but if A puts 3p, fold. Write this symbolically as (1 → F; 3 → F). His other strategies are: (1 → F; 3 → S), (1 → S; 3 → F), (1 → S; 3 → S).

2.5 To see the strategies, draw a game-tree.
(Confess on first round; if B confesses on first found, then I confess on second

round, but if B refuses on 1st round, I confess on second) is a typical strategy for A. Write this symbolically as (C; C → C, R → C). A's other strategies are: (C; C → C, R → R), (C; C → R, R → C), (C, C → R, R → R), (R; C → C, R → C), (R; C → C, R → R), (R; C → R, R → C), (R; C → R, R → R). Lavel these as 1–8. B has the same strategies. The outcome matrices are (leaving out the negative signs)

	B's strategies							
	1	2	3	4	5	6	7	8
1	10(10)	10(10)	5(12)	5(12)	5(12)	5(12)	0(14)	0(14)
2	10(10)	10(10)	5(12)	5(12)	7(7)	7(7)	2(9)	2(9)
3	12(5)	12(5)	7(7)	7(7)	7(7)	5(12)	0(14)	0(14)
4	12(5)	12(5)	7(7)	7(7)	7(7)	7(7)	2(9)	2(9)
5	12(5)	7(7)	7(7)	7(7)	7(7)	2(9)	7(7)	2(9)
6	12(5)	7(7)	12(5)	7(7)	9(2)	4(4)	9(2)	4(4)
7	12(5)	7(7)	12(5)	7(7)	9(2)	4(4)	7(7)	2(9)
8	14(0)	9(2)	14(0)	9(2)	9(2)	4(4)	9(2)	4(4)

GE3.1 If it is transformable to a zero-sum game, there exist numbers s and t such that $sU + t + U^T = 0$. Consider the first two elements: we require $-4s + t - 4 = 0$, and $-4s + t + 111 = 0$, and these are incompatible.

3.2 $s + t - 2 = 0$ and $-2s + t + 13 = 0$ imply that $s = \frac{3}{2}$, $t = -10$. Then the first matrix transforms into the second.

3.3 See solution (GE2.3) for labels. The outcome matrix is:

		B's stragies			
		1	2	3	4
A's strategies	1	0	0	$\frac{1}{2}$	-1
	2	0	0	$\frac{1}{2}$	$\frac{1}{2}$
	3	$-\frac{1}{2}$	$\frac{1}{2}$	0	$-\frac{3}{2}$
	4	1	$-\frac{1}{2}$	$\frac{3}{2}$	0

3.8 The game has to be symmetric for all pairs of players. For two players, $U_B = U_A^T$; if zero-sum, $U_B = -U_A = U_A^T$ and the matrices are skew-symmetric. symmetric.

3.9 Typical strategy is: 'if I win toss, I play Ai, but if I lose, I play Bj'. Write this symbolically as (W, Ai; L, Bj). Against the strategy (W, Ak; L, Bl) the pay-off is $\frac{1}{2}((U_A)_{il} + (U_B)_{jk})$. There are mn pure strategies in this game.

3.10 Typical strategy is: play Ai on first game and Bj on second. This can be symbolically written: (Ai; Bj). Against (Bl; Ak) the pay-off matrix for the first player is $((U_A)_{il} + (U_B)_{jk})$, which in a zero-sum game is $((U_A)_{il} - (U_A)_{kj})$. This is twice the pay-off matrix of Exercise 3.9.

GE4.1 (i) Maximin at (2, 3). (ii) Maximins at (2, 2), (2, 4), (4, 2), (4, 4).

4.2 (i) A plays $(\frac{2}{5}, \frac{3}{5}, 0)$, B plays $(\frac{3}{5}, \frac{2}{5})$.
(ii) $A2$ dominates $A1$; $B1$ dominates $B2$ and $B3$. So B plays $B1$, so that A plays $A2$.
(iii) A plays $(\frac{5}{7}, \frac{1}{4}, \frac{3}{14})$, B plays $(\frac{1}{2}, \frac{1}{2}, 0)$; value $\frac{3}{2}$.
(iv) Add one to the pay-offs. The vertices are at $(\frac{7}{27}, \frac{1}{9}, 0)$, $(\frac{1}{5}, \frac{1}{5}, 0)$, $(\frac{1}{3}, 0, \frac{1}{15})$, $(0, \frac{1}{2}, \frac{1}{10})$. The maximum occurs at the last one, with value $\frac{5}{3}$. So B plays $(0, \frac{5}{6}, \frac{1}{6})$ and gains $(-\frac{2}{3})$. A plays $(0, \frac{2}{3}, \frac{1}{3})$.

4.5 (i) Maximin at (2, 2); value = 6.
(ii) A plays $(\frac{3}{8}, \frac{5}{8})$, B plays $(\frac{1}{2}, \frac{1}{2})$; value $= \frac{1}{2}$.
(iii) A plays $(0, \frac{1}{13}, \frac{9}{26}, \frac{15}{26})$, B plays $(0, \frac{1}{13}, \frac{6}{13}, \frac{6}{13})$.

4.6 Suppose A chooses to fire at a distance x and B at a distance y apart. Then the pay-off to A is:

$$\begin{array}{ll} \text{if } x < y & -p_B(y) + p_A(x)(1 - p_B(y)) \\ \text{if } x > y & p_A(x) - p_B(y)(1 - p_A(x)) \\ \text{if } x = y & p_A(x) - p_B(x). \end{array}$$

GE5.1 The strategy for A on the second play depends on the strategies A and B chose on the previous play. To prove last part, use induction.

5.2 The game is fair, as it is symmetric.

5.3 (See solution to GE2.5.) Strategies 2, 3, 4 are dominated by strategy 1; strategies 6, 7, 8 are dominated by 5. Removing the dominated strategies leaves

$$\begin{array}{c c} & \begin{array}{cc} 1 & 5 \end{array} \\ \begin{array}{c} 1 \\ 2 \end{array} & \begin{bmatrix} -10(-10) & -5(-12) \\ -12(-5) & -7(-7) \end{bmatrix} \end{array}$$

showing that the strategy 1 is the 'best' strategy. Nevertheless the pay-off matrix of GE2.5 has no immediately dominating strategies, as strategies 5 and 6 are preferable to strategy 1 if player B plays strategies 2 or 6.

PE2.1 $dx/dt = x/(0.4 + 10^{-7}x)$; hence $0.4 \ln(x) + 10^{-7}x - 0.4 \ln(10^8) - 10 = t$. $t = 90.4$ min.

2.2 (i) $dn/dt = na_1^{1/2}$ for small n, so that $a_1 = \beta^2$. Equilibrium is given by $n = a_1/a_2 = \beta/\sigma$, so that $a_2 = \beta\sigma$.
(ii) Put $u^2 = (a_1 - a_2 n)$: $dt = -du((\beta + u)^{-1} + (\beta - u)^{-1})/\ln(\beta + u) - \ln(\beta - u) = -\beta t +$ constant. Hence $(\beta + u)/(\beta - u) = A \exp(-\beta t)$: thus $u = \beta(A \exp(-\beta t) - 1)/(A \exp(-\beta t) + 1)$.
(iii) $n = N$ when $A \exp(-\beta t) - 1 = 0$, i.e. when $t = \ln(A)/\beta$. Now $A = (\beta + u_0)/(\beta - u_0)$; expand u_0 in a binomial series: $u_0 = (\beta)^{1/2}(\beta - \sigma n_0)^{1/2} = (\beta)(1 - \sigma n_0/2)$, to get answer.

2.3 When $b = 2d$, $dn/dt = nd(N - n)/(N + n)$. Thus $n(N - n_0)^2/(n_0(N - n)^2) = \exp(dt)$.

2.4 The number of seeds at a given time $= k_1 n$. Their probability of reaching maturity $= k_1 n$ (times (probability that a seed finds a vacant site)) $= k_1 n(k_2(N - n))$.

2.5 $dn_{AB}/dt = cnn_B$. Now $n_{AB} = N - n = 2N - n_B$. Thus $dn/dt = -cn(N + n)$. $n/N = \exp(-Nct)/(2 - \exp(-Nct))$.

2.6 $dn_3/dt = n_1 n_2^2/(kT(k + n_3))$; $k - n_3 = n_1$; $k - 2n_3 = n_2$. Separate the variables and use partial fractions, i.e. $(k + n_3)/((k - n_3)(k - 2n_3)^2) = (2/(k - n_3) - 4/(k - 2n_3) + 3k/(k - 2n_3)^2)/k$.

2.8 There is always one root of $f(x) = 0$ at the origin. When $y_1 = \frac{1}{3}$, there are no more real roots; when $y_1 = \frac{1}{4}$, there are two equal roots, and when $y_1 = \frac{4}{25}$ there are two distinct real roots. For (i) the equilibrium value of x is small, so that this is not a suitable case; for (ii) fluctuations may make the population tend towards the small stable equilibrium value, so that $\frac{1}{4} \leqslant y_1 \leqslant \frac{4}{25}$ ensures that the population remains near the stable larger equilibrium value.

2.9 Equilibrium is given by $n(m) = n(m - 1) = N(\alpha - 1)$. When $n(m - 1) < N(\alpha - 1)$, $N(\alpha - 1) > n(m) > n(m - 1)$.

2.10 Leslie matrix is

$$\begin{pmatrix} 0 & 5 & 0 & \frac{16}{3} \\ \frac{3}{4} & 0 & 0 & 0 \\ 0 & \frac{1}{2} & 0 & 0 \\ 0 & 0 & \frac{1}{2} & 0 \end{pmatrix}.$$

$a = \frac{15}{4}$, so that $\lambda^2 = (15 + 17)/8 = 4$ or $-\frac{1}{4}$. The eigvector for $\lambda = 2$ is $\mathbf{x} = ((\frac{128}{3}), 16, 4, 1)$. The population is then $3(2^n)\mathbf{x}$, in year n.

PE3.3 The equilibrium points are (0, 0), (0, 600), (600, 0), (500, 500). The origin is an unstable improper node, the next two are saddle-points and the last is an asymptotically stable improper node. The reason why the species co-exist is that the competition between them is not great: here $\sigma_1 = \sigma_2 = \frac{1}{5} < 1$, whereas in P3.4.5, $\sigma_1 = \sigma_2 = 2 > 1$.

3.4 The equilibria are at (0, 0), (0, 600), (600, 0). The first is an unstable, the second, an asymptotically stable improper node and the last a saddle-point.

3.5 The equilibria are at (0, 0), (0, 600), (1200, 0), (300, 900). The first is an unstable improper node, the second and third are saddle-points, and the last is an asymptotically stable spiral point.

3.7 In the equation $dx_1/dt = 2x_1(1 - (x_1 + 2x_2)/600)$, the term $2x_1$ represents the (birth–death)-rate when the species X_1 is on its own and with an infinite supply of food. The term $-2x_1^2/600$ represents the logistic effect, due to the finiteness of the food supply. The term $-4x_1x_2/600$ represents the competitive effect of the species X_2, competing for the same food, etc.

3.8 There is competition between the species. The equilibria are given by (0, 0) and the part of the line $1 - x_1/N_1 - x_2/N_2 = 0$ that lies in the positive quadrant. Note that $dx_2/dx_1 = 2x_2/x_1$ so that $x_2 = Ax_1^2$. Thus all trajectories are parabolic and end on the above line.

3.9 These equations have a predator–prey interaction. $x(r + 1) - x(r) = x(r) - x(r)y(r)$ so that the term $x(r)$ on the right-hand side represents (birth–death)-rate when the predator is not present and the term $-x(r)y(r)$ represents the effect of predation on the species X. Now $y(r + 1) - y(r) = -3y(r)/2 + x(r)y(r)$; the term $-3y(r)/2$ represents the death-rate of predators when there is no prey, and $x(r)y(r)$ represents the rate of increase due to the presence of prey.

3.10 The equilibrium points, eigenvectors and eigenvalues are:

(0,0) $\eta_1 = (1, 0),\ \lambda_1 = 1$: $\qquad \eta_2 = (0, 1),\ \lambda_2 = 2$;

$(0,N)$ $\eta_1 = (7,2)$, $\lambda_1 = \frac{3}{2}$: $\eta_2 = (0,1)$, $\lambda_2 = -2$;

$(N,0)$ $\eta_1 = (1,6)$, $\lambda_1 = 2$: $\eta_2 = (1,0)$, $\lambda_2 = -1$;

$(2N,2N)$ $\eta_1 = (1, 3^{1/2} - 1)$, $\lambda_1 = -3 + 3^{1/2}$: $\eta_2 = (-1, 1 + 3^{1/2})$,
$\lambda_2 = -3 + 3^{1/2}$.

3.11 The maximum of H is given by $\partial H/\partial x = \partial H/\partial y = 0$. $\mathrm{d}H/\mathrm{d}t = (\partial H/\partial x)\mathrm{d}x/\mathrm{d}t + (\partial H/\partial y)\mathrm{d}y/\mathrm{d}t$. Thus if $\mathrm{d}H/\mathrm{d}t > 0$, H increases with time until H reaches its maximum.

3.12 Equilibrium points are (0, 0), (1, 1). The first is a saddle-point and the second a centre. $\mathrm{d}C/\mathrm{d}t = (\partial C/\partial x)\mathrm{d}x/\mathrm{d}t + (\partial C/\partial y)\mathrm{d}y/\mathrm{d}t = (1 - 1/x)x(1 - y) + (1 - 1/y)y(x - 1) = 0$. Write $u = x - 1$, $v = y - 1$. Then $C = u + 1 - \ln(u + 1) + v + 1 - (\ln(v + 1)$

$$= u + 1 - (u - u^2/2) + v + 1 - (v - v^2/2) \text{ for small } u, v.$$

For the second set of equations, $\mathrm{d}C/\mathrm{d}t = (1 - 4C)/200$, so that for $C < \frac{1}{4}$, C increases and for $C > \frac{1}{4}$, C decreases, so that $C = \frac{1}{4}$ is a limit cycle.

3.14

$$\mathrm{d}\mathbf{x}/\mathrm{d}t = \begin{pmatrix} 15 & -32 & 25 \\ 8 & -17 & 14 \\ 2 & -4 & 4 \end{pmatrix} . \mathbf{x}$$

The eigenvalues are 1, 2, -1, with eigenvectors (1, 2, 2), (3, 2, 1), (2, 1, 0). Write (x, y, z) as $a\mathbf{x}_1 + b\mathbf{x}_2 + c\mathbf{x}_{-1}$ to get $a = -x + 2y - z$, $b = 2x - 4y + 3z$, $c = -2x + 5y - 4z$. The equilibrium point is unstable.

PE4.1 Suppose δt is so small that at most only one person dies. Then $P(n, t + \delta t) = \sigma_0 \tau_0 P(n, t) + \sigma_1 P(n - 1, t) + \tau_1 P(n + 1, t)$, where τ_0 is the probability that no deaths occur in δt. $\sigma_0 \tau_0 = (1 - nr\,\delta t)(1 - ns\delta t) = 1 - (r + s)n\delta t$ to first order. $\tau_1 = (n + 1)\delta t$. Hence the equation. When $r = 0$, $\mathrm{d}P(n, t)/\mathrm{d}t = (n + 1)sP(n + 1, t) - snP(n, t)$, with $P(n, t) = 0$ for $n < N$ and $P(N, 0) = 1$, $P(n, 0) = 0$ for $n = N$. Then $P(N, t) = \exp(-sNt)$ and $P(N - 1, t) = N\exp(-sNt)(\exp(st) - 1)$.

4.2 $P(n, m + 1) = \sum_j \sigma_{n,j} P(n - j, m)$ where $\sigma_{n,j}$ is the probability that $(n - j)$ members have j offspring. Thus $P(n_0, m) = (1 - rT)^{n_0 m}$.

4.3 (i) $\begin{pmatrix} \frac{1}{4} & \frac{3}{4} & 0 \\ \frac{1}{2} & \frac{1}{2} & 0 \\ \frac{1}{2} & 0 & \frac{1}{2} \end{pmatrix}$; (ii) $\begin{pmatrix} \frac{1}{2} & \frac{1}{2} & 0 & 0 \\ \frac{1}{4} & \frac{3}{4} & 0 & 0 \\ \frac{1}{3} & 0 & \frac{1}{3} & \frac{1}{3} \\ 0 & \frac{1}{4} & \frac{1}{4} & \frac{1}{2} \end{pmatrix}$.

4.4 (i) Matrix is regular: the eigenvector with $\lambda = 1$ is $(\frac{4}{7}, \frac{3}{7})$: $p_1(m) \to \frac{4}{7}$. Alternatively $p_1(m+1) = p_1(m)/2 + (1 - p_1(m))2/3 = -p_1(m)/6 + \frac{2}{3}$: $p_1(m) = C(-\frac{1}{6})^m + \frac{4}{7}$.

(ii) $p_1(m+1) = p_1(m) + 2(1 - p_1(m))/3 = p_1(m)/3 + \frac{2}{3}$. Therefore $p_1(m) = 1 + C(\frac{1}{3})^m$. Thus $p_1(m) \to 1$ as predicted, it being an absorbing chain.

4.5 The transition matrix is

$$\begin{pmatrix} \frac{1}{4} & \frac{1}{4} & \frac{1}{4} & \frac{1}{4} \\ \frac{1}{3} & 0 & \frac{1}{3} & \frac{1}{3} \\ \frac{1}{2} & \frac{1}{2} & 0 & 0 \\ 0 & \frac{1}{2} & \frac{1}{3} & \frac{1}{6} \end{pmatrix}.$$

The eigenvector (r, g, b, w) with eigenvalue 1 is given by the equations:

$$\begin{aligned} \tfrac{1}{4}r + g/3 + b/2 \qquad\qquad &= r \\ \tfrac{1}{4}r + \qquad\qquad b/2 + w/2 &= g \\ \tfrac{1}{4}r + g/3 + \qquad\qquad w/3 &= b \\ \tfrac{1}{4}r + g/3 \qquad\qquad\quad w/6 &= w, \end{aligned}$$

giving $16g = 23w$, $b = 7w/6$, $r = 17w/12$. The eigenvector is $(68, 69, 56, 48)/241$. The player bets $(\frac{1}{4}, \frac{1}{4}, \frac{1}{4}, \frac{1}{4})$pence so that his average loss per go is $((2(68 + 69)/241 + 3(56 + 48)/241)/4 - 1)$.

4.6 Each bag has four balls. The number of balls of each colour in one bag, the red say, specifies the state. There are five pure states, labelled 1, 2, 3, 4, 5, with state n having $(5 - n)$ red balls in the red bag.

From state 1, the probability of a red and white ball being taken out is 1, so that there is a probability of $\frac{1}{2}$ of the red or the white ball being returned to the red bag. Thus if $\mathbf{p}(m) = (1, 0, 0, 0, 0)$, $\mathbf{p}(m+1) = (\frac{1}{2}, \frac{1}{2}, 0, 0, 0)$. The calculation from state 5 is similar. From state 2, there is a probability $\frac{3}{4}$ that a red ball is taken from the red bag. Thus the probability that two red balls are taken is $\frac{3}{16}$. There is then no change in the state of the system. If a red and a white ball are chosen there is a probability $\frac{1}{2}$ of a change, so that the probability of a change to state 1 is $\frac{1}{32}$. Thus if $\mathbf{p}(m) = (0, 1, 0, 0, 0)$ then $\mathbf{p}(m+1) = (\frac{1}{32}, \frac{11}{16}, \frac{9}{32}, 0, 0)$. Similarly if $\mathbf{p}(m) = (0, 0, 1, 0, 0)$ then $\mathbf{p}(m+1) = (0, \frac{1}{8}, \frac{3}{4}, \frac{1}{8}, 0)$. The transition matrix is

$$\begin{pmatrix} \frac{1}{2} & \frac{1}{2} & 0 & 0 & 0 \\ \frac{1}{32} & \frac{11}{16} & \frac{9}{32} & 0 & 0 \\ 0 & \frac{1}{8} & \frac{3}{4} & \frac{1}{8} & 0 \\ 0 & 0 & \frac{9}{32} & \frac{11}{16} & \frac{1}{32} \\ 0 & 0 & 0 & \frac{1}{2} & \frac{1}{2} \end{pmatrix}.$$

This is regular; the left eigenvector with eigenvalue 1 is (1, 16, 36, 16, 1)/70. This is the long-run behaviour.

4.7 There are four states for a letter, i.e. A's, B's, C's in-trays and C's file. Label them 1, 2, 3, 4. If $\mathbf{p}(m) = (1, 0, 0, 0)$ then $\mathbf{p}(m+1) = (0, \frac{3}{8}, \frac{1}{8}, \frac{1}{2})$; if $\mathbf{p}(m) = (0, 1, 0, 0)$ then $\mathbf{p}(m+1) = (\frac{1}{3}, 0, \frac{1}{6}, \frac{1}{2})$ and if $\mathbf{p}(m) = (0, 0, 1, 0)$ or $(0, 0, 0, 1)$ then $\mathbf{p}(m+1) = (0, 0, 0, 1)$.
The transition matrix is

$$\begin{pmatrix} 0 & \frac{3}{8} & \frac{1}{8} & \frac{1}{2} \\ \frac{1}{3} & 0 & \frac{1}{6} & \frac{1}{2} \\ 0 & 0 & 0 & 1 \\ 0 & 0 & 0 & 1 \end{pmatrix}.$$

State 4 is an absorbing state. The characteristic matrix is

$$\begin{pmatrix} 1 & -\frac{3}{8} & -\frac{1}{8} \\ -\frac{1}{3} & 1 & -\frac{1}{6} \\ 0 & 0 & 1 \end{pmatrix}^{-1} = \begin{pmatrix} \frac{8}{7} & \frac{3}{7} & \frac{3}{14} \\ \frac{8}{21} & \frac{8}{7} & \frac{5}{21} \\ 0 & 0 & 1 \end{pmatrix}.$$

The initial state is (1, 0, 0) so that the lengths of time spent in A's, B's and C's in-trays are $\frac{8}{7}$, $\frac{3}{7}$, $\frac{3}{14}$ days respectively. As the probability of A, B replying is $\frac{1}{2}$ each they reply to $\frac{4}{7}$ and $\frac{3}{14}$ letters respectively on average. The average length of time before a letter reaches the file is $\frac{25}{14}$ days.

4.11 Suppose the pay-off matrix is

$$U = \begin{pmatrix} a & b \\ c & d \end{pmatrix},$$

then $p_1(m+1) = p_1(m)\,(ap_1(m) + b(1 - p_1(m)))/(\mathbf{p}(m) . U . \mathbf{p}(m))$. If $p_1 = 0$ is an equilibrium then $\mathbf{p} . U . \mathbf{p} = (a - b)p_1 + b$. Thus $(p_1 - 1)\,(p_1(a - b - c + d) - (d - b)) = 0$. There is a mixed strategy equilibrium if $0 < (d - b)/(a - b - c + d) < 1$, i.e. if $a > c$ and $d > b$ or if $a < c$ and $d < b$. Then $p_1^e = (d - b)/(a - b - c + d)$ and $p_2^e = (a - c)/(a - b - c + d)$, and $\mathbf{p}^e . U . \mathbf{p}^e =$

$(ad - bc)/(a - b - c + d)$. Equation (P4.8.14) is then

$$\epsilon_1(m+1) = \epsilon_1(m)\,(1 + (d-b)\,(a-b)/(ad-bc)).$$

For stability we require

$$|1 + (d-b)\,(a-b)/(ad-bc)| < 1.$$

In the Hawk–Dove model, $a = w/2 - i$, $b = w$, $c = 0$, $d = w/2 - t$. Assume $0 < d < b$. Then there is a mixed strategy if $a < c$, i.e. if $w/2 - i < 0$. Now $1 + (d-b)\,(b-c)/(ad-bc) = 1 + (w/2+t)\,(w/2+i)/((w/2-t)\,(w/2-i)$ $(w/2-i))$, which is less than 1 but can be less than -1 in some circumstances.

Index